WORLD JEWRY

AND

THE STATE OF ISRAEL

WORLD JEWRY

AND

THE STATE OF ISRAEL

Edited by
MOSHE DAVIS

ARNO PRESS
A New York Times Company

Publications of the Continuing Seminar on World Jewry
under the auspices of the President of Israel

Vol. I   The Yom Kippur War: Israel and the Jewish People

Vol. II   World Jewry and the State of Israel

Vol. III Zionism Today (in preparation)

© Copyright, 1977 by the
Institute of Contemporary Jewry
The Hebrew University of Jerusalem

Arno Press
A New York Times Company

Manufactured in the United States of America

Library of Congress Catalogue Card Number: 77-72730
ISBN: 0-405-10305-0

אחינו כל־בית־ישראל הנתונים בצרה ובשביה...
המקום ירחם עליהם
ויוציאם מצרה לרוחה,
ומאפלה לאורה,
ומשעבוד לגאלה...

To our brothers of all the House of Israel,
in distress and captivity.   .   .
  May the Heavenly mercy bring them
    from oppression to deliverance
    from darkness to light
    from slavery to redemption.   .   .
                    (Daily Prayerbook)

Foreword

Professor Ephraim Katzir

This book is the second to emerge from the Seminar on World Jewry and the State of Israel, which I first convoked in Jerusalem at the end of 1973. The Seminar was assembled very soon after the crucial experience of the Yom Kippur War and was then summed up in a volume published in 1974, *The Yom Kippur War: Israel and the Jewish People,* edited by the Seminar's chairman, Moshe Davis.

The War and its aftermath demonstrated the extraordinary sensitivity and closeness of the relationship between Diaspora Jewry and Israel. This relationship was analyzed in depth by the international group of scholars and men of action meeting in the first Seminar, at the President's Residence in Jerusalem in December 1973. They were profoundly concerned with a number of fundamental questions: What can the Israel-Diaspora bond mean in the life of modern Jewry? How can it stem the dangerous erosion of Jewish knowledge and devotion in the open societies of the Western world? How can the sense of Jewish identity be deepened? What accounts for appearance of new types of hostility aimed at the Jewish People? What is the special function of the State of Israel in the struggle for creative Jewish survival?

In continued pursuance of answers to these questions the second Seminar turned to detailed presentation and consideration of three basic issues. The analysis and discussion of all three are now published in this volume. Its first section, delineating the present complex situation of Jews in many parts of the world, deals with "current manifestations of anti-Jewishness." The inner problem of both individual and group is skillfully examined in the section on Jewish identity. Thirdly, the changing alignment of forces, the historic shift in Jewry of the mid-twentieth century, is the theme of the section on "the centrality of Israel and interaction among world Jewish communities."

World events conspire to give our subjects new pertinence and significance. The year that has passed has been marked by an extraordinary campaign of vilification against Zionism, Israel and Jewish historical existence. Reaction to this campaign involved Jewish as well as non-Jewish thinkers and public figures very deeply, and there is an obvious need for presentation and study of the actualities of Zionism and Israel. To such study this book can surely make a distinct contribution.

As a natural scientist who has been immersed for the last three years in the world of statecraft and in close contacts with so many representative Jewish individuals and groups from so many countries, I have found myself reaching a number of conclusions and seeing Israel in a new perspective. To see it thus is to understand the vast difference between it and every other Jewish community, no matter how well organized or culturally rich. The difference, in a word, is *sovereignty*—the capacity of the State itself to make its own decisions and to carry them out in the fields of economics, education, immigration, social policy, security, planning for future development of the people and country. Sovereignty brings with it a new sort of psychological independence as well. It is my strong impression that precisely this aspect of sovereignty is what many Jews abroad cherish and what the world respects. But the State, for all its significance, is not an end in itself. For all of us, I believe, sovereignty—statehood—is in essence a tool, a means through which to give concrete expression to the moral values of our heritage by building a society based on freedom, justice and equality.

The second aspect of the Jewish State most important to Jews abroad and aspired to by a large sector of us here, is intellectual-cultural distinction. It is not easy to work at this in the economic and political conditions of Israel's life. But without dedication to, and achievement in, the pursuits of the intellect and spirit, our reason for being would be crucially diminished and injured. Zionism, after all, is rooted in the spirit, in centuries of longing and prayer. The diplomatic relationships and political contingencies of the nineteenth and twentieth centuries are only a modern and technical aspect of its story. International guarantees were the product, not the origin, of Zionism. The Messiah was born, Jewish legend says, the day the Temple was destroyed. Surely Zionism was born with the fall of the Second Commonwealth, and has had to wait for changed, modern conditions before it could be consummated.

These pages, I believe, can illuminate many complexities of the Jewish State's development, the Jewish People's modern existence and the problems we must face with determination and conviction.

Contents

-II-

Variant Patterns of Jewish Identification

-III-

The Centrality of Israel and
Interaction among World Jewish Communities

Contributors

MIKHAIL AGURSKY.
Oleh from Soviet Russia

SHLOMO AVINERI.
Professor of Political Science, The Hebrew University of
Jerusalem

HAIM AVNI.
Director, Division of Latin American Jewry, Institute of
Contemporary Jewry, The Hebrew University of Jerusalem

GERSON D. COHEN.
Chancellor; Professor of Jewish History, The Jewish Theological
Seminary of America

MOSHE DAVIS.
Head, Institute of Contemporary Jewry; Professor of American
Jewish History and Institutions, The Hebrew University of
Jerusalem

EMIL L. FACKENHEIM.
Professor of Philosophy, University of Toronto

ELI GINZBERG.
Director, Conservation of Human Resources; Professor of
Economics, Columbia University

ZVI GITELMAN.
Associate Professor of Political Science, The University of
Michigan; Visiting Associate Professor, Tel Aviv University

IRVING GREENBERG.
Professor, Department of Jewish Studies, City College of the City
University of New York

SIMON D. HERMAN.
Associate Professor, Institute of Contemporary Jewry and
Department of Psychology, The Hebrew University of Jerusalem

IMMANUEL JAKOBOVITS.
Chief Rabbi of the British Commonwealth of Nations

ZEV KATZ.
Department of Russian Studies and School for Overseas Students,
The Hebrew University of Jerusalem

EPHRAIM KATZIR.
President of The State of Israel

AHARON LICHTENSTEIN.
Rosh Yeshiva, Yeshivat Har Etzion

CHARLES S. LIEBMAN.
Associate Professor, Bar Ilan University; currently, Visiting
Professor, The Jewish Theological Seminary of America

MOSHE MA'OZ.
Academic Director, Harry S. Truman Research Institute, The
Hebrew University of Jerusalem

PETER Y. MEDDING.
Reader in Politics, Monash University, Melbourne

ALBERT MEMMI.
Director, Department of Social Sciences; Professor, Université de
Paris, Nanterre

SHULAMIT NARDI.
Assistant to the President of The State of Israel

NATHAN ROTENSTREICH.
Professor of Philosophy, The Hebrew University of Jerusalem

EPHRAIM E. URBACH.
Professor of Talmud, The Hebrew University of Jerusalem

GEOFFREY WIGODER.
Director, Oral History Division, Institute of Contemporary Jewry,
The Hebrew University of Jerusalem

DORA CAMRASS.
Editorial Associate

LOTTIE K. DAVIS.
Editorial Coordinator

Discussants

BENJAMIN AKZIN.
Professor Emeritus, The Hebrew University of Jerusalem

AVRAHAM AVI-HAI.
Department of Political Studies, Bar Ilan University

SALO W. BARON.
Professor Emeritus, Columbia University

MORDECHAI BAR-ON.
Head, Youth and Hechalutz Department, World Zionist
Organization

EPHRAIM BROIDO.
Editor, *Molad*

HAIM CHAMIEL.
Director General, Torah Education Department, World Zionist
Organization; Senior Lecturer of Education, Bar Ilan University

JACK J. COHEN.
Director, B'nai B'rith Hillel Foundations in Israel

ARYEH L. DULZIN.
Treasurer, World Zionist Organization and Jewish Agency

MARVIN FOX.
Chairman, Department of Near Eastern and Judaic Studies;
Professor of Jewish Philosphy, Brandeis University

JONATHAN FRANKEL.
Senior Lecturer, Institute of Contemporary Jewry and Department
of Russian Studies, The Hebrew University of Jerusalem

MAURICE FREEDMAN.
Professor of Social Anthropology, Oxford University; Editor,
Jewish Journal of Sociology

ALEXANDER GOLDFARB.
Oleh from Soviet Russia

ALFRED GOTTSCHALK.
  President, Hebrew Union College—Jewish Institute of Religion;
  Professor of Bible and Jewish Religious Thought

SIMON GREENBERG.
  Vice-Chancellor; Professor Emeritus, The Jewish Theological
  Seminary of America

ABRAHAM S. HALKIN.
  Professor Emeritus, The City University of New York

AVRAHAM HARMAN.
  President, The Hebrew University of Jerusalem

ABRAHAM J. KARP.
  Professor of Religious Studies, The University of Rochester

JACOB KATZ.
  Professor Emeritus, The Hebrew University of Jerusalem

ERNEST KRAUSZ.
  Professor of Sociology, Bar Ilan University

DAVID LAZAR.
  Institute of International Affairs, The Hebrew University of
  Jerusalem

NATAN LERNER.
  Executive Director, World Jewish Congress, Israel Branch

MICHAEL A. MEYER.
  Professor of Midrash, Hebrew Union College—Jewish Institute of
  Religion

CHAIM PERELMAN.
  Professor of Philosophy, University of Brussels

MOSHE RIVLIN.
  Director-General, Jewish Agency for Israel; Deputy Member,
  World Zionist Organization Executive

MICHAEL ROSENAK.
  Center for Jewish Education in the Diaspora, The Hebrew
  University of Jerusalem

SHALOM ROSENBERG.
  Department of Jewish Philosophy and Kabbala, The Hebrew
  University of Jerusalem

AVRAHAM SCHENKER.
  Member of Executive, World Zionist Organization

DAVID SIDORSKY.
  Professor of Philosophy, Columbia University

EZRA SPICEHANDLER.
Dean, Jerusalem School, Hebrew Union College—Jewish Institute of Religion

ERNEST STOCK.
Director, Jacob Hiatt Institute; Associate Professor, Brandeis University

MARIE SYRKIN.
Professor Emeritus, Brandeis University

JACOB TSUR.
World Chairman, Jewish National Fund

MARVIN F. VERBIT.
Associate Professor of Sociology, Brooklyn College and Graduate School, The City University of New York

MORDECAI WAXMAN.
Past President, Rabbinical Assembly of America; Vice-president, World Council of Synagogues

LENI YAHIL.
Associate Professor, Department of Jewish History, University of Haifa

ZVI YARON.
Editor, *Forum*, Jerusalem

I

Current Manifestations of
Anti-Jewishness

Aspects of Post-Holocaust Anti-Jewish Attitudes

Shlomo Avineri

One of the chief political and moral consequences of the Holocaust has been the virtual disappearance of anti-Semitism as a political force in the West. No matter what people may have felt or what Jews experienced individually, Nazism made even mildly anti-Semitic *public* utterances wholly unacceptable during the period following 1945.

Now, however, thirty years after the end of World War II, the picture seems to have changed once again. With younger generations not having endured the agony of being silent witnesses to the Holocaust, they do not experience the inner shame and revulsion of those days. As a student at a German university put it, the Holocaust for him is as much a part of history as the massacre of the Anabaptists at Münster; obviously he condemns it, but it is history to him, not experience.

Anti-Semitism—A New Framework

The recent emergence of a new kind of anti-Semitism in the contemporary West cannot, however, be traced exclusively to a generational change. While traditionalist Zionism saw the emergence of a Jewish national state not only as a solution to the plight of Jews but also as a therapy for the sickness of anti-Semitism, the picture now seems to be much more complex. Today it is not the Diaspora Jew as such who is the target of anti-Jewish criticism; it is Israel—its legitimacy, its politics, its links with Diaspora Jews, its very existence—which is the main target of this new wave of anti-Jewish attacks. The sad irony is obvious, and the natural tendency is to deny or belittle the significance of this phenomenon. Yet it cannot be denied that it is Israel (especially its post-1967 successes and post-1973 agonies) which appears to have granted a new appearance of legitimacy to a

3

criticism of Jews; and even if this criticism starts with Israel, it occasionally reverts very quickly to traditional anti-Semitic patterns. De Gaulle's "Sermon to the Hebrews" in 1967 was perhaps the first significant public expression on a political level of this new legitimacy.

One can discern five areas in which this new anti-Semitism is being expressed: (a) the Arab world; (b) the Communist countries; (c) New Left circles; (d) the Black Power movement; and (e) radical theology.

The first two are outside the scope of this paper, although certain phenomena, such as the policies and public statements of Idi Amin, possibly are extensions of both (a) and (d). With regard to (b) I limit myself to one observation: While in some Soviet and other East European statements a very careful distinction is claimed to be made between Zionism and Judaism, there have been a number of publications (notably those of Trofim Kichko) which suggest an intrinsic relationship between the two. (See Addendum 1.)

The New Left

A number of studies of this movement by Lipset, Glazer, Chertoff and reports by Jewish American service organizations concentrate mainly on the American scene. There is little material on German, Dutch or English New Left groups, where the impact of Arab propaganda was felt some years earlier and where Israeli involvement with American policy became much more of a political issue than in the United States itself. The bill of particulars against Israel is coherently expressed, for example, in Rodinson's writings by linking Zionism with Western imperialism, its character as a national liberation movement is overlooked so that basic legitimacy of Zionism and of Israel is undermined. Complex issues of religion and ethnicity in Judaism, exacerbated by problems of religious freedom in Israel, are linked with theocracy and racism, further deligitimizing the raison d'être of Israel. Certain religiously inspired hawkish expressions both in Israel and in the Diaspora help to sustain some of the arguments, the basic nature of which is similar to particular pre-Holocaust universal oriented socialist arguments against Zionism. The pernicious difference, however, lies not only in the disregard of the Holocaust but also in the fact that while Karl Kautsky may have been arguing in the 1920s against a vision, these same arguments, in the political context of 1975, call for the disestablishment of an existing body politic. Although some of the New Left arguments are, to a certain extent, a re-hash of old left-wing criticisms, their significance is of a completely different order: the ideological and partly hypothetical debate of the 1920s becomes a debate about "politicide" if not consequent genocide.

Black Power

The identification of Israel with the white world's oppression of the Third World is seen as qualitatively similar to the confrontation between Black and Jew in North American ghetto areas. Again, a number of American studies on the subject point to a co-relation between Black anti-Semitism, the actual conditions of American Blacks, and their concept of these conditions. Occasionally, Jewish studies on the subject appear to be somewhat apologetic when they argue, for example, that the number of Jewish slumlords in Harlem is in reality much lower than appears in the customary image of Jewish economic activity in the ghetto. Although this seems to be true, it is beside the point. Concepts, distorted as they may be, are part of reality, and similar statistics did not help the Jews in Europe against Nazism. Whatever the differences, the Black population in the United States is the only North American Gentile group which relates to Jews economically on a level similar to that in which Eastern European peasants related to Jewish merchants and peddlers in the Pale of Settlement. For the Jew, America was historically different from Europe because both Jew and Gentile were free from the mutually abrasive socioeconomic relationship where the Jew was characterized as the middle man in so many facets of European (mainly East European) society. With relation to the Blacks, however, the image of the Jew could be construed on lines similar to that of the East European *muzhik* vis-à-vis the Jewish population. Just as Jewish revolutionary activity in Eastern Europe did not help to endear the Jews to the peasantry there, so Jewish participation in, if not leadership of, the Civil Rights movement in the United States did not endear the Jews as a group to the ghetto Black. The causes of social anti-Semitism in Eastern Europe and the North American ghetto are similar, and it is this new anti-Semitism that, more than other forms, is reminiscent of the traditional patterns of pre-Holocaust anti-Semitism.

This new version can be violent indeed, at least rhetorically, where the existance of Israel only adds another to the traditional images. (See Addendum 2.)

Radical Theology

Since radical theology in general has to be explained in terms related to the emergence of a modern, new critique of democratic societies as, for instance, the New Left, much of the imagery concerning Israel and Zionism derives from the same roots (e.g., Daniel Berrigan, as well as some Dutch radical theologians). But there is a deeper strain which can be discerned in regard to Israel: The basic theological delegitimization of the people of Israel, so fundamental to the Church's understanding of itself, appears to reemerge in a secularized form in many of the radical theological critiques of Israel. When Berrigan says he speaks "as a Jew" in criticizing Israel, what he really means is that he, the true Christian, is also *versus Israel*. The real Jews, the Pharisees, to use Church phraseology, can then be conveniently referred to as "the Zionists." When such secularized theological delegitimization of the people of Israel is coupled with New Left criticism of the alleged social, economic and military role of Israel, the consequences are obvious: Jewish support for Israel in the Diaspora has immediate repercussions on the civic position of Jews whose support for Israel is thus delegitimized as well.

Anti-Zionism—The New Anti-Jewishness?

People who have in recent years expressed anti-Israel or anti-Zionist views have frequently added that their opinions on Zionism or Israel should not be construed automatically as expressing something akin to anti-Semitism. People such as Rodinson, or some of the extreme members of the American SDS (Students for a Democratic Society) are themselves Jewish or of Jewish descent, and a glib identification with anti-Semitism of every statement which is critical of Israel or of its policies is obviously too simple. Moreover, the issue cannot be reduced by pointing out that in certain publications, whether Arab, Communist or Black, "Zionist" is merely a code word for "Jews." Accounts of the anti-Jewish purges in Poland in 1968, as well as Soviet writings about Czechoslovak liberals during the

Prague Spring, referred to many of the Jews under attack as Zionists, even though it was known that they had no attachment to Israel and that they had never been involved in activities that could be labeled "Zionist" by any stretch of the imagination. The Arab quibble that they cannot be called anti-Semitic because they are themselves Semites can, of course, be answered by referring to the fact that the Nuremberg Laws did not apply to the Mufti and his henchmen when they spent the war years in Berlin. Historically, to anti-Semites, only Jews are Semites; the term "anti-Semitism" evolved as a polite euphemism for "anti-Judaism." Is the same happening today with regard to anti-Zionism?

The problem goes much deeper than merely labeling people or categorizing opinions. It must be insisted quite bluntly that it is the Jew who must decide whether an anti-Zionist statement is, or is not, anti-Semitic, not the person who makes the statement. After all, it is the Blacks who define a racist attitude, and what offends their sensibilities is regarded as bigotry. (If Blacks find the term "Negro" derogatory, then it is derogatory, even if the person who uses it does not so intend it; racism is not exclusively in the eye of the beholder.)

However, in addition to this analogy with Black consciousness or sensibility, there is a further element to be considered—the degree to which anti-Zionism is *ipso facto* anti-Semitic is now related to the centrality of Israel (and Zionism) in the general Jewish consciousness. If Israel were a marginal phenomenon in Jewish life (as it was until the Holocaust and the establishment of the State of Israel), an anti-Israel or anti-Zionist line would not necessarily be contradictory to a generally favorable attitude to Jews. But, for better or for worse, since 1945, and especially after 1967 and 1973, Israel has become central to the Jewish experience. More Jews are now prepared to define themselves as Jewish in relation to their attitude to Israel than through any other medium; moreover, identification with and sensitivity to Israel appears today to be the core of Jewish self-definition and self-understanding. The establishment of the State of Israel has, without a doubt, resulted in a great revolution in Jewish life. It created, even if only as an ideal, a Jewish polity which is meaningful not only to Jews who live there but also to Jews who do not live there, will never wish to live there, yet feel (as both American and Soviet Jews felt in 1967 and 1973) that its survival is crucial to their own understanding of being Jewish.

Israel in Jewish Consciousness

The existence of Israel is thus raised from a "merely" political matter, open to controversy like all other political attitudes, to one of fairly general Jewish self-identification. Today Israel is the epitome of Jewish self-consciousness; hence, to question its existence means striking at the core of Jewish self-understanding in our contemporary world. *A delegitimization of the State of Israel is therefore a delegitimization of Jewish existence as understood now by a majority of Jews in and outside of Israel.* Anti-Semitism cannot be defined by reference to a static concept of Judaism, eternal and unchanging. It develops through a determined misunderstanding of Jewish existence as this existence is defined in relation to a changing Jewish self-consciousness. Today, Jewish self-understanding is centered on Israel. Hence, a delegitimization of Israel (not, of course, merely a criticism of this or that policy of the Israeli government) is now equivalent to an expression of anti-Semitism.

In eras when the Gentile world was consciously religious, anti-Jewish feelings were focused on religious and theological issues; in a world which became aware of ethnic and racial differences, anti-Jewish feelings were expressed in racial terms; and in a world which is today politicized to an unprecedented degree (and in which the existence of the normative polity representing the self-consciousness of the Jewish People is menaced by political and military means), a criticism of this polity is the contemporary expression of anti-Jewish feelings. Historical anti-Semitism was not directed against the Jews per se. The devout Christian merely wished to convert him; the racist nationalist only wished to protect his land and people from contamination by the Jew, while the anti-Zionist was ready to accept him everywhere except in that place to which he himself felt chiefly attached. In each case, the Jew was and is denied his self-identity.

Addenda

(1) From an article on Zionism published in *URSS*, official information bulletin of the Soviet Embassy in Paris, September 22, 1972:

> In Israeli schools, the greater part of the school curriculum is devoted to the study of the Holy Scriptures which 'teach the feelings of the national conscience'—during 24 hours of the day. With what subject do these books deal? What kind of moral values do the schools of the Zionist State impart to the young generation?
>
> According to the essential concept of these 'textbooks,' particularly of the book *Shulkhan Arukh*, the world belongs to the believers in the Almighty *Yahve*, through whom they can wear the mask they assume. The property of the non-Jews belongs to them only temporarily, until it is turned over to the hands of the 'chosen people.' When the latter will outnumber the other peoples, 'God will deliver them to the Jews to be slaughtered to a man.'
>
> These are the concrete rules governing the relations between the Jews and the gentiles who are scornfully called *goya, akums,* or *Nazareens*. The *akums* are not to be considered human beings (*Orah-Hayim*, 14, 32, 33, 39, 55, 193): 'It is strictly forbidden for a Jew to save from death an *akum* with whom he is living at peace.' 'It is forbidden to cure an *akum* even in return for money, but it is permissible to try out the effects of medicine upon him' (*Yereh Dea*, 158). 'When a Jew witnesses the last moments of an *akum*, he must exult in joy' (*Yereh Dea*, 319, 5).
>
> To concede something to an *akum* or to give anything to him is sacrilege. It is better to throw a piece of meat to a dog than give it to a *goya* (*Hoshen-Mishpat*). However, it is permissible to give alms to poor *akum* and to visit their sick so that they may think that the Jews are their good friends (Yereh Dea, 151, 12).
>
> Such religious prescriptions, that may be quoted without end, constitute the 'moral' code of the Zionist society. The Israeli authorities have set up a special Department for the diffusion and propagation of the Torah, Talmud and other Zionist ideological material on a nationwide scale. It is from this 'cultural and moral' basis that the 'authentic Zionist' takes his concept of the world. He must learn all these precepts from childhood and quote them by heart during the ceremony of his Bar-Mitzvah (confirmation), so as to prove his 'ideological maturity.'
>
> These abject and detestable rules, hate towards other peoples, have been implanted from birth in the whole generations of Israelis who are commanded to 'slaughter the goyas under the vault of heaven' (*Orah-Hayyim* 690, 16). Jewish laws form part of the regulations of the Israeli army and their infringement is punished by disciplinary measures. They are the very essence of the policy of the Zionist State.

(2) Poem published in the magazine *Black Power* (June, 1967):

Jew-Land, On a summer afternoon
Really, couldn't kill the Jews too soon
Now dig, the Jews have stolen all our bread
Their filthy women tricked our men into bed
So I would rest until the Jews are dead
In Jew-Land, Nailing Rabbis to a cross
Really, don't you think that would be boss?
You know the Jews don't really want to fight
They're gonna say that we're just anti-Semite
But I don't care because the Jews are white
In Jew-Land, Don't be a Jew on Israel's side
Really, Cause that's where Christ was crucified,
No-no-no-no
We're gonna burn their towns and that ain't all
We're gonna piss upon the Wailing Wall
And then we'll get Kosygin and DeGaulle
That will be ecstasy, killing every Jew we see
Jew-Land, Not another day should pass
Really, Without a foot up Israel's ass
No-no-no-no
Jew-Land, Uh-huh-uh-huh, Jew-Land.

Post-Holocaust Anti-Jewishness, Jewish Identity and the Centrality of Israel[1]

Emil L. Fackenheim

The Term "Post-Holocaust"

The prefix "post" in the title of this paper may have two meanings. One signifies a merely temporal relation, so that any event after 1945 is "post-Holocaust." The other is historic in a pregnant rather than a merely trivial sense. An event succeeds another historically if the first somehow enters into its substance: if it is different from what it would have been if the first had never happened. Thus, much history is merely temporal. More important, historic events in the deeper sense are always of unpredictable import while they happen and even long after. Only when they are assimilated by the historic consciousness of succeeding generations are they capable of transforming the future and, thus, become historic in a deeper sense.

At least certain current anti-Jewish attitudes are post-Holocaust in the historic sense, as is shown by the very terminology that is forced upon us. Prior to the Holocaust, many antisemites would protest—rightly so—their friendship for some Jews and, thus, were called—rightly so— "decent" antisemites. Since the Holocaust, virtually all antisemites go to any length to deny, always to others (and often to themselves), that they *are* antisemites. The term, a nineteenth-century code word for anti-Jewishness, can no longer be used by anyone seriously concerned with identifying and comprehending post-Holocaust anti-Jewish attitudes.[2]

Only a few anti-Jewish attitudes may seem post-Holocaust in

---

1. This paper seeks to explicate the inner unity of the three topics of this book and of the conference in which it had its origin.
2. We shall generally use "antisemitism" for pre-Holocaust forms of anti-Jewishness. As James Parker pointed out, the spelling ought to be "antisemitism" without the hyphen, dispelling the notion there is an entity "Semitism" which "anti"-Semitism opposes.

the historic sense, and these seem bound to fade still further as the dread event passes from experience into history.[3] However, it is worth considering that on both scores the opposite may be true. Not all forms of anti-Jewishness which look unrelated to the Holocaust are in fact so. And while the Holocaust doubtless is passing from experience into history, it is only beginning to be absorbed by historic consciousness—the consciousness both of those living in history and those writing about it.[4]

No one presently alive can answer questions raised by the relation between the Holocaust and historic consciousness. But we must, at least, pause to ponder its momentousness. Will the Holocaust ultimately be forgotten or—more precisely—be consciously and unconsciously expunged from people's minds? Or will it, on the contrary, increasingly permeate both the lives of people in various civilizations and the consciousness of writers, philosophers, and historians? In that case, the event may well assume a world-historic significance.

The question just raised can only be answered in the future. In contrast, we can even now observe the fact that not all forms of anti-Jewishness, seemingly unrelated to the Holocaust, are indeed unrelated to it. Several examples may illustrate this.

First, Germans of the new generation protest rightly that they are not guilty. This does not alter the fact that *any* form of anti-Jewishness displayed by present and future Germans is historically post-Holocaust, for the slate of *no* people's history can be wiped clean—including that of Germans. Unless they choose not to participate in German history—that is, emigrate—Germans are burdened with the past and responsible for the future.

Second, Soviet Russia and other Iron Curtain countries actually try to wipe the slate clean, sparing no effort to make the Holocaust either a non-event or a non-Jewish event. (There are no memorials, or they are erected to the "victims of fascism.") This crime against truth is sufficient to make all anti-Jewishness in these countries historically post-Holocaust.

Third, the Arab world protests that the sins of Christian Europe have been visited on its Palestinian sector. Such a protest is in bad faith when—not to mention others—it excises two facts from the

3. See Shlomo Avineri in this volume.
4. Raul Hilberg's assertion to this effect, made in 1961, is still substantially correct. See his *The Destruction of the European Jews*, Chicago, 1961, p. v.

record: the active participation of Haj Amin al-Husseini, Grand Mufti of Jerusalem, in Hitler's murder of Jewish children, and the link between Auschwitz and the war on the newly-born Jewish state waged by five Arab armies. This attempt at politicide was encouraged by the way in which Hitler had just practiced genocide with almost total impunity. And, of course, the victim in both cases—in the one case, actual, in the other, intended—was the same people.

To be fair, one may wish to doubt whether the third example of anti-Jewishness is historically post-Holocaust or even anti-Jewish at all. In this spirit one may wish to consider the two excised events—the activities of the Grand Mufti during World War II and the Arab invasions in the 1948 war—as correctly excised; that is, not as events which, themselves shaped by the Holocaust, continued to shape subsequent history but, rather, as random facts of the dead past. But attempts to view these events as not historically related to the present become futile when one considers the present Arab propaganda system (assiduously aided by the communist) when it declares Israelis to be the new Nazis; the PLO to be the new French freedom-fighters, that is, the new anti-Nazis; Arab refugees victims of a holocaust; Zionism a form of racism; and, by a mathematical tour de force, Arab victims of Zionism, in American terms, equivalent in number to six million.[5] It is impossible to view this system as innocent, as truly ignorant of what happened a generation ago. One can only view it as an attempt to wipe out the Holocaust as a Jewish event, indeed, to appropriate it as an Arab one—to rewrite Israeli history as a "final solution of the Arab problem."

That none of these forms of post-Holocaust anti-Jewishness can be equated with the unsurpassable Nazi kind is self-evident. (We specifically mention it here because of a widespread dismissal of *all* Jewish explorations of *any* post-Holocaust manifestation of anti-Jewishness as products either of a neurotic complex about the dread event or of an attempt to exploit it. This extraordinary dismissal itself requires scrutiny, which cannot be attempted here.) At the same time, they cannot claim or recapture the "decency" of pre-Holocaust antisemitism. Only two decent Gentile relations toward the Jewish people remain. One has remained truly and genuinely innocent of the fact that just one generation ago the Nazi

5. Yassir Arafat's address to the United Nations General Assembly in 1974.

regime first persecuted and then murdered the Jewish People, while, at the same time, the rest of the world first shut its gates to Jews fleeing for their lives and then failed to bomb the railways to Auschwitz. (This antisemitism is a fossil, a relic from earlier, more innocent, times. Its own innocence may be barbaric, but it is nevertheless an innocence.) The other Gentile relation to the Jewish People has always been free of anti-Jewish animus, or else, in response to the catastrophe, is now trying desperately to rid itself of such animus. Apart from these two attitudes, all historic post-Holocaust forms of anti-Jewishness are posthumous victories for Hitler and witting or unwitting continuations of his work.

The Gentile Problem

These consequences follow from the fact of Nazism. No historic fact is decisive proof of anything. However, Nazism comes as close as possible to proving that *no* form of anti-Jewishness is ever caused by Jewish behavior. This is not to say that the conduct of Jews does not matter. It matters greatly, both in and for itself and in response to manifestations of anti-Jewishness. In causal terms, however, *all* forms of anti-Jewishness are strains of a Gentile disease. In nineteenth-century Europe right-wing antisemites hated the Jews because they were revolutionaries, while left-wing antisemites criticized them because they were capitalists, and universalist liberals and particularistic nationalists complained, respectively, that the Jews mixed too little or too much with Gentile society. Occasionally, anti-Jewishness *was* recognized as a Gentile disease. Lessing did so in the eighteenth century,[6] while in the twentieth century the late, great Reinhold Niebuhr wrote:

> When a minority group is hated for its virtues as well as its vices, and when its vices are hated not so much because they are vices as because

6. In Lessing's *Nathan the Wise* a Templar approaches a Christian patriarch with the hypothetical case of a Jew who had pity on a Christian orphan and raised her in his home. He is told that the Jew must burn on the stake. The troubled Templar asks: What if he brought her up as a Jewess? What if he did *not* bring her up as a Jewess but simply as a decent person? What if the Jew could not save her soul, yet God in His power can do so? All questions receive the same reply: "No matter! The Jew must burn!"

they bear the stamp of uniqueness, we are obviously dealing with a collective psychology that is not easily altered by a little more enlightenment.[7]

These words were written in 1942, before the worst was known. Now that it *is* known, anyone responding by word or deed with the proverb "where there is smoke there is fire" is not a diagnostician of anti-Jewishness and its causes but himself a victim of the disease. This fact is in no way altered by assurances that the smoke is out of all proportion to any possible fire.

Like all theses about history, the present one requires qualifications:

First, an exposed social situation (whether of their own choosing, such as religious separatism, or of the world's making, such as spatial or social ghettoization) makes Jews convenient scapegoats on which knaves and fools can blame the current ills of society. This theory is fashionable among the enlightened of all ages, Gentile and Jewish. It turns the mind to a rational cure—the healing of the true ills in question. More important still, it denies the disease itself that uniqueness which is at all times anathema to the enlightened. However, by itself, the scapegoat theory of antisemitism explains neither the tenacity of anti-Jewishness nor the variety of its forms, to say nothing of the fact that other groups, no less exposed, have been turned into scapegoats rarely, differently, or not at all.[8]

Further, Jews can, in fact, behave in ways that may appear to cause anti-Jewish attitudes. Jewish usury in the Middle Ages is a case in point. However, the fact that (to paraphrase Niebuhr) Jews were hated for their virtues as well as their vices would in itself suffice to overthrow this theory. Add that Jews were driven into usury by state and church policies that were *already* anti-Jewish in inspiration and purpose, and the Jewish "vice" in question emerges, not as a cause of anti-Jewishness, but rather to effect self-fulfilling

---

7. "Love and Justice," *Selections from the Shorter Writings of Reinhold Niebuhr*, D.B. Robertson, ed., New York, 1967, p. 133.
8. In his *Anti-Semite and Jew*, New York, 1948, J. P. Sartre achieves some deep insights into antisemitism but loses them totally when at one point he lapses into the scapegoat theory, p. 54. In a celebrated joke, an antisemitic speaker at a meeting shouts: "The Jews are our misfortune!" Heckler: "The Jews and the cyclists!" Speaker (puzzled): "Why the cyclists?" Heckler: "Why the Jews?" This joke, a classic illustration of the scapegoat theory, has never cured a single antisemite. However, its enlightened tellers have always fondly believed it could.

anti-Jewish prophecies.[9] Never was the principle behind such
prophecies expressed with such cynical openness as when Goebbels
announced a policy of robbing Jews of their livelihood, thus driving
them into crime, and then punishing them as a criminal group.

Cases of victimization must be distinguished from authentic
actions. The most clearly authentic case of a collective Jewish action
in recent history is the founding of the State of Israel. Obviously,
there could be no anti-Zionism without Zionism, and no Israel without Zionism. Somewhat less obviously, anti-Zionism may "spill
over" into anti-Jewishness. Hence, it may seem that here at least is
one *bona fide* case in which Jewish behavior can actually *cause* anti-
Jewish attitudes where none existed.

However, even so drastic a Jewish action can at most only
reinforce existing anti-Jewish attitudes. It cannot create them. Why,
in the First World, are Jews criticized for their passivity in Nazi Europe—and for their "aggressiveness" and "intransigence" in Israel?
Why do those who praise Algerians and Vietnamese when they fight
for liberty blame Israelis when they fight for life itself? Why, in the
Second World, is acquisition of territory through conquest legitimate for large and secure nations—the Baltic countries by Soviet
Russia, Tibet by Red China—but illegitimate for a small and beleaguered nation and, of all small countries, only for that of the Jews?
Why, in the Third World, was an exchange of populations possible
between India and Pakistan but remains inconceivable to this day
between Arabs and Israelis? That Palestinian Arabs should have become hostile to the "invaders" is understandable, perhaps natural,
even inevitable. But were these so-called invaders not Jews, it is
questionable whether their hostility—to say nothing of that of the
Arab world—would have remained implacable. Indeed, except in
the context of Muslim and post-Muslim Arab anti-Jewish attitudes,
Arab policies toward Israel would appear to be unintelligible.[10]

Moreover, while in some quarters the disease of anti-Jewishness may have been aggravated by the existence of Israel, it may be
asked whether, in other quarters, it has not helped to alleviate or

---

9. In 1784 Moses Mendelssohn wrote: "We continue to be barred from the arts, the
sciences, the useful trades and occupations of mankind . . . while our alleged lack of
refinement is used as a pretext for our further oppression. They tie our hands and then
reproach us for not using them . . . ," *Jerusalem and Other Writings*, A. Jospe, tr.,
New York, 1969, p. 146.

10. See below, pp. 25–26.

even cure it. Since we cannot replay history we cannot answer this question. However, we would be fainthearted if we did not at least pose it. In our age anti-Jewish attitudes in North America and other Western countries have reached their lowest ebb since pre-Christian times. Doubtless the Holocaust has generated thought and contrition among Gentiles and thought and militancy among Jews. However, except for Israel, would anyone *really* remember? But for this unique witness, would either Jews or Gentiles understand the *radical* fact that Jews *need* not be tolerees when they are not victims; and, having understood, would they seek to cure the Gentile world of its anti-Jewish disease, or the Jewish People of its effects?

The Nature of Anti-Jewishness

If anti-Jewishness is a Gentile disease, we must ask, especially in view of the persistence of the phenomenon, why it should always be necessary to rediscover it. One answer, applying to a variety of group prejudices, will be readily accepted. However, this answer must be supplemented by a second, applicable to anti-Jewishness alone.

We set the word "prejudice" in quotation marks, for a disorder far deeper than obtuseness to facts is involved in relations between racist and victim or between colonizer and colonized. Thus enlightenment by itself is no cure. First, the oppressor believes that the oppressed is inferior. Second, he acts upon his belief so as to make it true. Third, his success is complete only when one who is oppressed accepts his own inferiority and the truth of his oppressor's belief. In that case, there is a certain false harmony in the relationship—the final reason why it can endure. In the eyes of neither the oppressor nor the oppressed is the oppression "real." A master-slave relation is not a case of oppression if it is understood as "natural." Each knows—and has—his place.

This insight, first stated by Hegel and developed (in ways sound or not-so-sound) by such thinkers as Marx, Kojève, Sartre and Fanon, is today widely accepted wherever serious attempts are made to end (rather than merely to alleviate) such social ills as racism and colonialism. The slogan "Zionism is the liberation movement of the Jewish people" illustrates the belief that the social disease of anti-Jewishness and its cure are wholly parallel to these others. Even the relation between antisemite and self-hating

Jew is not entirely parallel—and not all Jews are self-hating. The self-hating Jew hates his Jewishness, while the antisemite considers his Jew hatred to be both caused and justified by the other's Jewishness. On his part, the Jew who is not self-hating detests, not his Jewishness, but rather his condition of exile which distorts his Jewishness; he seeks to liberate his Jewishness from exile, not himself from his Jewishness. As for the antisemite, he hates (as we have already stressed) Jewish virtues as well as Jewish vices. If forced to justify his hatred of *these*, he emerges as hating the Jew, not for his actions but because they are the actions of a Jew. He hates the Jew for existing at all.

As we have seen, there can be a relation of false harmony between colonizer and colonized, or between racist and victim. The antisemite (as Sartre has rightly said) is a criminal who seeks the Jew's death.[11] In such a relation the Jew should not exist at all—or should commit suicide. In fairness to all so-called decent oppressors—racist and colonizer as well as antisemite—we must add that there are degrees of hostility, as well as ways of disguising it from others and, above all, from oneself. In fairness also to the antisemites of pre-Holocaust times, we must further add that the group death of the Jewish People could be achieved in two ways—by genocide and radical assimilation. As decent a thinker as Kant could assert that the "euthanasia" of the Jewish People was desirable for Jews and Gentiles alike. That this particular expression sounds singularly unfortunate two centuries later cannot, in fairness, be considered his fault.

If racism, colonialism and anti-Jewishness were completely parallel phenomena, we should expect opponents of the first two to be firm supporters of the State of Israel, however critical they may be of this or that policy of an Israeli government. This, of course, is not so. In one quarter the Jewish State is hated because its Jews are not victims or tolerees of anyone; in other quarters it is hated because it willfully considers itself Jewish. (In 1944 Sartre wrote that "the anti-Semite reproaches the Jew with being Jewish; the democrat reproaches him with willfully considering himself a Jew."[12]) That fascist and communist United Nations representatives should have joined hands to denounce Zionism as a form of racism will always remain incredible. It would have been impossible were there not two

11. *Anti-Semite and Jews*, p. 49.
12. *Ibid.*, p. 58.

ways of destroying Jewish existence—by destroying the existence and by destroying the Jewishness.

What elements, then, added to those of racism and colonialism, enter into anti-Jewishness—its unique persistence, mutability, and nature? Its persistence may seem to be accounted for in terms of Diaspora history, a history longer and more varied than those, for example, of black slavery in America and European colonialism in Africa. But this answer only raises further questions: Why was the Jewish Diaspora accompanied by antagonism (which is not true of all diasporas), and why did even radical changes (such as that from the premodern to the modern world) not end the antagonism but merely change its nature, rationalizations and self-definitions?

We are driven, then, to pursue further the insight articulated by Reinhold Niebuhr. Had the Jews been hated only by the virtuous for their alleged vices (such as usury in the Middle Ages or lack of refinement at the time of Mendelssohn), anti-Jewishness should have ended with the disappearance of those vices or the standards which looked upon them as such. Had they been hated only for their virtues by the vicious, anti-Jewishness should at no time have had the social and spiritual respectability which has made it so uniquely powerful, lasting and deadly. *It is the anti-Jewishness of the saints (in secular terms, the idealists), far more than that of the sinners, which characterizes the uniqueness of the disease.*

This conclusion disposes of a theory of anti-Jewishness long fashionable among traditional Jews and now also found in secularist form. There is *Sin'ah* (Jew-hatred) because of Sinai, a Jewish tradition affirms. Jews are hated, claims its secularist counterpart, because they brought respect for human life into the world. This theory fails to explain why Jews are hated for their vices by Gentile fellow sinners. Far more seriously, it fails to account for the startling fact of saintly hatred, the more so when its object includes Jewish virtues. We are here considering people of love, grace and humility, who care for the poor, for widows, for orphaned children, for strangers within their gates, and who would lay down their lives to save another. These are people whose own lives declare the sacredness of human life, their oneness with all human suffering, their refusal to justify evil and violence and even the shedding of a single tear. Yet there is one exception to their virtues: hatred of "the Jews." Why should religious saints hate rather than love Jews because of Sinai? Why should secular idealists hate rather than love them for having brought respect for human life into the world? The failure to answer these questions implies that anti-Jewishness is incurable so long as there are Jews, when, in fact (as we shall see), it must be viewed as obdurate but not beyond cure. In failing to ask these questions the theory fails to confront anti-Jewishness in that aspect which lends it its unique power, and fails to confront it among those who, once challenged, might be better able to cure themselves. We are referring, of course, to the anti-Jewishness of saints and idealists.

Anti-Jewishness has its effective origins in Christianity and reflects those origins to this day. This thesis, like our earlier one, must be qualified, and in this case (lest it be misunderstood) before it is even explored.

Anti-Jewish attitudes predate Christianity in pagan antiquity. However, the saints of the Greco-Roman world did recognize Jewish virtues. Although the philosopher Theophrastus "recoiled" from Jewish animal sacrifices, he admired Jews as "philosophers by race."[13] Christianity not only perpetuated but also transformed pre-Christian anti-Jewish attitudes, and the transformation was crucial.

Again, anti-Jewish attitudes postdate Christianity in modern secularism, that is, in pseudo-Christian right-wing nationalism, anti-Christian left-wing liberalism and radicalism, and, most important, Nazi idolatry which aimed at the destruction of Christianity as a goal second in importance only to the destruction of the Jewish People.

However, without Christianity modern nationalist pseudo-Christianity would have been impossible. The modern liberal-leftist aim to make Jews—and no one but Jews—into men-in-general is a transformation of the Christian opposition to Jews-in-particular. And the Nazi murder camps were the apocalyptic nemesis of an anti-Jewishness which has persisted (whether in dormant or violent form) among Christian saints throughout the centuries. At its bravest and most authentic, organized German Christians resisted the Nazi onslaught on the Jewish People only because they were considered attacks on Jesus Christ.[14] We can imagine that Theophrastus would

13. *Greek and Latin Authors on Jews and Judaism*, M. Stern, ed., Jerusalem, 1974, vol. 1, pp. 8 ff.
14. T.A. Gill writes: "And even after it got rolling, the Confessing Church was late in its perceptions. I cannot get gooseflesh over the systematic refinement in Barmen's discovery that the attacks on the Jews must be resisted because they were in reality attacks on Jesus Christ. That is not high theology. That is blasphemy, the unwitting

consent to attacks on Jewish animal sacrifices. But we cannot imagine that he would defend "philosophers by race" on grounds no more forceful than that what was really being attacked was philosophy.

Not all Christians are, or were, afflicted by the disease of anti-Jewishness. In view of the content of the thesis stated above, this qualification is crucial. However, while its truth would seem obvious, its significance is complex, obscure and, possibly, even beyond present comprehension.

In the present context, it must suffice to reject a false view of its significance. The distinction between the anti-Jewishness of "mere Christendom" and a "true Christianity" free of all hatred (and hence necessarily free of Jew hatred) is obviously apologetic. That it is also false is demonstrated by the fact that there were anti-Jewish saints, among them St. Chrysostom, St. Augustine and Martin Luther. That this fact of saintly Christian anti-Jewishness is significant beyond its Christian limits is indicated by the presence, in all post-Christian forms of the phenomenon, of anti-Jewish idealists. Thus, nineteenth century secularist antisemites—right-wing, left-wing, and liberal—all included secular saints, that is, enemies and critics of the Jews who were inspired not by low passions, but by high ideals. Had the target of these saints been only Jewish vices, real or imagined, that target would not have been "the Jews." Yet while Jewish defense organizations of those times kept stressing precisely that point, their labors were quite in vain.

Nazism escalated the logic of anti-Jewishness to its unsurpassable extreme. Jewish virtue and vice were irrelevant. Jewish birth was itself a crime, deserving torture and death. The most shocking fact about the most shocking Nazi crime, however, is that, in essence, it was an idealistic enterprise—the work not of petty scoundrels or vicious sadists but of men and women sacrificing all to the "Final Solution."[15]

---

blasphemy, I hope, of men playing a dandy hand at doctrine. It was played out to the end, too. In the letter sent around preparing for the Stuttgart confession after the war, was there much about the guilt against the Jews? Was there anything? [There was not, E.L.F.] We have little to learn from any church or any prophet who cannot recognize murder until it is murder in the cathedral." See "What Can America Learn from the Struggle?" in *The German Church Struggle and the Holocaust,* F. H. Littell and H. G. Locke, ed., Detroit, 1974, p. 286.

15. In a secret address to the S.S., on October 4, 1943, Heinrich Himmler declared: ". . . 'The Jewish people is going to be annihilated,' says every party member. 'Sure,

Indeed, so shocking is this fact that it would be thought to have made impossible all historically post-Holocaust anti-Jewishness on the part of religious or secular saints. It is all the more startling, and depressing evidence of the tenacity and mutability of the anti-Jewish virus, that this impossibility is only apparent. "Saintly" anti-Jewishness has not ended but rather developed a wholly new strain which, for the first time in history, goes to any length to deny that Jews are its target. Pre-Nazi, "decent" antisemites would salve their consciences by citing exceptions when attacking "the Jews." Nazism did away with the exceptions.[16] Post-Nazi "saintly" anti-Jewishness shrinks from this horror and claims to attack only those Jews who are not "true" Jews.

From this point, only one step is needed to identify the "false" Jews; they are, of course, the Zionists—the more undefined the Zionism, the easier the step. That this new distinction between "true" and "false" Jews is simply the old disease in yet another form is obvious once we discover the nature of those who belong to these two groups. The "false" Jewish Zionists include, first, *all* Israelis, whether right or left, religious or secularist, "hawks" or "doves"—so long as they refuse to submit to politicide. They include, second, *all* Jews *anywhere* so long as they refuse to abandon the State of Israel to politicide. As for the "true" Jews, they reduce themselves to two kinds: those who allow their Jewish identity to disintegrate for the sake of mankind and those who are prepared—one generation after Hitler—to entrust their Jewish destiny to the mercies of the world. This new strain of the ancient anti-Jewishness finds its climax when the one who calls the "false" Jews back to their "true" Jewishness claims himself to be—symbolically, to be sure—the true Jew.[17]

---

it's in our program, elimination of the Jews, annihilation—we'll take care of it.' And then they all come trudging, 80 million worthy Germans, and each has his one decent Jew. Sure, the others are swine, but this one is an A-1 Jew. Of all those who talk this way, not one has seen it happen, not one has been through it. Most of you must know what it means to see a hundred corpses lie side by side, or five hundred, or a thousand. To have stuck this out and—excepting cases of human weakness—to have remained decent, that is what has made us hard. In our history, this is an unwritten and never-to-be-written page of glory . . ." *A Holocaust Reader,* L. Dawidowicz, ed., New York, 1976, p. 133.

16. In the Himmler address quoted in the preceding note, the "decent" antisemites of earlier times have become insufficiently idealistic, and the new "decency" of Jew hatred consists precisely of considering Jewish virtue and vice equally irrelevant to the crime of Jewish birth.

17. A. Roy Eckardt has analyzed this strain of anti-Jewishness as it erupted among

The inquiry into the uniqueness of the disease of anti-Jewishness—its nature, tenacity, and mutability—is thus refocused into an inquiry concerning the hatred of Jewish virtues by Gentile religious saints and idealists. There are attempts within the Christian community, few as yet to be sure, but compelling in their courage and relentlessness, to discover the primal roots of the dread plague within the Christian tradition itself. "The antisemitism in the New Testament" is no longer an uncommon expression, although it still awaits thorough exploration by Christians. For our purposes, it does indicate the profound ambiguity of the books of the New Testament, which, on one hand, affirm God's promise to keep His people Israel yet, on the other, deny that very peoplehood: "Only the faithful," but not all of Israel is Israel; read back into the "Old Testament," these faithful reduce themselves to a few isolated individuals. The flesh-and-blood people is lost. Thus, it is no wonder that for centuries the Church considered herself either as the "true" Israel opposed to one always false, or else the "new" Israel opposed to one already long dead.

Some Christians go even further. Is hatred of Jews built into the Christian gospel itself? Is it so much a part of the kerygma itself that only the most radical attempt to identify the evil and transform the teaching can save the Good News?

Whatever the answers to these radical questions, hatred of Jewish virtues by Gentile religious saints and secularist idealists may be said to have found its first systematic expression in the patristic *anti-Judaeos* literature. There, Jews are guilty both for obeying "the law" *and* for disobeying it; of "legalistically" observing the Sabbath *and* of giving to God only one day out of seven; their wickedness is both imputable as though it were willed *and* incurable as though it were hereditary.[18] Add to this page from the "Dark

---

certain liberal Christians following the Yom Kippur War, among them Professor Robert Cushman who asserted that decent respect for the opinions of mankind dictated that the price for Israel's existence was too high, and Father Daniel Berrigan who set himself up, before an Arab group, as the true—if symbolic—Jew. (See "The Devil and Yom Kippur," *Midstream*, Aug./Sept. 1974.) However, this strain has been evident at least since the Six Day War when voices from Geneva thought it a duty to remind Jews in Israel of their prophetic heritage—after the victory. Earlier, when Israel was threatened, Geneva showed no signs of concern.

18. The focusing of attention on the *anti-Judaeos* literature, for purposes of Roman Catholic self-criticism, is one of the great merits of Rosemary Ruether's *Faith and Fratricide*, New York, 1974, ch. 3.

Ages" the fact that Luther rewrote just that page even while writing
the first page of modern history,[19] and it is no longer altogether obscure why nineteenth century European nationalist idealists considered even patriotic Jews suspect because they *were* Jews; why their
no less idealistic internationalist opponents considered even radical
Jews suspect so long as they *considered themselves* Jews; why, during the apocalypse, German Nazis treated Jewish birth as a crime not
in spite but because of their idealism; and why, today, high-minded
post-Holocaust rightists and leftists unite to deny the legitimacy of
the State of Israel—the one because this state is composed of and
governed by Jews, the other because it is composed of and governed
by people who willfully consider themselves Jews.[20]

What still remains obscure in all these forms of saintly anti-
Jewishness is its relentlessness and centrality in the respective
schemes of things. What drove some Church Fathers into the radically un-Christian assertion that even baptism cannot redeem "the
Jews"? What caused Eichmann's priorities when he redirected trains
from the Russian front to Auschwitz?

In the nineteenth century, Bruno Bauer, ex-Protestant theolo-
gian turned left-wing atheist and anti-Jewish arch-ideologue, made
the following assertions. It is not the Christian daughter who is guilty for wishing to get rid of the Jewish mother; the Jewish mother is
guilty for wanting to live. The Jewish mother *had* to die for the
Christian daughter and her secularist offspring to live.[21] This piece

19. In our context it is worth recalling that the early Luther was decidedly pro-Jewish
but in his old age matched or even exceeded his medieval predecessors in anti-Jewish
venom because Jews proved to be no less stubborn in their insistence on surviving as
Jews vis-à-vis the new form of Christianity as they had been vis-à-vis the old.
20. Here is one reason why liberals and leftists are so easily taken in by the fraudulent
idea of a "Palestinian secular democratic state in which Jews, Muslims and Christians
can live together." That Arab propaganda does its best to exploit this liberal-leftist
weakness was to be expected.
21. Bruno Bauer, in *The Jewish Problem*, Helen Lederer tr., Cincinnati, 1958, writes:
"The hostility of the Christian world towards the Jews has been called inexplicable. Is
not Judaism the mother of Christianity, Jewish religion predecessor of Christianity?
Why this hatred of the Christians, this enormous ingratitude of the consequent for
the cause, of the daughter for the mother?" (p. 7). He answers his own question as follows: "Not the daughter is ungrateful toward the mother, but the mother
does not want to acknowledge her daughter. The daughter has really the higher right,
because she represents the true nature of the mother . . . If one wants to call both
sides egotistical, then the daughter is selfish for wanting her own way and progress,
and the mother because she wants her own way but no progress." On Bauer, see my
Encounters Between Judaism and Modern Philosophy, New York, 1973, pp. 142 ff.

of imagery diagnoses brilliantly, if unwittingly, the Gentile disease of anti-Jewishness—its nature, tenacity, and mutability. Why do certain Christian and post-Christian saints and idealists consider, in Jews and Jews alone, those characteristics as vices which, anywhere else, they would consider as virtues? Why, to them, is the "viciousness" of Jewish virtue a vice both unredeemable and central in the scheme of things? In Bauer's imagery because the mere survival of the "mother" threatens the "daughter's" very life. Put otherwise, *for these saints and idealists their self-affirmation is inseparable from the negation of the Jew.* On this point, the noblest saints afflicted by the disease are at one with depraved sinners. Julius Streicher wrote: "Who fights the Jew fights the devil. Who masters the devil conquers Heaven."[22]

However, Bauer's imagery also shows that the disease of anti-Jewishness is neither inevitable nor incurable. The mother-daughter relationship normally need not be antagonistic, to say nothing of being a life-and-death struggle. Minimally, the two can part company when the daughter has reached maturity. Maximally, each can continue to find strength and joy in the otherness of the other.

Contemporary Arab Anti-Jewishness

Why do anti-Jewish attitudes exist outside the Christian world? There is almost no part of the globe which is wholly outside Christian or post-Christian influence. Moreover, the Streicher-inspired cartoons prevalent in the pre-1967 Arab press and Arab translations of European antisemitic tracts are evidence of the ease with which even the most noxious strains of the anti-Jewish virus can be exported. Still, unless these exports found a positive response their effects would surely be marginal. In the Arab world this is not so. A segment of Palestinian Arabs has opposed, to a self-destructive extreme, any form of Jewish state in their neighborhood. The most moderate of current Arab statesmen has described the small Jewish island in an Arab ocean as a dagger in the heart of his own far larger and more populous country. Arab nationalism is so inextricably

---

22. Quoted in *The Yellow Spot: The Extermination of the Jews in Germany,* London, 1936, p. 47. This book, its title, and its date of publication all refute the accepted view that "it wasn't known and couldn't have been predicted." Its anonymous compilers and the Bishop of Durham (who wrote a moving preface) were voices in the wilderness.

bound up with negation of the "Zionist entity" that we may doubt whether Arab nationalism would not indeed disintegrate were this negative support ever to be removed.

We need not go beyond the evidence given elsewhere in this volume[23] to recognize that Islam, the second "daughter" of the Jewish "mother," has also fallen prey to the disease of anti-Jewishness, quite apart from any influence of her "sister." The ways are in some respects different, in others the same. The main difference is that Christian anti-Jewishness (and its derivatives) negates Jewish existence, while Muslim anti-Jewishness (and its derivatives) negates only Jewish equality, especially when it finds political expression. The main resemblance is that both forms of hostility include saints and idealists among their subjects and Jewish virtues among their objects.

The main cause of the difference is obvious enough: Christianity originated on Jewish soil, in the midst of a flesh-and-blood, still semi-autonomous, Jewish nation. When Islam originated, the Jews had already been in exile for centuries. They were in the eyes of the new religion no longer a nation but only a religious sect. In view of the vastness of this difference, the resemblance is all the more depressing; despite the "mother's" shadowy existence, the younger "daughter" has found herself threatened by the "mother's" feeble signs of life, is shocked to the marrow by her mother's miraculous new youth. It is fortunate, however, that Muslim and post-Muslim secular Arab anti-Jewishness is neither universal nor inevitable. In this case, too, antagonism is not the only possible mother-daughter relation.

Jewish Identity

The Gentile disease of anti-Jewishness can only be cured by the patients themselves—the two daughters of the Jewish mother and their respective offspring can be healed by no one but themselves. However, the Jewish mother can assist in two interrelated ways. She may remove herself, so far as she is able, from the power of her daughters. (Of this more will be said below.) Again, she may cure herself insofar as she has been infected by the daughters' disease; that is, it is necessary to break the circle in which the oppressor

23. See Ma'oz, pp. 33–51.

becomes a just accuser and the victim confesses guilt. The negative task of breaking this circle has as its positive counterpart the search for an authentic identity.

Such a search, obviously, must seek to end all Jewish self-hatred, open or disguised. Less obvious is the need to end or transform a plethora of qualified Jewish self-affirmations which are unauthentic to the extent to which they reflect a plethora of qualified anti-Jewish negations. The nineteenth-century German (or French or Hungarian) superpatriot of the Mosaic faith; his internationalist contemporary who expressed his Jewishness by dissolving it, thus leading all peoples in the march toward universalist mankind; the open-minded Jew who kept his Jewishness from his sons and daughters lest he deprive them of a free identity of their own when "they were old enough to choose"—these and other Jewish identities were all unauthentic. Yet they survive to this day. Moreover, others have been added by the events of this century. One is the Jew who forgets the Holocaust as if it were a guilty secret or as if it were selfish for a Jew to remember it. Another is the true Jew who outdoes all other anti-Zionists in opposing the false Jewish Zionists. An authentic Jewish identity is possible only if two questions are clearly separated: How should a Jew respond to anti-Jewish attitudes—indeed, what Gentile attitudes should be viewed as anti-Jewish? And what shall it mean to be a Jew today and tomorrow?

This separation by no means marks the end of the contemporary Jewish identity crisis. It would be more correct to say that it only reveals it; for just as there are unauthentic Jewish identities so there are authentic identity crises. The fact that the search for a Jewish identity has been emancipated from the tyranny of all forms of internalized anti-Jewishness only brings into clear focus the truth that the authentic identity crisis of the contemporary Jew is without precedent. The pre-modern Jew knew his identity: he was covenanted to the God of Israel. His secularist modern descendant could seek a new Jewish identity by abolishing those "abnormalities" caused by a religious tradition to which he yet owed his existence. However, the present-day religious Jew no longer can view the Jewish secularist as nothing but an apostate, and the present-day secularist Jew can no longer view the religious Jew as simply a relic of the past. Each must include the other when defining his own Jewish identity, and while the problem is with us, the solution has yet to come. This unprecedented crisis in post-modern Jewish identity is the result of two enormous facts. One is the State of Israel. The other, however, has an enormity which forces us to view it quite by itself: *Every Jew alive today would either be dead or unborn but for a geographic accident.*

This is a novum in the human condition, without parallel in Jewish or any other history. Philosophers have not yet noticed this novum—nor have Jewish thinkers done much better. Its significance for Jewish identity is as yet obscure. Only one thing is clear: The Jewish identity crisis cannot be confronted authentically unless the novum is faced in all its stark uniqueness. It is said that this is the first time in Jewish history that a Jew can cease to be a Jew without being compelled to adopt another identity, and, consequently, that the present Jewish identity crisis can authentically be solved by its simple dissolution. But it is not at all obvious that the conclusion follows from the premise. A generation ago, Franz Rosenzweig realized that he could not authentically become a Christian without first knowing the Judaism he was about to leave. He never did leave, and subsequently helped to write a new page in Jewish history. No Jew today can genuinely abandon his Jewish identity without asking whether in so doing he is helping to close the book of a history which should be closed, or is abandoning those who are writing a new page which cries out to be written; whether he is leaving the ranks of past victims whose death has retroactively become pointless, or he is joining the ranks of possible future murderers and bystanders; whether he is serving the cause of God and man or betraying it.

The Centrality of Israel

It is doubtful whether the Jewish People could effect its own spiritual cure from the disease of anti-Jewishness were it not for the fact that one of its parts has removed itself physically from the reach of anti-Jewish power—by founding the Third Jewish Commonwealth. This event, momentous in Gentile as well as Jewish history (the former minimally to the extent that it has suffered from the disease of anti-Jewishness), has transformed the Jewish condition in two respects which are related to our present purpose. Israel, a small yet independent state, has given a new dimension to the unauthentic position of the Jew who allows his Jewishness to be defined by others. And, building the Law of Return into its very substance, Israel has given a new dimension to the unauthenticity of the Jew who is voluntarily a toleree (to say nothing of being a victim) of societies, theologies, philosophies and ideologies of others. Thus, it has come to pass, as a corresponding fact, that in search for an authentic Jewish identity the State of Israel is central.

These assertions may seem frivolous or downright foolish at a time when the new, post-Holocaust, anti-Zionist strain of anti-Jewishness has become so worldwide as to have given rise, among certain Jews, to complaints that the Jewish State, intended as a solution to the Jewish problem, has *become* the Jewish problem, and that, intended as a spiritual center, it resembles more closely a beleaguered fortress.

Yet Herzl and Ahad Ha-Am, while wrong in one respect, were right in another. Herzl was wrong in his naive belief that a Jewish State would establish a natural Jewish existence and end the disease of anti-Jewishness; he was more right than he could have known in his belief that the Jewish People must stop tolerating what, since the Holocaust, has become absolutely intolerable: Jewish acceptance of the status of victim for those sick with anti-Jewishness or of the status of toleree of the semi-cured. Not long ago a Zionist leader proposed that Israel become a ward of the world community. Only a few years later it is clear that, so long as the world community remains infected with the disease of anti-Jewishness, the guardian is unsuitable and that, if and when the disease is vanquished, the guardian will not be necessary. Herzl was more correct than many who came after him.

Ahad Ha-Am too was wrong and right. The Jewish State does not abound with synagogues which are centers of superior piety or universities of superior excellence. The life-style of its citizens is too harried by the petty problems of daily existence, and by the deep worries concerning national existence, to be of much help to Jewish visitors in search of a Jewish life-style of their own. (There is more leisure for spiritual matters at the periphery than at the center.) The Jewish State is not, so far, a spiritual center of world Jewry in this sense. Yet Ahad Ha-Am was right in a way he could not have anticipated. Without Israel, the Diaspora's own spirituality would shrivel into mere fideism. Without the Jewish State, Diaspora Jews, even after the Holocaust, would belittle "mere" Jewish survival unless it served ideals acceptable to those who would allow Jews to live, provided they served exactly those ideals.[24] Without Israel's Law of Return, Diaspora Judaism would make Jewish homelessness into a blessing, viewing the bitter fact of persecution as meaningful martyrdom, and the degrading condition of toleree as an opportunity to turn the other cheek. This would be true of the Judaism of the modern-minded. As for the orthodox, they would try to rebuild ghetto walls which have crumbled beyond repair.

Epilogue

A modern view of great longevity has it that the Jewish People has survived through the ages only because of the pressures of its enemies. Friends holding this view have always hoped for the end of the enmity; foes have always hoped for the end of the Jewish People. Still others, neither friends nor foes, or a little of each, have always desired an end of both. The pre-Holocaust version of this view extends to both the People and its faith. The post-Holocaust version professes to respect the intrinsic value and vitality of the faith, seeking an end only of the People, and of those only insofar as they insist on *being* a People. Only the "Zionists" and their "entity" are without intrinsic value and vitality, a pseudo-nation bound to dissolve once enemies cease to threaten it. Zionism and antisemitism belong together, and the first is the product of the second.

Such is said to be the rationale of the current policies of Egypt, Israel's most peaceful Arab neighbor state. Peace with Israel is not considered incompatible with seeking her destruction but, on the contrary, the surest way to bring it about. An Israel at peace would be destroyed internally by factional strife—between secularists and orthodox, Europeans and Orientals, rich and poor; she would be externally abandoned, on the one hand, by Diaspora Jewry; on the other, by what is left of a world conscience.

---

24. A decade ago Milton Himmelfarb exclaimed: "After the Holocaust, let no one call Jewish survival 'mere'!" Now Terrence des Pres has written *The Survivor*, (New York, 1976), a profound meditation that questions "a tradition which speaks of 'merely' surviving, as if in itself life were not worth much; as if we felt life is justified only by things which negate it" (p. 5). He finds "the grandeur of death . . . lost in a world of mass murder" (p. 6), and sees a significance both profound and universal in the defiant affirmation of life shown by inmates of the death camps. He quotes a Belsen survivor as saying: "In my happier days I used to remark on the aptitude of the saying, 'When in life we are in the midst of death.' I have since learned that it's more apt to say, "When in death we are in the midst of life'."

Jews cannot speak on behalf of world conscience. On their own behalf, however, they should accept this challenge—both the explicit challenge to Israel and the implicit challenge to the whole Jewish People. Let her enemies make peace with the State of Israel! And let it be shown by future history whether Jewish rebirth at Jerusalem after Jewish death at Auschwitz was, after all, a mere illusion—the birth a stillbirth—or whether, on the contrary, it was a live birth, with the prospect that the new Jerusalem might grow to be a blessing which would match or even surpass the old.

In the pre-modern world Yehudah Halevi wrote: "Jerusalem can be rebuilt only when Israel yearns after it to such an extent that we love even its stones and dust."[25] A post-Holocaust Jew might add: "In loving the stones and dust of Jerusalem, the Jewish People will rebuild itself after its greatest catastrophe; only in rebuilding itself can it be a light unto the nations."

25. *Sefer ha-Kuzari*, v. 27.

The Image of the Jew in Official Arab Literature and Communications Media

Moshe Ma'oz

Introduction

Although the Koran and other Muslim classic writings contain grave anti-Jewish expressions, they are not arranged within a consistent frame of reference, as in Christianity. Side by side with such expressions, there are in the Koran and in Islamic literature certain positive expressions regarding Jews, as well as an inherent recognition of the partial revelation in Judaism.

Even more positive attitudes towards Jews and Judaism are to be found among a great many Arabs before the rise of Islam, on the eve of the modern era, and throughout long periods in the history of the Muslim lands. Generally speaking, the traditional approach of the Muslim Arabs to the Jew has been ambivalent: ethnic kinship and cultural affinity on the one hand, together with a belief in their political superiority and religious supremacy on the other. This attitude is by no means similar to the unequivocal anti-Jewish attitude of medieval Christian Europe and Nazi Germany which was based on religious hatred and racial animosity.

True, Islam imposed on the Jews political and judicial discriminatory laws, social and economic limitations and religioritual restrictions, while Muslim masses occasionally maltreated and sometimes even organized pogroms against Jews. Yet, these outrages, from which Christians suffered more than Jews, were in general not motivated by racial animosity, while the religiotheological factor was not always the predominant factor. Muslim anti-Jewish discrimination and pogroms were in no way similar to the institutionalized and systematic demonstration of anti-Semitism in the Inquisition cells of Christian Spain and in the gas chambers of Nazi Germany.

Alas, less than a generation after the horrible demonstration of anti-Semitism in Europe, we were witnessing the rapid development of official Arab Judaeophobia, the ideology of which includes

33

the essentials of medieval Christian and modern Nazi anti-Semitism, in addition to the anti-Zionist ideas of radical left movements.[1] These are integrated in, and adjusted to, the new anti-Jewish official Arab ideology, which is allegedly rooted in the Islamic culture and tradition.

Christian influences on the Muslim attitude toward Jews can be traced in the Koran and in early Islamic literature. Until the new era, however, these influences did not carry weight, mainly because in Islam there was no organized anti-Jewish movement. Only since the nineteenth century, with the impact of Western European ideas, have elements of European anti-Semitism, such as the "blood libel" and later the *Protocols of the Elders of Zion,* found their way into Arab literature and the communications media, particularly through Christian-Arab writers. In the 1930s, with Fascist and Nazi propaganda in the Middle East, further anti-Semitic elements were added to the developing Arab Judaeophobia.

However, it should be emphasized that despite these Christian-European influences, Arab Judaeophobia draws essentially upon Islamic religious literature and religious teaching, because of the centrality of Islam in modern Arab ideologies and cultural tradition. Moreover, the initiators or sponsors of this Arab Judaeophobia are to be found among the Arab-Muslim political and intellectual elite in the Arab states. Their motives are not religiocultural or socioeconomic, as in the anti-Semitic movements in other parts of the world, but are primarily nationalistic and political. Anti-Jewish expressions in the Koran and early Muslim writings are taken out of their context and given contemporary significance, with the aim of distorting the traditional image of the Jew in the Arab mind—an image which was ambivalent, never categorically negative. The new image which the Arab leadership has been attempting to create is that of an evil and demoniac Jew, who constitutes a grave danger to Arabism and Islam, as well as to human civilization.

THE JEWISH STEREOTYPE IN CLASSICAL ISLAM

It is true that several positive attitudes toward Jews can be found in the Koran and the *ḥadith.* Jews are considered among the *ahl al-kitab,* "people of the book," who believe in God and are to be treated as a protected people. In the Koran (*sura* II, v. 59) it is written:

1. See particularly Yehoshafat Harkabi, *Emdat Ha'aravim besikhsukh Israel-Arav (The Arab Position in the Arab-Israeli Conflict),* Tel Aviv, 1963, ch. v.

"Verily, whether it be those who believe, or those who are Jews or Christians or Sabaeans, whosoever believe in God and the last day and act aright, they have their reward at their Lord's hand, and there is no fear for them, nor shall they grieve."[2] Moreover, according to the *hadith*, Muhammad said: "He who harms a member of a protected nation—I shall be his prosecutor on the Day of Judgment."[3]

However, the Jewish stereotype, deriving from the Koran and the *ḥadith*, which finds expression in the Muslim literature of the Middle Ages and the modern period, is primarily negative, although it does not extend to the extreme rejection of the Jew found in the literature of ancient Greece and Rome,[4] or in the literature of Christian theology.

The conception of the Jew as it appears in Muslim literature may be described under three main headings which follow.

Abasement, Wretchedness and God's Wrath

One of the central anti-Jewish motifs in the Koran is found in *sura* II, v. 58: "Then were they smitten with abasement and poverty, and met with wrath from God. That was because they had misbelieved in God's signs and killed the prophets undeservedly; that was for that they were rebellious and had transgressed."[5] This verse, which is repeated in various forms in the Koran, refers to those people who break the covenant and are rebuked and cursed by God. The words, later removed from their immediate, contemporary context, have served for many generations as the basis for serious anti-Jewish charges, and have even achieved universal, eternal implications. As a Syrian Muslim religious leader of our own time has testified, "The description of the Children of Israel found in the Koran is not a description of a phenomenon which appeared during the period of Prophethood, but rather of an old disease which existed throughout the generations of the Jews, age after age."[6]

---

2. The Koran, trans. by E. J. Palmer, London 1938.
3. According to Baladhuri, *Futuh al-Buldan*, Leiden, 1866, p. 162; quoted in S. Rosenblatt, "The Jews and Islam," *Essays on Anti-Semitism*, K. S. Pinson, ed., New York, 1946, p. 114. Some scholars hold that this is one of a group of forged *ḥadiths*.
4 Cf. S. D. Goitein, "The Angry Religion," *Dinaburg Memorial Volume* (Hebrew), Jerusalem, 1949, p. 151.
5. The Koran, *sura* II, v. 58.
6. *The Fourth Conference of the Academy of Islamic Research* /Al Azhar/ Rajab, 1388 (Cairo, 1970), p. 530. This will be referred to in later notes as *Fourth Conference/Al Azhar/*.

On the basis of this verse and other expressions in the Koran the Jews were depicted in the Muslim religious literature of the Middle Ages and in the Arab political and educational writings of our own time as criminals and traitors, plotters, breakers of agreements, and distorters of sacred writings; in particular, they were depicted as a rebellious people who violate world order. Muslim historians and philosophers and Arab political leaders took the first part of the verse, "Then were they smitten with abasement and poverty . . ." and interpreted it as an irremediable heavenly judgment; from this, Muslims assume that it is their duty to debase the Jews to a state of complete humiliation. A *fatwa* (religious legal opinion) of the fourteenth century again affirms the official Muslim stand regarding the Jews: "It is known that the Jews and the Christians are branded with the marks of wrath and malediction of the Lord. . . ."[7] Ibn Khaldun, the great Arab historian of the same century, defines this in terms of the loss of collective consciousness of the children of Israel, their dispersion throughout the world, their alienation from the rest of humanity, and their living a life of disgrace and degradation. (He even claims that the Jews were infected with such evil character traits as corruption and deceitful plotting.)[8]

Similar opinions are expressed in our own day. For example, at the opening of the Fourth Conference of the Academy of Islamic Research in 1968 the Rector of Al-Azhar made the following statement with regard to Zionists of the State of Israel: "Those who adhere to Zionism are destined to dispersion by the Deity (as it is said), 'and humiliation and wretchedness were stamped upon them and they were visited with wrath from God'."[9]

Muhammad Anwar Sadat, President of Egypt, made use of the same verse before the Yom Kippur War. In a speech delivered on April 25, 1972, on the anniversary of the birth of the Prophet Muhammad, he attacked Israel, which was in control of Jerusalem, promising that he would crush its arrogance and return it to the "humiliation and wretchedness established in the Koran." Referring to the experience of the Prophet Muhammad, he argued that the Jews are "a nation of liars and traitors, plotters, a people born for deeds of

---

7. G. E. von Grunebaum, *Medieval Islam*, Chicago, 1962, p. 178.
8. Abd al-Raḥman ibn Khaldun, *Introduction to the Science of History/Muqaddima/* trans. into Hebrew by O. Koplevitz, Jerusalem, 1964, pp. 91, 155.
9. *Fourth Conference/Al Azhar/*, p. 2.

treachery."[10] In November 1971, King Faisal had proclaimed that the Jews, who had strayed from the laws of Moses and had attempted to kill Jesus, were cursed by God through the prophets. Similar statements may be found in Egyptian and Jordanian textbooks which appeared in 1966, a year before the Six Day War.[11]

The Jew as the Enemy of Muslims and Mankind

Another central anti-Jewish motif in the Koran is that which depicts Jews as great enemies of the Muslims: "Thou wilt surely find that the strongest in enmity against those who believe are the Jews and the idolators; and thou wilt find the nearest in love to those who believe to be those who say, 'We are Christians'."[12]

Based on this verse, a malevolent image of the Jew as one who plots to kill the Muslim at any opportune moment developed in the *hadith* and in classical Muslim literature. For example, a *hadith* of the eighth century (150 A.H.) declares that "A Jew will not be found alone with a Muslim without plotting to kill him." This statement also appears in the writings of Amr Ibn Bahar al-Jahiz (d. 255/869), a well-known writer and creator of the *adab* literature (i.e., writings of culture and enlightenment).[13]

The same motif, based upon the Koran as a holy and authentic source, appears frequently in literature dealing with the Arab-Israel conflict.[14] It also appears in Arab textbooks on the eve of the Six Day War in 1967, and again at the Islamic Conference held in 1968 at Al-Azhar.[15] One of the Egyptian textbooks prepared for use in a teachers' seminary contains the statement that the Jews tried to kill the Prophet Muhammad.[16]

Thus, the image of the Jew as an enemy of the Muslims

---

10. Radio Cairo, April 25, 1972.

11. "Indictments expressed in the textbooks used in the educational system in Jordan and the West Bank during the 1966 school year," published by the Ministry of Education and Culture, Dept. of Arab Education and Culture, Jerusalem, 1967, p. 18; "Indictments expressed . . . etc. . . . in Egypt and the Gaza Strip," *ibid.*, pp. 37–38, 74, later referred to as "Indictments etc." See also Hava Lazarus-Yafeh, "Guidelines for the Study of Arab Textbooks," *HaMizrah HeHadash*, vol. 17, 1967, pp. 207–221.

12. The Koran, *sura V, v. 85.*

13. Rosenblatt, p. 116.

14. Harkabi, pp. 246 ff.

15. *Fourth Conference/Al Azhar/*, pp. 397, 525.

16. "Indictments . . . in Egypt . . .," p. 74.

evolved in classic Muslim literature and particularly in modern
Arab literature as a demonological stereotype of a Jew who is also an
enemy of mankind. The comparison of the Jew to the devil is based
on the Islamic conception that the Jews, like the devil, are characterized by haughtiness and arrogance. The connection between the
Jews and the dark forces of the devil appeared in the classic Muslim
literature of the Middle Ages, along with the image of the Jew as the
enemy of mankind. For example, the Syrian Arab writer of the thirteenth century, 'Abd al-Raḥim al-Jawbari, discussed this subject in a
chapter of his book which sought to expose the cunning secrets of
the Jews. He reveals alleged secrets of the Jewish scholars as follows:

> It is known that this group are the most cursed of all God's creation,
> the most evil-natured, and the most deeply rooted in infidelity and ac-
> cursedness. They are the most evil-intentioned of mankind in their
> deeds, even though they are the most ostentatious in humility and
> self-abasement. . . . When they manage to be alone with a man, they
> bring him to destruction, they introduce, by trickery, a stupefying
> drug into his food, and then they kill him.[17]

The stereotype of the Jew as an enemy of mankind found wider expression in the literature of the nineteenth century which dealt
with the "blood libels" against the Jews (to be considered later). It
appears again and again in allegations against Zionism and the Jews
on the part of Muslim scholars and Arab politicians in various publications, in textbooks, and in the communications media of the Arab
lands in recent years. 'Ali Mahmud al-Shaykh 'Ali, Minister of Justice in the government of Rashid 'Ali al-Kaylani in Iraq, wrote in
1941 that Judaism constitutes a threat to mankind.[18] An Egyptian
textbook (prepared for use in a teachers' seminar) which appeared in
1966 contains the assertion that the Jews are "monsters of mankind,
a nation of beasts lacking the good qualities characteristic of humanity."[19]

Similar views were expressed at the Al-Azhar conference

17. C. E. Bosworth, "Jewish Elements in the Banu Sasan," *Studies in the History of
the Jewish Communities in Muslim Lands,* M. Ma'oz, ed., (in preparation).
18. Sylvia Haim, "Arabic anti-Semitic Literature," *Jewish Social Studies,* vol. 17,
1956, pp. 307–312.
19. "Indictments . . .," p. 33.

in 1968. The Mufti of Lebanon depicted Zionism as "the enemy of man, of truth, of justice, and the enemy of Allah," while the vice-principal of the Tanta Institute in Egypt held that the Jews were "hostile to all human values in this world."[20] At that same conference the Mufti of Tarsus in Syria, describing the alleged destructive role of the Jews among the nations, said: "They have always been a curse that spread among the nations and . . . sought to . . . extinguish all manifestations of civilization."[21]

A book by 'Abd al-Karim al-Khatib of the Academy for Qur-'anic Studies, *The Jews and the Qur'an*, which recently appeared in Egypt, called forth the following review in the Cairo newspaper *Al-Akhbar*: "The book represents pages from the history of our enemy who seeks to ensnare our nation and our monotheistic religion by means of conflict, plotting and destruction, for it nurtures in its heart hatred for all mankind and for all that is inherently good in man."[22]

The Jews as Deserving of Death

The motif of the danger to mankind inherent in Judaism or Zionism, as well as the threat it poses to Arabism and Islam, was particularly prevalent during the period of the Yom Kippur War. Israel was compared to the Mongols (Tatars) who burst upon the Islamic world in the thirteenth century and endangered civilization. A religious sermon delivered on Radio Damascus declared that "Zionism is the enemy of Allah throughout the world; the New Testament and the Torah denounced it. Muhammad, Jesus and Moses cursed it."[23]

The irrevocable conclusion to be drawn from such statements is that the Arabs are commanded by Islam to destroy this terrible enemy. Thus the Yom Kippur War, the "War of Ramadan" as it is called in Muslim countries, was officially declared by the Muslim authorities in Egypt, Syria and Saudi Arabia as a *jihad*, that is, a holy war—which the Muslim is commanded to wage against the infidels, the enemies of Islam. In a pamphlet specially published by the Egyptian Ministry of War, entitled *Our Faith—Our Way to Victory*, Chief of Staff Shazli, referring to a verse from the Koran, addressed himself

20. *Fourth Conference/Al Azhar/*, pp. 2, 361.
21. *Ibid.*, p. 527.
22. *Al-Akhbar*, Cairo, May 24, 1974.
23. Moshe Ma'oz, *Modern Syria* (Hebrew), Tel-Aviv, 1974, p. 94.

to the troops in these words: "The Jews have overstepped their bounds in [acts of] injustice and conceit . . . kill them wherever you find them."[24]

Here it must be pointed out that the Islamic injunction to kill Jews is not based solely on the concept of the *jihad* which sanctifies the killing of non-Muslims encountered in the "area of warfare" (*dar al-ḥarb*). Within the context of Shazli's statement there may be reference to another Islamic command regarding the protected peoples who have strayed from the bounds of the inferior status established for them: they have lost the protection of Islam, so it is permissible to shed their blood. This injunction is even more valid with regard to the Jews who allegedly seized control of Muslim areas within the heart of the Islamic world.[25] Another Islamic basis for the injunction to kill Jews may be found in the *hadith* attributed to Muhammad which appeared in Egyptian publications in the 1930s and 1940s: "The resurrection of the dead will not come until the Muslims will war with the Jews and the Muslims will kill them; until the Jews will hide behind the rocks and trees, and then the trees and rocks will say 'O Muslim, O Abdullah, here is a Jew behind me, come and kill him'."[26] Different versions of this *hadith* were cited at the Al Azhar conference by a Muslim religious scholar from Lebanon, who applied it to the contemporary reality of the Arab-Israel conflict.[27]

When Anwar Sadat was Minister of State in the Egyptian government, he also made use of Islamic religious sanction to declare war on Israel. At the close of the year 1955 he declared: "Our war against the Jews is an old battle which Muhammad began . . . It is our duty to fight the Jews in the name of Allah and in the name of our religion, and it is our duty to finish the war which Muhammad began."[28]

24. *Aqidatuna al-diniyya tariquna ila al-Naṣr*, Ministry of War, The Egyptian Arab Republic, 1973; cf. The Koran, *sura* II, v. 187.

25. Cf. Abu Ḥamid Muḥammad al-Ghazzali, *Ihya'ulūm al-Din*, P. II, Bk. 5, Cairo, 1356, p. 950, quoted in H. Lazarus-Yafeh, *Studies in Al-Ghazzali*, Jerusalem, 1975, p. 442.

26. Y. Harkabi, p. 250.

27. *Fourth Conference/Al Azhar/*, p. 122.

28. Radio Cairo, December 27, 1955, quoted in Bat Ye'or, *The Jews of Egypt* (Hebrew), Tel-Aviv, 1974, p. 132.

CHRISTIAN INFLUENCE ON THE JEWISH STEREOTYPE IN NINETEENTH-CENTURY ARAB LITERATURE

If we examine the stereotype of the Jew which permeated Arab literature under the influence of the Koran and Muslim tradition, along with other characteristics not yet mentioned, we shall see that in the image of the Jew there are many distinctive features. On the one hand there are such traits as a sense of inferiority, of abasement and wretchedness, and on the other, treachery, cruelty, malevolence and hatred. To this must be added divisiveness within the group, dispersion throughout the world, particularism, repulsion and alienation from man's natural surroundings, lack of loyalty to the state, and, along with these, haughtiness and arrogance. Other characteristics of the Jew, according to Muslim religious tradition, include being mercenary, practicing usury, cheating, lying and defrauding, as well as being morally corrupt and licentious.[29]

When we analyze this catalogue of negative traits, it may be concluded that the general stereotype of the Jew sketched in Muslim and Arab literature is similar to the stereotype of the Jew found in European Christian anti-Semitism. The conspicuous differences and emphases in the Christian anti-Semitism of the Middle Ages and the modern period are, as is well known, the accusation that the Jews killed God; that they kill Christians and use their blood for the Passover ritual; that they are racially inferior, yet seek to dominate; that they are members of an international conspiracy.

Modern Arab Judaeophobia is based largely on these anti-Semitic elements for which, it is alleged, there is a parallel in the Koran and in Muslim tradition. This is also true with regard to other elements of the Jewish stereotype which found greater emphasis in Christian anti-Semitism than in Islam. For example, with regard to the killing of Jesus, in addition to the reference in the Koran about the negative attitude of the Jews toward Jesus and his disciples, various Arab publications emphasize the Koran testimony that the Jews killed their own prophets; they even claim that the Jews tried to take the life of Muhammad. These claims may be based on the *hadith* (as well as on other sources), quoted by Jahiz, that the Jews tried to remove Muhammad from Medina by force.[30]

29. Harkabi, pp. 247–248.
30. Goitein, p. 154.

Notwithstanding the anti-Semitic image of the Jew, found in Muslim and other Arab writings, it is clear that Christianity has exerted a noticeable influence upon the formulation of the Jewish stereotype in the Muslim literature of various periods. This is true to some extent with regard to the Koran and some of the classic Muslim writings where the authors drew, as argued by Professor Goitein, upon anti-Jewish Christian polemics.[31] However, the Christian anti-Semitic influence is even more obvious in Arab historical writings of the nineteenth and twentieth centuries and in the new communications media. In this connection it should be remembered that many Christian Arabs were among the initiators of the Arab cultural renaissance, and included in their writings many rabid anti-Semitic references.

It is worth noting that there are isolated instances of comments in praise of Jews. For example, the Christian writer Shahin Makarius, in a history of the Jewish People published in Egypt in 1904, writes that the nations, envious of the Jews, disparage them because they are industrious and achievement-oriented; furthermore, they have continued to exist throughout history because of their intelligence and sharp wits, their solidarity and patience, and their faithful observance of the Jewish religious laws. The author adds that the Jews are compassionate and merciful, and help not only their own people but others as well. They are proficient in science and in business (but known for their tendency to give bribes in order to protect themselves).[32] The Muslim-Arab historian, Muhammad Kurd 'Ali, who lived in Syria at the turn of the century, deals in his great book *Khitat al-Sham* in a negative fashion with the Jews who lived in Syria and with the Zionists who settled in Palestine. At the same time he points out that the Zionist settlers have attractive habits, that they put emphasis on order, cleanliness, organization and thrift, in addition to which they show great ability in the field of agricultural development.[33] This dual approach is also characteristic of Rashid Riḍa, one of the leaders of the Muslim reform movement in Egypt and editor of the periodical *Al-Manar* at the end of the nineteenth and the beginning of the twentieth century.

31. Ibid., p. 159.
32. *Tarikh al-Israiliyyin*, Egypt, 1904, p. 262.
33. *Khitat al-Sham*, Damascus, 1925–28, vol. vi, p. 38.

In contrast to these isolated examples, the dominant tone in nineteenth-century Arab literature in Egypt and Syria on the eve of the Zionist immigration was clearly anti-Jewish. Traits of treachery, plotting, deception, extortion, cruelty and the practice of magic, which were attributed to the Jews, appeared in Muslim writings,[34] while accusations of extreme cowardice and avariciousness are mentioned in Muslim and Christian writings alike.

Jewish Domination

Another striking motif, stressed in both Muslim and Christian works of the same period, is that of Jewish domination. A Christian writer in Damascus at the turn of the nineteenth century describes Hayyim Farhi, the business and financial manager of the local Ottoman Pasha, in this fashion: "Hayyim the Jew held all the reins of rule and did whatever he wanted to. And there are those who say that a Jew rules over the Muslims and Christians, over the great and the humble, the near and the far—in absolute freedom."[35]

A Muslim author of the early twentieth century, dealing with this same issue, describes the position of Farhi and the Jews of his time by citing a poem written in the tenth century by Al-Suyuti, about Abu al-Faraj Ya'qub ibn Yusuf ibn Kilis, a Jew who served as vizir in the Fatimid court in Egypt: "The Jews of this time have attained their uttermost hopes, and have come to rule; glory is upon them, money is with them and from among them came the counsellor and the ruler. O people of Egypt, I advise you—turn Jew, for the heavens have turned Jew."[36]

A more explicit description of the dominating image of the Jew and of world Judaism appears in the *Protocols of the Elders of Zion*, which were translated into Arabic in the second decade of this century and have served since then as documentary support for not a few anti-Semitic writings. The malicious anti-Semitic *Protocols*, which have a wide distribution in the Arab world today, serve as the

---

34. For example, Abd al-Karim Gharayiba, *Suriyya fi al-Qarn al-Tasi Ashar 1840–1876*, Cairo, 1961–62, p. 47.
35. Ibrahim al-'Áwra, *Tarikh Wilayat Sulayman Basha al-'Ádil*, Sidon, 1936, p. 477.
36. Abd al Qadir al-Maghrabi, "Yahud al-Sham mundhu mi'at 'am," *Majallat al-Majma' al'ilmi al'Arabi*, 1929, p. 642. The poem appears in an English translation by Bernard Lewis in the anthology *Islam*, New York, 1974, vol. ii, p. 227.

primary source for the strengthening of the evil Jewish and Zionist stereotype in Arab political literature and the communications media—and this with the highest governmental imprimatur.

A few examples may be given here. The current president of Egypt, Anwar Sadat, quoted extensively from the *Protocols* in his book written in the mid-1950s when he was a minister in the Egyptian Government.[37] Gamal Abdul Nasser, too, gave a copy of the *Protocols* in 1958 to an important Indian journalist, urging him to study it, while in April 1967 the former president of Iraq, 'Arif, publicly expressed his appreciation to the Arab historian who published the work.[38] When King Faisal of Saudi Arabia presented copies of the *Protocols*, as well as an anthology of anti-Semitic writings, to French journalists who accompanied French Foreign Minister Michel Jobert on the latter's visit to Jeddah in January 1974, Saudi officials noted that these were the king's favorite books.[39]

Another motif which, under Christian anti-Semitic influence, is conspicuous in the new Arab literature is the mercenary quality of the Jew. I shall not deal with this subject in detail, but will merely note that an Arabic translation of *The Merchant of Venice* appeared at the end of the nineteenth century, and that a Jordanian school textbook of the 1960s includes excerpts from that play.

The Blood Libel

Just before the rise of Zionism one finds in Arab literature the allegation that Jews had a propensity for blood and murder. This finds its principal expression in the accusation that human blood is used in the Passover ritual, the Damascus blood libel of 1840 serving as incisive proof of that "truth." It should be emphasized that the blood libel was introduced from Christian Europe by Christian Arabs of the East, as well as by missionaries who came from the West. Even before 1840, an early nineteenth-century Christian Arab chronicler writes that "the laws of the Talmud permit [the Jew] to squeeze money and blood not only from Christians, but from anyone who is not a Jew."[40]

37. Muhammad Anwar al-Sadat, *Qissat al-waḥda al-Arabiyya*, Cairo, 1957, pp. 139–141, 156–158.
38. Harkabi, p. 217.
39. Haaretz, Tel-Aviv, January 29, 1974.
40. Al-'Awra, p. 90.

However, it seems that these concepts were not absorbed thoroughly by the majority of the Muslim population until the Damascus Affair. Although the libel was initiated by the local Christians and the French Consul, the accusation was soon taken up by many, Muslims as well as Christians. An Arab of our own generation, a university professor, describes the blood libel of Damascus in his study of the history of Syria in the nineteenth century. He presents so-called contemporary documents to affirm the validity of the accusation, claiming that the story became so widely known throughout the country that it served as a warning: "The mothers would caution their children not to go out alone late at night, lest the Jew Abu Al'afia would come and take their blood for the purpose of making matzot for Passover."[41]

Many additional stories of blood libel against Jews, published in writings and spread by word of mouth throughout Syria in the last century, were also circulated in Egypt during the latter part of the nineteenth and the early twentieth century.

The blood accusation motif is found in Egyptian literature and the communications media of our own time as well. In 1962, for example, the Egyptian Ministry of Education published a new edition of a book (in Arabic) by Ḥabib Faris, called *Talmudic Sacrifices*, which had originally appeared in Cairo in 1890. In the introduction, the editor notes that the book constitutes "an explicit documentation of indictment, based upon clear-cut evidence that the Jewish people permitted the shedding of blood as a religious duty enjoined in the Talmud."[42]

Similar expressions appear in other books published by government agencies in Egypt in the 1950s and 1960s. Among them are detailed references to alleged blood libels dating from the twelfth century to our own day. Some of these books even include detailed descriptions of the method of drawing blood from the victim by the Jews. 'Abdullah al-Tal, in his book (in Arabic) *The Danger of World Judaism for Christianity and Islam* (Cairo, 1964), claims that thousands of children and adults who disappear each year are for the most part victims of the religious rituals of the Jews; he adds that their blood settles in the stomachs of the Jews, together with the unleavened bread of their foul festivals.[43]

41. Gharayiba, p. 126.
42. Harkabi, p. 251.
43. Quoted in Harkabi, pp. 252–53.

Descriptions of blood libels against the Jews are found not only in books published by government agencies. On November 28, 1973, shortly after the Yom Kippur War, while the Egyptian leaders were still proclaiming their peaceful intentions, a historical play called "The Tragedy of the Good Father Thomas" appeared in the widely circulated weekly *Akhir Sa'ah*. The play, written by Mustafa Sa'adani, a former minister in the Egyptian foreign service, deals with the Damascus Affair and presents in words and pictures horrifying descriptions of the alleged murder of Father Thomas by the Jewish notables of Damascus in 1840.

On April 10, 1974, shortly after the Egyptian-Israeli "separation of forces" agreement, the same weekly carried a sharply anti-Semitic article (by a journalist named Anis Manṣur), which listed detailed indictments against the Jews who murder persons of other nations and use their blood. It also includes malicious references to the Jewish traits of domination, stealth and adultery. There is a long account of the ritual of Jewish burial (in connection with the Israel Defence Forces' attempt to find the bodies of soldiers killed in the Yom Kippur War). All this is allegedly based on detailed references to the history of Jewish sacred writings. Lastly, in an interview with a Lebanese periodical in November 1973, King Faisal also stressed the importance of the Father Thomas episode for an understanding of "Zionist crimes."[44]

These examples indicate that central motifs which were taken from Christian anti-Semitism have become the daily ration of this generation of Arab political and intellectual leaders. In order to provide an air of authenticity and credibility for extreme anti-Jewish indictments, occasionally the testimony is cited of Jews who converted to Islam, or of Christians who hold important positions in the Arab world, as, for instance, bishops and government ministers. Thus, an Egyptian Minister of State, the Copt Albert Salamah, in a radio program broadcast in honor of Christmas, attacked "the new Israel which has carried out the most terrible crimes in history and which bears the responsibility for the crucifixion of the Messiah; its hands will remain stained with his blood for eternity."[45]

44. *Al-Sayyad*, Lebanon, November 29, 1973.
45. Radio Cairo, January 1, 1975.

THE JEW IN CONTEMPORARY ARAB CONSCIOUSNESS

It may be stated, then, that political, religious, historical and educational Arab literature, as well as the various communications media, have produced an obnoxious Jewish stereotype which is composed of an accumulation of the negative traits of the Jew as portrayed in the Koran and in Muslim tradition, and the malicious image of European-Christian anti-Semitism in all its ramifications. This image is embellished with negative aspects allegedly drawn from the authentic Law of Moses. In other words, an anti-Jewish Arab ideology has been derived, so to speak, from the three heavenly religions and from the very wellsprings of human civilization—an ideology which claims to expose the danger to humanity posed by the Jewish People.

The question now to be considered is the extent of the correlation between the Jewish stereotype in Arab literature and the communications media, and the Jewish image in the various levels of Arab consciousness.

The answer to this question is extremely difficult and intricate and certainly requires more extensive research, but I shall here present only several preliminary comments. There is, without doubt, a gap between the image of the Jew in Arab literature and his image in the consciousness of the Arab masses; indeed, in the past that gap was very wide. In contrast to Christian anti-Semitism which spread from below, from a deep substratum of anti-Jewish feeling that existed among the masses, Judaeophobia in Arab literature was formulated from above by the political-religious and ideological-cultural elite, with the aim of influencing the Muslim and Arab peoples. Its goal was to distort and blacken the image of the Jew which had existed in the consciousness of the Arabs both in the early years of Islam and at the beginning of the modern period—an image that was not necessarily negative. Indeed, with the advent of Islam the image of the Jew among the Arabs was rather positive, and praise of the noble virtues of the Jews are to be found in ancient Arab literature: mention is made of their generosity, their kind hospitality, their loyalty to friends, and their willingness to help others. (The outstanding example of such a Jew is Samawil ibn 'Adaya.) These comments evidently reflected the stable, indeed positive, relations which existed between Arabs and Jews in that period. According to Professor H.Z. Hirshberg, these relations were also reflected in the fact that in

Yathrib (Medina) Arabs would send their children to be educated among Jewish families and that several Arab tribes had converted to Judaism.[46]

Muhammad, the founder of Islam, tried to destroy the positive image of the Jew in Arab consciousness during the Jahiliyya period, because of his ideological and political conflict with the Jews of the Arabian Peninsula. His tools of destruction were, in addition to arms and warriors, the Koran which he wrote and the tradition he left behind him. The political and religious leadership of classical Islam continued the policy which the Prophet had begun, despite the fact that, in contrast to Muhammad's experience in Arabia, the Jews in various areas of the Middle East aided the Muslim conquerors,[47] and even contributed greatly to the Muslim society of the Middle Ages in the fields of culture, financial administration and medicine. A certain sympathy toward the new religion of Islam was also manifested by the Jews.

Nonetheless, besides creating anti-Jewish literature, the Muslim state also imposed on Jews, as on Christians, political, social, and ritual limitations which led to the segregation, inferiority, and degradation of the Jew within Muslim society. The yellow badge and special articles of clothing were imposed upon the Jews in Islam centuries before they were instituted in Christian lands. Besides these formal limitations, the Jews of the Middle Ages also knew oppression, molestation, demolition of synagogues, forced conversion to Islam and even destruction at Muslim hands. The motivation for these deeds was partly economic—jealousy of Jews who occupied high-ranking positions and were successful in commerce, despite restrictions imposed by the state. But the religious element was a major motivation, as expressed in the reaction of the masses to the deviation of the Jews from the ritual limitations imposed upon them, and in the response to the anti-Jewish incitement of a fanatic ruler of religious zealots. Thus, for example, the slaughter of about 4,000 Jews in Granada in 1066 was largely the result of anti-Jewish agitation by a Muslim religious leader.[48] Similarly, when fanatic Muslim dynasties were in power, Jews fell upon evil times and frequently suffered from pogroms. This was the case of the al-Murabitun and

---

46. H. Z. Hirshberg, "The Jews in Islamic Lands," *Chapters in the History of the Arabs and Islam* (Hebrew), H. Lazarus-Yafeh, ed., Tel-Aviv, 1968, p. 265.
47. *Ibid.*, pp. 268–69.
48. Rosenblatt, p. 115.

al-Muwahhidun dynasties in North Africa (eleventh to thirteenth centuries) and of the Ayyubids and Mamluks in Egypt (twelfth to sixteenth centuries). Persecutions such as these led the Rambam in his twelfth century *Iggeret Teiman* to express the view that "never has there been a people which has caused us so much misery, humiliation and degradation as the Muslim."[49] And the words of Rabbi Bahya ibn Paquda, "the children of Ishmael deal more harshly with the people of Israel than the children of Esau."[50]

Despite all this, it must be noted that there were also long periods of calm and prosperity in the lives of the Jews in Islamic countries, notably the Ottoman Empire; it is also well-known that in the Middle Ages relations between Muslims and Jews were better than those between Christians and Jews in Europe. Moreover, the day-to-day attitude of the Muslim to the Jew was more positive than his attitude to the Christian, despite the fact that in the Koran, it would seem, the Christians are presented in a less negative light than are the Jews. Christians in the Islamic lands were subjected, during the Middle Ages, and more particularly in the modern period, to persecutions and even massacres to a greater extent than were the Jews. A Jewish traveler who visited Eretz Israel in the mid-nineteenth century expressed, with some exaggeration, the difference in the Muslim attitude to the Christians and to the Jews. He also claimed that "the Ishmaelites (i.e., the Muslims) and the Jews do not hate one another; on the contrary, they like one another; but as for the uncircumcised (the Christians), the Ishmaelites hate them."[51]

The difference in the Muslim attitude to Jews and Christians in that period stems from a variety of factors, the primary one being, it seems, the political-security element. Unlike the Jews, who were a religious minority with almost no external affiliation, the Christians were long identified in Muslim eyes with Christian Europe, which was an enemy of the Muslim-Ottoman state. Thus Christians were suspect as a potential "fifth column" and constituted a security problem. However, from the end of the nineteenth century the tide has gradually turned, and the Jews have become the principal focus of Muslim-Arab opposition and hostility. The primary motivation for this shift was the political threat posed by the Jewish settlement

49. Quoted in S. D. Goitein, *Interfaith Relations in Medieval Islam*, Columbia University, 1973, p. 27.
50. *Iggeret Teiman*, Halkin edition, New York, 1942, pp. 94–95.
51. A.Ya'ari, *Masa'ot Shliah Tzfat*, Jerusalem, 1942, p. 19.

of Palestine and later by the State of Israel (from the viewpoint of the
Arabs of Palestine and the Arab states).

This hostility was stimulated to a great extent by Christian
Arabs who sought to divert the deep hatred of the Muslims from
themselves to the Jews. During the thirties and the forties Judaeophobia was also propagated in the Arab world by Fascist agents who
added anti-Semitic elements to the new hatred of the Jews. National
and intellectual Arab leadership has adapted these elements for its
own purposes; and, like the Muslim leadership of the Middle Ages,
it has sought to distort even the nondamaging image of the Jew
which was widespread in the Arab lands on the eve of the Israel-
Arab conflict. In order to provide a basis for the negative stereotype
of the Jew which it was attempting to create in the consciousness of
the Arab people, the leadership made use of anti-Jewish references
in the Koran and the *hadith*, taking them out of their context, magni-
fying them out of all proportion and giving them contemporary
significance.

Still more unfortunate is the fact that the present Arab leadership exploits prevailing conditions to instill in the broad Arab public the negative stereotype of the Jew which it has been formulating
during the last two or three generations through religious, political
and educational indoctrination.

First, the majority of the Arab masses, loyal to Islam and the
values of the Muslim tradition, tends to accept almost without question the new anti-Jewish ideology which is presented to the public
as being rooted in Islam and its tradition. (Thinkers of Arab nationalism and socialism also based their teachings on the values of Islam.)

Second, the seeds of this new ideology fall upon fertile
ground, for the wide Arab public, having been involved in the conflict with Israel for over two generations, has developed latent feelings of anger and hostility against the Jewish state and the Jewish
People. These feelings have been cultivated assiduously by the political and spiritual leadership, in the name of Arab nationalism and
solidarity, and by submitting the populace to a constant stream of
Islamic, Christian, or even Marxist slogans.

Third, political leadership in the Arab world currently has at
its disposal a widespread system of indoctrination which utilizes
books, newspapers, caricatures and, of not less importance, television and radio networks which reach almost every Arab home.

Prominent among the most effective tools of indoctrination

which are under government control is the national education system, at all levels, which has expanded at a tremendous rate in recent
years. The schools have been educating Arab children and youth for
over two generations, on the one hand to respect Islam and the Arabs,
and on the other, to hate Israel and the Jews. This is accomplished
not only by the teaching in schools but also by means of textbooks
which include, *inter alia*, substantial anti-Jewish and anti-Semitic
material.

It is worth noting, regretfully, that the results of this
anti-Israel and anti-Jewish education and indoctrination among
adolescents and the younger generation of Arabs can already be seen
side by side with the anti-Zionist anger and hostility of the previous
generation. This finds expression in anti-Jewish and anti-Semitic attitudes voiced at meetings and discussions, as well as in written
material—poetry, prose, and art. Such popular manifestations provide nourishment for the communications media, which in turn
feeds it back to the masses. In this way a situation of mutual sustenance is created between the media and the people. The danger that
is implicit in this situation is that the Arabs are gradually losing
their earlier deep-rooted image of the Jew, an image which was
ambivalent rather than one-sided and negative, as was the image of
the Jew in Christianity; there was an attitude of affinity, kinship and
respect concurrent with a sense of rejection and contempt. In place
of this dual-value image, there has gradually developed among the
Arab people an extreme and absolutely negative stereotype of the
Jew, deriving from a new Arab ideology which is allegedly based
upon the Muslim-Arab and universal Christian cultural heritage.
Unfortunately, this new ideology has not only intensified the Arab-
Israel conflict, it has also turned the Arab states into new and active
centers for an international anti-Semitic revival.

Anti-Semitism in Latin America after the Yom Kippur War—A New Departure?

Haim Avni

From items which frequently appear in the news media, the impression is gained that Latin American Jewry has been faced in the 1970s with sharper, more dangerous anti-Semitic attacks than other Jewish communities. "Sitting on a volcano that can erupt at any moment"—such is the picture that is presented openly, or by implication, in the reports of visitors to Latin America, or in occasional despatches in the Israel press devoted to the Jews living there. The few scholarly works on Latin American Jewry point out their specially problematic position from the very beginning. Some of these works, published as recently as 1972, have not focused on direct, aggressive anti-Semitism as the main source of danger for Latin American Jewry. Rather, the social and economic stratification of the Jews within societies going through constant change and ferment, is emphasized in academic deliberations on the critical position of the Jewish communities.[1]

Latin American Jewry is characterized by two internal contradictions: (a) It lives in countries where the foremost problem is the poverty of the majority of the people and the vast economic and social gulf between classes, whereas Jews are found mainly among the wealthier strata of the population; (b) At a time when the Latin American states, like most of the Third World countries, are witnessing an increase in nationalism which aspires to be monolithic, the identity of the Jews, as an organized community in nearly all these countries,

---

1. *Proceedings of the Experts Conference on Latin America and the Future of Its Jewish Communities, New York, June 3–4, 1972*, London, 1973; see particularly pp. 115–158; "Fourth Session, The Position of the Jewish Communities in the Light of the Political, Socio-Economic and Cultural Developments"; Haim Avni, "Latin America," *World Politics and the Jewish Condition*, Louis Henkin, ed., New York, 1972, pp. 262–274; Irving Louis Horowitz, "Jewish Ethnicism and Latin American Nationalism," *Midstream*, vol. xviii, no. 9, November 1972, reprinted in I. L. Horowitz, *Israeli Ecstasies, Jewish Agonies*, New York, 1974, pp. 121–132.

is bound up with distinctive Jewish national traits. The history of Latin America and a consciousness of most of its inhabitants have been shaped in the Ibero-Catholic tradition; moreover, the connection between the local nationalisms and Christian, or even Catholic, civilization is accepted not only by the right-wing nationalist movements but also by the majority of the left. This puts even those Jews who do not identify themselves as national Jews, in a problematic position.

The internal contradictions of social stratification and national consciousness have been recognized as constituting a threat to the future of Latin American Jewry. Latent anti-Semitism, the existence of which is never questioned in academic deliberations, has, however, been presented as a matter of secondary importance, liable merely to aggravate the main difficulties. However, Latin American Jewry may be at the turning point. The question is whether events since 1973 and increasingly anti-Semitic trends of thought have, in fact, turned the old anti-Semitism into an immediate threat to the survival of Latin American Jews.

It is not intended here to offer a comprehensive answer to this problem, since several variables and their relative weight and potential influence would have to be analyzed before a reliable conclusion could be reached. Only the following questions will be discussed: (a) What outstanding motifs were used in the attacks on the Jewish People in Latin American countries between the Yom Kippur War and the summer of 1975; (b) To what extent do these attacks represent official attitudes or responses of circles close to the centers of power; (c) Has there been any change during the last two years (as compared with the period preceding the Yom Kippur War) in the essential nature of anti-Jewish motifs and in the attitude of authorities with regard to hostility toward Jews?

The twenty months dealt with in this paper were marked throughout the world by painful adjustment to the new economic and political realities created by the oil producing countries. The sudden increase in Arab influence and prestige was paralleled by weakening of the Israeli and Jewish positions. These developments may have influenced governmental policies towards the Jews, and it is therefore necessary to examine whether negative attitudes regarding them did indeed become official policy in Latin America.

Throughout the millennia-old history of the Jewish People, enmity toward the Jews has been fed from a variety of sources and supported by diverse arguments. If deeply rooted among the masses, it has a tremendous capacity for harm and can become very dangerous indeed. When anti-Semitism becomes an instrument in the hands of those in power, a means toward achieving their aims, state instruments at their disposal are used with grave consequences. This happened in modern times in tsarist Russia; in Eastern Europe between the two world wars; in much of Europe during the period of Nazi rule in Germany. If, therefore, we find that anti-Semitism was fostered on government levels in Latin America, it could be viewed as a clear indication that a threat is developing on a scale that could not have been foreseen at the beginning of the seventies.

This study is based for the most part on published (if, unfortunately, incomplete) material, such as newspaper reports and official statements. What follows must, therefore, be considered as no more than indications, which may have to be reconsidered when the documentary basis is widened to include more diversified source material. Owing to the vast size of the Latin American continent and its great diversity, attention will be focused in this paper on two states only, Peru and Argentina, each of outstanding importance in its own way. In both countries, for different reasons, the summer of 1975 marks the beginnings of political changes that put an end to the preceding period.

PERU

When the countries of Latin America are studied in terms of the ethnic composition of their populations and of the number of variables indicating the degree of progress or backwardness, it is obvious that the Peru of the sixties was one of the more backward, least European countries of Latin America. In 1968 average life expectancy in Peru was only 55 years; nevertheless, the yearly rate of natural increase was then about 3.1 percent, one of the highest in the world. National per capita income was then $246, and even this small sum as an *average* figure masked the fact that millions of Peruvians were living on the fringe, or even outside the framework, of the national economy.

> In Peru, outside Cuzco, we met men working their landlord's fields for 45 cents, a good wage in an area where others must work three days with no pay beyond the right to cultivate a small mountainside plot for themselves. . . .

This is an extract from the evidence given by United States Senator Robert Kennedy on his return from a Latin American tour in 1966. John Gunther, another experienced and knowledgeable traveler, reinforces this painful impression of the realities of Peru.[2]

Some 85 percent of the population of Peru is of non-European extraction, and by far the greater part are Indians and cross-breed *mestizos* (known as "cholos"). Immigration has rarely been encouraged throughout the history of Peru and only in a very few instances have the authorities permitted the entry of immigrants. The small Jewish community, numbering, by its own estimate, no more than 5,000 souls, was established by groups of immigrants who succeeded in entering the country at different periods in the twentieth century. This small community lives closed-in among a majority population that is predominantly Indo-Iberian in origin and culture. Since in this respect the position of the Jewish community in Peru resembles that of a number of other Jewish communities in Latin America, it can be considered representative for the purpose of the present discussion. But we are particularly interested in Peru because of the regime that has been in control of the country after 1968 and because of the special status of Peru in the international arena.

The "Inca Plan"

On October 3, 1968, army leaders seized power in Peru, and six days later they nationalized International Petroleum Company (I.P.C.), affiliate of Standard Oil of New Jersey. This nationalization was not an isolated move; it was the first step in the implementation of a detailed plan of action which heads of the revolution appropriately named the "Inca Plan." Even in the years preceding the revolution, the Peruvian army, unlike the armies in most Latin American countries, saw itself as destined to bring about a profound social change in Peru. In their goals, the officers regarded themselves as following a model where the army was the seat of power, that model being the regime created by Colonel Gamal Abdel Nasser in Egypt in the fifties.

Unlike the army revolution in Egypt, however, the leaders of

---

2. *United States Congressional Record*, May 9, 1966, quoted by John Gunther, *Inside South America*, New York, 1968, pp. 418–420.

the revolution in Peru did not abolish most of the old political parties. With the end of the constitutional regime and the absence of elections it seemed to them that the scope of activity of the politicos was sufficiently limited. At the same time, they set out to create a new political infrastructure, based on direct encouragement of the masses of peasants and workers, to support the regime. This course of action, which awakened the political consciousness of widely varied strata of Peruvian society that had previously been far removed from all direct participation in political life, was supported by important changes introduced into the main production systems in Peru.

Soon after seizing power in June 1969, the new rulers started on the energetic implementation of agrarian reform, which was, and still is, the burning issue in the interior agricultural provinces. About a year later it was industry's turn: Original methods were introduced whereby workers would share in the ownership of various concerns, though there would be no nationalizaion or drastic confiscation of property.[3] These changes, of course, struck at the interests of the *latifundia* (large estate) owners and the local capitalists. Attempts to change the spheres of oil exploitation, fishing and mining brought the new rulers of Peru into an open and serious confrontation with the United States. By 1966 the International Petroleum Company had extracted 76 percent of all the oil produced in Peru and had refined about 85 percent. For many years it was feared that nationalization of the International Petroleum Company would be a dangerous step, liable to provoke serious reprisals on the part of the United States government. However, the latter did not react as vigorously as had been expected, and October 9 (the anniversary of the takeover of the I.P.C.) is now celebrated in Peru as the *Dia de la Dignidad Nacional,* "The Day of National Dignity." Peru was involved in a further confrontation with the United States when it attempted to establish sovereignty over rich fishing grounds lying off its coast by extending the limits of its territorial waters to 200 miles. However, this conflict of interests was minimal compared with tension created between Peru and the United States when the Peruvian government ventured to nationalize foreign companies that

3. Juan Velasco Alvarado, *La Revolución Peruana,* Buenos Aires, 1973, pp. 7–20, 120–123.

controlled the mining industry—first and foremost a giant concern, the Cerro de Pasco Corporation.[4]

Protracted confrontation with United States interests was also accompanied by revolutionary innovations in foreign policy. Peru, having established close diplomatic and commercial relations with Eastern bloc nations, became an enthusiastic supporter of the attempt to raise the blockade of Cuba. This defiance of the much-resented "boss" in the North raised the prestige of the regime in the eyes of the peoples of the South, particularly those in the left-wing and nationalist camps. Measures introduced to improve the material conditions of the Indians and stress laid by leaders on the pre-Columbian heritage as a primary basis for Peru's entity and identity awakened a deep response from the masses. In fact, the "Inca Plan" was aimed not only at transferring control of the country's economic resources to the Peruvian people, but also at rehabilitating the descendants of the Incas, exalting their civilization over that of the descendants of the Conquistadores and giving their language an official status that would eventually put it on a level with Spanish.[5]

Peru and the Third World Bloc

The social, economic and foreign policy revolution in Peru gave the country a leading role in the Third World bloc. On October 28, 1971, Peru was host to the second conference of foreign ministers of the seventy-seven so-called non-aligned countries. Speaking at the opening session, President Velasco Alvarado declared in the name of Peru: "Our country proposes that this Conference take the first steps towards setting up the permanent organs that will make it possible to coordinate systematically the actions which the peoples of the Third World will henceforth initiate in order to face the problems they have in common."[6]

Peru then became a member of the permanent coordinating

4. Carlos Malpica, *Los Dueños del Peru*, Lima, 1970, 4 Edición, pp. 160–169. This contains a detailed description of the ramifications of this concern.
5. This process reached a peak at the beginning of June 1975, when President Alvarado proclaimed Quechua as the second official language of Peru. In 1961, 35 percent of the population of Peru gave Quechua as their mother tongue. In the provinces of the High Andes the percentage was 90 percent and over. (To implement this decision in administrative practice and in education remains a matter for the future.) See *Latin America*, June 6, 1975, vol xi, no. 22, p. 175.
6. Alvarado, *ibid.*, pp. 207–208.

committee of the non-aligned bloc. At a conference of the countries of that bloc which met in Algiers in September 1973, a Peruvian delegation was present when Cuba dramatically declared its intention of breaking off diplomatic relations with Israel. At the same time, in Chile, there was a military revolt which overthrew the socialist regime of President Allende in a merciless bloodbath. Peru remained the only revolutionary country in the Latin American bloc of the Third World countries maintaining formal relations with the State of Israel.

Special importance should be attached to Peru in view of the following significant factors:

a) The enthusiastic support automatically given by Peru to any country to exploit its oil resources independently for its own national purposes;

b) The protracted confrontation of Peru with the United States, the main supporter of the State of Israel;

c) Its leadership status in countries of the Third World bloc;

d) Its crying need for generous credit to promote industrial development of its natural resources;

e) The fact that Peru has been more directly involved in the Arab-Israeli conflict than other Latin American countries because after the Yom Kippur War it sent a military contingent to the United Nations Emergency Force. All these factors, together, create a delicate "parallelogram of forces" which is liable to affect the scale and nature of anti-Semitism in Peru and may, in turn, be influenced by such anti-Semitism.

How Jews are Regarded by Anti-Semites in Peru: Anti-Semitic Motifs

The themes stressed by writers who treat the subjects of Jews and Israel in an anti-Semitic vein emerge with clarity from a collection of press cuttings, dating mostly from 1974 and 1975. They include editorials, signed articles, second-line journalistic commentaries, caricatures and other humorous or satirical features.

The figure which stands out as representing a Jew is the classic stereotype of the money-grabber, the dubiously honest merchant, the usurer. This motif is personified in two types of caricatures: One is "Jacoibo" (i.e., the name "Jacob" with a Spanish-Yiddish inflection), a contemptuous, derogatory nickname for Jews, in customary use in Peru but not in any other Latin American country; the other is a caricatured figure that recalls the Jew in Nazi publications (with the *Stuermer* in the lead). He is bearded, hook-nosed, generally dressed in black coat and striped trousers and wearing a battered top hat. Both "Jacoibo" and the *Stuermer*-type figure busy themselves with debt collecting, investment, and buying and selling deals that smell of fraud and high interest rates. A satirical columnist, who writes for one of the economics papers, found rich source material in the stories of the patriarch Jacob to show his readers that "Jacoibo the First" and his family were the fathers of deception, the ancestors of crooked dealings; that to this day their descendants behave like their forefathers. The writer ends one of these notes with the following instructive moral: "Is it surprising then that today the International Monetary Fund, full of Jews, plays foul and exploits the poor countries? It is the atavism of 10,000 years."[7]

"Jacoibo" and the *Stuermer*-Jew do not represent simply the concept of Jew; they also represent the Israeli. One newspaper in a satirical tone puts the following prayer in the mouth of Anwar Sadat: "Oh, Allah! If the Russians don't keep their promises and give me arms, what shall I do to face up to these dumb Jacoibos?" The caricaturist of another paper sees the prisoner exchanges with Syria in the shape of three little Arabs returning to a large Arab, while three little *Stuermer*-type Jews are being returned to a large Jew-figure of the same type. The web of anti-Semitic fantasies associated with these two figures is thus transferred to the Middle Eastern conflict; this is the second aspect that stands out among the various anti-Semitic trends distinguishable in the source material.[8]

Another traditional anti-Semitic motif is linked almost entirely with Zionism and the State of Israel. This is the myth, taken from the *Protocols of the Elders of Zion,* that Jews control banking and communications media. For example, General Brown's assertion that the Jews have too much influence over United States policy has been accepted by several writers as convincing proof of their assertions that international Zionism and the financial interests of Wall Street are essentially united. Thus, a dispute which arose over a proposed Japanese loan to finance the laying of an oil pipeline (from

7. *Extra,* May 22, 1974. "La Economia en mini falda." This series appeared in May and June.
8. *El Correo,* June 11, 1974; *El Comercio,* January 19, 1975.

new oil wells in the jungles of the Amazon Basin to the Pacific coast)
was presented by a columnist as a Zionist attempt to prevent Peru
from shaking off the shackles of American-Zionist capital.

The legend of Zionist omnipotence has not prevented these
writers from embroidering another fairly new legend, this time describing the Zionist movement and the State of Israel as a tool created by Imperialism to promote its own ends and to be used against
Third World countries. Moreover, it is claimed, Zionism encourages
racial oppression, so that Palestinians are driven from their country
and even killed. "Jews, get out!" "Jews, exploiters!" Workers on
strike in a Jewish-owned textile firm daubed the factory walls with
these slogans, and their paintings were stamped with a swastika.
The Communist Party newspaper rebuked the strikers for this but, at
the same time, took the trouble to clarify matters for them by ex-
plaining: "Anti-Semitism is like Zionism—they are two sides of the
same coin, which is flashed before the eyes of the people by imperialism, by the merchants of hate and warmongers." Another paper,
one of the most important in Peru, published a leading article on the
United Nations Assembly resolution inviting the Palestine Liberation Organization (PLO) to take part in the Assembly debate with ob-
server status; the article, enthusiastically supporting the Arab cause,
affirmed: "Israel is occupying Arab territories and has officially sub-
jugated the Palestinian people for the last twenty-five years, not to
mention the massacres committed in the name of Zionism since the
beginning of the century."[9]

Classic economic anti-Semitism is here reinforced by anti-
Zionism based on anti-Semitic myths, old and new. In contrast to the
first motif, the second is based on clear and explicit political arguments: Third World identification and solidarity on the one hand
and anti-imperialism on the other. Unqualified support for the PLO
is represented by such writers as being, by its very nature, bound up
with these two attitudes. But the political-ideological basis does not
detract from the seriousness of this new anti-Semitic myth. To what
extent does the spread of such motifs constitute an innovation, and
how close are these anti-Semitic and anti-Zionist ideas to views held
in circles near the center of power in Peru?

9. *Unidad,* October 24, 1974; *La Prensa,* November 25, 1974.

The Press after the Yom Kippur War

From press cuttings covering a wide range of opinion at the time of the Yom Kippur War, it is evident that the more important papers held to an objective line on the entire Middle Eastern conflict. Israel's cause was, in general, adequately presented, and events reported without prejudicial overtones. Even when one of the papers headlined a report from Washington, "The situation is not easy for the Jacoibos," the report itself was balanced and in no way hostile.[10]

Two newspapers, the *Expreso* and the *Extra,* stood out in sharp contrast because of their hostile attitude toward the State of Israel and their attacks on "international," "inhuman" Zionism with its "filthy," unfair tactics. And precisely these two papers were owned at the time by circles close to power. The government which had requisitioned them from their owners at the beginning of 1970 had handed them over to a cooperative of newspaper workers. The Communist Party of Peru, which supports the military regime, gained a decisive influence over the workers' groups on these newspapers, and their attitude toward Zionism, the State of Israel and the Jews in general was hostile even before the Yom Kippur War. Other papers, in particular *La Prensa,* which claims to be the morning paper with the largest circulation, as well as *El Comercio* and *El Correo,* were still independent and continued to criticize the authorities. Indeed, they fought for freedom of the press as far as the Press Law of December 1969 permitted.

However, the independence of these very influential papers came to an end on July 27, 1974, when their offices were seized by the police; nominal editors and control committees were put in charge and ownership was handed over to loyal supporters of the regime, to trade unions or to other social organizations. In this way, the revolutionary government secured exclusive control over the main communications media. Although the bodies which assumed control of the newspapers were vastly different, and although there is a still wider range of differences among the circles supporting the regime, articles published from then on against the Jews and Zionism must be construed in terms of this new, official control of the press. True, there is no way of proving that any explicit government decision has dictated the handling of the relevant themes, but

10. *Ultima Hora,* October 10, 1973.

it may be assumed that expressions of hostility toward Jews and Zionism would not be published if they were in fact contrary to the wishes of those in authority. Especially significant in this context is the fact that it is precisely the *Expreso* and the *Extra* which have published the most virulent anti-Semitic material. These two papers have thus maintained the traditional line which they followed before the Yom Kippur War, in spite of the fact that in July 1974 the *Expreso* was transferred to the control of a different group, closer to central power. But, after that date, in the columns of *La Prensa* (the paper which reported the Yom Kippur War objectively and even supported Israel) there are statements taken straight from hostile anti-Zionist myths. Two other papers, *Ultima Hora* and *Correo,* which also reported the Jewish side in the Yom Kippur War fairly, have passed into the hands of circles close to the authorities; they, too, made use of some of the more classic anti-Semitic and anti-Zionist expressions. At the same time, it should be pointed out that *La Cronica* (in which most of the shares were held by the authorities even before the takeover of the independent press) has kept to a line more favorable to the Jews and Israel than the other papers, indicating that there are different shades of opinion in the ruling circles with regard to the Jews; but it cannot be ignored that, in the papers which were expropriated, there was a hardening of the unfavorable attitude characteristic of the two papers under government control before the Yom Kippur War.

Certain anti-Semitic and anti-Zionist motifs bear a striking resemblance to arguments found in two non-Peruvian sources, which, however, are published in Peru. One such source is material in Spanish, originating in the Soviet Union and published in organs such as *Panorama Internacional;* the material includes attacks both on Zionism and on the protest campaigns against the treatment of Jews in the U.S.S.R. The other source, which is of particular importance to us, is the material published by the *Comité de Solidaridad Arabe-Palestino-Peruano.* This committee, established in May 1971 to support the struggle of the Arab terrorist organizations and the PLO, published leaflets from time to time that were glaringly anti-Semitic in content. One of the leaders of the committee, Godolfo García Rendón, used the paper *Clarín* as a convenient platform from which to launch his attacks, until the paper was closed down at the beginning of 1972.

Major motif in the propaganda of the Solidarity Committee,

which identifies Zionism with all imperialism, attempts to shift the center of gravity from the Middle Eastern arena to Peru itself. "We have powerful Zionist-imperialist bases or enclaves here in Peru, no less than the Cerro de Pasco Corporation, which has caught the government and the people of Peru in its web . . . ," states a November 19, 1973 publication of this committee; elsewhere in the same publication it is stated that ". . . the Zionist Fifth Column in Peru, the enemy of the miners and of the people, whom it exploits in the building industry, which is in the hands of Zionism, possessor of most of the buildings and housing estates is, therefore, the enemy of the Urban Reform."

The publication of such declarations at a time of rising tension in the negotiations with the Cerro de Pasco Corporation, just when the Urban Reform was being introduced, was, of course, intended to incite the population against the Jewish community in Peru. In their efforts to cast suspicion on Peruvian Jewry as being loyal only to the State of Israel, the anti-Semitic propagandists did not even spare the popular television commentator José ("Pepe") Ludmir, who was also head of the Jewish community in Peru.[11]

From the material available, it would appear that the anti-Semites did not succeed in achieving their aims, for the time being at least. In the propaganda attacks on the Jews and incitement against Zionism, there was no definite indication of any attempt to draw conclusions regarding the Jews in Peru. In published reports of a scandal connected with Jewish doctors who owned a private clinic, there was no explicitly anti-Semitic observations that might be intended to arouse resentment against the Jews as a whole. Indeed, Jews who distinguished themselves in any way were given favorable publicity. The highlight in this connection was the admiration expressed for the above-mentioned "Pepe" Ludmir by the entire press (as well as by personalities of the highest authority), when he celebrated twenty-five years as broadcaster and editor of television programs and again when he retired. The Jewish community celebrated his jubilee by planting trees in his name in the "Peru Forest" of the Jewish National Fund in Israel.

11. Comité de Solidaridad Arabe-Palestino-Peruana, *La Situación en el Medio Oriente*, Lima, Peru, November, 1973, pp. 6, 8.

Clash of Interests

The writers of hostile articles abusing the Jews, particularly Zionism and Israel, justified themselves by the argument that Peru owes a debt of solidarity to the Third World. There were also reminders of the power of Arab oil and Arab money which can be seen in Peru's efforts to obtain material support for her development projects from Libya and other Arab countries. Such reminders gave expression to the practical recognition of the changes that have taken place, changes which mean that the Arabs now weigh far more heavily in Peru's immediate balance of interests.

This Third World solidarity and its practical considerations were exploited by the Arab states and the Peruvian Arabs, as well as their supporters, in order to propagate new anti-Semitic myths in Peru. In this way government-inspired anti-Semitism from the Near East was transplanted to Peru; in addition, multiplication of anti-Jewish and anti-Zionist expressions in Peruvian papers controlled by circles close to the government is evidence of the danger that Arab anti-Semitism might eventually take root in Peru on the government level. The influence of such Arab anti-Semitism is all the more dangerous in a country where there is a widespread negative image of the Jew in economic areas. Moreover, Peru, a Catholic country, has deep-rooted, traditional Christian trends of thought and being.[12]

"A strange situation has arisen: the word 'Israel'—and the State of Israel—has a positive significance, the word 'Jew' is generally of negative significance, and at the same time Peruvians as a whole consciously recognize an absolute identification of the Jews with Israel . . . ," writes Netanel Lorch, former Israel Ambassador to Lima, on the eve of Rosh Hashana, 5729 (September, 1968). He goes on, "You have here an open-ended triangle—but its illogicality does not cancel out its accuracy." Signs are now evident that the processes which were begun on Yom Kippur 5734 (1973), were calculated to blacken the name of Israel, and that new anti-Semitic myths may "close the triangle" of enmity to the Jews.[13]

---

12. *Ojo*, January 26, 1975—article on the Jewish community. See also article on the ceremony of Christ's Passion in Comas, *ibid.*, March 29, 1975.
13. Netanel Lorch, *Hanahar Halohesh* (The Whispering River), Tel Aviv, 1969, p. 136.

During the summer of 1975 Juan Velasco Alvarado's power faded rapidly. On August 29 he was deposed by the Peruvian generals headed by Prime Minister Francisco Morales Bermúdez. Shortly afterwards the "Second Phase" of the Peruvian Revolution was announced. The political pendulum has since then been swinging to the right, as is reflected in the expropriated press. The left-wing members of the revolutionary coalition lost almost all the positions previously entrusted to them in the papers.

ARGENTINA

The Argentine Republic is in many respects the antithesis of Peru. Its economy is one of the most highly developed in Latin America, almost the entire population is literate, life expectancy at birth is among the highest in South America, and the annual rate of natural increase is very low, approaching that of developed countries—1.5 percent at the beginning of the seventies. The Argentine was preeminently a country of immigration throughout the second half of the nineteenth and the first third of the twentieth century, as a result of which over 90 percent of the population is of European extraction. Since the bulk of the newcomers were Italian and Spanish, the Argentine—unlike Indo-American Peru—must be regarded as a *Latin* American country. The process of immigration has been accompanied by the powerful ideology of *crisol de las razas,* the Argentinian version of the United States melting-pot concept. Argentine society is well aware that it has been formed by successive waves of immigration; now descendants of the immigrants fill the highest positions in all walks of life.

The Jews in the Argentine comprise the largest, oldest, and most deeply-rooted Jewish collective unit in Latin America. According to recent research, they number 275,000 souls now, the great majority of them being Argentine-born.[14] Many Jews who have risen from the lower economic strata of Argentine society play leading roles in the fields of culture, science and the economy and, to a lesser extent, in politics. The heterogeneous nature of the majority immigrant society has made it possible for Jews of the Argentine to regard themselves as members of a Western-type open society.

14. O. Schmelz, S. Della Pergola, *The Demography of the Jews in Argentina and Other Latin American Countries* (Hebrew, mimeographed), August 1974, p. 160.

Whereas from 1973 on there was political continuity in Peru under a military-revolutionary government, the Argentine Republic experienced a stormy transition filled with upheavals. On March 11, 1973, general elections were held in Argentina for the first time since the army took over the reins of power in June 1966. About 49.5 percent of the electors voted for Héctor Cámpora, the candidate backed by General Juan Domingo Perón (who was prevented by the army from presenting himself as a candidate for election). Circles opposed to one another in their social backgrounds and programs, some with completely right-wing ideology and others with left-wing revolutionary concepts, joined forces under Perón's leadership. The military government, surprised by the wide support given to the Peronists and their allies, decided to hand over power to the President-Elect, and on May 25 Héctor Cámpora was sworn in as President. After eighteen years in exile, Peron triumphantly returned to Buenos Aires, where millions of Argentinians welcomed him with almost messianic expectation. Cámpora resigned less than a month later, and in new elections, held on September 23, General Perón and his wife, María Estela (Isabel) Martínez, were elected President and Vice-President respectively by a majority vote of 62 percent. Perón was installed as President of the republic on October 12, during the Yom Kippur War.

On the very morning of the inauguration, the left wing of the Peronist movement realized that their leader—unlike Héctor Cámpora—was in favor of a conservative, rather than a revolutionary policy. However, Perón's charismatic personality and the mystic faith of the masses in his ability to solve Argentina's problems succeeded for a time, though shakily, in bridging the extreme contradictions in the group that had been formed to bring him back. Thus, his death on July 1, 1974 resulted in a still sharper struggle for power.

During the year that elapsed after Perón's death, his widow succeeded in continuing as head of government, with a tough *éminence grise* at her side, José López Rega, formerly Perón's private secretary and Minister of Welfare. Behind these two personalities stood the right wing of the Peronist movement, the apparatus of the main trade unions and the army, drawn up against the Peronist left and the revolutionary groups. The latter, who had left or been driven out of the broad front which brought Perón back to power, attacked the new regime in the name of the dead leader by appealing to the principles of his doctrine of social justice—*justicialismo.*

In Argentina, as in Peru, affiliation with the Third World and hostility to the United States serve as a kind of flag brandished not only by all the Peronist factions, but by non-Peronist groups as well.

In Peru, far-reaching reforms were carried out without upsetting the course of daily life through acts of violence committed by underground groups. It is true that stormy demonstrations, accompanied by violence on a serious scale, did take place after the government expropriated the more important newspapers. After August 1974, an attempt was made on the life of the head of the government, General Edgardo Mercado Jarrín, bombs were set off in public places, and there was an uprising on the part of the police force in Lima. Some of these incidents were connected with opposition to the revolutionary reforms, but they were also related to the serious illness of the head of the army regime, General Velasco Alvarado, and the struggle for the succession. Declaration of a state of emergency, which was enforced for three months (until May 5, 1975), enabled the regime to repress the outbreaks of violence, at least temporarily.

The situation in Argentina, however, was quite different. Political violence, characteristic of life in the Republic under army rule before 1973, did not cease even after power was handed over to the Peronists and their allies. On the day General Perón returned to Argentina, shooting broke out among armed groups in the crowds that came to Buenos Aires airport to welcome their leader, and scores of people were killed. When it became clear that General Perón did not intend to take the revolutionary measures demanded by his left-wing supporters, bloodshed and violence increased. In the last weeks of his life, the sick and aging leader was in open confrontation with the left-wing underground, which stepped up its activity still more after his death. The Peronist right wing also organized strong-arm groups, and terrorism increased on both sides. "We are all of us afraid," declared the Jewish editor Jacob Timerman, on the front page of his widely read liberal paper, La Opinion; other Argentinian papers were outwardly stoical when the men guilty of one of the most appalling political murders proudly published a detailed description of the killing.[15]

15. La Opinion, September 6, 1974. The details of the political murder of Gen. Pedro Eugenio Aramburo, President of the Republic in 1955, were published in La Causa Peronista, a leftist Peronist periodical.

Soon after this, attacks and bloodshed multiplied. There were constant assassinations of university people, of elected deputies, army officers, soldiers, reporters, businessmen and workers, either by the left-wing underground or by the right-wing organization calling itself A.A.A. (Alianza Anti-imperialista Argentina, and then Alianza Anti-communista Argentina). According to the prevailing view both in Argentina and elsewhere, this organization was supported by high levels in government, mainly by López Rega himself. In addition to these urban guerrilla activities, rural guerrilla fighting has continued since Perón's death in the northern provinces of the Argentine, and the army's suppression of these activities has constantly produced headlines in the newspapers.

According to an announcement made in the Senate by the Minister of the Interior, there were no fewer than 5,799 acts of violence in the two years from May 25, 1973 to May 1975. A Buenos Aires newspaper reported that during the eleven months following Peron's death there was a total of 503 political murders. By other estimates, the real number of victims was between 800 and 1,200.[16]

This state of affairs must be kept in mind when examining the line taken by anti-Semites in the Argentine Republic, as well as the changed attitudes of the authorities toward the anti-Semites from the Yom Kippur War to July 1975.

"Sinarquía"

A systematic record of known anti-Semitic incidents against Jewish people throughout the world shows that there are more reports of such incidents from Argentina than from any other country. In a classification of the incidents recorded, it will be seen that, while most of them were sharp propaganda outbursts against the Jews, there was also no lack of actual violence. Though it is far from certain that the record includes all the incidents which actually occurred, we may assume that it certainly reflects those that were the most striking. Among the acts of violence reported were: a bomb thrown into a cinema showing films which the assailants thought were pro-Jewish; explosives laid at the entrance to Jewish institutions—synagogues, schools—some of which were damaged; attacks

16. *La Nación,* June 4, 1975; *Latin America,* vol. ix, no. 22, June 6, 1975, p. 172.

on Jewish youth groups and their club premises; and written or oral threats of murder.[17] No lives were actually lost and if anti-Semitism in the Argentine were to be judged by the scale and effectiveness of these incidents, it might be concluded—especially if the chronic murderous violence of political life there is considered—that the anti-Semites there need not be taken too seriously. Unfortunately, such a view does not hold good when the dominant motifs of anti-Semitic propaganda are examined.

The following analysis focuses on organs of political opinion with an anti-Semitic content, all of the right-wing Peronist trend.[18] These sources began to appear after Perón returned to power. Though they all stress the Christian character of Argentinian nationalism, their hostile attitude toward the Jews is based mainly on one idea, charged with exceptional significance—"Sinarquía"—a product of General Perón's thinking. In Perón's doctrine, this stands for the international forces and institutions that, by their very nature, aim at domination and are inimical to the national sovereignty and greatness of the Argentine Republic. According to Perón, "Sinarquía" is a compound of freemasonry, capitalist imperialism, communism, the Catholic Church, and international Zionism (according to another version, international Judaism). These are forces working in secrecy, and the difficulties of Argentina and the rest of the underdeveloped countries are the direct result of their action. This mystic interpretation of historical realities has been seized upon by the anti-Semites, who represent Judaism and Zionism as standing at the center of these powers of darkness, but they exclude the Catholic Church, about which, for obvious reasons, not a single hostile reference is to be found in all the relevant texts.

The first anti-Semitic interpretation of "Sinarquía" is bound up with the idea of a world Jewish organization that supposedly has control over all the gold in the world, as well as over mass communications media everywhere; it is thought that the group now, as in earlier times, acts as if it were only a part of the capitalist world but in reality constitutes its motive force. This world Jewish organiza-

17. *Bulletin of Events on the Subject of Anti-Semitism* (Hebrew, mimeograph) no. 25, March 1974, pp. 34–42; no. 26, March 1975, pp. 44–59. In 1974, 56 incidents were recorded in the Argentine, 17 of which could be classified as acts of violence. In 1973, 59 incidents were recorded, 28 of them acts of violence.
18. The main papers are the *Patria Peronista, El Caudillo, Consigna Nacional* and *Union.*

tion is embodied in well-known institutions: the Alliance Israelite Universelle, the Order of B'nai B'rith and the Anti-Defamation League. The tentacles of this Jewish organization reach everywhere. . . .

Jewish "Sinarquía" is linked not only with the capitalist right wing, but also with the left—it has been bound up with the history of socialism and communism from Karl Marx to the Fourth International. It was behind the outbreak of the anti-De Gaulle events of May 1968 in France. Its sinister aims in the Argentine Republic find expression in the left-wing guerrilla movements, and, should civil war break out, Jewish "Sinarquía" will be to blame, it is alleged.

In the press which we examined, these contradictory aspects of Jewish "Sinarquía" are based on explicit or implicit authority in the *Protocols of the Elders of Zion,* as may be gathered from the following quotation: "[this is done]. . . in order to achieve—in great measure in accordance with the C.I.A.—the realization of the dream of the great prophet, Theodor Herzl: world domination on the part of the Jews through the Marxist creed."[19]

The "Andinia Plan"

The alleged aims of Jewish "Sinarquía" in Argentina are even more far-reaching than elsewhere. Its supposed final intention is to split up the Argentine Republic and tear away the provinces of Patagonia in order to establish a Jewish State there. The Zionists of the Argentine are supposed to carry out that task by bringing the country to a state of economic collapse, by inciting the people to social and class warfare, by splitting the Peronist movement, and, finally— the "Andinia Plan"—by bringing about the secession of the southern provinces from the Argentinian Federation. International Zionism has decided that by carrying out this plan Argentine Jewry will insure the future of the Jewish People should the Arab states eventually succeed in wiping out the State of Israel. A certain Rabbi Gordon, the special emissary of the New York *kehillah* (community), supposedly brought this decision to the Jews of the Argentine and made them swear an oath to carry out the task imposed on them. The shortage of raw materials and vital consumer goods, the rise in prices,

19. *Patria Peronista,* no. 20, October 1974, pp. 11–13.

economic and political tension—all these are said to be the first signs of this Jewish operation.[20]

International Zionism also appears in a more realistic context: the Arab-Israeli conflict. These propagandists, of course, gave their absolute support to the Arabs, as a result of which the State of Israel was accused of genocide, of exiling millions of Arabs (one such publication referred to six million refugees) and other atrocities. The very existence of the State of Israel is represented as being the consequence of an imperialist crime committed by the United Nations in 1947. The propaganda sources feel, however, that this crime will now be undone, thanks to the power of Arab oil and capital and the power of the Third World.

Anti-Semitic Attacks

This old-new diabolizing of the Jewish People is also accepted—as far as can be judged from the material which reached us—by long-standing anti-Semites, such as Juan Queraltó, leader of an old anti-Semitic nationalist organization, the Alianza Libertadora Nacionalista, who, after a long period of quiescence, staged a comeback into public life in 1973. Although the left-wing is traditionally hostile to these circles, it shares their views on Jews on one count at least: enmity to Zionism and unreserved support for Arab extremists.

Anti-Jewish propagandists in Argentina do not limit themselves to dissemination of old and new negative stereotypes of Jews to their readers. Much of their energy is devoted to inciting the masses to act against Argentinian Jewry and particularly against those Jews who have become prominent in political life. At the head of the list of those under attack was the Minister of Economic Affairs, José Ber Gelbard. Born in Poland, he immigrated to the Argentine as a child and later became a successful industrialist. He was active in the Peronist movement—during the first period of Perón's rule—and it was the leader himself who appointed Gelbard to the highest government position. Though the latter never concealed the fact that he was Jewish, he was never active in organized Jewish public life. Gelbard's program, *Acuerdo Social,* intended to insure cooperation

20. *Consigna Nacional,* no. 7, March 1974, p. 18. This plan is also frequently referred to in "El Caudillo."

between the workers and employers by means of wage restraint and price stability, provoked criticism from the right and the left alike. The anti-Semitic attacks directed against him, against Julio Bronner, head of the Employers' Union, against Jacob Timerman, editor of *La Opinion* and against other Jews spilled over from the press into the street.

Not only individual Jews but Argentinian Jewry as a whole were attacked in leaflets, in inscriptions painted on the walls of houses, and in slogans chanted in chorus at public meetings. Two motifs in particular stand out in these attacks: on the one hand, a tie-up with Nazism and Nazi practices such as using the swastika, arranging memorial services for Hitler, and at the same time describing Zionism as a Nazi movement; on the other hand—a summons to kill Jews or exile them from the Argentine Republic.

The motifs revealed in such propaganda and in the anti-Semitic attacks are more extremist and more uncompromisingly hostile than it would appear from the number of violent clashes recorded.

Old and New Anti-Semitism

Is there anything new in the content of Argentine anti-Semitism after the Yom Kippur War?

If we return to the anti-Semitic publications of the late thirties, in particular the organ of the right-wing anti-Semitic organization *Accion Antijudía Argentina* (which used the sign of A.A.A.), we discover an astonishing similarity to the arguments put forward above. Diabolical Zionism, as conceived by the forgers of the *Protocols of the Elders of Zion*, is divided in these publications into western capitalist-imperialist Zionism and eastern Marxist Zionism. The Zionist movement appears under the headline *"El sionismo internacional—Nueva forma de Imperialismo."* Another theme is the establishment of the Jewish State in Argentina instead of in Palestine.[21]

Twenty-three years later, in 1964, the Peronist deputy Juan Carlos Cornejo Linares demanded that a parliamentary inquiry committee investigate the activity of the Zionist movement in Argentina–its military and educational activities, insidious undermining

---

21. *Accion Antijudia Argentina*, no. 11, 12, 13, November, December 1938, January 1939.

action, the flight of capital, all the usual charges, in exactly the same
way that Nazi activities in the Argentine Republic were investigated
in 1941. Cornejo Linares quoted those who called for that investigation, saying: "Replace 'Germany' by 'Israel' and 'National Socialism'
by 'Zionism,' and the words recited before this Honorable Chamber
by the Deputies Damonte, Taborda and Silvano Santander in 1941
are fully applicable, vigorous and eloquent today, twenty-three years
later, in 1964."[22]

The virulent anti-Zionist campaign was accompanied by the
publication of a great deal of material which gave expression to even stronger views after the Six Day War. It reached a high-
water mark with Walter Beveraggi Allende's so-called revelation at
the beginning of 1972 of the "Andinia Plan," already referred to. Allende, lecturer in political economy in the law faculty of Buenos
Aires University, sent an open letter to the head of the Trade Unions
Federation in that town describing the plan in detail; on the strength
of that letter a local attorney in Tucuman demanded that a federal
court launch a legal investigation to uncover the truth about the conspiracy. Echoes of this plan and the demand for an inquiry were
soon heard throughout Argentina.[23]

Extremist support for the Arabs from high-ranking Peronists
is, of course, not new. In October 1971, after a propaganda campaign
by Arab missions and ambassadors of Arab countries, a committee
was set up in the Argentine—Comité Justicialista de Palestina
Libre—under the chairmanship of Andrés Framini, an outstanding
Peronist leader. He was elected governor of Buenos Aires province
in 1962, as a result of which the army at that time annulled the elections. The committee's declaration of identification with the Palestinians and the serious charges made against Israel bore the signa-
tures of Peronist leaders of both left and right wings, as well as those
of long-standing anti-Semites.

Anti-Semitism in Argentina has apparently changed little
since October 1973. The anti-Semites of the sixties (and some of
those prominent in earlier years) were among the antagonists. But
the great change which took place between the Yom Kippur War and
July 1975 was their alarming closeness to the ruling power groups

22. *Cámara de Diputados de la Nación*, Reunion 33a, July 15, 1964, pp. 1653–54.
23. *Noticias* (Tucuman), January 29, 1972; February 3, 4, 1973.

and the extent to which they became involved in the vital economic and political interests of the Argentine Republic.

In the first half of the sixties anti-Semites did not enjoy the support of the political circles in power. Radical Presidents, such as Arturo Frondizi (1958–1962) and Arturo Illia (1963–1966), who had had earlier political careers in the thirties and were members of the united front of left and center parties against anti-Semitism and racialism, took legal measures and even made use of the police against nationalist anti-Semitic terrorist groups. Cornejo Linares' anti-Zionist proposals received no serious support in Parliament, and members of the Chamber of Deputies in the province of Córdoba joined together to support a resolution condemning the Linares proposal in the following terms:

. . . [this] proposal is plainly anti-Semitic in stamp, under the pretext of investigating the anti-Argentinian activities supposedly attributable to our Hebrew compatriots, who have worked so hard and are striving for the Zionist ideal, that is, for the creation and survival of the State of Israel.[24]

During the period of army control, anti-Semitic nationalists were indeed allowed to organize openly and ruling circles were certainly in favor of their nationalist, Catholic ideology, but—whether from consideration of foreign or internal policy—the central authorities were careful to avoid identifying themselves with these groups. The rise to power of General Carlos Onganía was acclaimed with sympathy and declarations of support by the anti-Semitic organizations, but he repeatedly tried to prove to the world that he personally was not an anti-Semite and that the Jewish community would not be exposed to any kind of persecution under the military regime.

When Cornejo Linares, Andrés Framini and other Peronists voiced their approval of anti-Zionism, questions were asked about the attitude of Perón himself. In February 1972, Dr. Noé Davidovitch, a member of the central roof organization of Argentinian Jewry, the *Delegación de Asociaciones Israelitas Argentinas* (DAIA), and one

---

24. *Repudia la Cámara de Diputados de Córdoba el Proyecto de Cornejo Linares*, p. 6. Record of the deliberations of the Chamber of Deputies on August 4, 1964. (There is no indication of publisher or date of publication.)

of the leaders of the *Mapam* (Zionist socialist) party in the Argentine, was accorded a meeting with exiled Gen. Perón in his home in Madrid. The following day, Perón authorized publication of this written statement:

> I have considered the information you reported to me yesterday, and have reached the conclusion that in the cases in question (which I have been able to check in my files) the matter involves persons who, though connected with the National Justicialist Movement politically, have no authority to speak in the name of our movement. It should be understood that they and they alone are responsible for their personal activities.[25]

This response is striking in its similarity to another declaration made by Perón at the very outset of his political career. During his campaign in 1945 (when he was elected for the first time), he had the enthusiastic support of the anti-Semitic nationalists, and his opponents took good care to brand him as a fascist and a supporter of Nazi Germany. At that time, he also issued a declaration:

> Nazi and racist ideas are being attributed to me because some of those who are acclaiming me have their heads in the clouds and are attacking people and principles they dislike. . . . I declare that they have no authority, and I deny that people who act in this way share my principles and ideals.[26]

The general spoke in a similar vein to a delegation of Jewish community leaders in the Argentine on November 8, 1973, after his return to power. According to him, the Peronist movement is opposed to discrimination on grounds of race or religion, and the idea of "Sinarquía," which is the basis for the attack on the Jewish community in the Argentine, does *not* refer to Jews of the Argentine. As proof of his stand, he explicitly referred to the fact that he had appointed a Jew, José Ber Gelbard, as Minister of Economic Affairs, maintaining him in that post in spite of anti-Semitic intrigues against him.[27]

25. *Nueva Sión*, March 3, 1972, giving photograph of Perón's letter dated February 2, 1971.
26. *La Epoca*, November 28, 1945.
27. *La Luz*, November 16, 1973, p. 18.

Anti-Semitism and the Ruling Power Group

To what extent had things changed during the period under review?

Increasing dependence on the right wing of the Peronist movement—where the anti-Semitic nationalists are to be found—became even more striking after Perón's death. The decision to wrest control of the universities from the Peronist left wing led to the appointment of an extreme nationalist and fascist, Dr. Alberto Ottalagano, Rector of Buenos Aires University; along with him were appointed a number of similarly disposed deans of faculties, who continued in their posts even after the rector was removed. When José Ber Gelbard was dismissed, anti-Semite Cornejo Linares—now a member of the Senate—was appointed head of a joint House of De- puties–Senate Inquiry Committee, which investigated Gelbard's business activities in exploiting aluminum deposits in the period preceding the Peronist return. As was expected, the committee found that the accusations leveled at the former minister were justified. The anti-Semitic, nationalist paper, *El Caudillo* with its slogan, "the best enemy is a dead enemy," in assessing its achieve- ments in the first year of publication, reported that the majority of those it had attacked no longer held their former positions. These successes continued until the paper bade farewell to its readers in April 1975 with the declaration, "The time for words is over; now is the time for deeds."

The right-wing terrorist organization A.A.A., in the same month, threatened the lives of sixteen eminent personalities, includ- ing certain Jews (writers, artists and journalists) in order to foil an al- leged Judeo-Marxist conspiracy. The anti-Semitic and nationalist character of the members of this organization and its direct or in- direct reliance on López Rega, the strong man in the government of President Isabel Perón until July 1975, were widely known in the Ar- gentine and among the foreign press.[28]

A no less serious symptom of the change that took place in the position of anti-Semitism in Argentina was the increase in anti-

28. *Visión* (Mexico), January 15, 1975, pp. 22, 24. Interview of the journalist Federico Branco from the Brazilian paper *Estado de São Paulo*, with a representative of the A.A.A., who gave him the *Protocols of the Elders of Zion* as his authority for his opin- ions on the Jews. See also *Latin America*, June 6, 1975, vol. ix, no. 22, p. 172.

Semitic attacks in the nationalized communications media, first and foremost on government television channels. In a number of instances, vicious anti-Semitic attacks have been televised and broadcast as part of programs on Syria and other Arab countries. The most striking attack evoked the surprise and outspoken gratitude of the head of the Arab League mission in Buenos Aires.[29] The willingness of the Argentine authorities to accept the image of the Jewish People and the State of Israel that the Arabs wish to disseminate is a sorry fact connected with another fundamental change that took place in the period under review.

The Arab League's efforts to attack Argentinian Jewry as the rearguard of the State of Israel began as early as the fifties. In the first half of the sixties, propaganda attacks were intensified, and close ties were established with strong-arm anti-Semitic groups. The uproar over the activity of the then head of the Arab Office, Hussein Triki, led to the cancellation of his visa, but someone was soon found to carry on in his place. Arab propaganda continued—as well as the financial support for such activity. These propagandists repeatedly tried to spur the Arab immigrants in the Argentine (and the sons of immigrants) to engage in anti-Israel and anti-Jewish activity. As a result of their efforts, increased after the Six Day War, a federation of Argentinian Arab organizations was created, and a high point was reached, by chance apparently, precisely when the Yom Kippur War broke out. From that time, local Arab activity has grown considerably; this movement, together with the prestige of the Arab organizations, was reinforced by close ties that were created between the Republic of Argentina and the Arab countries soon after the Yom Kippur War.

Even before the end of 1973, a trade delegation headed by an Argentinian Arab went on a tour of the Arab countries. The report of its activity, as well as a flood of news about the economic upswing of the Arab oil-producing countries, called forth in the Argentine communications media exaggerated hopes and expectations of a flow of capital. "Reports Confirmed: The Arab Dollars Are Coming"— declared a headline in the Peronist paper *El Mundo*, and a news report under the same headline spoke of a loan of $2,300,000 on easy

29. T.V. programs such as these appeared on Channel 11 on December 7, 1974; January 8, 1975; April 19, 1975; and on Channel 7, on February 27, 1974; April 12, 1975; April 19, 1975. Comments on the last two programs were made in a leading article in *La Prensa*, May 3, 1975.

terms to be granted to the Argentine Republic by the combined Arab states.[30]

In January 1974, when Minister López Rega went to Libya at the head of a comprehensive mission of experts, large-scale agreements were signed in the spheres of commerce, industry, technology and culture. On his return to the Argentine, López Rega presented these agreements as an impressive and unique achievement from the point of view of the Argentine economy. At a meeting in the presidential residence, López Rega gave a detailed report on his mission and the agreements reached; the governors of the provinces and the parliamentary deputies of Arab origin, representing Argentinian Arab institutions, and the ambassadors of the Arab states, were also present. In this report he recounted the difficulties that his mission had encountered, one of them being the mistaken belief prevailing in Tripoli with regard to his country's attitude to the Arab-Israeli conflict—"a problem aggravated by religious aspects connected with the composition of the Argentinian Government." In a still broader reference to the Jewish Minister of Economic Affairs, López Rega described as a further stumbling block "certain news items arriving from Buenos Aires by telex, received through local government channels and distorted when it was noticed that they were signed by Argentinian officials of Jewish origin."[31]

The details of the agreements and their implementation continued to arouse interest in the Argentinian press throughout the period under review, and the positive image of Libya and its leader, Colonel Muammar al-Qaddafi, has been progressively reinforced with the implementation of each phase of the trade agreement. "If this operation can be described as extraordinary from the commercial point of view, it is, in our judgment, still more important as a means of bringing closer together two peoples who adhere to the same ideals of grandeur and liberation, and are guided by the spirit of two great patriots, Colonel Qaddafi and General Perón," declared López Rega in December 1974.[32] This comparison between the two leaders mentioned by others on various occasions, was naturally repeated frequently in the anti-Semitic press. In 1975, about eighteen months after the signing of the agreements in Tripoli, it became known to the people that, under one of these agreements, the

30. El Mundo, January 25, 1975.
31. Crónica, Noticias, February 19, 1974.
32. La Razón, Clarín, December 14, 1974.

Argentine government also undertook to cooperate with the government of Libya in the research and development of atomic energy, allegedly for peaceful purposes.[33]

At the same time, the Argentine strengthened its ties with the other Arab countries. Lebanon, the Persian Gulf emirates, Algeria and Syria all became close friends of the Argentine Republic. A cultural cooperation agreement signed with Syria included an undertaking to exchange publications, exhibitions, and radio and television programs. Such presentations with an anti-Semitic slant should, therefore, be seen against the background of these changed foreign relations.

The new aspect of hostility toward the Jews in the Argentine between the Yom Kippur War and the month of July 1975 can thus be summed up as follows:

1. Anti-Semitic circles, which were by no means close to the center of power in the past, have clearly come very close to it during that period;
2. Arab anti-Semitism, which in earlier periods, too, existed in the Argentine but remained on the fringes of Argentinian international relations and political life, has, after the Yom Kippur War, become firmly connected with vital economic and political interests.

These changes bring with them a clearly discernible, new phenomenon: government-level anti-Semitism imported into the Argentine from the Near East, an import which has fallen on fertile soil among those who wield authority. At the same time it should be pointed out that there was no outspoken, anti-Jewish policy, certainly not a systematic one, so that formal relations between Argentina and the State of Israel have not been impaired.

Against a background of growing violence and political change at a frenzied tempo, distinctions should be made between transitory events and those that signify permanent change.

Right-wing anti-Semitic personalities have come close to power in the Argentine at various periods in the past—in 1930, 1943 and 1966. Yet, each time anti-Semites failed to undermine Jewish existence there. Such a situation is not impossible this time, too, either

33. *La Prensa*, May 14, 1975.

because those in power now may lose their positions or because they will refrain from going beyond a certain point in their enmity to the Jews. The development of government-level anti-Semitism in the Argentine is thus not necessarily bound to happen.

However, this is not valid for imported governmental anti-Semitism. Connections with the Third World and economic and political links with the Arab states are well entrenched in the Peronist and non-Peronist left no less than in the Peronist right, and perhaps even more so. It is true that during the period under review there were political elements in Argentina critical of the agreements with Libya and even of unreserved identification with the Third World; but it is doubtful whether strong ties that were woven with the Arab countries can be cut, even if those elements will eventually influence Argentine policy. To this must be added the awakening and the systematic organization of Arabs in the Argentine Republic, a fact which is likely to affect permanently the degree of hostility to Jews and the State of Israel.[34]

Summing Up

Both Peru under the presidency of Velasco Alvarado and Peronist Argentina belonged to the bloc of nonaligned countries in spite of the fact that the regimes were different. Arab anti-Semitic propaganda has penetrated into both countries, creating relatively new anti-Semitic myths in Peru and revivifying the veteran anti-Semitic groups in the Argentine, for whom these myths are not really new. This process was the direct result of the bloc allegiance of these two countries and the pressure of their economic and political interests. As a consequence, Latin American Jewry is now, for the second time in history, faced with an assault by government-level anti-Semitism imported from outside. The Latin American situation

---

34. In July 1975, after a chain of dramatic political developments, José López Rega had to leave Argentina. Estela María de Perón's power base disintegrated rapidly and on March 24th, 1976, a military coup brought General Jorge Videla into the presidential chair. Very few Argentinians mourned the disappearance of "Isabelita" from the government. All the energies of the new regime were immediately directed towards the physical elimination of the left-wing guerrillas. A.A.A. killing squads, as well as leftist terrorism, along with extreme measures of suppression, became the day-to-day experience of the Argentinian population. The anti-Semites hailed the military regime and particularly the extremist factions in the ruling Junta.

since the Yom Kippur War is thus potentially different from that of the sixties.

Will the situation in the late seventies in fact resemble that of the years of the Nazi German, anti-Semitic assaults of the thirties and forties? It is beyond the scope of this paper to discuss these eventualities but, when comparing the two periods, one should weigh the influence of the German communities in Latin America then as compared with the potential influence of the Arab diaspora today; the ties of vital interest among countries in the region with Nazi Germany at that time as compared with their ties with the oil-producing Arab countries today; their affiliation with the bloc of American countries in the thirties as compared with the changes in bloc allegiance in recent years as a result of the growing strength of the Third World; and, finally, the capacity of the Jewish communities within Latin America to take their stand in the face of anti-Semitism then and now. In this last respect, the State of Israel has a significant part to play.

Russian Nationalism and the Jewish Question

Mikhail Agursky

In the U.S.S.R. today, as in the Western world, there are crises in the fields of economics, social relations, politics and religion, but in none is the crisis so acutely felt as in the sphere of nationalism. There are powerful forces, generated by the imperialist structure of the state, which under given conditions might even destroy the Soviet empire. Some nationalist movements have developed because peoples, such as the Crimean Tartars, Germans and Meskh-Turks, were driven from their territories. Other movements have developed in the so-called republics, such as the Baltic States, Central Asia, the Caucasus and the Ukraine. It is in the Ukraine that local nationalism is particularly strong and a potentially dangerous centrifugal movement, since it is the largest republic and economically the most independent. Moreover, it can become the center of attraction for other national movements. This, in fact, was the case when the group led by Petr Shelest (first Secretary of the Ukrainian Communist Party) was in power. Even though that group was defeated, the problem of Ukrainian nationalism has by no means been solved; it has only been postponed. Of the two main types of local nationalism, pro-communist and anti-communist, the former is at present the main driving force, since the use of communist ideology as a camouflage ensures its survival, as in Rumania and Albania.

Local nationalist movements have consolidated their position on the basis of anti-Jewishness, and the degree of their separatism is judged by the intensity of their anti-Jewishness. In such republics as the Ukraine and Lithuania, the Jews have been attacked as being mainly responsible for russification, since they are oriented to the Russian language.

Russian Nationalism before the Revolution

Russian nationalism, which assumed organized form during the 1905 revolution, is a complex phenomenon and it is impossible to evaluate it in simple terms. Yet, an analysis is extremely important, since it dominates the complex set of factors determining the position of Jews in the U.S.S.R.

By 1905 Russian nationalism was already a definite conglomerate of tendencies, frequently contradictory, even antagonistic. Among its adherents were the religious nationalists, who considered Orthodoxy the only true faith on earth and Russia its only sanctuary. They considered monarchy a form of theocracy and the expansion of Russia a religious duty. They held identical views on russification of aliens. They, too, were against the Jews, though anti-Jewishness had a religious basis. The most prominent representative of that trend was Metropolitan Antony (Khrapovitskii).

Another trend was political nationalism, which considered national and state interests all-important and justified. The attitude of political nationalists toward the Jews was extremely hostile, their actions revealing racial motives. However, political nationalism did not reduce the entire intrastate conflict to the Jewish question, as was the case with the extreme trend of Russian nationalism—racism. The racists, quite irrationally, imputed all difficulties of Russia and the world in general to a global Jewish-Masonic plot.

Racist Tendencies

From its emergence Russian racism was spearheaded almost exclusively against the Jews. This form of Russian nationalism has much in common with German national socialism. Both emerged from the ruins of Christian civilization in their countries and, essentially, possess many features which warrant their being classed as a modern form of gnosticism.

In the view of the gnostic racists the Jews are obviously endowed with certain divine attributes: omnipresence, omniscience, and absolute prescience. They are also considered extraordinarily sly and treacherous. Russian racists see the relations between Russia and Jews as a cosmic struggle, while the Jews have the upper hand with respect to their antagonists in terms of malice and, naturally, wealth. Russian gnostic racism is essentially a projection of the ontological role of the Jews in the history of Christianity, which has left an indelible mark on the subconscious of the racist, even if it has lost its religious sense for him. Racists have preserved the old structure of religious consciousness, but without the earlier values, which have been replaced by the dualism of good and evil, drawn from the former religious system. Russian gnostic racism has become transformed into a deification of the people, precisely as was the case with German racism. However, like German racism, it also includes immanent suicidal tendencies, for it was based on a false and irrational view of the world.

Russian racism was grouped mainly around the Union of the Russian People and the Union of Michael the Archangel, the most prominent leaders and ideologists of which were Alexander Dubrovin, Nikolai Markov II, Vladimir Purishkevich and Georgi Butmi de Katzman. Another prominent racist ideologist was the non-party journalist, Mikhail Menshikov. The slogan which formally consolidated Russian nationalism was "Orthodoxy, Autocracy, Nationality." However, already in the pre-revolutionary period racism, like political nationalism, displayed a tendency to departure from this credo.

While political nationalism set no value on religion, racism from the very outset revealed anti-Christian tendencies. Recognition of the Hebrew Scriptures was extremely undesirable for the gnostic racists, because Jewish history would thereby be acknowledged as the holy history of the Russians. Moreover, recognition of the Hebrew Scriptures was demanded also by the New Testament, where, in certain gospels and in the Epistles of St. Paul, Judaism remains the positive fulcrum of world history. Finally, there was a deep watershed between religious and racist anti-Jewishness, so that the Church became an obstacle to racism, even though at the very beginning the organized forms of racism by inertia endeavored to use the Church as their basis.

Gradually the racists became dissatisfied with the monarchy too. Thus, one of the leaders of the Union of Russian People, Boris Nikolsky, in private correspondence with Metropolitan Antony, said outright that it was necessary to destroy the ruling dynasty, and the leader of the Union of Michael the Archangel, Vladimir Purishkevich, participated in Rasputin's murder. Subsequently the anti-Christian stand of the racists and their ambiguous attitude toward the monarchy made it possible for them to draw close to the political system of the Stalin period.

Russian Nationalism after the Revolution

It seemed as if nationalist parties, disbanded after the February

Revolution, had ceased to play a part in the life of the country. It would, however, be strange if such large movements were to disappear without a trace, even if those prominent Russian nationalists who emigrated did exert little influence on the political life of Soviet Russia.

At the same time there are reasons to believe that the rank and file members of nationalist parties were with the Bolsheviks shortly before the October Revolution. The diocesan newspaper, *Moskovskyi Tserkovnyi Golos* (Moscow Church Herald), pointed out as early as December 1917 that in Moscow the Bolsheviks were supported by former members of the Union of the Russian People. It cannot, however, be maintained that these people acted as nationalists in the course of the events marking the first period of the revolution; then any manifestation of Russian nationalism was mercilessly suppressed, and prominent nationalists were ruthlessly destroyed. They did, nonetheless, become part of the new system in various spheres, so that they could play a role in the formation of the system which emerged twenty years later.

The restoration of Soviet Russia virtually within the former State borders definitely evoked sympathy among some of the political emigrés who published the journal *Smena Vekh* (Change of Landmarks). The interests of Russian statehood were placed above everything and the Bolsheviks were regarded as a force which would restore Russia as a single and indivisible state. Those ideologists grouped around the journal undoubtedly expected Soviet Russia sooner or later to become a traditional state and they saw in the New Economic Policy (NEP) proof that this was really happening.

Sympathy for the state mission of the Bolsheviks was noticeable among the political nationalists, who had openly fought with the Bolsheviks. Vasilii Shulgin,[1] in his book *1920* (Sophia, 1921), expressed sympathy for the Bolsheviks who, to the author's surprise, shared his aim—the restoration of a single and indivisible Russia. Indifferent to religion, Shulgin predicted with some sympathy that Soviet Russia's development would lead to the restoration of the Russian Empire and to the advent of a dictator who would destroy his comrades. Shulgin further maintained that a Jew could not play such a role. He represented nationalists who attached no value to religion, against which Soviet Russia waged a bitter fanatical struggle.

---

1. Deputy Chairman of the All-Russian National Union.

Reaction against Jews and Aliens

As a result of the revolution the Jews won many civil rights. It was now possible to move *en masse* to the metropolitan cities and to the central parts of Russia, where formerly few Jews had lived. Moreover, in the twenties and thirties the Jews became the second most influential national group and were even dominant in important spheres. The leadership of the country included, among others, Leon Trotsky, Grigorii Zinoviev, Yakov Sverdlov, Grigorii Sokolnikov, Karl Radek, Yuri Larin, Lazar Kaganovich, Arkadii Rosengoltz, Rosalia Zemlyachka, Maxim Litvinov, Lev Mekhlis, Emelyan Yaroslavsky and Solomon Lozovsky. Until the mid-thirties a large number of Jews held key posts in the party and state apparatus, the secret police and the army. Suffice it to say that about thirty percent of key figures in Cheka, GPU and NKVD were Jews. This resulted from a spontaneous process, since Jews never acted as an organized national group with a common aim. Similarly, the political role of other minorities, such as the Latvians, Poles and Finns, was elevated.

The sharp increase in the role of Jews and other aliens and their mass influx into the central parts of the country inevitably evoked a sharp reaction on the part of the indigenous population, resulting in the growth of anti-Jewishness. Since, at first, the anti-Stalin opposition consisted predominantly of Jews and other aliens, the struggle within the party immediately assumed a nationalist coloration. Thus clashes with alien elements among the elite became one of the main, even if hidden, motives of the struggle, which ended in the domination of the Russians. By the end of the twenties symptoms of the imminent reaction against Jews and other aliens were already evident. During the November 1927 demonstration in Moscow (as reported in *Pravda*) the dispersal of the opposition was accompanied by anti-Jewish slogans, inspired by the then secretary of the Moscow Committee, Nikolai Uglanov, whom Stalin used against his opponents. According to A. Avtorkhanov,[2] Stalin had already in 1926 shown his anti-Jewish attitude in his struggle with the Leningrad opposition. The defeat of Trotsky and Zinoviev indicated that the indigenous population was pleased to see the awe-inspiring Jews become the object of attacks. Thus the struggle against the

2. See *Stalin and the Soviet Communist Party*, Munich, 1959.

opposition in 1925–27 showed Stalin that the reaction against the sharply increased Jewish influence could be effectively used to strengthen his power, without rejecting communist ideology. Stalin did not invent Russian nationalism; he only realized that it could be used as a powerful weapon to strengthen his reign.

In 1928 the Soviet press launched a campaign against anti-Semitism, indicating that Jews of the lower social class were harassed by rabid spontaneous hostility, while Jews of the upper class were as yet protected from it. There is reason to believe that this campaign was inspired by Stalin to camouflage the gradual transformation of anti-Jewishness into state policy at a higher level. Apparently, Stalin was already preparing for the ouster of aliens, notably Jews, from the country's political life, but since the old internationalist-oriented elite still stood at the helm of the state, such slogans could not be used officially.

Framed Trials

Stalin gradually began to suggest to the population that the Jews were not all so loyal. Several Jews of the older generation were indicted at the completely framed Shakhty Trial in 1928, and although Jews were not cast in the role of the main accused, the press listed names of the accused, mentioning first engineer Rabinovitch, former member of the State Duma. In 1930 the Jewish Section (*Yevsektsiya*) was abolished and in 1931 the Menshevik Trial was staged. Virtually all the accused were Jews and their indictment on fabricated evidence had far-reaching aims. It may be surmised that already in the early thirties the ideology of Russian nationalism was being transformed into the secret ideology of an influential circle in Stalin's entourage.

However, Russian nationalism among Stalin's followers developed not only as a political movement, but assumed an irrational gnostic form—a development which was due to the antireligious fanaticism of the Soviet system; in destroying religious values fertile ground for such a trend was created. The events of 1936–38 were no historical accident. A revolution generally raises to power forces other than those who are active in it. Reality generally makes short shrift of the revolutionaries, even though a new situation is always created in the aftermath of a Thermidor.

Soviet Thermidor

The Soviet Thermidor of 1936–38 was the result of real social, economic and national forces in an enormous country. Stalin did not invent this Thermidor, but he used it shrewdly. He foresaw the course of historical events and swam with the tide. Otherwise the Thermidor might have swept him aside too. The national reaction of the indigenous population, sharply aggravated by the end of the twenties and the beginning of the thirties, threatened the very existence of the new system, but Stalin succeeded in transforming it into the state system.

It was impossible to implement such doubtful national experiments in a vast country with conservative national formations, without evoking a strong reaction. The purges in 1936–38, which led to the destruction of the entire elite, had a clearly expressed nationalist character. Jewish and other alien influences on the country's political life were destroyed, although the nature of the purges was scarcely realized, since in official propaganda no changes were indicated.

At one of the main trials of 1936-38—the Pyatakov[3]-Radek[4] trial—a provocateur called Arnold was accused of being a Mason.[5] Hardly anyone noticed that the attempt to connect Masonry with "Trotskyism" heralded the legalization of the most extreme anti-Jewish propaganda emanating from Russian racists, whose bible was the *Protocols of the Elders of Zion*.

Of special note also was the so-called trial of the "Jewish Fascist Center" during the purges, which came to light only after the publication of Samuel Agursky's letter of 1940 to Shakhne Epstein (*Soviet Jewish Affairs*, no. 2, 1974).

A New Nationalism

An entirely new social element emerged during the purges— one that hailed from the peasantry and rural lower middle class.

3. Grigorii Pyatakov (1890–1937), prominent Party functionary and one of the economic leaders. Executed.
4. Karl Radek (1885–1940), one of the leaders of the German Left Social Democrats. He came to Soviet Russia in 1919; held important positions in the Komintern. Died in prison.
5. *Sudjebny otchjet po djelu antisovjetskogo fashistitskogo tzentra* (Legal Proceedings of the Anti-Soviet Fascist Center), 23–30 januarja, Moskva, 1937.

With the advent of this group to power nationalism became a component part of the system, without its former political, cultural and religious content. Its aims were to dominate other national groups and consolidate state power and expansion, while preserving communist ideology only as a pragmatic instrument for the attainment of these aims. This ideology, however, was, at times, an impediment to the vital interests of the new system. The triumph of the new nationalism was not perceived in the lower layers immediately after the purges, but the leadership at the top level was consciously guided by it.

The fact that state nationalism of the new type began to reveal gnostic tendencies at the end of the thirties was the inevitable result of the spiritual vacuum created by the bitter anti-religious struggle and the ineffectiveness of communist ideology felt, first and foremost, at the top.

Part of Stalin's entourage regarded itself as a force in opposition to so-called Zionism (i.e., Jewish influence in the country). According to oral testimony, the *Protocols of the Elders of Zion* was the manual of Andrei Zhdanov, Stalin's closest collaborator. This led to the rapprochement between Stalin and Hitler immediately after the 1936–38 purges and was based on Stalin's belief in Hitler's ideological closeness. The removal of Jews from power continued after 1938; the war with Germany only strengthened that tendency. Thus a month before the war of 1941 virtually all the Jews remaining in the Party Central Committee were removed from it.

Russian Nationalism after World War II

The postwar years were a triumph of state nationalism. The victory over Germany and the great expansion of the empire brought a rapid and open growth of nationalist sentiments in all spheres, though without cultural and religious content. This was most vividly expressed in the attempt to justify the entire colonial policy of the earlier regime; to ascribe to Russia priority in all fields of science and culture; and, finally, to exacerbate open anti-Jewishness. The intensification of anti-Jewishness during that period, as distinct from that before the war, could no longer be justified by pragmatic considerations. That Stalin himself realized his actions were specifically anti-Jewish is vividly demonstrated in Svetlana Allilueva's memoirs. In a conversation with his daughter about her marriage to a Jew, Stalin remarked that "the entire generation was infected with Zionism, and were now teaching it to the young people too."

This remark is of enormous importance, for it sheds light on Stalin's secret ideology. His observation can only be understood in the light of the ideology of gnostic racism, which looks upon Zionism as the Jewish attempt to dominate the whole world. Stalin's remark implies that the Russians had allowed themselves to be lulled by internationalist slogans: They had failed to notice the secret aims of world Jewry, the representatives of which, it must be assumed, were the Jewish Communists in the U.S.S.R. His remark also shows that he considered it necessary to eradicate any feeling of sympathy which the Russians had for the Jews.

The irrationality of this position, even the absence of Stalin's former pragmatism, can be deduced from the fact that in the postwar period the people were consolidated because of the general terror. The population began to feel its supremacy over other countries as a result of the victory over Germany; they also felt that the Soviet people were ideologically superior to the whole world, an idea which had been suggested to them by official propaganda. The Jews by that time had been ousted from key state positions so that the attempt in 1952–53 at a "final solution" to the Jewish question could not be justified even by Machiavellian considerations. It resulted purely from the development of gnostic racism, which by that time was of the same mystical nature as German racism.

However, the negative consequences of state nationalism were being felt even by the Russians. First of all, to forestall dissatisfaction in the borderlands the standard of living there was maintained at a higher level than in Russia. Further, the Russians, now the backbone of the army, had to bear the main burden of preserving and expanding the nation. They were developing also as the chief physical force in industry throughout the country, especially in mining. On the one hand, this led to extensive Russian colonization of the national republics; on the other, it depopulated the Russian villages which had been the main source of industrialization in the U.S.S.R. in its progress toward a consumer society. The absence of traditional cultural and religious life and the weakness of the ruling ideology also had a negative effect on the moral state of the Russians, among whom, for example, drunkenness soon assumed biologically dangerous dimensions.

The change of power following Stalin's death temporarily

stopped the development of racism, preventing physical destruction of the Jews. Khrushchev's reign was an unsuccessful attempt at communist restoration; having rejected extreme nationalism in internal policy, he sharply intensified the imperialist strivings of the country, not even showing Stalin's undoubted caution.

The brunt of imperial policy was again borne mainly by the Russians; despite the general improvement of material conditions in the country, there was still a gap in the living standards of Russia and the national borderlands. When Khrushchev's communist restoration had spent itself, intensified gnostic nationalism became extraordinarily influential in the life of the country. It was apparently one of the main reasons for the overthrow of Khrushchev.

Development of Russian Nationalism

After Khrushchev, racism required both internal and foreign political justification. This was not easy, for Russian Jews had been removed from power almost completely and were no longer enjoying equal rights. Foreign political affairs as, for instance, the Arab-Israeli conflict and the events in Czechoslovakia, received priority. These events were portrayed as a manifestation of the Zionist threat and the Jewish attempt to achieve world domination. Irrational nationalism, in sharp contradiction to the official communist ideology, now became a dominant social force in the country.

There emerged influential ruling circles for whom the ideology of extreme anti-Jewishness proved to be a pragmatic instrument. Even though these circles do not as yet exert a dominant influence on the country's policy, they have sufficient authority to publish literature in which all critical events in international and internal affairs are said to result from a secret world-wide Jewish plot. Among such publications are Yuri Ivanov's *Beware of Zionism*,[6] Yuri Kolesnikov's *The Promised Land*,[7] as well as books and articles by Ivan Shevtsov,[8] Yevgenii Yevseev,[9] Vladimir Begun,[10] and Dmitrii Zhukov.[11] Moreover, an attempt is made to vindicate Nazi Germany's murder of Jews. Kolesnikov's book maintains that Eichmann

6. See author's review in *New York Review of Books*, November 16, 1972.
7. *Oktjabr*, no. 9, Moscow, 1972.
8. *Vo imja otza i syna* (In the Name of Father and Son), Letchworth, 1972.
9. *Fashism pod goluboj zvezdoj* (Fascism under the Blue Star), Moscow, 1971.
10. *Polzutchaja kontrrevolutzia* (Creeping Counter-revolution), Minsk, 1974.
11. *Ogonjek*, October 12, 1974.

was a secret Jewish agent so that this mass murder was in fact the handiwork of the Jews themselves.

No less effective are propaganda lectures, which often mold Soviet public opinion; they leave an indelible impression on the listeners and in recent times have disseminated the most rabid anti-Jewish propaganda. Thus, for example, Emelyanov's notorious lecture was read in the main lecture hall of the *Znaniye* (Knowledge) Society in Moscow. In the Academy of Pedagogical Sciences the lecturer maintained that Zionism aims at establishing world domination by the year 2000: Maps of Greater Israel, allegedly published in Israel, show that its borders extend south of Kiev. The lecturer asserted that the struggle against world Zionism will be even more difficult and sanguinary than was the war against Germany.

Documents of the nationalist *Samizdat,* some of which have recently been made public, give an idea of modern Russian racism. One of these, written at the end of 1973, resembles Nazi propaganda, but "Jew" has been replaced by "Zionist," and "Aryan" by "Indo-European." The document claims that the Russians are the oldest of the "Indo-European Peoples," and, therefore, a superior race. It is also claimed that the Jews intend to use gas chambers for the physical destruction of the Russians. A typical feature of that document is its formal loyalty to the existing system and to communist ideology, which, however, must be freed from Zionism.

An important, though not a novel, feature of the document is the sharp antagonism toward Christianity. This anti-Christian trend is rooted in the common world picture of racism and was given expression even before the revolution. The document sharply criticizes the old triple formula, "Orthodoxy, Autocracy, Nationality," for having included Orthodoxy and Autocracy. Now, however, Russian racism does not don the cloak of atheism, but of neo-paganism, precisely as was the case with German racism.

Racism, at present growing stronger, is entering the political arena and displaying a tendency to discard communist ideology, which it considers an imposed evil.

Independent Russian Nationalism

Russian nationalism of an independent, even anti-communist, form, which always existed in the U.S.S.R., was cruelly suppressed in the antireligious terror of the twenties and thirties, though it survived in the emotions. Nationalism had religious as well as nonreligious forms, although most of the nonreligious nationalists merged with the existing political system. However, many religious nationalists cast their lot with the Russian Orthodox Church. At the beginning of the war against Germany, Stalin decided to permit the Church to exist legally, mainly with a view to channeling non-communist nationalism into the Church—a policy which provided an acceptable compromise for many people. During the post-war period the official organ of the Russian Orthodox Church even featured a well-known religious nationalist of the pre-revolutionary period, I. Aivazov.

Until the end of the sixties, the authorities made no attempt to use the Church for anti-Semitic purposes. But since then the religious figures have been ordered to adopt a sharp anti-Israel position in various religious and procommunist organizations. At the same time the Russian Orthodox Church was criticized by the racists who considered it the main obstacle to the spread of racism among the masses. However, the incompatibility of racism and Christianity did not exclude religious anti-Jewishness. Even before the war some religious nationalists sided with the very small "Genuine" Orthodox Church (Istino Pravoslavnaya Tserkov—IPT) which, though now underground, played a major role in developing religious nationalism with a political trend. Russian nationalism had no independent expression till the sixties, but then the situation began to change. A semi-legal opposition emerged and Russian nationalism also took the form of an opposition trend. Two independent sources of the Russian nationalist movement emerged, one of them in the forced labor camps in Mordovia, and the other among many Russian intellectuals.

In these camps in the early sixties a group of young Russian nationalists with a sharp anti-Jewish tendency was formed by prisoners. It is said that the founder of this group was a follower of the IPT. According to some sources the camp administration, in its attempts to sow strife among the inmates, encouraged national tendencies, as a result of which separate groups emerged—Russians, Jews, Lithuanians, Ukrainians and others.[12]

From the group of Russian nationalists emerged people such as the priest Grigorii Petukhov, and Vladimir Osipov, Viacheslav

12. E. Kouznetzov, *Dnjevniki*, Paris, 1973.

Rodionov, Vladislav Ilyakov, Deacon Varsonofy (Khaibulin), the main activists of the independent national movement. By the mid-sixties a circle of about sixty people, headed by the orientalist Igor Ogurtsov, was formed in Leningrad. Calling itself the All-Russian Social-Christian Union for the Liberation of the People (V.S.C.C.O.N.),[13] it planned armed struggle against the existing system. The Jews, who were regarded as an alien element in Russia, were not accepted into the group, although the program was not officially anti-Jewish. The circle was exposed in 1966 and all its members arrested. An active role continues to be played by some of its members, since then released. Ogurtsov, the leader of that circle, and Sado, his deputy, are still in prison.

At this time some intellectuals in Moscow were centered around the newly established club *Rodina* (Motherland), the official aim of which was to safeguard ancient monuments. These intellectuals had a predominantly negative, even racist, attitude toward the Jews. Among the most extreme were the artist Ilya Glazunov, the journalist Dmitrii Zhukov, and the literary critics Petr Palievsky and Dmitrii Kozhinov. The writer Vladimir Soloukhin is one of the more moderate followers of that trend.

Veche

By the beginning of the seventies the independent Russian nationalists had grown so strong that they decided to publish a journal, loyal to the state system, though it was non-communist. The journal *Veche* (People's Assembly) appeared in 1971, its first editor being Osipov. Various groups rallied around this journal: religious nationalists, monarchists, national democrats and racists.[14] *Veche* played an important role in forming an independent Russian nationalism. Although none of the articles were openly anti-Jewish, some were implicitly so. The journal also criticized the system as being responsible for the decline of the Russian people and culture.

Veche proclaimed the religious revival of Russia as its main aim. But there was an anti-Christian tendency championed mainly by Anatoly Skuratov (Ivanov), who had spent four years in a mental

13. V.S.C.C.O.N.—*Vserossiyski sozialno-khristiansky sojuz osvobozhdenja naroda*, Paris, 1975.
14. See D. Pospelovsky in *Survey*, London, 1973.

hospital because of his democratic opposition activity. Later, the journal became a house divided and collapsed. This was preceded by many developments, one being Alexander Solzhenitsyn's entry into political life. He became known as a national and religious writer and as early as 1966 many regarded him as a potential leader of the Russian national movement.

The watershed between him and a majority of nationalists was his novel *August 1914*, which was considered by them antipatriotic because in it the Jews were not shown to be the cause of Russia's defeat in the war and the revolution. Moreover, he described some Jews in the novel in positive terms. Another hidden cause of the hostile attitude toward Solzhenitsyn was his marriage to a half-Jewess.

In order to understand the attitude of the nationalists to Solzhenitsyn, it is essential to read the manuscript, "Letter of Ivan Samolvin to Solzhenitsyn,"[15] which appeared at the end of 1971. This document, highly popular in nationalist circles, accuses Solzhenitsyn of promoting world Zionism, and alleges that the U.S.S.R. is still under the complete power of the Jews, who are said to control the government itself. *Veche* also began to attack Solzhenitsyn as a betrayer of national interests. Soviet liberal, democratic dissidents believed *Veche* to be the unofficial mouthpiece of the authorities, even of the KGB. However, this was not so. There were those in political circles who, desiring to use the independent Russian national movement for their own ends, hoped to make *Veche* their mouthpiece, but in a manner that would enable them to dissociate themselves from the magazine, if necessary. It became quite clear by the end of 1973 that this plan had gone awry. In the autumn of that year the present writer sent an open letter to *Veche* criticizing the attitude of the journal toward the Jews[16]—an attitude at odds with the interests of the Russian people. The publication of this letter coincided with a sharp controversy among the members of the editorial board. One group proposed that the journal adopt a pro-Arab position in the Arab-Israel conflict, and take its orientation from the Palestinians and Qaddafi. However, Osipov and others objected. The editorial office then received an unofficial ultimatum, which declared that the main shortcoming of the journal was its

---

15. *Novy Zhurnal*, New York, 1975 (but not printed in *Veche*).
16. *Le Messager*, no. 108–10, Paris, 1973.

Christian orientation, as well as its sympathy for the democratic opposition. Obviously the position of the religious nationalists was the
main obstacle to the transformation of the journal into a racist organ.
Finally the journal collapsed and the religious-oriented group, headed by Osipov and Borodin, dissociated themselves from the extreme
program of *Veche.* Adopting a moderate position on the Jewish question, they established contacts with the Jewish national movement.
The changed position is evident in the new manuscript journals—
Zemlya (Earth) and *Moskovsky Sbornik* (Moscow Collection)—published by Osipov and Borodin respectively. To suppress independent religious nationalism, a trial was instituted in 1974 against
Veche and Osipov was arrested. However, the journals *Zemlya* and
Moskovsky Sbornik continued to appear.

From the beginning of 1974 Solzhenitsyn and his group,
among them the widely-known mathematician Shafarevich and the
historian Borisov, became the actual leaders of the Russian religious
movement. Solzhenitsyn's social program, outlined in his *Letter to
the Leaders,* was misinterpreted in the West. European liberals, and
some prominent members of world Jewry, regarded his program as
tantamount to extreme Russian nationalism. Actually, however,
Solzhenitsyn's program was the only real humanistic alternative to
racism and neo-Nazism in the U.S.S.R. Solzhenitsyn unambiguously
proclaimed solidarity with Israel, at the same time condemning Jews
who use visas to emigrate from Russia to countries other than Israel.

Solzhenitsyn clarified his position on the national question in
Iz Pod Glyb (From under the Rubble), where he advanced the idea of
national atonement and self-limitation for every nation.[17] Some Jewish leaders also misinterpreted *Gulag Archipelago* in which were
published the names and photographs of Jews who worked in the
NKVD and GPU.[18] However, the Solzhenitsyn documents were the
only available ones on the slave-labor system in the U.S.S.R. Had
Solzhenitsyn wished to add material relating to Jewish participation
in the system of terror and violence, he could easily have done so.
Unfortunately, it is known that Jewish Bolsheviks in the 1920s and
30s were among the proponents of the monstrous terror which later
destroyed them. Solzhenitsyn used extremely soft colors in painting
the picture of Jewish involvement and made no generalizations. In

17. Little, Brown, New York, 1975.
18. Soviet Security Police.

Gulag Archipelago he shows that there were a great number of Jewish martyrs in contrast to the number of Jewish executioners. He is accused of not describing in detail the Jewish trials, but it should be remembered that he did not set himself the task of giving a full description of everything that was taking place in the U.S.S.R. For example, he did not write about the persecution of Moslems in the U.S.S.R., who, prior to World War I, probably suffered more than any other religious group in the U.S.S.R.

Solzhenitsyn is decidedly anti-communist; however, following the appearance of *Iz Pod Glyb,* Shafarevich became the main anti-communist theoretician of that trend. Both believed that a national revival of Russia would be possible only after the elimination of communism, which is being coercively imposed, and the restoration of religious values. A complex situation has developed in the spiritual state of Soviet society. It appears that atheism and materialism have only opened the door for the spontaneous formation of various syncretic beliefs, beginning with the official pagan cult of Lenin and his associates.

Gnostic racism is one of these syncretic beliefs. It is countered among the people only by traditional Christian denominations, mainly by Russian Orthodoxy. The Orthodox clergy are, however, under full state control and therefore hampered in their struggle against anti-Christian tendencies. A new movement, in unison with the religious nationalists or liberal-democratic dissenters, has emerged within the Church to oppose state control. The Church position, however, is weak. This is explained by the traditional subordination of layman and clergy to the hierarchy, which is subjected to state control.

In the remote future, however, the Orthodox Church, in alliance with religious nationalism, may be one of the few forces which will be able to act against racism in Russia. At present, the Christian opposition is strongest in Protestant sects, notably the Baptists and the Pentecostals. Together, these denominations, which have over a million followers, do not support the anti-Jewish stand. Indeed, a large group of Pentecostals from the Soviet Far East recently submitted applications for emigration to Israel. Both the Baptists and the Pentecostals are major obstacles to the spread of racism among the Russian people, and their influence is spreading.

Special mention should also be made of the Church of Old

Believers.[19] At the turn of the century, Russian nationalism began to develop, it was bound up with the interests of the ruling Orthodox Church and was sharply hostile to the Church of Old Believers, which was at that time experiencing an upswing. The Old Church was not connected with political nationalism either before or after the revolution, and remained isolated in their form of religious nationalism. Approximately 200 parishes of the Church of Old Believers, which are still extant, have attracted Solzhenitsyn's attention. Russian religious nationalism will possibly turn its sympathies toward the Church of Old Believers, since it has preserved the ancient Russian culture. The Church of Old Believers is also incompatible with racism.

If the traditional Christian values of Russian society will not acquire their former importance it can be expected that the most extreme racists will begin to flourish and will, at best, strive for the eviction of the Jews from Russia; at worst, for their physical extermination. Since the liberal democrats in Russia have no political prospects, they will not be able to set up any serious alternative to racists and nationalism in general.

The Outlook

It is important to realize that the inevitable growth of nationalism in all its forms is spearheaded against the Jewish presence in Russia. Some of them aim at the physical extermination of Jews, others favor emigration and approve of Zionism but demand the assimilation of those Jews who remain.

Anti-Jewishness is also a pragmatic means of strengthening Russian nationalism in virtually all its forms. Attacks on Zionism, external as well as internal, are frequently camouflaged criticism of official ideology. The ideological apparatus, however, pandering to Soviet imperialism, is itself the main vehicle of state nationalism and anti-Jewishness.

It should be noted that the political circles which have decided to use racism as a weapon in the political struggle are playing a dangerous game; this trend has innate suicidal tendencies which

19. Branch of the Orthodox Church, separated in the seventeenth century; was subjected to harsh suppression till 1905.

may end in catastrophe. Irrational racism cannot be introduced without causing the country's political life to become irrational as well.
Any internal or external conflict with Russia will only exacerbate
hostility toward the Jews. Thus it is possible, on the one hand, to
foresee a growing desire of Jews to leave the country, but, on the other hand, this will undoubtedly cause apprehension as to the fate of
Russian Jewry.

Since the country's evolution does not warrant the hope that
the Jewish question will lose any of its poignancy, it is irresponsible
to appeal to Jews to fight changes in the existing system. Those who
do not understand that the Soviet Jews can be saved from a new
national catastrophe only by mass emigration and not by
assimilation are working toward a new Jewish tragedy.

Discussion

MAURICE FREEDMAN

One is bound to be struck by the heading of this section—Manifestations of anti-Jewishness—and the vocabulary used in the main papers. The term "anti-Semitism" has not been abandoned, but is "anti-Jewishness" meant to hint that something new has come upon the face of the earth? A newer threat to be contemplated when an older one, under an older name, has already been coped with intellectually? But the papers tell against that view. Nothing could more vividly demonstrate that what we now see in all parts of the Diaspora is a reactivation and reshuffling of the old ideas. Some deep programs of anti-Semitism, religious, political, economic and racial, are embedded in the ideas recorded in all the countries surveyed at the present time. Does "anti-Jewishness" embrace anti-Semitism as we have long known it to exist as well as the modern hostility to Israel?

It is that last phenomenon that must dominate our thinking. The Zionists preached a solution to the Jewish question which, in assuming a Jewish State, assumed, too, the end of the problem. I should not go so far as to assert that they were naive: they were falling into one of the traps laid untiringly by history.

It would be absurd to argue that but for the State of Israel the Jews would have settled down comfortably into the second half of the twentieth century. Even in the Middle East, where on an optimistic interpretation the Jewish position was favorable, the process of modernization would probably have shaken up the old structures into which the Jews fitted had the State of Israel never emerged. I do not see how it is possible to discuss anti-Semitism at the present time without giving first place to the impact of the State of Israel upon the world.

To ensure that Israel survives, the Jews in the Diaspora have to pay a price. The money they pour into Israel is the least part of it. Their real contribution is in the political and moral support they offer, and for that they must be prepared to suffer. For their support of Israel they are often disliked, and worse may come. Speaking as a

101

Diaspora Jew (and one with no commitment to Zionism in its classical form), I say that we shall have to be stoic about it. But there is a more important message: Our Israeli friends should shake themselves out of their old attitudes toward that wicked world in which the Diaspora has its being. They too easily write off anti-Semitism as a chronic disease of that world, thinking of Israel as the clinic to which the afflicted Jews may retreat for rehabilitation. In fact, Israel is one of the causes of the disease and one would prefer to see some recognition of the responsibility. Israel has by and large a very poor perception of what the world outside is like. It tends, as a result, to seize upon all evidence of anti-Semitism to feed its sense of righteousness. It strikes a foreigner that Israelis are remarkably, and laudably, self-critical at home, but uncritical about themselves in relation to the external world, including the Jews in it.

This brings me back to the relationship between anti-Semitism in its classical forms and modern anti-Israel attitudes. I do not for a moment deny that old-fashioned anti-Semitism may be disguised or expressed by anti-Israel sentiment, but I suggest that a lack of perfect congruence between the two phenomena may have serious implications among Diaspora Jews. It is surely important to realize that, whatever its deep motivation, a generalized anti-Israelism that professes itself free of anti-Semitism makes it possible for some Jews in the Diaspora to be hostile or indifferent to Israel without suffering the guilt of self-hatred. (Among non-Jews anti-Semites may be pro-Israel, either dissociating Israelis from Jews or being content to envisage a country that will absorb what they do not want among them—and which, moreover, has the great merit of challenging the Third World of which they disapprove.) In the wake of the Yom Kippur War, Professor Daniel Elazar made the point at the first seminar of this series that an effect of the crisis in the United States was to sort Jewry more clearly into the unambiguous supporters of Israel and the group of the doubtful, the indifferent, and the hostile. Anti-Israelism, instead of helping to mass Jewry together, may mutilate it. The danger lies not in extremist opinion—opinion that is obvious from afar—but in general attitudes, especially among intellectuals, that jeopardize Israel by situating it within the haughty imperialist world.

Moreover, people are now less touched by the Holocaust. I do not mean simply that memory fades; it is changed by events and the tensions set up by events. Believing as I do that what the Germans did they could do again, and many other Western countries along with them, I find myself constantly surprised in England by views that the Holocaust was an aberration and its historical uniqueness should have no effect upon one's perceptions of the possibilities of the future.

JACOB KATZ

It has been said that it is not the anti-Semite but the Jew who is entitled to define anti-Semitism. I think that scholars, who try to analyze as historians, social scientists or philosophers, and are used to looking at reality with some detachment, should attempt to analyze contemporary anti-Semitism. As long as we accept the idea that prejudice is simply transmitted from generation to generation and is responsible for anti-Jewish or anti-Israeli reaction we blur our vision of the present situation.

I dislike the word anti-Semitism. Nineteenth-century anti-Semitism represented a change in the position of the Jews, because in the pre-Emancipation situation, the Jews were a special, underprivileged group, and whatever was said then against Jews was said as justification of the entire situation. But in the nineteenth century, when Jews had already been emancipated—at least in the Western countries—the anti-Jewish movement, returning to its former position, became an attack against people who were now members of the general society. To define the situation the brand new term anti-Semitism was created.

Today the situation has changed once again. We cannot understand in former terms either the struggle of the Jewish teachers in New York against Blacks, or the problem of the emigration of Russian Jews, and certainly not the particular situation of Israel. We may ask what anti-Semitic motivation lies behind the argument against Jews in Israel. But if we assume that it is just a repetition of the anti-Semitic attitude we will certainly be misled and be incapable of doing justice to the present situation.

Nor do I believe that we can easily define modern anti-Jewish or anti-Israeli attitudes. The fact that someone is against what is being done, or claimed, by Jews is not an indication of anti-Semitism.

We should try to understand the residual of anti-Semitism, and how far it influences the present situation. But we should dismiss the notion that a universal explanation for anti-Semitism can be found.

JACOB TSUR

Unquestionably, we need to understand the change in anti-Semitism as expressed in the 1970s, when its influence is no longer

decisive as was the case until the end of the 1940s. In many countries anti-Semitism is endemic, but it is no longer a danger to the
physical existence of the Jews. That danger exists only in the
U.S.S.R. In Western Europe its influence has lessened considerably,
whereas in Latin America there is a danger to Jewish existence due
to general factors of social development, and not necessarily to Jew-
hatred.

The reasons for this change are: (a) the shift of the geographic
center of gravity of the Jews; (b) changes in their occupations and social standing; (c) the change in the economic structure of the surrounding society; (d) a respite in the anti-Semitic pressures of the
Church; (e) the existence of a Jewish State—a factor which has positive and negative implications.

In Western Europe, where the Jew is, generally speaking, accepted socially, and the forces of assimilation continue unabated,
his economic position hardly differs from that of the community of
which he is part (in contrast to his struggle in all the East European
countries in earlier times). It is now impossible to assert that only
Jews are merchants, industrialists, entrepreneurs, lawyers, doctors;
the same is true of his non-Jewish neighbors. The hatred of the
masses is directed more toward foreign laborers (North Africans in
France, Italians in Switzerland). Jews are part of the middle class
community. The Church has mitigated its campaign against them,
especially since the time of Pope John XXIII. The existence of Israel
has put an end to the attitude of contempt for Jews, an attitude which
was previously an important factor of anti-Semitism; hatred of the
Jews is now transferred to the Jewish State. And other factors are involved: the struggle of Communism for political influence in the
Middle East; Arab wealth and propaganda; the self-hatred of various
Jewish groups (not necessarily due to ideological assimilation);
dreams of a cosmopolitan *Weltanschauung*; concern lest the economic crisis should spread in the West due to Israel, and so forth.
The weakness of Zionist ideological propaganda is a contributing
factor. Nevertheless, I do not see anti-Zionism as a central factor, liable to endanger the existence of the Jews.

Even in Argentina there have always been manifestations of
anti-Semitism because of the teachings of the Church, and struggle
between town and city. Another factor has been repeated attempts
to stabilize an ideology of Argentinian nationality in a community of immigrants from different European backgrounds. In the
political arena, hatred of the United States and the tendency to see
Argentina as part of the Third World are additional factors which
work against the Jews.

We should remember that when Juan Perón spoke of the

"Third Position" he was not referring to "the under-developed world," but rather to the neutral countries which do not follow either the United States or the U.S.S.R. Argentina and Latin America in general are insulted when compared with the new countries of Africa or Asia. I often think that Israel has not taken advantage of South America's pride in its European-American cultural roots.

The standing of the Jews in Latin America is poor not because of Jew-hatred, but because of the general situation on that continent. In most of these countries, the government is not stable and a socio-economic crisis is threatening. In any uprising, the Jews, as part of the middle class, will be first to be hurt; and they will not recover, because they will not find their place in any other social structure.

Thus, I do not see any short-range danger to the situation of the Jews in Latin America, but it is certain that in the long run there is no future for them on that continent. There may be a crisis in the Jewish communities but it is doubtful if migration to Israel will increase. The Jews may move from country to country, some to the United States, and others to countries such as Mexico, Brazil and Venezuela.

The increasing tendency toward nationalism in Greater Russia and in the National Republics (Ukraine, Belorussia) undoubtedly portends an uncertain future for the continued existence of Jews in Russia. In the Soviet Union there is a competitive factor among the nationalities, which creates anti-Semitism as it developed earlier in history in Poland, Croatia, Slovakia and the like. We must also remember that the Soviet Union is the only multiple-nation state with a large Jewish community.

To understand the special conditions of Judaism in the Soviet Union it is worth quoting remarks made in the twenties by the first Soviet Foreign Minister, George Tchicherin, to Albert Einstein (see Kurt Blumenfeld, *"The Jewish Question as an Experience,"* p. 121, quoted in my book, *Anatomy of a Diaspora,* p. 229):

> The Jews tried at first with the help of liberalism, and after the Emancipation with the help of socialism, to appear like Germans in every possible way. And if the Russian Jews now try as Bolsheviks to seem to be Russians within the Soviet alignment, then their attempt will be their downfall in the future. In the Soviet state the plight of people belonging to a nationality consisting of individuals scattered throughout the land will be a hard one. It is almost certain that these individuals will quickly be felt to be anachronisms, remnant of a time which the Soviet government has already overcome. And for any manifestations which may come from this later, one is not to hold the Soviet government responsible.

Thus, from a certain point of view we may see anti-Semitism in the U.S.S.R. as the only form of anti-Jewish feeling in accord with the classical Zionist analysis formulated toward the beginning of the twentieth century.

NATAN LERNER

When analyzing anti-Semitism *today*, a preliminary question must be asked: Are we dealing with a phenomenon which is really *new* and quite different from those forms of anti-Jewishness which virtually disappeared after the Holocaust? Or, are we confronting a twofold situation in which, on the one hand, anti-Jewish criticism starts with Israel and then reverts to some of the traditional anti-Semitic patterns, and, on the other, the ugly past reinforces traditional motifs?

I believe that a combination of both factors characterizes the current situation, and here I would like to single out the role of the Radical Right. While the extreme Right is no longer the main factor in originating and disseminating anti-Semitism, as in the thirties or forties, it is not an insignificant source of racial hatred. This is true of several countries in Western Europe and certainly in Latin America—particularly in the south, where it has considerable influence on important Populist movements. To a lesser extent this is also the position in the United States.

While the pro-Arab Left does not attempt to draw a clear borderline between political hostility to Israel and typical anti-Semitism, the Right in Argentina—and to a lesser extent in other Latin American countries—uses the unsophisticated anti-Jewish approach already well-known through the writings of Father Meinvielle, the Fascist priest, who devoted several decades to imitating the *Protocols of the Elders of Zion.*

Objective non-Jewish observers have repeatedly issued warnings against the danger involved in strengthening the right wing in Argentina. They cite anti-Semitic television programs and the anti-Jewish flavor of publications sometimes sponsored by government bodies, "with Teutonic condors and almost-swastikas on the masthead." A brutal example of how far anti-Semites in Argentina go today is a poem, printed in the Peronist *El Caudillo,* entitled *Rompan todo* (Destroy Everything), which openly calls for a pogrom against the Jewish quarter in Buenos Aires. This kind of incitement became frequent and deeds sometimes followed words.

In Uruguay, old-fashioned anti-Semitic implications were evident in the expressions of Right-oriented Army circles, while, in

Chile, the higher authorities felt it necessary to convey to Jewish leaders their anxiety about "Marxist content of the prohibited film 'Fiddler on the Roof'." In Mexico, Jews have been accused of loyalty "only to the Jewish State of Israel," while the "Zionist regime" has been called "the instrument of American imperialism."

One must also mention the dangers inherent in the new wave of leftist, Populist nationalism which has gained preeminence in Latin America and is quite different from the old-style right-wing clerical nationalism. This neo-nationalism aims at inner growth, is hostile to the United States, cold to the Soviet Union and inclined toward the Third World. It is not *New* Left. It has, clearly, no sympathy for Israel, which is too much under American influence, too "white," too "capitalistic" for its taste. Nor can it accept the fact that hundreds of thousands of Latin American Jews express their solidarity with Israel in political action, economic support for, and even emigration to, Israel. From such nonacceptance to hostility toward the Jewish communities—the distance is indeed short.

The picture of anti-Semitism today is thus a complex one. Jews come under fire both from the Left and from the Right. There is little that we can add to the traditional means of fighting anti-Jewish outbursts. But a new approach is required to the anti-Jewish campaign which denies Jews the right to identify as a group, as a people, with the problems and destiny of the State of Israel.

A serious intellectual effort to confront the anti-Jewish campaign seems imperative if we are to help non-Jews understand and accept the legitimacy of Jewry's concern with the State of Israel. The Catholic Church, for instance, has, rather timidly, recognized the need to respect the way in which Jews define themselves. To help formulate that definition, Israel itself should play a central role.

LENI YAHIL

The development from classical anti-Semitism to the anti-Jewish approach expressed as anti-Zionism and anti-Israelism can be called the process of politicization of Jew-hatred. Emphasis has shifted to the new, political function, which the Jewish nation has undertaken by centralizing Jewish national life in the State of Israel. Modern anti-Zionist and anti-Israel ideology and politics correspond to this change. Incidentally, the political trend developed much earlier than the founding of the State of Israel, though its forms in the nineteenth century were entirely different from those of today. Emancipation was basically a political movement and

achievement, but the Jews had been required to break up their autonomous and compact organization. They entered the political realm
as individual citizens. Still, modern racial anti-Semitism related itself again to Judaism as a social and ethnic body. The racial basis,
from an ideological and political point of view, led logically to the
demand for destruction. Hitler's aim to annihilate Judaism invalidat-
ed the political rights of the individual by destroying the community. In the Holocaust, the political motivation was a decisive factor
and one of the tragedies is that this was not understood either by the
Jews or by the nations of the world.

Hitler left behind a legacy which the world has not forgotten,
even though today Jew-hatred is no longer officially proclaimed;
first, the fact that an ideology may justify the slaughter of the Jews,
and second, that the world need not protect the Jews, as long as their
persecution does not harm national interests, and sometimes may
even be a convenience. These two approaches the Arabs have adapted to their own use.

The anti-Zionist argument is purely political, and it is today
evident even in countries where there are no Jews. This is demonstrated at international conventions where states which have no direct interest in the Middle East conflict use the anti-Israel argument
to achieve their political goals.

JACK J. COHEN

The theological dimension deserves some consideration. It is
too simplistic to describe anti-Semitism as sickness of Gentiles, to
maintain that there is no relationship between what we do and the
response of the anti-Semites. True, causes of anti-Semitism lie more
in the psychology of the anti-Semites than in behavior of the Jews.
But the fact does not imply that there is no connection between
Jewish behavior and the phenomenon of anti-Semitism—certainly in
regard to its elimination. To argue that no connection is possible is
to posit a dogmatic theology.

Properly, we reject the theological position that the Holocaust
was the punishment wrought by God upon the Jewish People for its
sins. We recoil from the idea that anti-Semitism is the response
to Jewish misbehavior. Yet, is there no relationship whatso-
ever between what we do and the way in which the world reacts, insofar as content, style and intensity of anti-Semitism are concerned?
What is the point of scientific research if not to devise a
strategy of response, not only by non-Jews but by Jews as well? True,

a particular response may not bring a solution—we have not progressed far toward elimination of human indecency. On the other hand, is not our disclaimer theologically irresponsible? We are on firmer theological grounds when we are self-critical, because then, at least, we express trust and hope in an underlying (or transcendent) law of society which forbids us to divest ourselves of all responsibility for the elimination of a social blight in which we are involved, even as victims.

It is not the task of the Jewish People to suffer and to bear witness to human sickness. But is not this the implication of the view which states that no matter what we Jews do we cannot solve the problem of anti-Semitism because it is *their* problem?

SALO W. BARON

Recently, at a meeting conducted by the Conference on Jewish Social Studies, I presented a paper entitled, "Changing Patterns of Anti-Semitism" (see *Jewish Social Studies,* Winter, 1976, pp. 5–38). I recalled my appearance in Jerusalem at the Eichmann trial, where, after my testimony, I was asked by the Defense Attorney: "Why has anti-Semitism lasted for thousands of years? How can you, as a historian, explain that?" The intention was to prove that anti-Semitism has been a sort of biological force; hence we cannot blame a little man—Eichmann—for being an anti-Semite and for doing things which other people would not do. In the course of that discussion I simply referred to the old phrase: the dislike of the unlike. The very fact that Jews were unlike others sufficed to make them disliked.

Reasons for the dislike have differed throughout the ages. The latest form—Jews as imperialists or as colonialists—shows quite a remarkable change. First there was praise of the Jews for their contribution to European colonialization. If Columbus was of Jewish descent then Jews deserved praise, for they helped discover the New World.

In other ways, too, Jews have been pioneers in the United States, Latin America and elsewhere. Next to the pioneers of the brawn, so frequently emphasized in the American mystique, there were pioneers of the brain, among whom Jews played a significant role. The Jews have, indeed, contributed greatly to the development of American civilization through their pioneering efforts in science, economics and many other areas.

Today, colonialism has become a dirty word. Perhaps it was a little unfortunate that we originally spoke of Zionist "colonization," of "establishing colonies in Palestine," and so on, but that is only a minor detail. Basically, the Jews have become a colonial rather than colonizing people.

Whatever Jews do is of no real importance—they are always found to have done something wrong. I am, therefore, pessimistic about the total disappearance of anti-Semitism in the foreseeable future. I think that anti-Semitism may last so long as there is a Jewish dispersion, so long as a Jewish minority exists anywhere.

We have time and again seen that anti-Semitism cannot successfully be combated by Jews on their own. An effective example is the Dreyfus Affair: Liberal France showed that when the Republic was in danger, Zola, Clemenceau and others rose up and destroyed the myth of Jewish disloyalty. This meant that Christians tried to defend Jews against anti-Semitism only when they themselves felt endangered.

Whenever a Jewish minority is accused of being alien, of wanting something other than the majority, there is always danger that anti-Semitism will be intensified. That is certainly the case to a large extent in the Latin American countries today.

MARIE SYRKIN: Summary Comment

Creation of Israel did not wipe out anti-Semitism as Zionist ideologists confidently expected and as Herzl never tired of assuring his followers would be the case. Israel rather than the individual Jew now readily serves as the target of anti-Jewish agitation. The existence of a Jewish State permits the discharge of anti-Jewish feeling without the onus attached to overt anti-Semitism. In the post-Holocaust era the most rabid anti-Semite can, if he so desires, gratify his emotions under cover of opposition to Israel. Not every anti-Semite resorts to this camouflage, or is sensitive to the accusation of anti-Semitism. But after Hitler, only the extreme Right and in some cases the extreme Left are likely to preach a crusade against the Jews without reference to Israel. For groups inhibited from professing a crude anti-Semitism, Israel is a semantic as well as an ideological convenience.

At the same time, a corrective should be added to what would otherwise appear to be a totally negative picture. Notice should also be taken of the part played by the Jewish State in countering traditional anti-Semitic stereotypes. The new image of the Jew as farmer, fighter and creative figure in contrast to Diaspora clichés should be taken into account. The rise of Israel has forced anti-Semitism to run in new channels. Instead of the "sniveling, cowardly Jew" we now get the ruthless "imperialist aggressor." The shift in the anti-Semitic stereotype indicates no lessening in the virulence of anti-Semitism but in view of the positive images from which the present stereotype proceeds, the end result is favorable. The revolutionary change in the image of the Jew because of Israel's achievements has had a profound effect on the world's consciousness, if not conscience. It will be very hard to peddle the old wares. I think we may properly suggest that while Israel does not provide a cure for an ancient ill, it does offer therapy in a measure previously unknown. The anti-Semite is not disarmed; he has new weapons in his arsenal, but his task has been rendered more complex and difficult by a Jewish State which has captured the imagination of the world and has compelled a revision of attitudes and preconceptions. Israel has tapped sources of pro-Jewish sympathy previously non-existent, and has taken the Jew out of the spectral and mystical into human reality. When the balance is drawn the classic Zionist thesis may not prove misleading as we sometimes now tend to believe, for in the complete calculation there are more pluses than minuses.

In this connection, I should like to comment on a point in Professor Avineri's paper: "Is anti-Zionism identical with anti-Semitism?" Obviously, in the blatant instances where "Zionist" is merely a code word for "Jew," the question answers itself. A considerable portion of current anti-Zionism may be defined as traditional anti-Semitism in a contemporary guise. However, the problem has many facets and cannot summarily be reduced to one blanket explanation.

We must concede the existence of an anti-Zionism which, whatever its intellectual confusion, cannot be dismissed simply as anti-Semitic. Such an anti-Zionism may originate in deeply held universalist convictions or an honest humanitarian concern for "displaced Palestinian people." This concern may be ill-founded and derived from ignorance of Zionism and the course of its realization; nevertheless, it cannot be automatically labeled anti-Semitic. The policy of the anti-Zionist may lead to the same end as that of the anti-Semite, yet it is not mere quibbling to insist on the distinction between the two. The distinction must be maintained not only out of an abstract respect for intellectual rigor, but because far-fetched accusations of anti-Semitism are self-defeating in that they vitiate the force of any better grounded charge that may be brought. An anti-Zionist can escape from argument in a cloud of righteous indignation because he has been called an anti-Semite.

The centrality of Israel in the consciousness of contemporary Jewry depends upon what Jews feel. All those who do not share or appreciate this centrality may be strictured for insensibility without categorically being pigeonholed as anti-Semites. Anti-Semitism belongs in a special category of irrational prejudice, but nations and individuals have been and are injured and betrayed for reasons of stupidity, indifference or cruelty not allied to anti-Semitism. The latter is too *sui generis,* too unique in human history, to be merged with other forms of evil.

Among the components of the *New* anti-Semitism—whose object is primarily Israel—Professor Avineri comments on the New Left and points out wherein the arguments of the New Left differ from the standard criticism of Zionism indulged in by the old Left. The New Left's refusal to recognize Zionism as a national liberation movement in a period when the Left has abandoned former internationalist dogmas and glorifies ethnic and national separatism, no matter how ludicrously fragmented, highlights its bias against Israel. We should also note that just as in Soviet Russia the line between anti-Zionism and anti-Semitism is repeatedly and shockingly crossed, the same tendency may be found in contemporary utterances of the Left.

Another component of the new anti-Semitism that Professor Avineri examines is Black Power. The chief arena of confrontation between Jews and Blacks has been in the field of what is derisively described by its opponents as "meritocracy"—the old-fashioned democratic concept that individuals should be given the opportunity to advance freely in accordance with their capacities. The Jewish "slumlord" or merchant is far less of an irritant in Jewish-Black relations than the Jewish teacher, student or civil service worker. This situation is the reverse of what took place in Eastern Europe. American Jews emancipated from the confinement of European quotas for Jews now see themselves threatened by Black demands for preferential treatment in education and the professions, just as working-class whites object to preferential hiring practices. Traditional notions of justice and equality—long the fundamental tenets of American democracy as previously conceived—have been challenged by a strident ideology which subordinates the rights of the individual to group rights, and gives the dreaded idea of quotas respectability. This is hardly the pattern that obtained in the East European ghetto where Jews suffered from quotas. In the United States disadvantaged minorities seek the establishment of quotas while Jews fear their reimposition in an American setting.

The anti-Semitic propaganda of the Black Power movement—propaganda which should no more be dismissed as rhetoric than similar programs of Nazis yesterday or of Arabs today—has reached far from negligible proportions. However, there have been indications of change. The Black Panthers have muted some of their ferocity in regard to Israel and the Jews. Furthermore, some Black spokesmen have begun to reassess the profits of their contention with the Jews, and have been surveying the advisability of reestablishing the former alliance between Black and Jewish liberals. Under the sponsorship of Bayard Rustin, the well-known Black moderate and liberal, a group associated with him has issued a statement of principles in support of Israel. The statement reaffirms the belief that "Blacks and Jews have common interests in democracy and justice," supports "democratic Israel's right to exist" and declares that "Arab oil policies have had disastrous effects upon Blacks in America and Africa."

The tensions in American society are inevitably exploited by Arabs and their sympathizers in the United States in ways with which we are familiar. Arab alignment with the Left goes hand-in-hand with alliances with rabble-rousing anti-Semitic groups of the extreme Right. None of this is new except in its extent. Nor is the utilization of the United Nations as a forum, not only for anti-Israel vituperation but for anti-Semitic outbursts, a departure from what has become accepted practice in the Assembly.

More serious than blatant incitement at an international forum which has long since discarded any pretense at impartiality or fair play is the systematic effort made by the Arab states to infiltrate American universities through the provision of funds for Middle East Departments or allied disciplines. The temptation to accept generous endowments for research is a blandishment hard for a financially pressed institution to resist.

So far the various elements enumerated by Professor Avineri as contributors to the new anti-Semitism have made no deep impact, even though American Jewry's passionate identification with Israel lends itself to anti-Semitic exploitation. No purpose will be served by dwelling on the utterances of the lunatic fringe of the extreme Right since these do not differ in tone or substance from scurrilities in Latin America, Soviet Russia or elsewhere. Up to the present their influence on the great body of American public opinion has been slight.

The refusal of the American people to make the Jews the scapegoat during the Arab oil embargo after the Yom Kippur War was notable. But it would be a mistake to assume that Arab financial clout is without effect. Though the Arabs in their present dizzying affluence can no longer successfully maintain the image of pitiful victims, their astute, highly financed propaganda apparatus in the United States has managed to convince large sectors of the American public of the justice of the Palestinian claim and to obscure the measure in which Arabs expect this claim to be realized at the expense of Israel.

I am primarily concerned with assessing the formation and expression of attitudes, insofar as these can be discerned, in the heartland of the United States—the so-called "silent majority." This center is affected by winds that blow from the periphery or that emanate from integral sectors of the population such as various ethnic groups. The dichotomy between what people admit privately and what they profess when questioned is sufficiently great to be a factor worth weighing in any candid estimate. For a variety of reasons— urban crime, preferential hiring, forcible busing—more intense anti-Black feeling exists in the North today than at any time that I recall; yet very few of the individuals affected by the problems of achieving an integrated society would openly admit to anti-Black or racist prejudices in any questionnaire offered to them.

The same holds true for latent anti-Semites. If the price for the support of Israel were to become high, American Jewry's espousal of a rightful cause might serve as an irritant. This is a different matter from the specter of double loyalty or of the influence of Jewish pressure groups raised by such discreet antagonists as the former Senator Fulbright. For today we are engaged not in theoretical discussions of American geopolitical interests, but we are dealing with such immediate realities as oil, rising unemployment and the lucrative possibilities of Arab investments in the American economy.

It would be folly to underestimate the possible corrosive effect of such considerations. Traditional anti-Semitism, irrational in origin and not subject to argument, requires merely excuses, not genuine causes, for its stimulation. Such classic Jew-hatred has enjoyed no recrudescence in the United States of the post-Holocaust era. Except for the lunatic fringe it has been muted and driven underground. Nor have concerted Arab efforts been successful in reviving attitudes long dormant. Yet the record, though reassuring, should not blind us to the dangers inherent in the present situation—dangers resulting not from the sudden flourishing of irrational prejudice or from conscious malice but from the discomfort that may be involved in upholding the just demands of the Jewish People.

The real test, however, for American Jewry and the strength of the Jewish position in the United States may be in the making. Should American Jewry and the United States Government find themselves at odds in regard to shifts in American policy in the Middle East, the true worth of Jewish equality in the United States will be measured by the degree to which American Jews will feel free to assert their independent judgment as Jews and as Americans. Any suggestion that docility is obligatory will have to be viewed as evidence that American Jews are not as secure as they assumed.

American Jewry may find itself isolated and subjected to the kind of criticism to which it would be most sensitive—namely, the old bugaboo of "dual loyalty." In the forties, the courage and dignity of British Jews in opposing the Mandatory Government's Palestine policy were matched by the degree to which the British Government accepted such freedom of expression without impugning the motives of those in opposition. The inner assurance of American Jews as well as solidity of their status will be indicated by their response should a similar challenge be posed.

II

Variant Patterns of
Jewish Identification

Equality and the Shrinkage of Jewish Identity

Peter Y. Medding

> The more equal conditions are, the less explanation there
> is for the differences that actually exist between people;
> and thus all the more unequal do individuals and groups
> become.
>
> —Hannah Arendt*

Contemporary Jewish Identity: Historical Perspective

To examine contemporary Jewish identity in proper perspective, it is necessary to refer briefly to the "traditional society" which
characterized Jewry prior to the Enlightenment and the Emancipation.[1] In this society religion as a way of life and traditional authority
as a pattern of thought, which related values and goals to ancient
and revered traditions, were dominant. Religious performance and
religious legitimation were the cement which held this society
together, were the very society itself. In theory, only that which was
demanded, or legitimated, in religious terms was valued. Thus all
social activity was directed to religious ends and new forms had to
be adapted to traditional purposes. Similarly, intellectual activity
was of the traditional variety, and external intellectual currents
needed the legitimation of religious authority and tradition.

Jewry was set apart from surrounding society by residential
segregation, religious hostility, social distance, economic
concentration, political autonomy and communal self-government
(based upon religious and traditional law), as well as different
language and dress. In these circumstances the distinctions between

---

*The Origins of Totalitarianism, New York, 1958, p. 64.
1. See Jacob Katz, Tradition and Crisis, Glencoe, Ill., 1961.

119

Jews and their neighbors were obvious in all spheres. They had little in common and seldom engaged in common pursuits. In terms of modern psychology, it may be said that Jewish religious identification filled completely the cognitive, affective and behavioral spheres.

Jewish religious definition affected all levels of existence, identity and role performance. It encompassed the ethnic ties of blood, family, kinship, people and territory; the psychological aspects of man's identity and place in the greater universe; the cultural values by which a man gave expression to his ideals, goals, aspirations, and the meanings attached to them and to the universe at large. This religious definition was continually reinforced by the exclusive social interaction, economic concentration and political autonomy. It operated strongly at the level of historic memory in past and future terms, encompassing both the glories and persecutions of the past, the intimacies of joy and sorrow, and the recognition of a shared fate in the future. All these levels were bound together in an inextricable set of roles and loyalties which constituted Jewish identity.

Moreover, no matter how inhospitable the world may have been to Jews and Judaism, this kind of socioreligious structure at all levels was regarded as legitimate. The only universal feature of the world at the time was that it consisted of many parochialisms, the particularistic traditions and social organizations of various peoples. There were no universal movements of thought or consciousness which transcended particular religious traditions. Even the major universal movements, Christianity and Islam, were themselves large-scale parochialisms and particularisms.

Emancipation, by permitting Jews to participate in the larger society, afforded choices where none existed before. What is more, these possibilities were in a larger society that had changed considerably in its sociopolitical organization, as well as in some of its major intellectual and religious orientations. The basis of the change lay in the concept of *equal* citizenship, which granted everyone equal rights to participate in the economy, in civic and public life, in secular education and in professions. In the social sphere it broke down involuntary residential segregation. Vexing problems for Jewry, however, developed in regard to the cost of exercising such choices. These related specifically to the core areas of religion and culture or what some sociologists would call "the intrinsic group values."[2]

The problems can be stated concisely, even though the varying responses to them constitute much of modern Jewish history. In the sphere of religion the problem was twofold. First, how should Jews relate to their Judaism now that they were free to participate in a society where the majority was Christian, and particularly in those nation-states where there was a close interrelationship between Christianity and nationalism? Would their religious distinctiveness set up barriers between Jews and other citizens—barriers which might prevent, seriously limit, or undermine their participation in that society?

The other aspect of the religious question related to the development of secular thinking: neutral scientific reason which claimed objectivity, universality of scope, and the ultimate validity of its methods and patterns of thought. How should Judaism relate to this powerful intellectual movement which lay at the basis of all scientific and professional intellectual pursuits? If it was held that these secular patterns of thought were of universal validity and undermined the basis of all religion, how did this affect Jews or Judaism? If commitment to reason meant severing all connections with Judaism as a religion, what role, if any, was left for Jewish identity? Was general secularism the only option, or was there an authentic Jewish secular option? If the latter did exist, of what would it consist, and would it be accepted by society?

The second broad problem is related to national values and national identity. In the nation-states which granted equal citizenship after the Emancipation the national basis of the state was far from universal; in fact it was parochial and particularistic. The relation of the individual to the state was that of citizen. But when and how do national values and national identity become coterminous with citizenship?

Where demands were made for the development of an exclusive national identity that was coterminous with citizenship, the Jew was caught in a state of conflict, which called for resolution, because, in the last resort, the individual can be loyal to only one set of national identity obligations. The problem for Jews was compounded

2. Milton M. Gordon, *Assimilation in American Life,* New York, 1963, p. 79.

to the extent that religion as the basis of Jewish identity became far less important for many individuals and was even consciously rejected, while ethnic notions of peoplehood and nationality became more important as the basis of group ties. But how could the Jew be a member of two peoples at one and the same time? Would his primordial ethnic loyalty interfere with his citizenship and national loyalty to his nation-state?

These questions are still with us, more or less in the same terms in which they were stated when they arose two hundred years ago. At the end of the eighteenth century there was public debate on the emancipation of Jews in Germany and their capacity to become fully fledged equal citizens of the secular state. Opposition to Jewry, as well as their rejection as citizens, was expressed by an expert on Jewish matters, Johann David Michaelis, in terms of the two fundamental issues that still confront Jewry in contemporary times. His arguments went to the heart of the predicament of the Jews, pointing to their religious distinctiveness on the one hand and their national ties on the other:

> As long as Jews keep the laws of Moses, as long as for instance they do not take their meals with us, and at mealtimes or with simple folk over a glass of beer are not able to make friends, they will never (I do not speak of individuals but of the greater part) fuse with us like Catholics and Lutherans, Germans, Italians (Wende) and Frenchmen living in the same State.[3]

Similarly, it was considered that dietary laws and Sabbath observances would prevent the Jew from performing such citizenship obligations as, for instance, serving in the army.[4] Moreover, according to Michaelis, Jews would never be able to regard the country in which they were living as any more than a temporary abode "which they hope one day to leave, to their great happiness and return to Palestine . . . . A people that has such hopes will never entirely feel at home or have patriotic love for the paternal soil."[5]

In sum, the Enlightenment and the Emancipation produced three major challenges for Jewry which obtain even today and are key factors in analyzing and assessing the possibilities of developing

3. Quoted and discussed in Jacob Katz, *Out of the Ghetto*, Cambridge, Mass., 1973, p. 91.
4. *Ibid.*
5. *Ibid.*, p. 92.

Jewish identity in the contemporary world. First, the challenge of equality: Equal participation, as Arendt pointed out, made all kinds of distinctiveness less legitimate and less justifiable, and in the end re-created inequality. There are, second, the challenges of religious and national particularism: the claims of the nation-state on behalf of the majority religion, the religious values interwoven in the national tradition and history, and the desire to fashion a citizenry that is integrated in its national cultural values and not divided by external national ties and loyalties. Third, the challenge of the various forms of universalism, whether of the secular scientific, rational variety that sweeps aside all claims to religious and ethnic particularism, or of the internationalistic "scientific," political variety further sweeping aside these claims as well as those of national political distinctiveness and existence. It is instructive to examine their combined effects upon Jewry by analyzing briefly the "de-Judaization" of contemporary Jewry at the various levels of social existence as compared with Jewry of the "traditional society" outlined above.

The De-Judaization of Contemporary Jewry

In the contemporary economic and occupational spheres the vast majority of Jews conduct their lives outside the framework of the Jewish community. Even allowing for concentration in certain industries and occupations Jews do not, in most instances, represent a majority of those engaged in them. The patterns of organization, and the norms, ethics and laws which govern these occupations are external to the Jewish community and its value system. This is particularly noticeable in the professional spheres where the criteria of performance, the rules of the profession and the methods of scholarship, as well as occupational role fulfillment, advancement and judgment, are subject to criteria that are universal in character and intent and often international in scope. They represent autonomous communities with their own highly articulated and independent value systems.

Jews today rarely live in completely Jewish residential areas. Despite preferences for propinquity with their own kind, Jews generally live in mixed neighborhoods where only rarely are they in the majority. Moreover, their overall residential life pattern, with its suburban character and its mobility, follows the general middle-class pattern. In the social sphere the evidence suggests that most

Jews mix in predominantly Jewish friendship circles. At the more formal level there is participation in both general non-Jewish as well as Jewish organizations, with a tendency toward more intense involvement in the latter. Yet, despite the existence of a strong particularistic ethnic social network, the content and substance of that system are not solely ethnic; that is, many of the organizational patterns, concerns, and pursuits, and their substantive content are general in purpose and outlook rather than particularistically ethnic. As has been observed, it is common for Jewish organizations in the United States to facilitate the integration of Jews into the wider society and the transmission of general and national social values to the Jewish community. In short, they are ethnic solely in membership, not in content.[6] To see how far Jewish organizational forms have been expanded to introduce more general content, one need only consider the typical synagogue sermon—a review of the latest bestseller, an analysis of current political problems or a discussion of social conflicts. Inevitably this leads to a shrinkage of Jewish content. Similarly, a close analysis of intimate Jewish friendship circles would show the extent to which their interaction was general or was of specifically Jewish concern.

These contrasts are even greater in the educational, philosophical, cultural and religious spheres. In the educational sphere, at all levels, general secular education has taken precedence over Jewish education, for it is this education that equips one for living in contemporary industrial societies. In such societies pride of place is undoubtedly accorded to secular scientific values and methods; indeed nowhere is this more apparent than in the professions which, based upon universal scientific values, do not recognize either particularistic membership or ascriptive criteria as being of any value. In that sense the professions claim to transcend all those particularistic traditional patterns of thinking and authority which are based upon interpretation of ancient and revered traditional and religious values: for many people, this is their special appeal.

In particular, there is the problem of conflicting attitudes to authority. Scientific authority to be valid must be demonstrated; the more modern approach has greater authority, because it is competent to determine for itself the validity of previous approaches and

6. Charles Liebman, "American Jewry: Identity and Affiliation," *The Future of the Jewish Community in America,* David Sidorsky, ed., New York, 1973, p. 132.

can accept or reject them accordingly. Contemporary scientists are sovereign in that sense. Religious authority of the traditional type, to be valid, must be revealed; whatever is more ancient and closer to the source of revelation has greater authority. Since contemporary practitioners of religious authority are not recognized as having the legitimate capacity to determine the validity of previous approaches, the contemporary era, in that sense, is not sovereign. Briefly stated, this conflict has led to a shrinkage of the Orthodox belief till it now encompasses only a small proportion of Jewry; to the rise of movements of religious accommodation and religious reform; and, for many, to the growth and supremacy of secularism and secular patterns of thought.

To these effects in the sphere of religious authority and philosophy, must be added the contribution of cultural developments in Western society. Jews participate actively as consumers in the world of literature, drama, the arts, music. In giving free expression to their tastes they also express a set of values, standards and commitments, which in their origins lie outside the sphere of their Jewish existence. These cultural pursuits create for Jewry a new set of values and standards that are external to their Jewishness (although they may become internalized to the extent that certain values, standards and criteria may be more characteristic of Jews and more appealing to them than to others). This list could probably be extended to cover Jewish participation in politics and in most other areas of civic life where the standards maintained and the reciprocal values incorporated generally owe little to autonomous or authentic Jewish values and tend to be external to them. For example, it has been demonstrated that Jewish political liberalism, where it exists, owes its origins not to Jewish values but to the history of the Jews and to their position in society.[7] This liberalism is, in fact, much more common among Jews who are marginal to the Jewish community than among those deeply involved in it and committed to its values.[8]

The pattern of Jewish identity has altered completely; from occupying most of the cognitive, affective, and behavioral life and

7. Discussed in P. Y. Medding, "Towards a General Theory of Jewish Political Behavior and Interests," *The Jewish Political Tradition*, Daniel J. Elazar, ed. (forthcoming).
8. P. Y. Medding, "Factors Influencing the Voting Behavior of Jews in Melbourne," *Jews in Australian Society*, P. Y. Medding, ed., Melbourne, 1973, pp. 141–159. See also Charles Liebman, *The Ambivalent American Jew*, Philadelphia, 1973.

time-space of individual Jews, it now occupies only a small fraction
of it. Or, put in Simon Herman's terms, the extent to which Jews
were like only *some* other men (the Jews) has greatly decreased, and
the extent to which they are like all other men (the rest of society)
has dramatically increased.[9] A previously integrated identification
has been broken down into a larger number of separate identifications. If this is so, it would be instructive to examine the extent to
which these various identities do or do not overlap, or to which they
exist in some other form of relationship. In order to do this it will be
useful to examine those areas where distinctive Jewish values and
cultural patterns and practices still continue to exist, that is, to explore the boundaries of Jewish distinctiveness.

The Limits of De-Judaization

At least six separate elements of Jewish distinctiveness in the
contemporary world can be identified. There is, first, the nonbelief
in Christianity, or, in positive terms, belief in Jewish monotheism
(to the extent that there is any belief in a Divine Being) as distinct from Christian Trinitarianism. Second, among the *rites of passage* there is fairly universal majority support for, and participation
in, circumcision, *Bar* and *Bat Mitzvah* ceremonies, Jewish marriage
and Jewish burial. Third, there is common ritual participation in
such festivals and ceremonies as the Passover *Seder*, the lighting of
Hanukkah candles and synagogue attendance on High Holy Days—
arbitrarily chosen by individual and group practice and custom rather than by articulated religious argument. Significant in this context
is Marshal Sklare's analysis of the criteria which operate in determining the rituals to be preserved. They are "capable of effective
redefinition in modern terms"; do not "demand social isolation and
the following of an unique life style"; "accord with the religious culture of the larger community while providing a 'Jewish' alternative
when such is felt needed"; are "centered on the child"; and are "per-
formed annually or infrequently."[10] Fourth, there is a sense of belonging to an international people, an identity currently focused on
Israel, awakened by its trials and troubles and kept alive by its bat-
tles for existence. Fifth, and connected with the above, is concern for

9. See Simon Herman's contribution to this volume.
10. M. Sklare, *America's Jews*, New York, 1971, pp. 110–22.

Jewish survival, both for its own sake, or for the sake of the values that Jews espouse or formerly espoused, with Israel now providing a meaningful and physical rationale for survival. Sixth, there is the sense of historical consciousness termed by Daniel Bell "memory," both personal and collective, involving that awareness of separateness and uniqueness which has developed out of Jewish history with its persecutions, and is maintained by a sense of interdependence of fate and the continuing threat of further persecution.[11]

This pattern of distinctiveness, seen in the perspective of the various societal and intellectual changes outlined above, is tribal rather than intellectual, and ethnic rather than theological, philosophical or even cultural. In other words, it engages the affective and behavioral levels rather than the cognitive level of content and substance. Jewish identity for most Jews thus occupies only a very small part of their life- and time-space, although as Herman has pointed out, this may, for various reasons, still be quite central, valent, and salient,[12] because these elements of Jewish identity lie close to the core of personality. Consequently, it may infuse other aspects of life with the special meaning that comes from Jewishness, or it may be so deep-seated and self-understood as not to require constant reinforcement. Perhaps the closest analogy here is the sexual one. One may not spend a great deal of time fulfilling a male role, and masculinity may not influence the other spheres of one's life to any great degree, yet it would be futile to deny that the sense of masculinity lies very close to the core of personality; this is evident from the intensity of response when masculinity is questioned or is threatened. In a sense, there is a close correlation between an ethnic or a sexual insult in its capacity to wound.

The second characteristic aspect of these six elements is that they continue to separate Jews from other members of society. They establish a clear line of demarcation, aligning Jews with each other and arousing those tensions of distinctiveness of which Arendt speaks. They create distinctions which the ideology of equality of the leveling kind finds difficult to justify and to accept as legitimate. To alleviate these tensions Jewry has lent its support to a different form of egalitarian ideology, one which permits and legitimates the ideology of cultural pluralism. The latter sees value in the richness

11. Daniel Bell, "Reflections on Jewish Identity," *The Ghetto and Beyond,* Peter Rose, ed., New York, 1969, pp. 465–76.
12. See Simon Herman's contribution to this volume.

of cultural variety and creativity and promotes an equality based upon diversity, permitting every group and culture equal opportunity to follow its *own* particularistic course within the limits of a minimum of national integration and common values. Cultural pluralism thus posits as its universal goal not a substantive, but a procedural, set of values which affirm the benefits of diversity and the legitimacy of particularism.

Strategies and Possibilities of Cognitive Identity

Contemporary Jews have adopted a number of strategies in order to cope with the problem of a shrinking Jewish identity arising from these challenges. It is instructive to examine such strategies in order to assess the future possibilities of developing a substantive, cognitive Jewish identity which has content as well as affect.

(a) Compartmentalization. This is the attempt to keep the two worlds apart in order to preserve what is regarded as valuable in both realms, with the assumption that closer cooperation is not possible. It is thought that these areas of response cannot be integrated further either because they are on different planes of thought and analysis or because they are kept separate in order to avoid direct confrontations with the conflicts. This is not a new strategy; it was already practiced in the *Haskalah* (Enlightenment) period with a famous dictum: "Be a man when you go out and a Jew in your home." Currently this seems to be the major strategy of large sections of modern Orthodoxy, particularly those involved in the professions and in academic and scientific pursuits. It is perfectly clear that many accept universal scientific secular reasoning (and even if they do not accept it, make use of it). "Yet, at the same time, they subscribe to an intense form of Jewish identity and commitment to religionational values. It is also apparent that the latter values have little or no influence upon the manner in which professionals pursue their scientific work. There is no distinctive Orthodox Jewish way of being a biologist, a physicist or a mathematician. Thus, ethnoreligious values and scientific work are kept in separate compartments. To the extent that these areas are brought together it is more likely to be in the direction of assessing the effects of science upon religion, as, for example, in using science to solve problems of *Halakhah* (Jewish law) and to discuss the *halakhic* consequences of new scientific discoveries. Rarely, if ever, is there an attempt to use Jewish religious insights to cast light upon scientific problems.

An interesting aspect of such compartmentalization is the disproportionate choice among modern Orthodox scientists of fields such as mathematics and the natural sciences rather than the social sciences or philosophy. One reason, clearly, is that the former do not seem to represent such a direct threat to religious faith. Science and religion are seen to operate on separate levels; take, for example, the argument that "the Torah is not a science text." It is also believed that science reveals what already exists in the Divine scheme. Mathematics is the safest of all, as its concerns bear no apparent relation to the sphere of religion. The social sciences and philosophy, on the other hand, are more involved with questions of ethical judgments and values, with the problems of relativism, and with activities of human beings as agents acting outside a theological framework and set of assumptions; they generally proceed to deal with these questions in a positivist manner which can be corrosive of the metaphysical assumptions of religious belief. Compartmentalization enables the scientist to solve the authority problem raised earlier—in science, one set of rule applies, in the religious sphere, another. This results in two worlds, two value systems, two identities.

(b) Synthesis and Integration.   This is a much more difficult course than was discussed in (a) because it involves the degree to which it is possible to combine, in a logical and consistent whole, values which on the surface seem to be mutually exclusive. The problem occurs specifically in relation to the conflict between universal and particularistic ethnoreligious values. The problem also occurs in relation to particularistic national values and particularistic ethnic peoplehood values which compete at the same level of integration. In the general value area the closest approach to synthesis and integration is that of incorporation, that is, the continuous attempt to take valuable and important features from the universal secular world and use them for a better understanding of the religioethnic tradition. This is particularly noticeable in the philosophic world where currents such as existentialism have been synthesized with the Jewish tradition or have been used to illuminate previously hidden aspects of Jewish philosophy and theology. Similarly, political philosophies such as liberalism, socialism and democracy have all found exponents who have attempted to integrate them into an authentic Jewish viewpoint by uncovering or illuminating Jewish sources which point in a similar direction. In general, one can say that each significant social, political and philosophical movement is examined to see whether it can be accommodated with Judaism, either by emphasizing those elements in Judaism that are sympathetic to it and in consonance with it or by using its tools to illuminate and add to an understanding of the Jewish tradition. Some, of course, are so directly in conflict that no synthesis or integration is possible.

These dominant patterns of synthesis and integration among Orthodoxy have been stressed because of the latter's total and articulated commitment to the entire corpus of traditional values, their avowed refusal to compromise, and commitment to the maximal form and content of Jewish identity.

Other Jewish religious and secular movements have adopted the paths of synthesis and integration in a different manner. For many, the claims of modernity have exercised greater sway; integration has been accomplished by placing greater emphasis on those elements that are shared in common and by shedding values that seem to be in conflict, thus preventing integration and accommodation. The differing responses of Orthodoxy, Conservatism and Reform to the questions of the relation of Jewish tradition to modern scholarship and to the demands of contemporary society are classic examples of those differing patterns.

For secular Jews the problem has been both easier and more difficult. The denial of religion and the avowal of modern secular values have aligned them with progress, civilization and science. But to the extent that secular Jews have emphasized Jewish peoplehood without its religious basis, their task has been more difficult. They have directly encountered the problem raised by Hannah Arendt: that having been granted citizenship and enabled to participate they no longer have a satisfactory explanation for the ethnic and national claim to distinction. This was particularly so since it conflicted with an important element in the nation state, the claims of national identity as part of citizenship loyalty. Zionists raised specifically (and Jews committed to Israel and the Jewish past raise implicitly) the question of whether synthesis is possible between two particularistic identities, the national identity of citizenship and the national identity of Jewish peoplehood. In this context it is clear that there are competing particularisms which on lower levels are capable of integration but on higher levels to which both aspire, the conflict between them remains and cannot be resolved except by choosing one or the other. This may be achieved either by separation or by total assimilation, if that is possible. As Erikson once put it in relation to the American Negro, the "alternative to an exclusive totalism is the wholeness of the more inclusive identity."[13] But he goes on (I transpose his words to insert Jew instead of Negro), "If the Jew wants to find that other identity which permits him to be self-certain as a Jew (or a descendent of Jews) and *integrated as an American*, what joint historical actuality can he count on?"

In other words, the possibility for Jews of a completely integrated identity as both Jews and Americans seems remote because of the absence of a positively valued shared past; on the contrary, the Jewish attitude to their past in non-Jewish societies is such as to preclude this. The result then is integration on lower levels where Jews can respond as integrated Americans, but lack of integration on higher levels—a situation which arouses feelings of unease, anxiety and tension.

Jewish Identity in Confrontation with Marxist Universalism and National Particularism

The problems of Jewish identity within Western, secular societies have been considered, but the Marxist situation and the position of Jews within that framework should also be discussed.[14] Many Jews, both in the past and the present, have sought to synthesize Marxism with Jewish existence (that is, to examine the possibilities of Jewish identity), within a Marxist perspective. They usually point out that Marxism initially sought to bring brotherhood and equality to mankind; its ideology was based upon universal and secularizing impulses wherein the particularisms of faith and ritual, class and nation, were to be eliminated and a new society created in which the individual freed from all repressive bonds would find personal fulfillment. The problem for the Jew was that the equality demanded was of the leveling variety, which sought the disappearance of all differences, particularly of faith and national origin. To the extent

---

13. See Simon Herman's contribution to this volume.
14. See Albert Memmi's contribution to this volume.

that the differences did not fade, either because the Jews did not wish them to fade or because society did not permit them to fade, Jewry was subjected to the pressure of a militant universalism which left no room for Jewish particularism as a legitimate goal. This problem was exacerbated with the resurgence of the national dimension in many communist societies. Here the Jew was caught in a blistering cross-fire; his particularism offended the universalism of the secular internationalist ideology on the one hand and the new militant nationalist particularism, which arose contrary to Marxist ideological expectations and criteria, on the other. The result, of course, is not compartmentalization or synthesis or any capacity for integration. The Jew is faced with several conflicting possibilities: He must (1) stridently reassert Jewish particularism; (2) live in a state of permanent ambivalence, tension and marginality; (3) become as indistinguishable as possible, intermarry, and drop all pretense of ethnic identity; or (4) seek the future of Marxism in a national Jewish framework.

These various options give rise, in fact, to the very real dilemmas of the Jewish situation in the Soviet Union. Except for the last possibility (with which the Soviet state experimented fleetingly in the past but to which no real meaning was given), they correspond to the three current major alignments and divisions in Soviet Jewry:[15] Jews who identify positively with their Jewish heritage in either traditional, Yiddish, or Zionist ways; those who have a neutral attitude to Jewish matters but regard Jewish identity as an existential fact of life; and those who seek to rid themselves of their Jewish identity.

The Soviet Union, however, does not permit a free choice of ethnic identity, nor does it permit individuals to change their ethnic identity; thus, the option of assimilation and indistinguishability and the complete extinction of all aspects of Jewish identity implied in both the universalist and the national Marxist positions is not open to them. It is in this context that the contrast between the Soviet Union and Jews in Western liberal democracies is most marked. Jews in the West are under pressure from the universal and particularistic elements in those societies that have been analyzed above, but, within broad limits, they are free to develop their Jewish identity in cognitive, affective, and behavioral directions.

15. See Zvi Gitelman's contribution to this volume.

The Jew in the Soviet Union, on the other hand, is faced with an even stronger combination of universal and particularistic pressures, which do not regard the development of a cognitive, positive, and substantive cultural Jewish identity as permissible or desirable. But, at the same time, by virtue of the legal and social definition of nationality in the internal passport, the state and society *impose* an affective and behavioral identity upon Jewry. While the possibilities of developing a substantive identity in this situation are narrow, the growth of the *aliyah* movement in this context is instructive. The Soviet government by its system of stamping "Jew" on the internal passport reinforces and affirms for Soviet Jewry an ethnic sense of peoplehood and community of fate, which at this level is not greatly different from that of Jews elsewhere, although it is difficult to develop it further. Yet, for the mass of Jews in the West, one may well ask how much further has this Jewish identity been developed in a substantive cultural sense? The similarities and differences may be demonstrated in tabular form:

	U.S.A.	U.S.S.R
Nationality	American	Jewish
Citizenship	American	Soviet
Cultural Identity	American-Jewish	Russian
Legal Status	American	Jewish
Social Status	American-Jewish	Jewish

The Emancipation brought the challenge of equality to Jews in both the West and the East, while the Enlightenment added to these the challenge of universal values which could not simply be ignored or evaded as either insignificant or particularistic by Jews who wished to live fully in the modern world. Faced with these challenges, the Jewish response, as we have seen, has been varied. Despite a decline in content and substance, Jewish identity in recent years has become strengthened at the affective level because of the State of Israel. But Zionism, which was instrumental in the establishment of the State of Israel, was itself at one time a cognitive form of Jewish identity which provided substantive cultural content and answers to these problems. Whether Israel will succeed in reversing its current role and turning back the process of identity shrinkage that has taken place in modern times by adding content remains to be seen. But a question looms large: Will the current stock of cultural distinctiveness be sufficiently large and meaningful to maintain a significant contribution to individual identity?

Patterns of Jewish Identification and Non-Identification in the Soviet Union

Zvi Gitelman

It has been demonstrated many times in a wide variety of contexts that the subjective identification of an individual with a group has a direct and important impact on the behavior of the individual. His subjective perception of what he *is* (or to what entity he belongs) will greatly influence what an individual *does*. William Buchanan writes in regard to political self-identification:

> Of the psychological processes directly relevant to political behavior, perhaps none is more pervasive than a person's identification with a group, regardless of whether the group is ostensibly political or not. . . . In its most general sense . . . political identification means a person's sense of belonging to a group, if that identification influences his political behavior.[1]

Several studies of voting behavior in the United States and Western Europe have concluded that it is the voter's identification with one or another party, perhaps more than any other factor, that will most heavily influence his vote. Moreover, party identification is remarkably stable and voting behavior over relatively long periods of time can therefore be predicted.

Self-identification and a sense of belonging to a particular group are important not only for individual behavior, but also for the fate of entire communities and nations. Erik Erikson describes a process whereby individual "identity crises" are resolved, usually in adolescence, and lead the individual to "identity closure" and "ideology," which, in turn, create fidelity to a group. ". . . As positive identities are 'confirmed,' societies are regenerated. Where this process fails in too many individuals, a *historical crisis* becomes

---

1. William Buchanan, "Identification, Political," *International Encyclopedia of the Social Sciences*, New York, 1968, vol. 7, p. 57.

apparent. Psychosocial identity, therefore, can also be studied from the point of view of a complementarity of life history (of the individual) and of history (of the group)."[2] Changing technologies, cultures, and political systems lead to changes in identification and identities, so that both the size of a particular group as well as its qualitative character may shift over time. The fate of historical communities, therefore, is in no small measure determined by the way in which their individual components identify themselves. This is true not only in regard to the fundamental question of the continuity or disappearance of a particular community, but it also determines the quality of political and social life in the community. Stressing that political identity ("of what political unit or units does the individual consider himself a member") is "perhaps the most crucial political belief." Sidney Verba points out that unless "those individuals who are physically and legally members of a political system (that is, who live within its boundaries and are subject to its laws) are also psychologically members of that system (that is, feel themselves to be members) orderly patterns of change are unlikely."[3] The recent history of such disparate states as Nigeria, Belgium, Iraq, Canada and Yugoslavia lends support to Verba's assertion.

Identity Crisis

The same kinds of assertions may be made in regard to ethnic identity (it should be noted that ethnic identity is itself, in many contexts, a political question). If one is able to answer the question "Who am I?" or "What am I?" it is likely that one's social, cultural and political behavior will be determined, or at least heavily influenced, by that answer. Defining oneself as a Serb or Croat or Yugoslav, as a Jew, an American, or an American Jew will undoubtedly have behavioral consequences of great importance.

In Western Europe Jews were confronted with the necessity to define themselves when the Emancipation afforded them the opportunity to *choose* to be Jewish. For the first time Jewishness became not simply a natural and almost immutable state of being, but an identity and concept which had to be first defined and then evaluated in order that a rational choice could be made. Jewishness was

2. Erik Erikson, "Identity, Psychosocial," *ibid.*, p. 61.
3. Sidney Verba, "Comparative Political Culture," *Political Culture and Political Development*, Lucian Pye and Sidney Verba, ed., Princeton University, 1965, p. 529.

then defined largely in religious terms, and to choose not to be Jewish meant usually to convert to Christianity. In Eastern Europe the Emancipation was late in coming, but the question of "who is a Jew," more often conceived in terms of "what are the Jews," became a practical question for those who sought universal solutions to broad questions of social and political change, as well as for those whose major concern was the solution to the so-called Jewish problem alone. The former sought to locate the future role of Jews in a world which would be changed in a fundamental and far-reaching way, while the latter argued that the Jewish condition must be changed either within the context of wider secular change or even within the basic contours of the general status quo.

In the Russian Empire of the nineteenth century there was a Jewish identity crisis to which a wide variety of solutions was offered. At the two extremes were the solutions of retreat into the ghetto and total assimilation. Between these there developed a wide spectrum of ideologies which tried first to define Jewish identity and then to synthesize it with modernizing political, social, economic and cultural values. Zionists, Socialists, Hebraists, Yiddishists, and territorial autonomists, religious reformers, cultural reformers— these and others tried to redefine Jewishness so that it would be synthesized with modern values while retaining a distinctive identity.

Here it became crucial to determine the defining characteristic of Jewishness, religion, ethnicity, nationhood, culture, or genetic and historical accident. Some schools of thought chose one or another of these, while others combined such elements in various ways. The choices determined ideologies and platforms. Only if one assumed that Jews constituted a nation did it make sense to aspire to since Jews could be absorbed into larger groups. Over time nations would merge into one another, as the concept of nation itself was a product of a specific historical era and social order—capitalism With the disappearance of capitalism, a process would be initiated whereby nations would disappear.

The Bolsheviks began by denying Jewish nationhood, while at the same time treating Judaism as a transient historical phenomenon, like other religions. In the view of both Lenin and Stalin, Jewishness in the modern age had come to be an historical anachronism since Jews could be absorbed into larger groups. Over time nations would merge into one another, as the concept of nation itself was a product of a specific historical era and social order—capitalism. With

the disappearance of capitalism, a process would be initiated whereby nations would disappear.

Cultural Autonomy

Just as the realities of the multinational Russian Empire
forced Lenin to revise his expectations of the disappearance of nations, so too did tactical political considerations lead the Bolsheviks
to the position that a distinctive Jewish identity would remain for
the foreseeable future. Neither Lenin nor the Bolshevik movement
revised their ideological commitment to the eventual assimilation of
the Jews, but by 1918 in practice it was decided that the Jews were to
be given the status of a nationality—less than a nation, but more than
a "caste" (as Lenin had categorized the Jews in 1913). The operational consequences of this tactical retreat were that Jewish sections
were created within the Communist Party, and the Bolshevik regime
granted the Jews some cultural autonomy, in spite of Lenin's earlier
rejection of the Bund's demands for Jewish national-cultural
autonomy. If in order to bring the message of socialism to the
Jews it was necessary to treat the Jews as a linguistic and cultural
community, they would be so treated until such time as this was no
longer necessary.

As is well known, the Soviet policy on nationality began to
move away from cultural and ethnic pluralism and toward a position
of encouraging assimilation of the various nationalities. The Jews
themselves, attracted by educational, occupational and cultural opportunities denied to them by the tsars, spontaneously displayed a
preference for what they perceived as higher Russian culture, and
increasing numbers abandoned what they saw as sterile Soviet Yiddish culture. Jewish culture had been stripped of its traditional religious and Zionist elements for ideological reasons and what
remained was often perceived as an artificial creation or hollow shell
which could not compete with the dominant Russian culture. Moreover, after World War II even Soviet Yiddish culture was effectively
eliminated from the Soviet scene, so that what remained was formal,
legal identification as Jews, but almost no cultural or national content attaching to that identification.

At present, for many Soviet Jews, being Jewish is a matter of
form without meaningful content. Soviet policies have effectively
diminished the scope and content of Jewish culture, have severely

reduced the number of religiously identified Jews, and have eliminated even those elements of the Jewish cultural tradition that once
were not only tolerated but actively promoted by the Soviet regime
itself. At the same time, the regime has continued the policy of class-
ifying Jews as such and of making it very difficult for those officially
registered as Jews to change their nationality. Thus, most Soviet
Jews are officially identified as such but have no opportunity to infuse their official ethnic identity with cultural content. There is no
organized Jewish national or communal life in which they can participate and there is little communication between them and Jewish
communities the world over.

The Soviet policy of maintaining official Jewish identity
while emptying it of all positive content has produced a situation for
the individual which may be described as a kind of psychological
dissonance. On the one hand, the Soviet Jew is legally and socially
recognized as such; yet on the other hand, in most cases, his culture
is non-Jewish, usually Russian. Soviet Jews are acculturated—they
have adopted the culture of another social group—but they are not
assimilated; they have not adopted that other group's culture to
such an extent that they no longer have any characteristics identifying them with their former culture and no longer have any loyalties
to their former culture.[4] Most Soviet Jews consider themselves culturally Russian, and, as we shall see, there is good reason for them to
do so. However, since their internal passports designate them
officially as Jews, and since Soviet society (which places emphasis
on ethnic identity) regards Jews as such, they are in the curious
and uncomfortable position of being culturally Russian but legally
and socially Jews.

While in many Western societies Jews are similarly
acculturated into the majority culture, they have no legal, ethnic
identity and are thus free to define their Jewishness in any way they
desire without anyone forcing them to identify as Jews, on the one
hand, or dictating to them the meaning and content of their Jewishness. They can choose to define Jewishness in religious, cultural,
ethnic, or even political (Zionist) terms, or to combine these categories in any way they choose. This enables Western Jews to evolve
identities which can resolve to their satisfaction the problems of

4. On the difference between acculturation and assimilation, see Arnold Rose, *Sociology: The Study of Human Relations*, New York, 1969, p. 584.

dual belonging and multiple memberships. In most Western countries citizenship is the only officially recognized identity—and in some countries it is also socially the only relevant identity—in the U.S.S.R. both citizenship and nationality are official categories of identification and the latter is socially of great importance. In Western countries citizenship and nationality are often coterminous, while in the U.S.S.R. they are distinct. The strange position of Russian Jews is that while nationality is an official identification it is also commonly perceived as a category by which different cultures are identified and described. However, Jews by nationality are only rarely Jews by culture.

National Self-Assertion

Culturally Russian, but legally and socially Jewish, Soviet Jews have a split identity—that is, a psychological dissonance exists which can be resolved only by becoming wholly Russian, or wholly Jewish, or finding an identity that synthesizes these two. Thus, we see two simultaneous but diametrically opposed tendencies among Soviet Jews: Some try to lose their Jewish identity entirely, while others assert it and try to give it meaning. To become wholly Russian is very difficult, since only children of mixed marriages can choose a nationality (of one of the parents), while the nationality of others is determined by that of their parents. To be both Russian and Jewish is also difficult, since these are mutually exclusive categories of nationality. To become wholly Jewish is nearly impossible under Soviet conditions.

In recent years the realistic possibility of becoming wholly Jewish—but not Soviet—has become feasible with the opening of emigration to Israel. Thus, while assimilation (becoming Russian) is no more viable an option today than before, national self-assertion has become possible; there has been a strong movement in this direction, which is not to say that the psychological dissonance is easily resolved for most individuals, even those whose subjective preferences are clearly formulated in their own minds. Professor Alexander Temkin reports that in the 1970 Soviet census he declared his native language to be Hebrew, though he knew Russian best. As he says, "This is fact, not emotion."[5] Factually—that is, culturally—he

5. Alexander Temkin, "Who Am I, Who Are We, and What Are We," *Jewishness Rediscovered*, Aleksander Voronel and Viktor Yakhot, ed., New York, 1974.

was Russian; emotionally he was Jewish. The resolution of this difference came in the form of emigration to Israel.

On the other hand, Larissa Bogoraz, similarly dually identified, could not come to the same conclusion, and her reflections epitomize the emotional conflicts which many Soviet Jews must feel. "Who am I now?" she writes. "Unfortunately, I do not feel like a Jew. I understand that I have an unquestionable genetic tie with Jewry. . . . A more profound, or more general common bond is lacking, such as community of language, culture, history, tradition. . . . By all these characterizations, I am Russian. . . . And nevertheless, no, I am not Russian. I am a stranger today in this land."[6] For like many Jews before her who for various reasons were not well integrated into Jewish society in Russia and who also were not accepted into Russian society, Larissa Bogoraz has been actively trying to change the total society in which she lives, presumably in part to enable people to solve identity problems such as she describes. Whereas the Trotsky's and Zinoviev's et al. of an earlier age tried to resolve their dual alienation from both Jewish and Russian society by seeking to create a new Soviet society where ethnic identity would be irrelevant, Larissa Bogoraz and others are trying to reform Soviet society, perhaps in part to remove the disabilities and contradictions of being officially Jewish and culturally Russian.

Demography and Jewish Identity

Between 1959 and 1970 there was an absolute decline in the number of Jews in the U.S.S.R. More precisely, there was a decline in the number of persons reporting themselves as Jews to the census taker. Whereas in 1959 there were 2,268,000 Jews in the Soviet Union, in 1970 there were only 2,151,000. During a period when the total Soviet population grew by nearly 16 percent, only among Jews and six other, much smaller, nationalities, were there declines. This decline cannot be wholly explained either by Jewish emigration— which amounted to only about 17,000 in this period—or by the low Jewish birth rate and the age structure of the Jewish population, which is heavily slanted toward older persons. A good part of the

---

6. Larissa Bogoraz, "Do I Feel I Belong to the Jewish People?" *I Am a Jew: Essays on Jewish Identity in the Soviet Union*, Aleksander Voronel and Viktor Yakhot, ed. New York, 1973, pp. 63–64.

decline in the number of Jews may be attributed to a tendency not to identify oneself as a Jew. This does not necessarily mean that in their own minds those who identified themselves as Jews in 1959 no longer identified themselves as such in 1970. It is quite likely that they simply found it more comfortable to identify themselves as non-Jews to the census taker. We cannot, therefore, draw from the data any conclusions regarding trends in the subjective self-identification of Soviet Jews.

We can treat with greater confidence certain objective indicators relevant to the question of national or ethnic identification. We know that Jews are the most linguistically assimilated of the Soviet nationalities. Whereas in 1970, 93.9 percent of the Soviet population reported the language of their nationality as their mother tongue, only 17.7 percent of the Jews listed a Jewish language as their mother tongue (in 1926, 71.9 percent and in 1939, 21.5 percent of the Jews gave a Jewish language as their mother tongue). However, 25 percent in 1970 indicated substantial familiarity with Yiddish.[7] Seventy-eight percent of the Jews consider Russian their mother tongue; 95 percent have a command of Russian; and 33 percent command other languages in the U.S.S.R.[8] Even in the non-Russian republics Jews favor Russian over other languages. For example, in Kharkov 92 percent of the Jews listed Russian, and only 9.3 percent listed Ukrainian as their mother tongue. The tendency to acculturate into the Russian, rather than Ukrainian, Lithuanian or other cultures, derives from the belief that Russian is a more useful language as the lingua franca of the U.S.S.R., that it embodies a higher culture than other cultures of the U.S.S.R., and that it is a prerequisite to social mobility. Moreover, Russian is the dominant language of the cities of the Slavic—and some other—republics, and it is in the cities that the Jews are concentrated.

The linguistic assimilation of Soviet Jews should not be taken as an indicator of their overall assimilation but rather of their acculturation. Soviet scholars themselves have warned against identifying linguistic with psychological assimilation. I. S. Gurvich points to Russianized Germans and Jews and to Tatarified Bashkirs when he notes: "Even while losing the mother tongue and even cultural

7. Yakov Kapeliush, "Yidn in Sovetnfarband," *Sovetish Heymland*, no. 9, 1974, p. 177. Census data is taken from the 1959 and 1970 Soviet censuses.
8. *Ibid.*

characteristics, the national consciousness is often preserved."[9] Another Soviet scholar, asserting that ethnic change lags behind socioeconomic change, declared: "Linguistic switchover does not in itself mark a transition to a new ethnic state."[10] Naturally, it is inconceivable that one who considers his mother tongue to be Yiddish will not identify as a Jew; but it is not at all the case that having Russian as a mother tongue is an indicator of non-Jewish identification.

A better indicator of assimilation, if not of the present generation then of future ones, is marriage between Jews and members of other nationalities. Children of such marriages may choose the nationality of either parent, and fragmentary evidence on Baltic Jews and considerable data on other nationalities of the U.S.S.R. indicate that children, one of whose parents is a member of a national minority, overwhelmingly opt for the majority nationality. So, in Vilnius between 1960 and 1968 only 14 percent of the children of mixed marriages chose Jewish nationality; in Tallin, only 10 percent; and in Riga, only 6.7 percent.[11] This tendency is likely to obtain in most parts of the U.S.S.R. and so we can assume that children with only one Jewish parent are likely to have their legal identification become other than Jewish. In most cases a change in legal identification would also probably involve a change in subjective identification.

Marriage to non-Jews is clearly an effective means of reducing the number of identified Jews. It is not necessarily the case, especially in Soviet circumstances, that Jews who take non-Jewish spouses cease to identify themselves subjectively as Jews. (In the West, too, Jews with non-Jewish spouses sometimes identify strongly as Jews.) Some of the most militant activists in the Jewish national movement in the Soviet Union have non-Jewish spouses. While details and statistics on Jewish intermarriage have been reported elsewhere,[12] for the purposes of the present discussion it is sufficient to point out that as yet we have no nationwide data on Jewish intermarriage in the

9. "Nekotorye problemy etnicheskogo razvitiia narodov SSSR," *Sovetskaia etnografiia*, no. 5, 1967, p. 63.
10. Yu. V. Bromley, "Toward a Typology of Ethnic Processes," paper delivered at the Eighth World Congress of Sociology, Toronto, 1974, p. 10.
11. L. N. Terenteva, "Opredelenie svoei natsional' noi prinadlezhnosti podrostkami v natsional' no-smeshannykh semiakh," *Sovetskaia etnografiia*, no. 3, 1969, pp. 20–30.
12. See, for example, my "Assimilation, Acculturation, and National Consciousness among Soviet Jews," Synagogue Council of America, New York, 1973, and "Political Role of the Jews in the Ukraine," *Bekhinot*, no. 6, 1975.

U.S.S.R.; and we do know that there are substantial regional variations in this regard. In the country as a whole, for every 1,000 families 102 are of mixed nationality. The highest proportion of mixed families is in Latvia (158) and the second highest is in the Ukraine (150).[13] In the Ukraine, where, among the urban population, 26 percent of the marriages are mixed, in 1969 Ukrainian males married Ukrainian females in 83 of 100 cases; Jewish males married Jewish females in 63 of 100; and Polish males married Polish females in only 22 of 100 instances.[14] We have considerable data on marriages in the Ukraine in the 1920s, and from these we can see that mixed marriages are significantly more frequent today than they were fifty years ago. In Kharkov, for example, three times as many Jewish males were married to non-Jews in 1960 compared with 1923, and four times as many Jewish females.[15]

Nevertheless, in comparison with other national minorities the Jewish intermarriage rate is not very high, and in comparison with intermarriage among American and West European Jews it is not high at all. Again citing Kharkov data, in 1960 of 720 Jewish women who married, 235 of them (32.6 percent) married non-Jews. This was a lower percentage of exogenous marriage than among Russians, Ukrainians, Belorussians and Tatars.[16] A 1970 sample survey of the Kiev marriage registry showed that Jews have the highest "index of attraction" for their own nationality.[17] Though Jewish intermarriage in the Ukraine is more frequent than in Moldavia and the Asian and trans-Caucasian republics, it is comparable to intermarriage in Latvia[18] and is less frequent than one might expect, given the general acculturation of Ukrainian Jews. This may be an indication of high ethnic consciousness even among urban educated groups. It is true that traditional Jewish strictures against intermarriage are very strong and that even when the great majority of Soviet Jews no longer observe the tradition there may remain a kind of

13. A. A. Isupov, *Natsional'ny sostav naseleniia SSR*, Moscow, 1964, p. 38.
14. M. I. Kulichenko, *Natsional'nye otnosheniia v SSSR i tendentsii ikh razvitiia*, Moscow, 1972, pp. 499–500.
15. M. V. Kurman and I. V. Lebedinskii, *Naselenie bol'shogo sotsialisticheskogo goroda*, Moscow, 1968, p. 122.
16. *Ibid.*, pp. 126–127.
17. V. S. Zhuchenko and V. S. Steshenko, ed., *Vliianie sotsial'no-ekonomicheskikh faktorov na demograficheskie protsessy*, Kiev, 1972, p. 118.
18. A. I. Kholmogorov, *Internatsional'nye cherty Sovetskikh natsii*, Moscow, 1970, p. 84.

folkway which discourages intermarriage. However, it is also likely that in Soviet conditions Jewish intermarriage may not necessarily mean a loss of Jewish identity in the intermarrying generation; but it is more likely to lead to such a loss in the next generation.

Finally, to date, about 10 percent of the Soviet Jewish population has either emigrated or publicly expressed a desire to do so; thus, it would seem that a significant minority of Soviet Jews wish to resolve their psychological dissonance not by becoming wholly Russian, but by becoming wholly Jewish. It is impossible to be wholly Jewish in Soviet conditions, in their view, and so they choose to emigrate, usually to Israel. Of course, in the last few years the percentage of emigrants with non-Zionist and even non-Jewish motivations has grown considerably.

The Jews of the U.S.S.R.: Collectivity or Community?

It would be hard to conceive of the Soviet Jewish population as a community in conventional terms. After all, this is a collectivity which includes people of widely varying cultures (Baltic, European, Central Asian, Georgian, Caucasian), who speak different languages and who have no central or regional institutions and organizations which could provide communal identity and leadership. The appurtenances of a community in the West are lacking: buildings, organizations, schools, publications, group activities. Yet, Soviet Jews are most definitely a community of fate, and a great number of them are aware of that. Neither Hitler nor Stalin inquired into the level of consciousness or commitment of individual Jews when executing their policies directed at the group as a whole. Many Soviet citizens today also tend to see Jews as members of a distinct group with quite specific characteristics. Even the Jews perceive themselves as part of an in-group, for better or for worse, and this perception is reinforced—in some cases even created—by the perception of the outgroup that Jews are a separate group. As one Soviet immigrant puts it, "When they brought a new elephant to the zoo, the first question that was asked was, 'a yid or a goy?'" The combination of mass perceptions, self-perception and legal status insures that, despite the fact that Jews are the most acculturated major nationality in the U.S.S.R., they are still regarded—and regard themselves in most cases—as a distinct group.

As is well known, in recent years Soviet Jews have become

more aware of their Jewish nationality or at least have been willing to express their national identity more openly and decisively. The national consciousness of some Jews is of more recent vintage than that of others, but overall there is a higher level of such consciousness than there was ten or twenty years ago, and there seems to be less inclination to resolve the problem of split identity by striving for assimilation. Stimuli for such consciousness appeared at different historical junctures, but they seem to have had a kind of cumulative effect.

One of these stimuli was World War II, which disabused many Jews of the notion that they could lose their Jewish identity and which emphasized in a most terrible way the existential fact that they were indeed linked to a community of fate. Another factor was the influx of a large number of nationally conscious and even militant Jews from the territories annexed to the U.S.S.R. in 1939–1940. They reestablished contact between Soviet Jews and the mainstream of world Jewry. In many instances, it was newcomers, "Zapadniki" (Westerners), who taught the others Hebrew, Jewish history and Zionist ideology. It is not accidental that the emigration movement began in the Baltic cities of Riga and Vilnius and spread eastward, with the Zapadniki playing a leading role in the movement. A third stimulus to national consciousness was the State of Israel. Following the Holocaust, the establishment of the Jewish State (initially favored by the Soviet Union) fired the imagination of many Soviet Jews and made the Jewish People more respectable in their own eyes and those of their neighbors. The trial of Adolf Eichmann, which retaught the lessons of the Holocaust, served to remind the younger generation especially of the common destiny of the Jews.

Finally, as in other Jewish communities, the Arab-Israeli war of 1967 at first aroused among many Soviet Jews a realization that an Israeli defeat would be personally hard to bear and, later, a feeling of relief and pride in the Israeli victory. Just as important was the awareness of the Soviet Government's unequivocal support of those whose avowed aim was the destruction of Israel as a Jewish State.

Until June, 1967, Soviet Jews had illusions about co-existence with the regime, despite the fact that it wanted to spiritually destroy the Jews. But suddenly they realized that the Soviet government identifies itself with those who wish to destroy the Jewish state, the sole hope left for the Jewish people. Russia spat on the Jewish people, and "then we knew that we would never be able to live under such a regime."[19]

Soviet propaganda during and after the war was so shrill and one-sided that it could not but arouse the attention of even the most indifferent Jew, especially as it began to interchange the terms "Zionist" and "Jew" rather freely. Subsequently, the Leningrad trials of 1970 aroused memories of the late Stalinist period and led some Soviet Jews to ponder anew the meaning of being Jewish in the U.S.S.R.

Finally, one must take into consideration both anti-Semitism and growing Russian nationalism—and the two often go hand-in-hand—as realities of Soviet life. Russian nationalism manifests itself not only in *samizdat* publications but also in official policies and attitudes. Russian nationalism and anti-Semitism force Jewish consciousness, however resented, even upon those Jews who would much prefer not to have this particular national identity. In sum, consciousness of being Jewish, and hence the Jewish identity, under Soviet conditions, is engendered not by schools, literature, language and other normal appurtenances of ethnic belonging, but by social and legal realities and by historical truths from which it is difficult to escape. To be sure, perceptions of these realities and truths vary widely, and we can speak of different types or patterns of Jewish identity in the Soviet Union today.

Patterns of Jewish Identity in the Soviet Union

In the absence of survey data and systematic studies, it is impossible to describe with certainty the distribution of attitudes toward Jewishness among Soviet Jews. We cannot even say precisely how many people in the U.S.S.R. consider themselves Jews, let alone in what way and how they evaluate their Jewishness. Nevertheless, on the basis of available information, we can at least impressionistically describe some modal types and their characteristics. Since the discussion is of types, it would be misleading to generalize to individuals; these modal types serve only to indicate tendencies,

19. David Giladi, summarizing statements by Soviet immigrants at the Twenty-eighth World Zionist Congress, *Haaretz*, January 25, 1972.

likelihoods, and probabilities about Jewish identity patterns in various subgroups of the Soviet Jewish population.

One modal type finds a sort of positive evaluation of their Jewishness, another group is neutral to what is regarded as an objective fact of their existence, and a third mode has a negative attitude toward being Jewish.

In the first category are included three types: traditional Jews, Yiddishists and Zionists. By traditional Jews is meant those to whom Jewish identity is probably more a matter of inheritance than of choice, a natural identity which is passed on from generation to generation, almost without the interruptions of intermarriage. Obviously, this applies largely to the Georgian, Central Asian and Mountain Jews, whose family structure is more traditional and Asiatic than that of the Ashkenazic Jews. Growing up in extended families where parental and ancestral authority is still much respected, these Jews tend to be more observant of religious customs and of folkways than those in the European parts of the U.S.S.R. Russification and cultural deprivation have made inroads among such Jewish groups as well, but these processes came later to Asiatic Jews than to Europeans, and the forces of acculturation and assimilation were confronted by more powerful social and cultural resistance.

Traditional Jews in many ways reflect the cultures in which they have lived for many centuries; just as traditional folkways and customs have survived longer in the Caucasus and Central Asia than in European U.S.S.R., so have the Jews in these areas been more resistant to cultural and psychological change. Traditional identities are reinforced both by the internal dynamics of the Jewish family and the Jewish subculture, as well as by the values and attitudes of the larger Asian society. These identities are what Clifford Geertz calls "primordial attachments." Such attachments stem from the "assumed 'givens' of social existence: immediate contiguity and kin connection mainly, but beyond them the givenness that stems from being born into a particular religious community, speaking a particular language, or a dialect of a language, and following particular social practices." Geertz emphasizes the strength of such primordial attachments.

> These congruities of blood, speech, custom, and so on, are seen to have an ineffable, and at times overpowering, coerciveness in and of themselves. One is bound to one's kinsman . . . *ipso facto* . . . by virtue of some unaccountable absolute import attributed to the very tie

itself. The general strength of such primordial bonds, and the types of them that are important, differ from person to person, from society to society, and from time to time. But for virtually every person, in every society, at almost all times, some attachments seem to flow more from a sense of natural—some would say spiritual—affinity than from social interaction.[20]

For various cultural and historical reasons, primordial attachments seem to be stronger among the Georgian, Bukharan and Mountain Jews than among the others, and so Jewish identity, as historically defined in these communities, is more pervasive and more integral a part of the mental baggage of the individual.

In this category of traditional Jewish identity, the religious Jews should be included. To some extent, there is a congruity between the religious and culturally traditional categories, since religion is a hallmark of Jewish culture and cannot easily be separated from it. There are, of course, religious believers among the Ashkenazic Jews whose cultural ambience is different from the Asiatic. It is impossible to ascertain how many religious believers there are—it is also very difficult to define a religious believer—but one has the distinct impression that most of the publicly visible religious practitioners are old people whose religious convictions and education were inculcated in the prerevolutionary period.

However, in recent years an interesting phenomenon has emerged, no doubt as a result of the search by younger Jews for the meaning of their official Jewish identity. In an attempt to discover the substance and content that underlie the meaning of "Jew," some young Soviet citizens have tried to understand, learn and practice the Jewish faith. While opportunities for doing so are limited, one is greatly impressed by the devotion, sincerity and willingness to sacrifice that are exhibited by these people. The major component of their Jewishness seems to be a religious one and, while in most cases they did not arrive at religious conviction through traditional conduits, it is possible to include such people in the traditional category.

A second pattern of positive Jewish identification is involvement with the attenuated Yiddish cultural life of the U.S.S.R. There is a kind of elite culture, involving a creative intelligentsia whose

20. Clifford Geertz, "The Integrative Revolution," *Old Societies and New States*, Geertz, ed., New York, 1968, pp. 109–110.

medium is the Yiddish language. Probably a few hundrèd people are active producers of Yiddish culture and are involved in Yiddish literature, scholarship, theater and music. The number of consumers of Yiddish culture is far greater, though it is impossible to establish this number with any accuracy. Of course, Yiddish culture is severely restricted by the cultural-political constraints which obtain generally in the U.S.S.R. In the absence of any Yiddish schools or other means of perpetuating and developing Yiddish culture, it remains the preserve of older people or a middle-aged group originally from the Western territories, and a few individuals who, for all sorts of idiosyncratic reasons, have succeeded in overcoming the objective obstacles and have involved themselves with Yiddish culture. It seems probable that Soviet policies will succeed in reducing the scope of Yiddish culture and its adherents even further, and that long-term trends will erode this pattern of Jewish identity even more rapidly than they are eroding these traditional patterns described earlier.

Since 1967, many of those who were involved in, and committed to, Yiddish culture have become involved in the *aliyah* movement and have reached Israel. Thus, the traditional as well as the Yiddishist types have contributed to the third pattern of positive Jewish identification.

Zionist Identification

This brings us to a discussion of the Jewish national revival and the *aliyah* movement. We have already mentioned the stimuli for the Jewish national revival in the U.S.S.R. It remains to ask why this revival took Zionist form, that is, why it represents a movement for repatriation to the historic Jewish homeland. It must be remembered that among certain elements of Soviet Jewry the idea of a Jewish state has been enthusiastically received. While Georgian Jews and some Central Asian Jews may have seen Israel as the fulfillment of age-old dreams and the natural culmination of Jewish historical experience, other European Jews had developed a personal commitment to Zionism, either openly, in the independent Baltic states, Poland, or Rumania, or surreptitiously, even in the Soviet heartland. Soviet policies and circumstances prevented them from acting on their convictions; but these people kept the Zionist ideal alive and were able to pass on to others emotional commitment as well as factual information. Many of these people were Soviet-born Jews who had come to the conclusion that Jewish life was not viable in the U.S.S.R. and that not only would the national-cultural life of the Jews remain unrehabilitated, but that the personal fate of the individual Jew, irrespective of his outlook and convictions, was likely to become worse with time. To leave the U.S.S.R. became the only acceptable alternative for the group as a whole as well as for its individual components. This alternative became realizable when the Zionists organized a visible, widespread, and tactically successful movement within the country, at the same time that complementary supportive movements were organized in the West. Zionism pressed forward at a time when the U.S.S.R. desired more intensive and extensive relations with the West and was therefore more sensitive to internal and external pressures. These three factors, together with greater possibilities for open dissidence in the U.S.S.R. (compared with Stalin's day), made Zionist identification a viable reality.

Again, it is difficult to measure the scope of this pattern of identification. While over 100,000 Jews have gone to Israel (roughly 5 percent of the Soviet Jewish population), there is reason to believe that a like number is interested in emigrating from the U.S.S.R., though it is not known with certainty how many would actually emigrate or what would be their motivations. It should be clear that the great majority of those falling into this pattern have already arrived in Israel and it is likely that their numbers will continue to decline.

There are intermediate patterns of Jewish identity regarding which it is difficult to know what emotional valuation, if any, is attached. There are probably some Jews, relatively few in number, who are either officially or genetically Jewish but who are not very conscious of this fact, or, more likely, do not attach particular significance to it. Nor do those in their immediate milieu remind them of it or act as though it made a difference. Much more frequently one can encounter people of mixed parentage who may be officially identified as Jews or non-Jews but who consciously think of themselves as half-Jews and are thus identified socially. This is simply a fact, and such people may attach values to the factual status which will run the gamut from Zionist commitment to self-hatred as a Jew or half-Jew.

Jews in Urban Areas

Finally, we must consider a Jewish identity which is probably widespread among Soviet Jews and which is also likely to be the way many non-Jews perceive Jewish identity. Definition of this Jewish ethnic group is not in conventional terms of language, dress, specific customs or institutions, but in terms of a social group with specific social and economic attributes. The two chief characteristics of the group are urbanity and education. About 98 percent of these Jews are classified as urban dwellers; 26 percent of this Jewish population live in the three largest and most important cities—Moscow, Leningrad and Kiev. While Jews are a declining proportion of urban Soviet population, the urban proportion of the Jewish population has increased steadily and is likely to continue.

According to the third volume of the 1970 census, 39.9 percent of the Jews in the Russian Soviet Federated Socialist Republics (no data were published for Jews in other republics) who were above ten years of age had some sort of higher education. Of the second ranking nationality, the Georgians, only 10.5 percent had higher education, while Russians had 5.9 percent. Fully 82.4 percent of the Jews have more than primary education, which is nearly twice the national average (43.5 percent). Though Jews are the twelfth largest nationality, in 1973 they ranked third in the absolute number of scientific workers in the economy.[21] Thus, a high level of education has emerged as an attribute or trait of the Soviet Jew. Since education is highly correlated with position in the social-occupational structure, this also means that Jews are unevenly distributed in the social hierarchy and are concentrated in the professions, adding yet a third component to the definition of being a Jew in the U.S.S.R. There is little doubt that the Jews themselves associate these characteristics with Jews and that they have become as much a defining characteristic of ethnic affiliation as more conventional components of ethnicity.[22]

21. *Vestnik statistiki*, no. 4, 1974, p. 92.
22. Professor Voronel writes: "By now, Soviet Jews have become less (perhaps far from) an ethnic group than a social grouping with an educational level far above the country's average," in "The Social Pre-Conditions of the National Awakening of the Jews in the U.S.S.R.," *I Am a Jew*, p. 26. As is well-known, there have long been attempts to infuse Jewish identity with specific character traits, ranging from sharp business dealings to the capacity for critical thinking (Freud, Veblen) or love of freedom.

In fact, the educational attributes of the Jews are a source of pride and are a positive stimulus to Jewish identity. They are proud of the achievements of the State of Israel and have even been known to attribute to Israel fantastic accomplishments, particularly in the medical and scientific fields. Thus, the objective characteristics of Soviet Jews and Israeli successes may be positive stimuli to Jewish identification.

"Invalids of the Fifth Category"

There are at least two identity patterns that involve a negative evaluation of Jewishness, though the degree and substance of negation differ considerably. On the one hand there are those who see themselves, in the Soviet-Jewish expression, as "invalids of the fifth category" (the fifth paragraph in one's identity card lists nationality). To these people Jewish identity is largely a burden, a fact of life that brings with it many disadvantages and very few advantages. Were they free to do so, they would discard this identity. In practice they do not identify as Jews except when forced to do so by official policy. Jewishness is a kind of mark of Cain which is extremely difficult to erase. In instances when the opportunity arises to change one's nationality, such people will eagerly do so. Presumably, this identity pattern—or nonidentity pattern—which encompasses thousands of people, is often encountered in countries where being Jewish is not nearly so great a disadvantage as it is in the U.S.S.R. It is hardly surprising, therefore, that under Soviet conditions there would be a powerful tendency in this direction.

Finally, there is a group that does not think of itself as Jewish under normal circumstances. To some extent, this pattern overlaps with a reluctance to think of oneself as a Jew, but we distinguish it here for analytic purposes to encompass those who genuinely feel themselves non-Jewish in every way. Even in the nineteenth century there were numbers of Russian Jews who succeeded in assimilating into Russian culture and society and lost all trace of Jewish identity. Then, as now, for many the attractions of Russian culture were irresistible. Lev Navrozov, a recent emigré, writes of "the delight of being a Russian." His mother, born a Jew, "went to hear every great Russian poet and novelist—to see their gods in the flesh, to hear them speaking in the heavenly tongue called Russian"; and he testifies to his own "exaltation in *real* Russia [that country which

presumably existed before 1917] and in Europe—ah, Evropa!—as
seen through the Russian intellectual's eye at the turn of the century."[23] The large number of Jews who have become not only enthusiastic consumers of Russian culture but prolific creators of that
culture testifies to its attraction and to the identification of Jews with
it. Presumably, a high proportion of these most acculturated Jews
would also be assimilated when circumstances permitted.

Conclusion

It should be emphasized that such patterns of identity are
fluid and that individuals change their identification and hence their
behavior, sometimes with enormous social and historical consequences. After 1967 large numbers of Soviet Jews changed their
evaluation of their identity and even changed their (subjective) identity, with results that are well known. While under Soviet conditions
it has been difficult to change official identity, subjective identity has
been more changeable and will continue to be so. There are at least
three major influences shaping subjective identity; variations in
these influences will continue to shape Jewish identity and hence
Jewish behavior and history in the Soviet Union. First, there is Soviet policy. This establishes not only official identity but also heavily
influences subjective identity, as is clear from the entire history of
the Jewish population under Soviet rule. For example, should the
Soviets permit individuals to choose an ethnic identity, this would
undoubtedly result in a powerful tendency to full-scale assimilation
among Jews, accompanied perhaps by a weaker opposing trend
wherein some would adopt Jewish identity officially. Should Soviet
policy remain the same, as it is likely to do, it will perpetuate the
state of acculturation without assimilation, and this condition will
continue to create psychological dissonance which characterizes so
many.

A second factor is secular demographic, economic and social
trends. A continued decline in the Jewish birth rate, an increase in
the number of intermarriages, and a lowering of barriers to economic, social, and even political advancement would be the optimal

23. Lev Navrozov, "Getting Out of Russia," *Commentary*, vol. 54, no. 4, October 1972,
pp. 47–50.

combination for the growth of non-Jewish identity. Thus far, one trend seems to have been counterbalanced by another tending in a different direction. If intermarriages grow and hence the number of officially non-Jewish Jews rises, but anti-Semitism and official restrictions on Jews continue or grow, even nonofficial Jews are likely to be reminded of the Jewish component of their identities and to draw a variety of conclusions from this. The social forces influencing identity patterns are many and complex and are seldom likely to push individuals in the same direction. Rather, they are likely to produce conflict and dissonance.

In the shorter range, perceptions and evaluations of Israel are likely to influence identity patterns among Soviet Jews. Since Israel is presently the prominent alternative to Jewish existence in the Soviet Union, it must continue to be attractive to Soviet Jews if it is to remain a viable alternative. Otherwise, they will be forced once again to seek alternatives along the continuum of total assimilation at one end and national assertion in the form of immigration to Israel at the other. A combination of changes in Soviet policy and difficulties in Israel could well produce a tendency opposite to that which we have been witnessing in the past five years or so, especially if a new wave of committed Zionists is not forthcoming. Changes in Soviet policy, which in my view are unlikely, could also create Jewish alternatives within the Soviet Union. One cannot predict with any certainty the relative strengths of the various identification patterns. We can, however, identify those factors which will influence the development and maintenance of the patterns. As Erikson reminds us, ". . . In history, identifications and identities are bound to shift with changing technologies, cultures, and political systems. Existing or changing roles thus must be reassimilated in the psychosocial identity of the most dominant and most numerous members of an organization."[24] If we are even to guess at likely future patterns of identification in the U.S.S.R., we must give serious thought to the larger social forces operating both inside and outside of the Soviet Union and, if this is our concern, even try to influence them.

24. Erikson, "Identity, Psychosocial," *ibid.*

Is the Marxist Model Operative for the Jew?

Albert Memmi

Of identification models that offer themselves to the present-day Jew, I wish to examine the socialist, more particularly the Marxist socialist, model, even though I am not an expert on Marxism. It is imperative to discuss this subject for two reasons. First, a major part of the world today believes it is socialist or claims to be socialist. The second reason concerns the Jewish People specifically because an important section of Jewish youth, in particular students, calls itself socialist. It would be impossible, therefore, to ignore this manifestation in our analysis, even by those who have no socialist sympathies.

I am well aware of the objections to this idea. Some distinguished scholars feel that interest should be focused exclusively on the inner problems of Judaism, by the study of Jewish tradition; moreover, it is considered a waste of time to dissipate our efforts on doctrines and ideologies which are alien to the spirit of Judaism. Such assertions are alarming—they evidently derive from a ghetto attitude. The richness of Jewish cultural tradition does not derive from additional interpretations or from a new exegesis of this or that text (although these, naturally, are not to be ignored), but from confronting Jewish tradition with the day-to-day concrete problems which the Jew has to face in a contemporary life situation. Socialism is one of those possibilities which confronts non-Jews as well as Jews; it is of particular concern to Jewish youth.

Socialism—The New Messianism

Whatever the reasons, it is obvious that socialism has emerged as one solution to the oppression of contemporary Jews. Those who are familiar with my writings know it is my belief that the guideline to an interpretation of Jewishness (that is, the objective

157

and subjective fact of being a Jew) is to be found in the condition of the Jews. As this condition has always been one of oppression and, periodically, of catastrophe, the contemporary Jew—after first seeking sanctuary in religion—has enthusiastically welcomed, perhaps even more so than others, the solutions devised by ideologists for the liberation of all the peoples of the world.

Socialism is one of the prime answers to social, political, historical and cultural oppression. It became all the more welcome since religions were on the decline everywhere, with the Jewish religion following the general trend (in Europe at least). In a sense, socialism, particularly in its Marxist form, is one of the best replacements for the religions of non-Jews as well as Jews, because it promotes the idea of world organization free of the beliefs which constrain many modern intellectuals.

In the ethical sphere, where Jews are particularly sensitive, socialism contains an element of the moralization of history, part of which is the subconscious need felt by almost every Jew for a just, humane order. It seems fair to suggest that there is more to it than that: Mosaic messianism is replaced by another kind of messianism which implies the complete transformation of man and of society. Socialism is undoubtedly heir to the ethics and culture of Judeo-Christianity.

Finally, there is a more concrete aspect which cannot be overlooked. By adhering to a political party, a union or an action group, the Jewish individual (whose inclusion into a global society may be questioned) feels that he has found another kind of brotherhood, simpler and more direct, with his fellow citizens. Only those who have been close to Jewish members of a political party or a union can understand the feeling of warmth and kinship for which those Jews may even sacrifice their lives.

However, it must be conceded that the encounter between contemporary Jews and socialism has proved to be a serious failure. There are several reasons for this, the most important of which is based on a fundamental misunderstanding. The somewhat remote objective of socialism is to eliminate differences—to strive toward promoting a universality of man which would reach beyond frontiers, religious beliefs and cultures. The Jew, therefore, should not fight to save his Jewishness, but rather struggle for universal man; that, indeed, is what most Jewish activists have done, but it means, for the Jew, setting aside the specificity of his condition. In some countries he could fight against the same constraints as his fellow citizens but he could not fight against the odds which he suffered as a Jew. In other words, the Jewish activist was required to forget that he was a Jew. Naturally, anti-Semitism was seldom discussed openly by the union or party to which the Jewish activist belonged. This unsatisfactory position had a theoretical basis which was inherent in the socialist doctrine itself.

The Marxist form of socialism held that the driving force of the social struggle was primarily the class struggle. Jews were to be found in most of the social classes, but they belonged more often to the wealthier middle classes (in Western countries, at least); here, too, the socialist movement demanded that they repudiate their own social class.

This interpretation of history solely from the angle of social class is, in my opinion, one of the weaknesses of socialism. During the decolonization period in North Africa, I had the utmost difficulty convincing even my intimate colleagues that national dimension is occasionally just as important as social dimension. In my book *The Colonizer and the Colonized,*[1] I came to the conclusion (long before I took up the subject of Zionism in *Portrait of a Jew*)[2] that liberation from colonialism would most certainly be accomplished through nationalism.

Marxism and the Jewish Situation

Marxist analysts could not understand the Jewish masses inasmuch as the latter reacted in a relatively autonomous, that is, national, manner. Indeed, such a response is the basis of Zionism—a Jewish movement of national liberation. Because socialists mistrust all national movements—which they too hastily term "nationalist" in the derogatory sense of the word—mistrust of Zionism was inevitable. Socialists also feared that Zionism would influence desirable elements to abandon the ranks of the revolutionary movements. Indeed, it may be conceded that, at present, Jewish youth is caught in the midst of an underlying struggle between the Jewish national movement and the revolutionary parties; the outcome of this struggle will depend on Jewish grasp of the aspirations and difficulties of

---

1. New York, 1965 (American edition).
2. New York, 1962 (American edition).

Jewish youth. For that reason, it must be stressed repeatedly that the delicate problem posed by the confrontation of socialism and Jewish cultural tradition must not be ignored.

The ultimate point of this confrontation is embodied in the stand taken by the U.S.S.R. against Zionism and the State of Israel. Many Marxist Jews, forced to struggle against the only specifically Jewish political attempt to gain national independence, have reached the depths of despair during the last decade. A Jewish communist cannot take an interest in Jewish culture without being suspected of Jewish chauvinism and reactionary nostalgia.

Is there, then, a final contradiction between the socialist model and the Jewish condition? I think not. (Without seeking to vindicate the Marxist model, I must here confess to a great sympathy for socialism in spite of certain ideological objections.) Strangely enough, it is in contemporary socialism that an unexpected contradiction poses a dilemma.

National Consciousness

Marxism and socialism in general, did not foresee the extent, vigor and even the resurgence of national feeling among the peoples of the world. There has been an extraordinary remolding of the world into distinct nations while the majority of capable leftist minds believed that the trend was toward internationalism. Thus orthodox socialist thinking has proved to be wrong. I am convinced that even young, socialist nations are fighting for their collective, that is, national dimension—an unexpected contradiction of socialist fundamentals.

These national assertions have been a disaster for Jews in an unexpected manner: the Communist Party, for instance, hastened to exclude their Jewish leaders. It is noteworthy that this happened in Poland and in Czechoslovakia as well as in Algeria and Tunisia where I witnessed a similar elimination of Jews. Thus, neither the nationalism nor the socialism of others can provide a solution to the oppression of Jews. It means that the only solution for the Marxist Jew lies within a specifically Jewish national framework.

Only the Jewish national movement—Zionism—can provide a solution to the dilemma which arises for Jews who are also socialists. Jewish youth must be persuaded that for Jews socialism can prevail only if the Jewish condition is included within its framework; in other words, the Jewish socialist has to give up hope of finding an answer to the oppression of Jews in socialism alone. Let us, however, not forget the political contradictions between Zionism and its opponents (into whose ranks Jewish youth was accepted) and the anguish which such contradictions imply.

It seems to me, therefore, that the unease and confusion, which lead to a revision of the doctrine of many Jewish intellectuals today—in Israel too—must be dispelled. The socialism of others cannot provide an answer to the Jewish problem. Only a national Jewish socialism (with reservations as to this designation) can provide a solution for the Jewish condition.

To end on a personal note, I shall give just one illustration: I am convinced that if the problems of the Oriental Jews were reexamined in terms of socialism, they would be better understood. Or put differently, the problem confronting Israeli socialism today is not that of the socialist *kibbutzim* (which remain a wonderful accomplishment of Israeli society), but the problem of the integration and progress of the new Oriental Jewish proletariat.

Criteria for Jewish Identity*

Simon N. Herman

Despite the increased interest in recent years in the problems of ethnicity, little has been done by way of systematic analysis of the structure and dynamics of any ethnic identity. The social sciences have made important contributions to an understanding of the nature of ethnic group prejudice and of the factors calculated to promote intergroup cooperation. The studies of ethnic groups, however, fail to undertake a theoretical conceptualization of the identity with which they are dealing.[1] This is markedly so in the case of the growing literature on Black ethnicity, and—with few exceptions—it holds true also for studies of the Jewish identity with which we are here concerned. The studies of the Jewish group—as those of Black ethnicity—are generally limited, empirical explorations; their contribution is to our knowledge of specific questions only and they are not a source for wider derivations. In the absence of a systematic conceptual framework the various studies bear little relationship to one another; they do not add up.

Almost any study of Jewish attitudes is pretentiously called a study of Jewish identity. A glance at most studies of Jewish communities in the Diaspora shows that they are at best studies of Jewish *identification*. They may deal with the process by which the individual comes to see himself as part of the Jewish group and the form the act of identification takes; or they may describe the extent to which, and the circumstances under which, the Jews in a particular community are prepared to stand up and be counted as such, or, conversely, prefer to throw in their lot with the majority. But very few of

*This paper is an adaptation of a chapter in a forthcoming publication, *The Social Psychology of Jewish Identity*.

1. A recent contribution to the theory of ethnicity is *Ethnicity: Theory and Experience*, N. Glazer and D. P. Moynihan, ed., Harvard University, 1975.

them are studies of Jewish identity, of what being Jewish means, of what kind of Jew and what kind of Jewishness develop in the majority culture.[2] In the Jewish majority society of Israel, where Jewish identification is taken for granted (unless there are indications to the contrary), studies move more readily into the field of Jewish identity.

The present paper attempts a clarification—in broad outline—of the basic elements of Jewish identity. We shall limit ourselves to an analysis of the structure and content of Jewish identity and, while we shall have reason to refer to some of the influences at work, we shall not deal specifically with the dynamics of Jewish identity formation. We would, however, submit that an analysis of the basic elements is a necessary preliminary to systematic consideration of the dynamic factors.

The conceptual framework which we are setting forth has been utilized by us in a series of studies on Jewish identity conducted at the Institute of Contemporary Jewry and the Department of Psychology of the Hebrew University, and we shall have occasion to refer to these studies in the course of this paper. (i) The first of these studies had as its subjects a representative sample of all the eleventh-graders in the high schools of Israel and their parents and teachers. It was initiated in 1965, and—in order to take into account the impact of the Six Day War—was supplemented in 1968 by a substudy of high school students in Jerusalem and Haifa. The findings are reported in the book *Israelis and Jews: The Continuity of an Identity*.[3] (ii) A small-scale replication of the study was undertaken in 1974 (findings in preparation for publication). (iii) A study of American students in the One Year Program for overseas students at the Hebrew University, reported in *American Students in Israel*,[4] covered the years 1965 to 1969. (iv) A study, conducted in 1973–74, compared the Jewish identity of Israeli students with the identities of students from the United States, the Argentine, South Africa and the U.S.S.R. (in preparation for publication).

General Observations

(1) When we discuss an individual's identity as it is shaped in

2. A good example of such a study of Jewish identity is M. Sklare and J. Greenblum, *Jewish Identity on the Suburban Frontier*, New York, 1967.
3. New York, 1971.
4. Cornell University, 1970.

the course of social interaction, it is useful to distinguish—as does Daniel Miller[5]—between objective public identity (a person's pattern of traits as they appear to others), subjective public identity (his perception of his appearance to others) and self-identity (the person's version of his pattern of traits).

Let us turn to public objective identity; a particular individual may be regarded as a Jew by members of the in-group (i.e., by other Jews) or the out-group (by non-Jews), or both. When we refer to the definition of "Who is a Jew?" in Jewish religious law (*Halakhah*), we are in the realm of public objective identity. While this is a widely accepted definition it should be noted that some sectors of the Jewish in-group show greater latitude in their classification of individuals as Jews. The out-group on occasion may define as a Jew someone who is not regarded as such by Jews. Thus, the Nazi regime in its Nuremberg Laws adopted a sweeping definition embracing even those who were no longer in the Jewish fold but who had a Jewish grandparent. Even where no formal definition exists, individuals who have completely assimilated may still be perceived as Jews by Gentiles.

The individual's self-identity is influenced by subjective public identity, that is, by the way he believes others see him. What is crucial here is not simply whether the individual sees himself classified as a Jew—in most cases, this is not open to question—but how he believes others view a Jew. The question then arises as to whom the individual regards as the significant others—Jews or non-Jews. The answer will differ for a Jew in a majority Jewish society such as exists in Israel and for Jews in minority situations. While a Jew in Israel looks into a Jewish mirror, the member of a Jewish minority is influenced to a greater or lesser extent by the image of a Jew reflected in the mirror held by the Gentile majority. The extent will depend upon the individual's location in his group: A Jew seeking to be accepted into a majority group will be more greatly influenced by non-Jewish appraisal than will an identifying Jew. For the latter the image projected in the distorting Gentile mirror will be modified somewhat through the prism of his own Jewish subculture. But, even then, it will leave some trace.

(2) A Jewish identity, like any other ethnic identity, relates to

5. D. R. Miller, "The Study of Social Relationships: Situation, Identity, and Social Interaction," *Psychology: A Study of a Science*, S. Koch, ed., New York, 1963, p. 673.

a particular people with a particular history. What constitutes such identity is not a matter of arbitrary definition, nor is it something which is created entirely anew. There are certain minimal requirements for an identity to qualify as Jewish. (Thus, in the absence of such minimal criteria, the members of a religious sect of American Blacks, the Black Hebrew Israelites, were not deemed to be Jews by the Israel Supreme Court for the purposes of the Law of Return.) The study of Jewish identity cannot, however, confine itself to the investigation of just that part of the identity which constitutes a given, or fixed, datum. An identity does not exist as something completely preformed; as they make choices in life which commit them to certain attitudes and courses of action, individuals and groups are engaged in a creative process of building up an identity. A leading writer on the philosophy of education, Israel Scheffler, has expressed this well:

> Insofar as a group is specifiable, one may investigate its characteristics empirically, and perhaps try to determine which are common and peculiar to it. But those who speak of finding or searching for an identity do not seem to be addressing themselves to such a cluster of empirical traits. Rather they seem to be raising a set of normative questions: what to do as a member of a given group, how the group ought itself to act, etc. . . . The question is what we are to make of our historical group membership through our own deliberate choices, based upon an accurate awareness of our historical circumstances, and as reliable as possible an estimate of alternative possibilities open to us.[6]

(3) An identity may be exclusive or inclusive of other identities. One of the specific problems facing developing countries in Africa and Asia is how to foster a more inclusive national identity which will integrate segmental tribal identities without suppressing them. The Nigerian-Biafran conflict illustrated the tragic results of failure on this score.

It has been maintained that the pluralistic conception of the American identity is "neither one of separatism—with or without equality—nor of assimilation but one of full participation combined

6. I. Scheffler, "How Can a Jewish Self-Consciousness Be Developed?" *The Study of Jewish Identity: Issues and Approaches,* S. N. Herman, ed., Jerusalem, 1971, pp. 1–2.
7. T. Parsons, "Full Citizenship for the American Negro? A Sociological Problem," *The Negro American,* T. Parsons and K. B. Clark, ed., Boston, 1965, p. 750.

with the preservation of an identity."[7] In practice, however, cultural pluralism has meant "that immigrant communities, while adopting the dominant American culture, retained and contributed to America a form of subculture acceptable to the general consensus. The more superficial the cultural difference that immigrant groups brought with them the easier the naturalization of these differences in America."[8] In the new ethnic climate American pluralism is being reexamined, possibly resulting in lesser subordination of minority cultures to the dominant majority culture while preserving the common American framework.

"The alternative to an exclusive totalism," Erikson has observed, "is the wholeness of the more inclusive identity." But in respect to the American Black, this, he points out, leads to another question: "If the Negro wants to find that other identity which permits him to be self-certain as a Negro (or as a descendant of Negroes) and *integrated as an American* what joint historical actuality can he count on?"[9]

The problem of integration in Israel has been facilitated by the strength of the overriding inclusive Jewish identity which has provided a wide enough spectrum, allowing for the unquestioned maintenance of identities such as the Ashkenazic and Sephardic. A "joint historical actuality" clearly exists. But with increasing diversification in the Jewish world there is not the same degree of consensus as to which are the legitimate segmental variations which may be integrated into a Jewish identity.

A Definition of Jewish Identity

Identity has been used by psychologists, often loosely, as a broad concept under which are subsumed a number of phenomena. It has rarely been given precise definition.

Erikson (who, despite his insightful studies of identity, admits to the difficulty of definition) states in his *Childhood and Society* that "the ego identity develops out of a gradual integration of all identifications."[10] Discussing elsewhere Freud's formulation of his own "inner identity" with Judaism, Erikson speaks of the reflection

8. B. Halpern, *The American Jew*, New York, 1956, p. 84.
9. E. H. Erikson, "The Concept of Identity in Race Relations; Notes and Queries," *The Negro American*, p. 247.
10. E. H. Erikson, *Childhood and Society*, New York, 1950, p. 213.

in the individual of "an essential aspect of a group's inner coherence."[11]

Depending on the particular context, we shall use the term
"Jewish identity" to mean (1) the pattern of attributes of the Jewish
group as seen by its members, that is, how the group defines itself; or
(2) the relationship of the individual to the Jewish group and the reflection in him of its attributes, that is, how the individual sees himself (self-identity) by virtue of his membership in the Jewish group.
As Herbert Kelman has pointed out:

> Group identity is carried by the individual members of the group,
> but it is not coterminous with the sum of the conceptions of individual
> group members. For one thing, it has an independent existence in the
> form of accumulated historical products, including written
> documents, oral traditions, institutional arrangements, and symbolic
> artifacts. For another, different segments of the group differ widely in
> their degree of active involvement and emotional commitment to the
> group: various leadership elements and particularly active and com-
> mitted subgroups are far more instrumental in defining the group
> identity than the rank-and-file members.[12]

In developing a conceptual framework we shall focus on the
relationship of the individual to his being and becoming Jewish, but
in doing so we shall also keep the group identity in sight. While our
concern here is with Jewish identity, we would submit that the
framework is pertinent for the analysis of other ethnic identities as
well.

An analysis of the Jewish identity of an individual must deal
with (A) the nature of the individual's relationship to the Jewish
group as a membership group; (B) the content of a Jewish identity—
the individual's perception of the attributes of the Jewish group, his
feelings about them and the extent to which its norms are adopted by
him as a source of reference.

While it is useful to bear in mind the distinction between
"identification" and "identity," the two terms will frequently inter-
twine in the analysis which follows.

11. E. H. Erikson, "The Problem of Ego Identity," *Identity and Anxiety*, M. R. Stein et
al., Glencoe, Ill., 1960, p. 38.
12. H. C. Kelman, "The Place of Jewish Identity in the Development of Personal Identity," a working paper prepared for the American Jewish Committee's Colloquium on
Jewish Education and Jewish Identity, November 1974.

A. Membership in the Jewish Group

Identity reflects both likeness and uniqueness. In terms of a popular phrasing of the fact: Every man is (1) like all other men (he possesses universal human attributes); (2) like some other men (he shares certain attributes in common with specific social categories); (3) like no other man (he has a unique personality of his own).

Ethnic identity relates to that which the individual shares in common with other men, along with whom he is set off from still others "by inherited physical type (or race), by religion, language or national origin or any combination of these."[13] (This is the broader definition of ethnic identity. Sometimes it is defined more narrowly to embrace just those who have a common origin.)

A person with a certain ethnic identity is aligned with members of a particular group and, at the same time, is marked off, or marks himself off, from members of other groups. We shall first discuss the marking-off function and will then trace the implications of alignment with the Jewish group: the psychological need which underlies it, the bases of alignment, the sense of mutual responsibility which accompanies it, the temporal and spatial compass of the alignment.

Marking Off

Members of a minority—much more so than members of a majority—are conscious of being marked off. One of the most significant divisions of their world for members of a Jewish community is that between themselves and the non-Jews with whom they are in constant juxtaposition. Jews may be one of a number of minorities in a country but there are occasions when they feel that the boundary line runs between Jews on the one hand and all non-Jews—whatever their specific affiliations—on the other.

The individual members of a Jewish minority will differ in their relation to the non-Jewish majority according to their position in their Jewish group. Those at the center will tend to be more aware of their distinctiveness, of what sets them apart, while the marginal Jews are more anxious to stress what they have in common with the majority. The former often tend to be conscious of intergroup

13. O. Klineberg, "The Multi-national Society: Some Research Problems," *Social Sciences Information*, vol. 6, no. 6, December 1967, pp. 81–99.

dissimilarities, of the differences between the Jewish and Gentile groups, while the latter will underline intragroup dissimilarities, that not all Jews are alike and should not be branded as the bearers of identical "undesirable characteristics." Jews on the periphery would indeed have wished that they could be aligned with those from whom they are now marked off. But in regard to Jews of all categories a relation exists between their conception of the marking-off group and their conception of their own group.

Since in Israel Jews constitute the majority, the group from which they are marked off obtrudes less in their consciousness than it does in Jewish communities elsewhere. When Israelis do think of themselves as Jews, it is not so much in relation to any minority in Israel but as part of a Jewish People in the Gentile world: they place themselves in a global context. The group from which they are marked off is the general category of Gentiles—at times the Gentiles of whom they learn in Jewish history and at times the Gentiles in countries from which reports currently come of anti-Jewish discrimination. But these are Gentiles who are at a distance and of whose existence they do not have a constant reminder.

The Arab minority and other non-Jews living in Israel serve only a limited marking-off function. The Arabs serve this function more in relation to the Oriental Jews than in relation to the Ashkenazic Jews: for the Oriental Jews who have lived in Arab countries, in many cases the Arabs are the only non-Jews they have personally encountered; indeed, in Israel they are anxious to be seen as different from Arabs. At the same time they too—like the Ashkenazic Jews—are conscious of the wider Gentile world from which they are marked off as Jews. When the Israeli students (in the 1968 and 1974 studies) were asked to supply the missing word in the statement "We are Jews and they on the other hand are . . ." the most frequent response—on the part of both Ashkenazic and Oriental students—was "goyim" (Gentiles), with smaller numbers inserting such terms as "non-Jews" and "Christians." Only a minority inserted "Arabs," although the percentage was greater in 1974 than in 1968 (18 as compared to 7 percent). Within this minority the larger proportion were students from the Oriental communities.

It would seem that events after the Yom Kippur War (the continued isolation of Israel, the ovation accorded at the United Nations to the terrorist leader Yasser Arafat) have sharpened the sense of a line of demarcation in the minds of Jews.

Alignment—The Need to Belong

In a series of penetrating essays on the shaping of the identity of the Jewish child, Kurt Lewin has stressed how crucial is a clear sense of belongingness to his Jewish group and his acceptance of this belongingness as positive and meaningful. "One of the most important constituents of the ground on which the individual stands is the social group to which he belongs."[14] Uncertainty of belongingness implies instability of the social ground and leads to instability of the person.

Every individual belongs to a number of groups, some of greater and some of lesser importance in his life. Membership in an underprivileged minority group generally has far-reaching implications. This is particularly the case in regard to a group such as the Jews, who, for historical and other reasons, occupy a singular position in whatever society they find themselves. Some Jews may readily accept membership in the Jewish group and all that goes with it, regarding it as a mark of distinction even if it subjects them to certain difficulties. They know where they stand, and their membership in what they regard as a desirable group bolsters their self-esteem. Other Jews may see this membership as a stigma, and may develop inferiority feelings about their Jewishness. But they generally cannot escape it; they can only deny it by a formal act of conversion. Even then their Jewish origins are not always forgotten by their Gentile neighbors (and will also be remembered by the Jews in certain situations). In a sense such individuals are vainly trying to reject a part of themselves.

In the life-space of any minority group there are forces leading to positive identification with that group by its members, and other forces which lead to gravitation to the majority. Among those who gravitate strongly toward the majority will be persons who remain suspended between the two groups, the so-called marginal men, who do not reconcile themselves to membership in the minority and at the same time cannot join the majority because of the barriers erected against their entry. This position of marginality is often accompanied by feelings of isolation and insecurity and by a search for a substitute belongingness.[15]

14. K. Lewin, *Resolving Social Conflicts*, Gertrud Lewin, ed., New York, 1948, p. 145.
15. Cf. I. Berlin, "Benjamin Disraeli, Karl Marx and the Search for Identity," *Midstream*, vol. 16, no. 7, August–September, 1970, pp. 29–49.

Bases of Alignment

Alignment may be based on a perception of similarity or a feeling of interdependence or both.

Since Emancipation, Jewish society has become increasingly diversified. The migrations of the latter part of the nineteenth century and of the twentieth century and the consequent socialization of Jews in settings so different politically, culturally and socially have accelerated this process. If we compare two major communities—Israel and the United States—we find that they are much less alike now than they were at the beginning of this century when both American Jewry and the Yishuv in Eretz Israel were to a large extent composed of Yiddish-speaking immigrants from Eastern Europe who had taken different routes. In the meantime, two new generations have grown up, speaking different languages. Moreover, at least half of the Israeli Jewish population is not from Europe but from the Middle East.

In our studies of Israeli and American students we found that neither group saw much similarity between Israeli and American Jews; indeed, what impressed the Americans on arrival in Israel was the unexpected extent of the dissimilarity. At the same time, however, the feeling of interdependence has grown, and the overwhelming majority of students testify to the existence of this feeling. When we speak here of interdependence we are using the term in the sense of a change in the state of any part that affects all the other parts. In the context of Jewish life this means that whatever happens to Jews as Jews anywhere has implications for Jews everywhere.

Since there are a variety of models of Jewish life, a good deal of confusion exists among Jews as to how the Jewish group should be defined and what their relation is to other Jews whom they see as dissimilar from themselves in so many respects. On the other hand, the facts of Jewish existence, particularly since the Holocaust, are such that a feeling of common fate can be more easily invoked. Where interdependence is recognized as the basis of belongingness, even Jews who see themselves as dissimilar from other Jews regard themselves as belonging to a Jewish group. In our studies those students who are highest on the scale of Jewish identification affirm the existence of both similarity and interdependence, while those lower on the scale do not perceive similarity but do recognize interdependence. The feeling of interdependence represents the widest minimal basis of Jewish belongingness in our time.

There are, of course, kinds of interdependence as well as degrees of interdependence. Thus, there is the promotive interdependence which results from cooperation in the pursuit of a common goal as well as interdependence in the face of an external threat.[16] The cooperative effort on the part of Jews throughout the world in making possible an ingathering of Jews in Israel contains both elements. It is the external threat, however, which weighs most heavily on Jews. In the face of continuing attacks from so many quarters they see themselves as a beleaguered people "standing alone but standing together."

Sense of Mutual Responsibility

Social psychological experimentation has demonstrated that a concomitant to the feeling of interdependence is a sense of mutual responsibility.[17] A widespread recognition of the mutual obligations between Israel and Jews abroad is shown in studies of Israelis and of visiting students from the United States and other countries. In time of crisis, as during the Six Day War and Yom Kippur War, Jewish communities throughout the world rallied spontaneously and unreservedly to the aid of Israel. The feeling of responsibility exists not only between Israelis and Jews abroad but among Jews wherever they may be. It is summed up in the Hebrew phrase *Kol Yisrael arevim zeh la-zeh,* (All Jews are guarantors one for the other). In a long history of persecutions and migrations Jews always knew that they could turn to their fellow Jews for help. Moreover, Jewish communities do not make such aid contingent on the Jewish loyalties of their fellow-Jews—witness the assistance accorded to assimilated Jews compelled to leave Poland after the purges of 1968.

Our studies of Israeli students show that they feel particularly close to Jews who are under attack; indeed, it is such discrimination or persecution which underlines the element of common fate and activates a sense of mutual responsibility to the Jews of the U.S.S.R. and of Syria, whom they regard as the most threatened of Jewish communities. "To work for the ingathering of Jews from the Golah"

16. M. Deutsch, *The Resolution of Conflict,* Yale University, 1973, p. 20.
17. L. Berkowitz and L. R. Daniels, "Responsibility and Dependency," *Journal of Abnormal and Social Psychology,* vol. 66, no. 5, 1963, pp. 429–36.

ranks highest among the characteristics of a "good Jew" in Israel in
the opinion of Israeli students.

Alignment across Time

Alignment with an ethnic group implies a relationship to the
group beyond a given moment in time—to the past and the future as
well as to its present. An ethnic identity points to an individual's
link with the "unique values, fostered by a unique history, of his
people."[18]

An analysis of the relationship between historical time perspective and ethnic identity requires a breakdown of time perspective into its various dimensions. We have suggested in one of our
studies (*Israelis and Jews*) that the relevant dimensions are those
which relate to past, present and future orientation, to scope, to
structurization, to differentiation, to selectivity, to continuity and to
probability of locomotion. We shall here refer to just one of these dimensions, that of continuity, which concerns the interrelatedness of
past, present and future. Is a particular event relegated to the limbo
of the historical past? Or is it seen as exercising a continuing influence through the present into the future? A past cannot be adopted.
It is only when it consists of memories which still live on in the lives
of men and impinge on their present life-space that it plays its proper part in the development of an ethnic identity.

Just as it cannot be adopted, so the actuality of the past cannot
be artificially erased. A Jew anywhere is what he is because of the
centuries of Diaspora existence experienced by his people. Some
members of the younger generation in Israel have difficulty in identifying with this part of their past—seen by them as that of a passive
minority—so different from the conditions of their own lives. But to
deny this past would be to efface a part of themselves. (One of the
tasks of education in Israel is to develop a proper understanding of,
and relationship to, this past.)

The Jewish People is a group with a particularly long memory
which has contributed in no small measure to the preservation of its
distinctiveness across the centuries. It has been characterized

18. E. H. Erikson, "The Problem of Ego Identity," p. 38. See also "The Concept of
Identity in Race Relations: Notes and Queries," p. 243: ". . . Identity also contains a
complementarity of past and future both in the individual and in society; it links the
actuality of a living past with that of a promising future."

through the vicissitudes of time and place by a sense of continuity. An obvious example is the way in which, on Passover, when celebrating the exodus from Egypt, the Jew is urged to regard himself as personally involved in that event, as if he himself were among those liberated from Egyptian bondage.

As a touchstone of the relationship to the past it is particularly important to examine attitudes to the period of the Holocaust. In our studies of the identity of Israeli youth and of American students visiting Israel, we found the most significant question—in the exploration of a sense of historical continuity—to be whether this generation of young Jews, born after the Holocaust, saw themselves "as if they were survivors" and, as such, charged with the responsibility of ensuring the Jewish future. The consciousness of being survivors is the strongest expression of the sense of interdependence, and the data of our studies confirm that it is associated with an intensity of Jewish identity.

Not all historical events are deeply imprinted in the on-going life of a people. It would seem that much depends on the centrality of an event in the life of a people, its relevance to the conditions of their present and their aspirations for the future; much depends also on the educational measures taken to perpetuate the memory of such an event in a way which emphasizes its continuing pertinence for the present and the future. The Holocaust is an example of such a traumatic central event in the history of the Jewish People, a persistent memory which has been further sharpened by the constellation of happenings surrounding the Six Day War and the Yom Kippur War.

Alignment across Space

Alignment with so widely dispersed a people as the Jews has to be across space as well as time and has to bridge other differences as well. Some Jews think in terms of "one Jewish People," of *klal Yisrael,* and see themselves aligned with all Jews irrespective of differences in geographical location or communal background or ideology; there are others whose alignment is primarily with their local community or confined to a particular segment of it, with very little concern for Jews elsewhere.

In terms of our discussion of the criteria so far listed we would submit that a Jew would rank high on a scale measuring the *compass*

of Jewish identity if (a) he regards himself aligned with (and responsible for) the welfare of all Jews wherever they be, and (b) he sees
himself linked not only to the Jews of the present but to generations
past and those still to come.

B. The Content of a Jewish Identity

An ethnic identity implies more than the mere fact of affiliation with a group. The additional questions which arise are:

(1) On the cognitive level: How does the individual perceive
the attributes of the group? Furthermore, in what situations is the
group membership a salient factor in his consciousness, and how
central is the position it occupies in his life-space?

(2) On the affective level: How does he feel about the group
and its attributes? What attracts him (positive valence) and what re-
pels him (negative valence)?

(3) On the behavioral level: To what extent does he adopt its
norms, that is, to what extent does the membership group serve also
as a source of reference? Is his self-definition as a Jew purely class-
ificatory, with possibly an affective element, or is it seen also to include obligations for action?

Perception of the Group's Attributes and Its Position in Life-Space

Religious and National Components. Of particular importance is the question of whether an individual perceives his Jewish
identity in its full compass as a blend of religious and national elements inextricably interwoven. A weakening in any one of these
components leads to a weakening in the Jewish identity as a whole.
Our studies of Israeli youth have demonstrated the extent to which
religious observance is a crucial variable in the Jewish identity. The
religiously observant students ranked highest on all criteria—not
only, as could be expected, in regard to the content of their Jewishness but in their relationship to Jews everywhere. American studies
have similarly indicated a stronger Jewish identity among the religiously observant. A secular Jewishness has severe limitations, and
durability across generations is questionable. There are limitations
also to a strictly religious Jewishness of a kind that endeavors to strip
Judaism of its national component and to see in it only a religious

creed analogous to Christianity. The components are so intertwined that they cannot be isolated without disturbing their essential character. Jews have indeed maintained through the centuries that there is an indissoluble connection between all the Jewish People, the Land of Israel and the Torah.

An individual's perception of the nature of the Jewish group will be reflected in his relationship to other Jews. Thus, the Jew who sees the group as a religious entity only is more likely to limit his interest to the local community, although he may also come to the aid of a "coreligionist" further afield as a philanthropic benefactor; the Jew who perceives the group as a religionational group will have a stronger involvement in the fate of his "fellow-Jews" everywhere.

Salience and Centrality. Centrality relates to the breadth or extent of influence. The fact of an individual's Jewishness may affect the main spheres of his life, or it may have only limited implications for him. Thus, in our study of Israeli students, 62 percent of the religious students reported that their being Jewish played "a very important part" in their lives, and another 36 percent, that it played an "important part," whereas the corresponding percentages for nonreligious students were 7 and 39.

Salience refers to prominence in the perceptual field, the figure against the ground, the extent to which an object or activity captures a person's attention at a given moment.

Certain behavior settings, such as the synagogue, will bring to the fore, that is, will enhance the salience of, the Jewish identity of the person in Israel or in the Diaspora. Again, the Jew in the Diaspora may be reminded of his Jewishness in a particular situation by an anti-Semitic remark or by another form of discrimination. The frequency of these reminders, over a wide variety of situations, contributes to the centrality of the Jewish identity. There is indeed a relationship between salience and centrality, although, at the same time, the difference between the two should be observed. "Salience is a short-term phenomenon, that is, a function of the immediate situation; centrality refers to a much more durable interest on the part of the individual, in certain kinds of objects, with these objects remaining important for him in many different, specific situations."[19]

19.   T.M. Newcomb, R. H. Turner and P. E. Converse, *Social Psychology*, New York, 1965, p. 59.

Valence of Jewishness

The extent to which an individual will be willing to adopt the norms of the Jewish group will depend in no small measure on the preferences and/or aversions he has for various facets of Jewish life. Many Jews, while accepting their Jewish belongingness and recognizing the religionational character of the group, may reject some religious custom or may be completely antireligious. At times the aversions are based on reflections of the Jews which an individual finds in a distorting Gentile mirror. Thus, he may be very sensitive about so-called Jewish characteristics which are attributed to the group. Severe tension results where the salience of Jewish membership is high but the valence negative.

When an individual rejects his Jewish group, it becomes, at times, a negative reference group; that is, an individual may demonstratively indicate severance of the connection by adopting norms contrary to those of the Jewish group, which then serves as a yardstick for what he should not be or should not do.

As a test of the valence of the Jewish group, the Israeli students were given the following question: "If you were to be born all over again, would you wish to be born a Jew?" The great majority replied in the affirmative—the religious students more so than the traditionalists, the traditionalists more so than the nonreligious. When they were given a further question—"If you were to live abroad, would you wish to be born a Jew?"—a majority of religious and traditionalist students still replied in the affirmative, but only a minority of nonreligious students did so. For many nonreligious students, the valence of being Jewish is predicated upon living in Israel, while for religious students it is positive under all conditions.

Adoption of Jewish Norms—A Question of Distinctiveness

In the majority Jewish society of Israel the Jewish group can more easily serve as a source of reference as well as membership. In the Diaspora the Jew is immersed in a majority culture where the norms may run counter to those of the Jewish group. And even when they do not conflict, the norms of the Jewish group lose their specific Jewish quality when they become submerged in the dominant culture. Writing about the image the Lakeville Jew has of what constitutes a "good Jew," Sklare et al. comment: ". . . The *mitzvot* he prized most were often identical with virtuous acts enjoined by the general American culture. In other words, though the Lakeville Jew borrowed the traits that made up his model of the good Jew from traditional Judaism, he borrowed so selectively that the model came out more standard American than Jewish."[20] Again, in reviewing the position among American ethnic groups, Glazer and Moynihan observe: "The cultural *content* of each ethnic group, in the United States, seems to have become very similar to that of others, but the emotional significance of attachment to the ethnic group seems to persist."[21]

It is precisely the content of their Jewishness which constitutes a problem for the third generation of American Jews, grandchildren of immigrants who came at the time of the mass migration from eastern Europe. There are indications that the third generation—unlike some of their second-generation parents—are not in revolt against their Jewishness. But while they may quite readily accept their Jewish affiliation, the content of this Jewishness has been considerably diluted. They look upon themselves as Jews, they are looked upon by others as such and their social contacts generally are mainly with Jews. Yet, "each new generation is in part the product of its inheritance,"[22] and the homes of their second-generation parents already had less Jewish content than those of their immigrant grandparents. The problem of this third generation, thus, is not so much one of identification with the Jewish group as of giving distinctiveness to their identity as Jews. As Tajfel has pointed out, "a social group will . . . be capable of preserving its contributions to those aspects of an individual's social identity which are positively valued by him only if it manages to keep its positively valued distinctiveness from other groups."[23]

The Jewish cultural environment in which some of the communities in eastern Europe once lived allowed for the development of an intensive Jewish identity. The American and other Diaspora milieux, in contrast, do not provide conditions for the sort of Jewish living conducive to the production of such identities. In the great

---

20. M. Sklare, J. Greenblum and B. B. Ringer, *Not Quite at Home*, American Jewish Committee Pamphlet Series, no. 11, New York, 1969, p. 47.
21. Glazer and Moynihan, p. 8.
22. Sklare and Greenblum, *Jewish Identity on the Suburban Frontier*, p. 331.
23. H. Tajfel, "Social Identity and Intergroup Behaviour," *Social Science Information*, vol. 13, no. 2, April 1974, p. 72.

centers of Jewish culture in Europe before the Holocaust an important expression of Jewish identity, and one which gave it distinctiveness, was a specific Jewish language, Yiddish. Today, the overwhelming majority of Jews in the Diaspora know only the language
of the country in which they dwell. Although Hebrew is firmly entrenched in Israel, it has not succeeded as yet in becoming the second language of Jews in the Diaspora.

Secularization has further contributed to erosion of Jewish
identity. The religiously observant Jew knows, and in the daily contacts of his life gives expression to, what sets him off from others in
the non-Jewish society in which he lives. The secular Jew, constantly exposed to the pervasive influences of the majority culture, becomes engulfed by these influences unless specific Jewish content is
introduced into his life. There is no ideology of assimilation in the
United States—as there was in Europe—but there is a process of Jewish cultural attrition from generation to generation. The situation
lends cogency to the contention of those who urge that only the
more intensive forms of Jewish education, supplemented by study-
visits to Israel, are likely to provide the distinctive content.

In Soviet Russia, where Jews are denied the possibility of even
the most elementary Jewish education, many Jews, as one of them
has observed, "have no choice but to see themselves through the
eyes of others. They have no resources of self-knowledge. They have
been deprived of their literature, their history and their art. Dispersed among the nations, they think in the categories accepted
among those nations."[24]

In Israel the overwhelming majority readily accept their
affiliation with the Jewish People. There are, however, significant
differences between the *dati'im* (religiously observant), the *mesora-
ti'im* (traditionalists) and the nonreligious in regard to the content
and scope of their Jewish identity. The following are typical statements expressing these differences:

> My entire way of life is determined by my Jewishness. It influences my
> way of thinking and conduct. I am a Jew all the time and cannot even
> imagine myself being anything else.
>
> (Religious student)

24. A. Voronel, "The Social Pre-conditions for the National Awakening of the Jews in
the U.S.S.R.," *I Am a Jew: Essays on Jewish Identity in the Soviet Union*, A. Voronel
and V. Yakhot, ed., New York, 1973, p. 31.

What is important is to feel oneself Jewish, to consider oneself part
and parcel of the people and to observe at least some of the Jewish customs which symbolize the special character of the Jewish People.

(Traditionalist)

I think very rarely about Jewish affairs, mainly only when something
happens to the Jews abroad and also at the time of the holydays.

(Nonreligious student)

We may now summarize our discussion on the content of Jewish identity by stating that an individual will have a Jewish identity
of greater *intensity* if (a) he perceives the Jewish group as being both
a national and a religious entity, and not just exclusively one or the
other; (b) the Jewish group occupies a position of centrality in his
life-space; (c) being Jewish has high positive valence; (d) the Jewish
group serves as a source of reference in significant spheres of his life;
(e) he acts—more particularly in the daily conduct of his life—in
accordance with those norms of the group that have a distinctive
Jewish stamp.

In the development of our framework, the further phase—into
which we shall not enter here—seeks to provide a systematic basis
for the analysis of the relationship between Jewish identity and the
national identity with which it is linked and with which it interacts.
The Jewish identity of an American Jew can only be understood in
the context of his Americanism just as the Jewishness of an Israeli
Jew has always to be seen in relation to the Israeliness with which it
is associated.

A comprehensive analysis, furthermore, has to view a Jewish
identity in historical perspective. Although elements of quintessen-
tial sameness characterize Jewish identity in different climes and periods, significant variations also appear around a constant core.
There are variations which flow from the peculiarities in the historical development of various communities, from the need to adjust to
changes in the Jewish situation in the non-Jewish world, and from
the impact of political and social movements, of both a Jewish and a
general character, on Jewish life.

In such an analysis, special attention has to be given to the
two events in the past three decades which so profoundly affected
Jewish identity—the Holocaust and the establishment of the State of
Israel.

Patterns of Contemporary Jewish Self-Identification (*Hizdahut*)

Aharon Lichtenstein

Comprehensive treatment of patterns of contemporary Jewish self-identification—or, to use the reflexive Hebrew term, *hizdahut*—must operate on two planes. There should first be a descriptive account of the manner in which, in current practice, Jews identify themselves. Second, inasmuch as behavioral patterns are obviously a function of one's interpretation of Jewishness, substantive and perhaps even prescriptive issues should be dealt with. By way of preface to my statement, however, I confess to a certain bias. While I do not intend to ignore the first aspect entirely, I do find myself driven by temperament, training and conviction to focus upon the second. I do this not only because I am more at home with ideological than sociological categories but because the analysis must be grounded upon awareness of the archetypal modes of *hizdahut*. From a traditional perspective, the constant element in Jewish identity far outweighs the contemporary, and this relation is, and should be, reflected in the processes and patterns of Jewish identification.

Substantively, *hizdahut* comprehends two distinct, if related, components. In one sense, it constitutes empathy and/or commitment. We identify with a person or a people by the vicarious sharing of experience; and we identify with a cause or a party insofar as we possess a sense of common purpose. Thus, *hizdahut yehudit*—Jewish self-identification—is understood as adherence to Jewish history and Jewish values: the existential sharing of past experience, present anxiety and hope for the future; the acceptance, both intellectual and emotional, of a complex of norms and ideals.

Hizdahut is inherently relational. It is perceived as a positive stance vis-à-vis a given reality. There is, however, a second sense in which we neither align nor affiliate, but rather become the focus of a self-contained process. As the reflexive form of the term suggests, it denotes, above all, self-definition—identification not *with* but *as*. At this level, we are much less concerned with our stance toward others than with expressing the reality of our own being. To the extent that being is conceived in social categories, the relational aspect is never wholly absent. The quest for identity may very well lead to finding one's milieu. Nevertheless, there is a vast difference between personal definition and empathetic alliance.

Modes of Identity

Hizdahut yehudit encompasses both aspects; and both are enjoined and/or reinforced by specific Rabbinic sanctions. The need for empathy is stressed in a Talmudic passage in which insensitivity to suffering is equated with *carpe diem* hedonism. The Rabbis taught, the Talmud declares in *Ta'anit*:

> When the community is in distress one should not say, I will go home, eat and drink, and peace will be upon my soul. And if he does so, Scripture says of him (Is. 22:13): "And behold joy and gladness, slaying oxen and killing sheep, eating flesh and drinking wine—'let us eat and drink, for to-morrow we shall die.'" Now, what are the words that follow this verse? "And the Lord of Hosts revealed Himself in mine ears. Surely this iniquity shall not be expiated by you till ye die." One should therefore afflict himself with the community, for thus we find that Moses afflicted himself out of sympathy with the community, as it is said (Ex. 17:12): "But Moses's hands were heavy and they took a stone and put it under him, and he sat thereon." Now, did not Moses have a cushion or a pillow to sit upon? But Moses said to himself, as Israel is in trouble I will also share it with them.[1]

Such empathy is simply an aspect of fundamental humanity; but to the extent that it is universal in character, it is devoid of any identifying force. In this case, however, as the allusion to Moses makes clear, there is a sensitivity to specifically Jewish suffering. This sensitivity, in turn, simply exemplifies, within a Jewish setting, a natural and universal element—affinity for our sociocultural and ethnic confreres. In part, however, it includes a particularly Jewish component. It is grounded in the sense of mutual responsibility mandated by a common covenantal commitment, thus constituting the positive root of that "double ethic" with which, not altogether without justice, Max Weber and others have charged us. The *halakhic*

---

1. *Babylonian Talmud, Ta' anit 11a*, Henry Malter, tr., Philadelphia, 1928, pp. 74–75.

implications of this bond were formulated by the Rabbis in strictly legalistic terms: *Kol Israel arevim zeh bazeh* (All Jews are guarantors for each other).[2] However, beyond the liability of each Jew for the physical and spiritual welfare of every other Jew lies the dimension of love—that which, as Denis de Rougemont once observed, results not from two people contemplating each other, but rather from looking together at a common object.

Sinai produced no social contract. The *Gemeinschaft* which in one sense constituted its basis, and in another its issue, derived, not from reciprocal fealty, but from the reality of the gestation of "a kingdom of priests and a holy nation" with whose members and aspirations we could identify and to whom we could belong.

The kinship implicit in common commitment goes far beyond affiliation. It is in the nature of a brother's concern rather than a stranger's sympathy. Empathy is more the result of felt identity than an alternative to it or to its dialectical pole. From this perspective, both types of *hizdahut* are clearly related; and yet, in at least one important respect, they are fundamentally different. Empathy is essentially expansive. It projects an individual from the confines of his own being into the human reality beyond; and, through a process of imaginative transference—that existence as "the Proteus of human intellect" which Hazlitt so admired in Shakespeare—enables the individual to identify with the joys and sorrows of his fellows. Self-definition, by contrast, is inherently confining. As the term indicates, definition places bounds upon the individual, since he attains one identity at the cost of dissociation from others. At this level, *hizzdahut* requires choice between mutually exclusive options.

Singular and Unique

The significance of this element is reinforced, for our purpose, by a specifically Jewish factor. Judaism's blending of universalism and particularism has always included a strong element of separatism and even exclusiveness. As both adherents and critics have noted, the concept of a *goy kadosh*—a holy and therefore different nation—or of "distincton between Israel and the nations" has been central to Jewish thought and life from the very beginning. The sense of being not only singular but unique has lent Jewish national

2. *Babylonian Talmud, Shevuot 39a.*

consciousness a special dimension. "And who is like your People, Israel, a single nation upon earth?" the Jew asks God rhetorically in his Sabbath-afternoon prayer; and the implicit reply helps mold his self-definition.

The modes of self-identification as well as their substance are clearly determined by individual perception of the content and meaning of Jewish identity. What does it mean, personally and collectively, to be a Jew? Is Jewishness an axiological or a sociopolitical category? Is its primary axis normative or cultural? Does it impose spiritual demands or merely provide a historical locus? Must it be religious or can it be secular in character? The answers to these questions will determine the nature of one's *hizdahut*.

From my own *halakhic* perspective, the answers may seem fairly obvious; and yet we should beware of oversimplification. Ideally, Jewish existence is inextricably rooted in religious commitment. Nevertheless, the possibility of fragmentary Jewishness cannot be dismissed. The *Halakhah* has allowed for it—declaring that the secular Jew is "like a Gentile" for some purposes, while "a Jew, although he has sinned, remains a Jew."[3] The traditional Jew may be tempted to limit Jewish self-definition to spiritual commitment while relegating national *hizdahut* to empathy. However, such a view, comfortable as it may sometimes be, is simplistic. It is wrong logically, because nationality is no less defining than religion; and it is wrong morally and *halakhically*, because it understates and undercuts the bonds which link the secular and even the assimilated Jew to his fellows, and vice versa. Notwithstanding the profound importance of ideological considerations, there is a point beyond which they should not be pressed. On the basis of pure ideology, I should feel much closer to Gilson than to Weizmann. Do I? Only the grossest misinterpretation of Jewish identity could lead to greater existential kinship with a Damascus *qadi* than with a Mapam *kibbutznik*.[4]

We should also beware of a second error—the facile assumption that, while empathy need not entail self-definition, the latter

---

3. *Babylonian Talmud, Sanhedrin 44a.* I have treated some of the *halakhic* ramifications of this question in "Brother Daniel and the Jewish Fraternity," *Judaism*, vol. xii, 1963, pp. 260–280.

4. This point—the balance between spiritual affinity and physical kinship (in the broadest sense of the term)—is bound up with one's perception and definition of Jewish identity and obviously requires fuller elaboration. Here I confine myself to rejecting the total domination of pure ideology.

does include the former. This is not necessarily the case: a Jew may be conscious of his Jewishness and yet reject his patrimony. However, we should not dismiss this level of identification entirely. While full *hizdahut* embraces acceptance as well as awareness, even self-hatred reflects a sense—at times both profound and perverse—of one's roots. Blasphemy, Eliot often contended, is more religious than indifference.

Public Dimension

While identification is clearly a function of identity, the two are nevertheless distinct. The latter relates to essence and existence, the former to experience and expression. This distinction is relevant even to a discussion of the individual Jew *tout seul*. Primarily, however, it is reflected in his relation to others. While *hizdahut* may be a purely personal phenomenon, it generally includes, both consciously and unconsciously, a public dimension too. Empathy and self-definition are communicated as well as felt. Moreover, the process of communication is dynamic, and the inner reality is modified by its expression.

This public identification is itself dual. In some respects it may be largely or even wholly involuntary—the inevitable result of simply living and being observed and classified by others. Within a Jewish context, visible *hizdahut* is also a matter of conscious choice; and, as such, it is, like empathy, *halakhically* mandated: "Neither shall ye walk in their [the Egyptians' and the Canaanites'] statutes." This is elaborated by the Rabbis and codified by Maimonides:

> We should not follow the customs of the Gentiles, nor imitate them in dress or in their way of trimming the hair, as it is said, "And you shall not walk in the customs of the nation which I have cast out before you" (Lev. 20:23); "Neither shall you walk in their statutes" (*ibid.* 18:3); "Take heed to yourself that you be not ensnared to follow them" (Deut. 12:30). These texts all refer to one theme and warn against imitating them. The Israelite shall, on the contrary, be distinguished from them and be recognizable by the way he dresses and in his other activities, just as he is distinguished from them by his knowledge and his principles. And thus it is said, "And I have set you apart from the peoples" (Lev. 20:26).[5]

5. Maimonides, *Mishneh Torah, Hilchot Avodat Kochavim,* 11:1; translation in *A Maimonides Reader,* Isadore Twersky, ed., New York, 1972, pp. 74–75.

Put in these terms, the demand that one not only *be* but *appear* a Jew is largely inner-directed, as it serves to deepen personal identity. However, differentiation clearly has centrifugal significance. As an overt assertion of Jewish existence, it confronts the world with an implicit declaration of Jewish values and Jewish destiny. It reaffirms, publicly, the Jew's commitment to the God of Israel.

Patterns of Identification

Specific patterns of *hizdahut yehudit* may be divided into two broad categories—one consisting of fairly direct and even pragmatic activity, the other of predominantly symbolic elements, both cutting across the line between empathy and self-definition. Practical action ranges from support of Jewish causes through adherence and affiliation, to commitment to Jewish culture and full *halakhic* living. Support may be moral or financial, political as well as philanthropic. Overt affiliation translates itself into membership in a *kehillah,* a synagogue, or any other communal or fraternal organization—with widely divergent degrees of involvement. Finally, in a more private sphere, a sense of Jewishness finds expression in day-to-day personal behavior. Minimally, this entails marriage within the fold; maximally, the discipline of a comprehensive and intensive regimen of *mitzvot,* some of which, as the Torah tells us, posit the sharpening of Jewish identity as their immediate rationale, but all of which collectively advance this aim in an ancillary way.

As for identification through symbolic elements, there were three which, according to a *midrash,* distinguished the children of Israel in Egypt: name, language, dress. Naturally, these elements differ in character. Nomenclature generally belongs to that group of relatively superficial and accidental (in the scholastic sense) badges which set apart a given referent. Language, by contrast, as both the repository of past experience and the vehicle of present expression, is a symbolic order, organically related to the collective reality it signifies. Dress—which, for our purposes includes personal appearance—straddles the two. Nevertheless, each in its own way is a principal instrument of identification, its significance depending upon the degree of choice involved in its use. The halting Hebrew spoken by a Russian activist may reveal far more Jewish consciousness than fluent Hebrew prattled by an Israeli youngster.

Sociopolitical Impact

Thus far I have made minimal reference to particular contexts, preferring to focus upon constant elements. It now remains to discuss contemporary facets of our subject. The situation today is, for better or worse, significantly different from that which obtained for almost two millennia. The causes of this change are of two types. Some are attributable to the general course of modern history, and thus, as regards European or American Jewry, date back a century or two; others are the outgrowth of more strictly contemporary developments. The major changes in the fabric of Ashkenazi society, wrought by the transition from the medieval to the modern world, are too familiar to require recounting.[6] Here we need only note that the impact has been dual.

First, the overall level of Jewish identification has receded, because of the interaction of two related factors. On the one hand, the secularizing influence of modern culture has attenuated the scope and intensity of *hizdahut yehudit;* on the other, this ideological erosion has coincided with sociopolitical changes which, for the first time in centuries, have made integration into the broader Gentile world a very live and increasingly attractive option. During the last decade, the erosion of Jewish identification has been reflected in an alarming increase in intermarriage. But this is simply the logical culmination of a process which has dulled both the Jew's sense of his own uniqueness and the Gentile's reluctance to forge bonds with him.

Second, the impact of the Emancipation and the *Haskalah* has resulted in greater emphasis upon national, as opposed to religious, modes of identification. This was not true of the early champions of Jewish *Aufklärung;* Mendelssohn and his ideological progeny could have thought of nothing worse. However, nineteenth, and early twentieth-century Jewish society, especially in Eastern Europe, increasingly regarded language, culture and political aspiration as the focus of both the substance and mode of Jewish identification. This shift, too, has helped make intermarriage more acceptable and feasible. If religious, especially traditional, thought spoke of Jewish

---

6. With respect to large segments of Sephardic Jewry, the transition from quasi-medieval to modern culture has coincided with more strictly contemporary developments.

uniqueness and reciprocal covenantal commitment, secular nationalistic ideology could only tell the Jew that he belonged to one nation *inter alia*. Small wonder that so many have found ethnicity no obstacle to intermarriage.

The Zionist Impact

Emphasis upon nationality has found its most prominent expression in Zionism; and this brings us to more specifically contemporary aspects of *hizdahut yehudit*. The two major events which have stamped Jewish life in this generation—the Holocaust and the rise of the State of Israel—have molded patterns of Jewish identification. While the impact of the former has been more traumatic, the impact of the latter has certainly been broader. The existence of the State has affected Jewish identification both within and without Israel. At one level, it has restored identities, such as citizenship and soldiering, which had dropped out of Jewish history for two millennia. Concurrently, the resumption of political life has sharpened the need for renewed definition of the relation between material and spiritual elements within Judaism. At another level, Israel has become the focus of Diaspora Jewry's commitment to Jewish history. It has restored pride and generated anxiety. It has helped Jews relate to the past and reach for the future. For many, it has become the primary medium through which they can identify as Jews.

In practical terms, the sense of identification aroused by the State has found its primary outlet in a remarkable display of philanthropy. But the ethnic consciousness generated by the disproportionate prominence of the State on the international scene has been reflected in other ways, too. The increased use of Hebrew names in the West—almost unheard of in the thirties—is one manifestation. The quasi-Messianic hopes entertained by segments of Russian Jewry are another—if at quite a different level.

Nevertheless, the impact of the State should not be exaggerated. For one thing, with regard to most Jews, it has generated more empathy than self-definition, although, in practice, the two are related. Charity, as either *caritas* or philanthropy, is less demanding, above all less committing, than self-definition. It allows for a wide latitude of multiple loyalty. Second, in terms of Jewish identification, Zionism, along with the rise of the State of Israel, has had negative as well as positive results. It has enhanced the affinity of those who might otherwise have become wholly estranged; but by making possible and even encouraging the substitution of national for religious categories, it has diluted the content of Jewish identification for others.

On the collective plane, it has done even more. The gospel of "normal" national existence, that age-old dream which Ezekiel confronted—"We will be as the nations, as the families of the countries,"—often called, in effect, for collective assimilation and Jewish identification was accordingly impaired. As it happened, the pressure of history has outrun ideology, and the Yishuv has had to rediscover the reality of Jewish loneliness and even uniqueness. Nevertheless, the danger of assimilation *en bloc* remains very real.

The rise of the State has affected Jewish identification in yet another way. The very normalization of social and cultural life has emasculated the identifying force of certain elements. Language, for instance, once figured prominently as an aspect of *hizdahut.* It need not today. Can a Tel-Aviv student appreciate the value of Hebrew in tzarist Odessa? As visions have faded into the light of common day, and as they have often been less consciously sought, their symbolic potency has been reduced.

The Holocaust Experience

The second major experience, the Holocaust, has affected the Jewish identification of those within and without its range. Though the sensibilities of the former have been dulled by time, the searing effect of the torment has molded their Jewish identity and subsequent identification. For some, driven both to defy seemingly elemental forces and to ally themselves with "the powers above," the agony sharpened and deepened *hizdahut yehudit.* Many either rebelled or were left listless. In some degree, however, virtually all wrestled—none remaining unaffected.

For others, fortunate enough to have been spared the horrors of the Holocaust, the impact upon Jewish identification has been qualitatively weaker; but in their case, too, conflicting results have been produced. Some, overcome by skepticism and despair, have become totally disaffected. Many have reacted by identifying more fully. For those whose response to the Holocaust has been peripheral, the change has been limited—frequently confined to sympathy with suffering confreres but largely devoid of keener self-definition. But

Jews who have been more deeply involved intellectually and emotionally have responded in terms of the latter as well. The very scope
of the destruction has stiffened resolve to persist and strengthened
Jewish consciousness. Resolve has, in turn, produced a measure of
activism. Theoretically, it is formulated in Emil Fackenheim's
"614th commandment" not to give Hitler another victory. Practical-
ly, it is reflected in expressions ranging from the Jewish Defense
League's "Never Again" to aspects of Israeli foreign policy. It has,
above all, brought home the need to assert Jewish existence more
visibly and forcefully. In the wake of the Holocaust, many have
found J.L. Gordon's counsel, "Be a man when you go out and a Jew
in your home," totally unacceptable. The victory over Hitler and
those whose silence abetted him requires that one not only be Jewish
but be overtly Jewish.

The acceptance of this lesson, learned with such frightful
pain, is the legacy of the Holocaust. It may well have been reinforced
by the development of the State of Israel. For the individual, a low
Jewish profile may be feasible and, from a practical standpoint, often
advisable. For a State, especially one with such a sensitive relation
both to the international community and to Diaspora Jewry, such a
stance hardly seems possible. To the extent that it draws sustenance
from Jews in whom it strengthens Jewish identification, the State
must recognize and, overtly or indirectly, declare its Jewishness; and
to the extent that its political claims are rooted in Jewish history
and Jewish destiny, it is driven to identify with them actively. In this sense, the specifically contemporary aspects of Jewish
existence coalesce with the constant elements within it in the persistent quest for new and yet very old patterns of *hizdahut yehudit.*

Discussion

MICHAEL A. MEYER

Jewish identity is based in part on identification with the Jewish past. Such identification, however, is very different for Israeli and Diaspora Jews. For Israelis those periods of the Jewish past in which a significant portion of the people dwelt in its Land are the primary historical constituents of identity. Diaspora Jewish history is understood by many Israelis as essentially negative, composed either of suffering and passivity or, in the modern West, of rampant assimilation. In this view, the Holocaust and the high rate of mixed marriage represent complementary aspects of what was always potential in Diaspora Jewish existence. Those who resisted in the Warsaw Ghetto and elsewhere constituted an anomaly in the Diaspora and are to be linked more closely to the type of the Israeli than to that of the Diaspora Jew; those who currently resist assimilation are able to do so largely because of the existence of the State of Israel.

For Diaspora Jews, in contrast, the same periods of the Jewish past which fail to induce identification by Israeli Jews or even induce negative reactions contribute significantly to the historical basis of their Jewishness. Those times when Jews enjoyed a relatively secure physical existence and a creative spiritual life while living within a non-Jewish environment—whether in Babylonia, the Golden Age of Spain, or certain periods of nineteenth or twentieth century Europe and America—serve as the model for a Diaspora Jewish identity. The Diaspora Jew's subjective identity presumes his belief in the viability of Jewish life within a non-Jewish context despite the erosive forces of assimilation.

With regard to mutual identification in the present between Israeli and Diaspora Jews, it is important to stress that the degree of such identification is far from constant. For Diaspora Jews it rises to great prominence in periods of crisis, such as May 1967 or in the first hours of the Yom Kippur War, when another Holocaust seemed to threaten a portion of the Jewish People. But it recedes when the crisis is past. Likewise, Israeli Jews stretch their Jewish identification beyond the borders of the State most readily and fully when, in a period of stress and isolation, Diaspora Jewry seems to be their only source of wholehearted support. But here, too, the passage of time after the crisis seems to bring with it a drift in the opposite direction, toward a basic affirmation of Israeli identity with only a secondary attachment to the totality of the Jewish People. Perhaps this divergence was most evident in the period shortly before the Yom Kippur War when Israeli self-assurance contrasted most starkly with the self-questioning that has remained a characteristic of many Diaspora Jews even in periods of relative freedom from anti-Semitic pressures.

It is difficult, as yet, to judge the effects of the Yom Kippur War on Jewish identity. On the one hand, it brought Diaspora Jewish identification with Israel once again to a high point, and the *heshbon ha-nefesh,* the self-examination, which followed it shifted the Israeli moral temper away from a direction that had threatened to alienate it as far as Diaspora moral sensitivities were concerned. But the Yom Kippur War, like the wars which preceded it, was basically an event in Israeli history. Diaspora Jews played only a peripheral role. As the State of Israel's history lengthens, the identity-forming experiences which are primarily Israeli in character will necessarily increase for Israelis, while those which belong more directly to Jews in Europe and America as well as in Israel will recede.

It seems necessary for those interested in strengthening identification with the Jewish People to base that identification upon the realization that Diaspora and Israeli forms of expressing Jewish identity will necessarily differ both with regard to evaluation of the past and the significance of the present. It will serve little purpose to make Diaspora Jewish identity conform as closely as possible to Israeli identity. Israeli Jews and Diaspora Jews should be allowed to draw their identifications selectively in accordance with their own situation. However, each group draws from a common totality of past and present Jewish experience, and this totatlity is the shared heritage of the whole Jewish People.

Jewish messianism, which remains the preeminent distinction of the Jews, and which has its specific applications both in Israel and in the Diaspora, can serve as the spiritual basis for a unity of purpose extending beyond the crises that bring Jews together. Understood in terms of both national and universal elements yet to be realized, and understood as requiring a perpetual struggle against mere normality in the one case and against submission to assimilation in the other, it can assume a position of primary significance in the transmission of a comprehensive Jewish identity.

AVRAHAM SCHENKER

In the Jewish context, we tend to view cosmopolitan tendencies primarily as a phenomenon of leftist or radical movements. Yet from relatively early in its development, the Marxist model was confronted with the contradiction between the cosmopolitan and universalist objectives of its ideology and the national dimension in the countries in which it developed. In fact, post-World War II resurgence of national aspirations, especially as reflected in the so-called Third World, has sharpened this contradiction.

Yet, it would be erroneous to view this as a radical or leftist phenomenon only. The Western liberal model, under which the largest proportion of Jews live in our day, is no less faced by a similar contradiction. The liberal ideology with its focus on the individual's rights, initiatives and opportunities, has evolved its own cosmopolitanism.

The very concentration of Jews in the United States and in the Soviet Union has exposed them to the pressures and demands of life in the superpower society, not only in the political and economic spheres, but in the social and cultural domains as well. Both superpowers have, in distinctly different and opposing patterns, proclaimed pluralistic objectives with regard to minority (in the case of the United States) or national (in the case of the Soviet Union) groupings. Yet both have set limitations, overt or assumed, on the full development of minority cultures.

In the medium-sized countries in which there are smaller, yet substantial, Jewish communities, the national majority society finds itself in a constant struggle, especially in the cultural sphere, against the inroads of Americanization or Russification (depending on the sphere of influence). The aggressive nationalism which characterizes this defensive struggle leaves little room for minority cultural development or creativity. In the large number of countries where smaller or tiny Jewish communities reside, the minority cultural pattern is doomed.

The problem is general in nature and applies to all minority groups, but it is particularly true in the Jewish case, which, based on a combined and unique religio-cultural identity, comes into conflict with the national-cultural struggles of the surrounding society.

In the historical-sociological sense, there have been three basic factors in evolving Jewish self-identity: religion, community and family. Each provided an anchor and a mainstay for self-definition, even for those who were non-observant, or on the fringes of the organized community framework. All three factors are weaker today than they were a generation ago. They are weaker in society generally and this inevitably has an effect upon the Jewish community.

The rise and existence of the State of Israel has not only been a political solution to the "Jewish Problem"; Israel has gradually become a hinge and a substitute for each of these factors in determining self-identity for increasingly large numbers of Jews. In the affirmative sense, it has become an indispensible ingredient of Jewish existence everywhere. It may be noted that the process even operates in the negative sense, when the rejection of Israel, its centrality and its polity, paradoxically becomes a factor of self-identity to some.

Finally, a comment on the balance between the religious and the national in terms of Jewish identity. Zionism, particularly in its post-State metamorphosis, has led to two simultaneous processes. One is secularization in Jewish life, particularly in its political aspects and involvement. The other is the traditionalizing of secularism in Jewish life. It may be said that without the Zionist context, it can no longer be assumed that secular Judaism (or Jewishness, if you will) leads to assimilation.

In trying to come to grips with the modern world, the Orthodox Jew, in the traditional historical sense, has secularized his religion in order to find his place and exert his influence. The secular Jew, for his part, in attempting to find and maintain his identity, began a process of traditionalizing his secularism. Both processes have been profoundly affected by Zionism as an ideology and Israel as a Zionist state. In terms of the close relationship between the existence of the State of Israel and the evolution of Jewish identity in our time, these processes will surely affect the nature of Jewish continuity and existence in the future.

DAVID SIDORSKY

The rise of the modern nation-state limited the public role of religion and greatly expanded the domain of secular culture. Since that domain was neutral as regards religion, the growth of Jewish involvement in modern society followed: there was a movement for Jewish enlightenment and an increase in the potential for cultural assimilation. In consequence, in the nineteenth century, both poles of Jewish identity—the ethnic and the religious—were probed for new formulations of historic Judaism.

The probe of the ethnic dimension of Judaism led to movements that interpreted or transformed historic Jewish identity into a form of national self-consciousness, in which religion was viewed as a secondary, or even distorting, imposition. This tendency was exemplified in secular Zionism, in Dispora nationalism and in Yiddishist socialism.

A probe of the exclusively religious dimension of Judaism led to the classical Reform movement that interpreted or transformed historic Jewish identity into a form of prophetic ethical culture. It expressed a tendency within Jewish religious life to assert moral universalism, and to erode or transcend ethnicity.

This polarization of integral components of historic Judaism reflected the breakdown of integral nineteenth-century Jewish religious folk culture. The most obvious symptom of that breakdown, in my view, is the revolt against the Ghetto which motivates both much of Hebraic and Zionist literature, as well as the passion for moral universalism which found expression in Jewish socialism and religious reform in the nineteenth century. It is the heritage of these movements that has confronted Israelis with the need to reexamine their religious identity, although the possibility of an Israeli secular Jewishness remains. The failure of Socialism has forced some Soviet Jews to rediscover both the national and religious roots of their Jewish identity.

For the American Jewish community, this nineteenth-century experience can be symbolically understood as a kind of "trauma of ghettoization." With greater or lesser degrees of intensity, the record of Jewish adjustment to America is also a record of the effort to overcome the stigma of ghettoization, through the abandonment of Yiddish, the erosion of distinctive Jewish styles and the transcendence of ethnicity in liberal and universalistic social action. I believe this trend survives as the powerful motivation for assimilation within the American Jewish community.

In the postwar period, as a result of both the emergence of the State of Israel and of the abiding memory of the destruction of European Jewry, there have been countervailing trends within the Jewish community in America. The effort to transcend ethnicity has been checked for many by identification with, and concern for, Israel. The dramatic evidence for that has been the complete reversal of Reform Judaism on ritual, the Hebrew language and the State of Israel. Yet the resurgence of ethnicity has not involved a rejection of the religious aspects of Jewish identity. In a significant sense, the American Jewish community accepts the norm of a depolarized Judaism that combines both ethnic and religious components.

For many critics of the American Jewish community the acceptance of this norm seems to be contradicted by a lack of intensity or commitment to the norm by the majority of the community. Their criticism seems to be that the acceptance of such a norm commits

one to the intensification or maximalization of the values included
in the norm. Yet this, apparently, does not seem to follow. I believe
that most American Jews wish to assert Jewish religious values and
practices but do not wish to be particularly observant. They also
wish to support Jewish peoplehood and Israel, but are not willing to
commit themselves to immigrate to Israel.

From the critics' perspective, there is a contradiction between
their value assertions and their practices. At a symposium involving
both American Jews and Israelis there should be an attempt to understand that from the American Jewish perspective such criticism
seems unwarranted. Many American Jews seek to be faithful to a reasonable norm of Judaism: they seek to avoid both the "deficiency"
characterized by apathy, or by alienation from the Jewish heritage, as
well as an "excess" of extremely religious or Zionist passion. Excess
or deficiency would interfere with the goals and life styles preferred
by most American Jews.

MORDECAI WAXMAN

That American Jews almost entirely affirm their Jewish identity today reflects a significant historical change. In the 1930s and the
1940s there were many Jews who privately resented Jewish identity
and publicly denied it. It would have been reasonable to assume that
as a third and fourth generation of American Jews came upon the
scene, the sense of Jewish identity would have grown weaker and
weaker. Instead it has been strengthened.

Paradoxically, one of the major problems of American life—
intermarriage—proves the point. It is estimated that in the last few
years about 30 percent of American Jews have intermarried. In the
past, children of intermarriages were almost inevitably lost to the
Jewish People. In intermarriage today the conversion is by the non-
Jewish partners—virtually no Jews are today converting. Moreover,
even where there is no conversion by the non-Jewish partner, there
is often an intention to rear the children as Jews. The Jewish partner,
while usually denying religiosity, almost invariably insists that he
or she has no intention of giving up Jewish identity.

This almost universal affirmation of Jewish identity stems
from the general acceptance of ethnicity in America, the impact of
the Holocaust, the existence of the State of Israel, the remarkable
achievement of American Jews in entering into the heart of American cultural, political and economic life, and the idea that Judaism is
one of the three religions of America and that western civilization
reflects a Judeo-Christian outlook.

With regard to the meaning of Jewish identity in America now, three related questions arise. First, is the sense of Jewish identity sufficient to guarantee Jewish continuity and survival? The answer, at this juncture, must be—no. The obvious test is whether the sense of Jewish identity is strong enough to prevent intermarriage, that is, to induce younger Jews to sacrifice personal desires to ensure the survival of the Jewish People.

A second major question is whether the sense of identity is sufficient to induce Jewish behavior on a reasonably consistent basis. Here, again, the answer seems to be—no. The view of Judaism as a body of moral imperatives is widely held but little honored, even among nominally observant Jews, although the most frequent cliché heard in Jewish circles, designed to excuse violation of the practical observances, is that to be a Jew means to be a good person.

The third scale in which American Jewish identity must be weighed is that of content. By what myth (in its positive sense) are Jews going to live and what myth is going to form the substance of Jewish education in order to transform Jewish identity into true obligation?

The years since the end of World War II have been largely devoted throughout the Jewish world to a survivalist response to the Holocaust so that the questions of the meaning and content of survival have been ignored even within most of the Jewish religious institutions and schools of America. But now the myth of Yavneh and the basic Jewish myth of *ki vanu vachartah* (Chosen People) cannot really be evaded. They constitute a basis for translating identity into obligation and identification, and they must be formulated in a manner to which the majority of American Jews can relate.

Jewish identification is the translation of identity into patterns of behavior or into formal affiliation with the community and an acceptance of, at least, some collective goals. The plethora of Jewish organizations in America has made possible many forms of affiliation, so that the average affiliated American Jew is likely to be a member of several complementary, mutually reinforcing, organizations. However, that type of formal affiliation embraces perhaps 60 percent of American Jews. A more informal type of affiliation embraces many of the rest, including the tendency of Jews to congregate in neighborhoods and to mingle socially with other Jews.

What is needed is promulgation of a view of the Jewish community as a far-flung polis which is in essence a religio-cultural-national entity within American society. It would have been absurd to speak in these terms not long ago, and indeed, even Zionism never took this position in America. But in an America which is in a post–melting pot phase, with Black and Latin American groups having shown the way, it is no longer unthinkable.

Our problem is to develop a model, based on the American situation in combination with the Jewish tradition, of how a Jew should comport himself both morally and in terms of observance. It may be that the most important task of the next few decades is to develop a distinctive American Jewish style, which must inevitably have a religious base.

A third necessary element for a coherent community is common cultural recognition and shared elements of culture, whether it be songs or readily recognized phrases or cultural heroes. This is an area in which we have not yet used the resources or zeal of the Jewish community.

A further major element which must be recognized today in discussing American Jewish identity is that Israel and American Jewry represent the two primary elements in Jewish existence. American Jewry is an accident of history. But Israel is a cause into which world Jewry has put its dreams. Israel's sheer existence does strengthen American Jewish identity and identification today. But if we think in long-range terms, Israel can bolster Jewish identity in America only if it is a success. And that success will be measured by American Jews, who are citizens of a great power, less in political and military terms, vital as they are, than in moral, religious, cultural and societal terms.

In sum, if Jewish identity is to become significant identification, we need a new conception of the American Jewish community in which in-group language, style, common cultural ties and political activity buttress one another.

ABRAHAM J. KARP

By the end of the nineteenth and beginning of the twentieth century, it became apparent that, while a purely religious definition of Judaism might be acceptable to America, it could not serve Jewish survival needs. It deprived Judaism of its cultural-national vitality and made no provision for the growing number of Jews who defined their Jewish identity in terms other than religious.

Those who now proposed a redefinition argued that it should be based not on American models but on the Jewish historic tradition. Thus they sowed the seeds for an inner-directed definition of the Jewish communal identity which came to fruition a half century later.

Intellectual leaders could plead that American Jewry define its status and structure its community in response to inner cultural needs but the immigrant Jew and his children panted for acceptance in the American melting-pot.

In American Jewish life, the era of cultural pluralism between World Wars I and II saw a flowering of Hebrew and Yiddish culture, an expansion of artistic creativity, and a reconstitution of the synagogue from a churchlike house of worship to a cultural and social as well as religious synagogue center.

A "religious revival" marked American life in the decades following World War II. For the third-generation American Jew acculturation, which once was an assimilatory force, became spur for the retention of identity—identity no longer as a member of an ethnic group but again as part of a religious community. Sociologists have described postwar America as a society of "ethnic assimilation but religious differentiation."

American Jewry, seen as a religious community, was lifted out of the constellation of ethnic minorities to the status of one-third of the nation. Symbols of this new status abounded. A minister, a priest and a rabbi sat on the dais at every civic function, including the inauguration of a President; radio and television apportioned time equally to each of the three faiths.

However, the posture of a religious community did not reflect a true religious revival. It was more an expression of organization and form than a way of life or commitment.

American Jewry allowed itself to be designated a *religious community*, at the same time holding on to its own self-identification as a *People*. The establishment of the State of Israel, and the ready identification of American Jewry with its destiny, symbolize an identity beyond that of a "faith" group.

What had developed was a *dual image identity*, fashioned by the folk wisdom of the people. In simple words it says: Before the world we retain the identity of a *religious community*. Internally, in our understanding of ourselves, in assessing our needs, in ordering our priorities, we are a People possessed of our own unique *civilization*.

The central problem of Jewish identity in contemporary America is maintaining an identity distinctive enough to be capable of transmission to the next generation and sufficiently rich in content to win its acceptance and loyalty. The sardonic observation has been made that the children of the immigrants wanted to be like Gentiles, without becoming Gentiles, while the grandchildren of the immigrants want to be like Jews, without becoming real Jews.

ALEXANDER GOLDFARB

Jewish identity is the only alternative to Soviet Communism which intellectual and young Jews in Russia have been able to find during the last thirty years. The reasons for this phenomenon grow out of contemporary Russian history. After the war, and especially in the 1950s and 1960s, there was a rise of nationalism generally in Russia, and now national groups are the only reference in the search for identity. The reason is that before World War II, the basic national myth in Russia was the proletarian Marxist ideology, and the new generation of Jews, who grew up after the Revolution, believed only in this. They forgot their religion and their national heritage, and considered themselves orthodox Marxists.

When Khrushchev denounced the crimes of Stalin, this produced a shock among intellectuals, who became disillusioned with Communist ideology. The search for a new identity started, but Soviet intellectuals could find no ideology and no groups with which to associate. There were no religious groups, political parties or unions. Accordingly, everyone started to look for his own national heritage.

With Jews, this has posed a special problem. They belong with Jews because the word "Jewish" is stamped on their identity cards. But they cannot find their way to Jewishness because there are no Jewish schools, no associations and no Jewish family background. The only distinctive factor is Israel. Now in Russia if you start to do or study anything about Israel, you immediately turn yourself into a political criminal—not because Israel is a foreign country, and not because Israel is involved in a major political crisis in the world, but because Israel is a free country. Hence, everyone who tries to associate himself with Israel is immediately seen as representing a political challenge to Russian society.

Thus it is the search for Jewish identity that leads to the decision to emigrate.

ERNEST STOCK

The quest for identity is one of three ideological ingredients of secular Zionism, the other two being the quest for community and the quest for legitimacy.

During the pre-State period in Palestine, the problem of Jewish identity was secondary, because the Yishuv was a functional Jewish community, which was sharply differentiated. You had Jews, Arabs and the British, and there was no question about who the Jews were.

The problem arose with the creation of the State of Israel. In the first place it was a semantic problem, because we called the State Israel. If we had called the State Judea, as some people proposed at the time, we would all be *Yehudim* today, and our identity would be uniform, but I think the decision was good. We have to differentiate between Israeli identity and Jewish identity because the dynamics are different.

We are searching for a collective Israeli identity to replace the collective Jewish identity which was integral until the end of the Mandate. Now we must distinguish not only between Israelis and Jews, but between Israelis and Israelis, namely, between Israeli Jews and Israeli Arabs.

We further complicate the problem by a strictly legal perspective on the question, "Who is a Jew." The whole question of identity is a matter of the spirit, not of legal definition.

Zionism has solved the problem of Jewish identity on an individual level. In addition to their Israeli identity, secular Jews preserve their Jewish identity in a special way, although the latter is becoming more recessed. On the other hand, among religious Jews in Israel the Jewish identity remains dominant, and Israeli identity for the time being is in recess.

MORDECHAI BAR-ON

We speak a great deal of "identity" and "identification" but these designations themselves reflect a problem. We must see "identity" as an *objective* description of a condition which is mainly spiritual, but partly physical, whereas "identification" is the *subjective* description of the same condition. "Identification" is what a man thinks about his very nature, whereas "identity" is his nature in reality, and the two are not necessarily connected.

We can describe the situation of the Jewish People as follows: In Israel there is a problem of "identification," whereas in the Diaspora the problem is one of "identity." We may take the extreme case of a young Jew in Russia who does not know a word of Hebrew, nor scarcely any Jewish history, but dances in front of the synagogue in Moscow on Yom Kippur or Simḥat Torah to express his profound feeling of identification, or at least his desire to identify with the Jewish People. Despite his total lack of knowledge of anything Jewish we may say that he is at the peak of Jewish identification—but at the lowest point of Jewish identity. At the same time, the Israeli often has the strongest of Jewish identities—his life and existence —and nevertheless lacks identification.

The difference we speak of is not the accepted difference between the cognitive and affective levels. Both levels belong to the coordinate "identification," whereas "identity" belongs to the existential situation. One of the problems of the western Diaspora is the great gap between the desire to identify and the ability to achieve identity: Jewish identity demands a pattern of action, and it is not enough simply to want to be a Jew.

ERNEST KRAUSZ

Apart from the strong and enduring Jewish identities described, I wish to draw attention to the possibility of supporting a weaker, less positive form of a "void" identity, that is, an identity stripped of meaningful content, held together simply by *association*. That is to say, in many Western countries there are factors of residence, demography, occupation and organization which create a kind of emasculated Jewish identity. Being *Jewish by association* is in a sense the situation that developed in the Soviet Union—but there the lack of content in Jewish identity as well as the "associative" aspect have been imposed from above by the regime rather than induced by trends of acculturation or deculturation as experienced by Jews in the West.

The most interesting case of the maintenance of Jewish identity by association is Israel. The existence of a State with a Jewish majority *ipso facto* produces a whole array of associational factors, including fighting for independence and survival, which bring about a specific identity. It is true that if this specific identity is stripped of all traditional content, its definition as *Jewish* remains only in the sense of its past associations, and a redefinition in terms of *Israeliness* may then become necessary. The extreme possibility exists that such a new identity may be forged and that its content would have some kind of secular contemporary form composed of a mixture of Levantine and European culture, far removed from what most people would define as "Jewish."

HAIM CHAMIEL

We should acknowledge the composite basis of Jewish identity, namely: religion, nationality, state, language and even dress, with the prayer shawl and skull cap belonging on the list. The idea of completeness has a special implication. Judaism is not just a philosophy of life. It is a way of life according to a historical outlook which implies belonging to a society, land, culture and common identity.

All the alternatives to an identity based on faith have failed in the past, and it is dangerous to Jewish existence to suppose that there can be any other reliable basis in the future.

A debate recently took place between a group of Israeli youngsters and American youth from Kansas City. The latter—this happened in a Conservative school—asked the Israelis what substance there is to Judaism in Israel, to the Jewish faith, to the synagogue prayers. The Israelis answered: "We don't go to synagogue—we don't need that sort of thing any more." Afterward, the American group asked the principal of the school: "Were all those students Jewish?"

Eighteen years ago, I was in Uruguay at the time of the great debate on Jewish identity when Ben-Gurion asked, "What is a Jew?" I put this question to a class of twelve-year-old girls. One girl answered in Yiddish: "A Jew is a person who learns Torah." As Jews our educational function is to learn and teach the Torah, and if we can be true to that, our future will be assured.

MICHAEL ROSENAK

Educators who wish to strengthen the Jewish identity of the young must consider how to view the "fate" aspect of identity. It may be seen as a "last retreat," the ground-rock of an otherwise eroded identity—or it may be seen as a necessary aspect (or pole) of all identity situations, which must include passive or coercive elements as well as purposeful, freely chosen ones. It appears that an identity which is ideologically perceived as *only* "fated" cannot avoid the "fate" of being considered "absurd" or "tragic"; on the other hand, a comprehensive identity which appears to be *only* chosen invites misunderstanding of the human situation and miscalculations regarding the real range of choice available in a given set of circumstances. Thus, an important issue for deliberation is indicated: Which educational strategies are available (and on which philosophic grounds) for strengthening a total sense of Jewish identity among youth who tend toward the polarities of resignation (fate) and total "openness" and freedom ("Convince me to be Jewish") as though Jewishness were analogous to membership in a sports club.

MERVIN F. VERBIT

The characteristics of the alignment of Jews with the Jewish group with which Simon Herman deals can be organized along five "dimensions." One is its *extension* in time and space. The Jew who sees himself part of the worldwide Jewish People has greater Jewish

identity (all other things being equal) than does the Jew who
identifies only with the Jewish group in his country; and the Jew
who sees himself as part of the historic Jewish People has greater
Jewish identity than the Jew whose alignment is limited to the present period. A second "dimension" of alignment is its *bases*, as for
example, similarity and interdependence. A third "dimension" of
alignment is its *strength*. The more a Jew is aware of his Jewishness
(*salience*) and the more his behavior is affected by his Jewishness,
the greater his Jewish identity. A fourth "dimension" is the *valence*
of an alignment, which can be positive or negative. A Jew can like
his Jewishness and the Jewish group of which he is part, or reject
them. Finally, the fifth "dimension" of alignment is *content*, namely, a person's perceptions of the characteristics of the group with
which he is aligned (the cognitive element) and that group's expectations for his behavior (the normative element).

This paradigm, however, needs to be "doubled." Since Jews
are more an ideologically defined group than a "natural" group, one
can for analytic purposes distinguish the ideology from the flesh and
blood people. Judaism as a set of ideas, values, feelings and behavior
can itself be a significant Jewish referent. While Judaism requires a
living Jewish People as its instrument, nevertheless the actual ideas,
values, feelings and behavior of Jews in a given time and place are
not necessarily identical with those of Judaism—in any of its reasonably acceptable varieties. Granted that the practices of Jews shape
Judaism as it develops over time, it is simply wrong to claim that
whatever Jews—or a majority of Jews—do is *ipso facto* a form of
Judaism. Some popular practices of Jews enter the tradition, in pristine or altered form, but others are rejected in time as temporary behavior found unacceptable by the authorities or by the generations
themselves. Jewish identity, therefore, is not only a Jew's relationship to the Jewish group, but also his relationship to Judaism, and
the two can be viewed separately, at least in the short run.

Many American Jews of the "second generation" were strongly attached to the Jewish group without equivalent attachment to
Judaism. They manifested a powerful "fellow feeling" or "ethnic
tie" to other Jews, but theirs was a "commitment without content,"
with little use of Judaism as a referent for behavior. On the other
hand, there are Jewish "loners" who withdraw from and even reject
what they perceive as the "mainstream" or "established" Jewish
community in order to live—as they see it—more fully according to
the norms of Judaism. Granted that Judaism discourages "separation
from the community," there can be no doubt that the Jewish identity
of such people has a greater salience, centrality, positiveness and extension than that of most Jews.

A feeling of similarity to other Jews, a sense of shared danger and a feeling of shared goals can engender Jewish identity. However, a feeling of shared goals differs from the other two bases in two crucial ways. First, it rests on internal decision rather than on external facts. Every Jew differs from many other Jews, and there are times when the collective dangers we confront are minor. By contrast, the goal we share with other Jews—that is, the long-range goal we share *as Jews*—is initially a matter of commitment. The second difference is that commitment to a significant shared goal is itself a sufficient condition for alignment with the Jewish People, but the other two bases of identity, even when they are present, require accompanying conditions to generate Jewish alignment. Therefore, the most, perhaps the only *stable* basis for Jewish identity is full alignment with Judaism.

It has often been observed that after the Holocaust, after the Six Day War and after the Yom Kippur War, Jewish identity increased. We do not know whether those events were "causes" or catalysts which accelerated a process actually generated by more subtle and long-range trends inside and outside the Jewish community. Whether an external threat leads to cohesion or to a centrifugal "every man for himself" response depends on such factors as the nature of the threat, assessment of the likelihood of overcoming it, and commitment to group maintenance despite political, economic and even physical risk. In the recent threatening situations, many Jews did, but an unsettlingly large number of Jews did not, manifest an increase in their Jewish identity, and some went so far as to make it less obvious, at least to non-Jews.

Perceived similarity to positively evaluated attributes of a group is another basis of alignment, and the Jewish identity of many Jews does seem to rest primarily on their appreciation of the alleged or actual attributes found proportionately more among Jews than among other groups. But such similarity is often not salient or central enough to outweigh dissimilarity with regard to more powerful characteristics. When is Jewishness, as opposed to social class, for example, more determinative of, say, family patterns, personal relationships, social responsibility and other elements of life-style? Perception of similarity is both a basis for and a consequence of identity and understanding of their precise relationships must await the development of more sophisticated methods of research into the processes of referent-selection.

That brings us to the third basis of alignment, namely, interdependence based on a common goal. This is internally defined, and transcends the attributes of Jews at any time and place. If a Jew shares an historic goal of fundamental significance with other Jews, then their personal characteristics matter little to his Jewish identity, and the place and centuries in which they lived are incidental to that common goal. That goal also mandates resistance to threat. Such a goal is religious in the sense that it represents an interpretation of life's meaning and of the basic role of the individual and the group in history.

Judaism, as an interpretation of life and a definition of the Jewish People's role in history, not only makes the existence of a living Jewish People necessary, but also makes the individual Jew's alignment with that People a responsibility which transcends external threats as well as the characteristics of a specific set of Jews. In other words, alignment with Judaism is perhaps the only enduring, and certainly the most reliable, basis for alignment with the Jewish People.

SHALOM ROSENBERG

An analysis of the substance of Jewish identity leads us to contend that there are three general aspects. First, there are features which characterize Judaism as a faith. Second, there are features which characterize Jewry as an ethnic group, a nation and nationality. We may describe the long existence of the Jews in the Diaspora in terms of these two poles. The third aspect is political, and this pole is obviously necessary for an understanding of the Jewish reality today.

If we think in terms of a triangle, we can see the angles as establishing the extremities of Jewish identity; the sides suggesting their interrelationships. We can underscore the meaning of these sides by pointing out three central problems which have both a legal and political character, and yet are fused with the problems of Jewish identity. We refer to three laws: the Law of Return, the laws regarding the Sabbath, and the regulations regarding the entry for "nationality" on the Israeli identity card. The Law of Return symbolizes the Jewish character of the State; the laws regarding the Sabbath demonstrate the problematic as well as the meaningful areas of the relationship between religion and the State; the regulations regarding the "nationality" entry relate to the possibility of a Jewish nationality independent of the religious definition and even in opposition to it in actual cases which were ruled on in this connection.

If we consider that side of the triangle which connects the national and religious points, we may deepen our understanding of the ideological struggles in Jewish thought since the Emancipation. For generations the image of Judaism was that of unity between religion and nationality. The history of Jewish thought in recent generations demonstrates new problems which result from attempts to focus Judaism exclusively around one pole. The ideology behind the Emancipation in western and central Europe, which, in identifying Judaism as a religion, spoke of "Germans of the Mosaic faith," was a pure system of polarization. Growth of the nationalistic movements of leftist bent in Eastern Europe was a prime example of polarization, attempting to define Jewish identity on a nationalistic basis, without religious content. Zionism may be seen as the third political pole. As the expression of political development, it is dependent on both religious and nationalistic identity.

The recent history of Jewish ideologies illustrates the danger of polarization, from that pole which identifies itself only in relation to a particular territory or political entity. A parallel situation is normal in many nations, the classic example being the Latin American countries. Those states in which education is used to inculcate awareness of national history do not identify with the ancestors of the Spanish immigrants, but rather with the Indians—the inhabitants before the conquest. Analogously the Israeli identifies with the early Hebrew, or even the Canaanite, and not with the Diaspora Jew as the source of the Zionist impulse. This polarization doubtless contains a certain bitter historical irony: Zionism, which seeks to create political entity, is faced with the danger of bringing about the destruction of the national identity.

Most of the systems of Jewish identity are not theories which indicate factual positions, but rather programs determining ends and means. A discussion dealing with the problems of identity cannot therefore be concluded by a factual debate. An understanding of the various positions is dependent on an understanding of the various goals. Those goals which we can determine relate to a double system: 1) the promise of a Jewish character for the State; 2) the assurance of the unity of the Jewish nation. The first goal limits the development of an Israeli rather than a Jewish identity; but in conjunction with the second condition, it negates the possibility of a Jewish alternative in the Diaspora without relation to the national identity or its centralization.

The definition of Judaism according to national criteria alone does not allow for the term "one nation," since ethnic criteria, which do not take into consideration the elements which form the religious identity, could not mold eastern European Jewry and, for example, Yemenite Jewry into one nation. The many-sidedness of Jewish identity is a constant source of political and social conflicts. Sometimes the situation of conflict is so severe in everything connected with the short-term future, that it clouds the meaning of many-sidedness. But the strength of the nation and its power to overcome various crises over the generations is dependent precisely on this many-sidedness.

ALFRED GOTTSCHALK: Summary Comment

One of the fascinating and most revealing aspects of this discussion was how psychological (or social psychological) description, classification and interpretation of Jewish identification led over and over to the problem of normative regulation and authentication—a problem whose solution cannot be expected from psychological analysis. The patterns of Jewish identity, which came into view as the objective of Jewish identification, obtained and retained their structure by way of normative determination. To what extent and in what manner norm-determined, the components of a Jewish identity never became a main concern. Neither was there a *substantive*, systematic exploration of the minimum requirements that make an identity Jewish. The need for such an exploration was spelled out. Michael Rosenak, for example, feels that a fruitful deliberation on the question of identity as a programmatic problem will not be possible unless we admit to the existence of diverse *normative* models. (Italics mine.)

One of the reasons for this failure was the ever-present inclination to consider Jewish identification per se, that is, the subjective process leading to Jewish identity, as a form of identity. Professor Herman stated that the terms "identity" and "identification" might be used interchangeably. Thus one might gain the impression that the status of *being* a Jew, a status determined by objective criteria and requirements, minimal and otherwise, had been replaced by the act of *becoming* a Jew.

It is true that the act of Jewish identification has always played a special role in the life of the Jew. Prayer represents an act of Jewish identification confirming Jewish group identity, and so does Jewish *Lernen*, the process of traditional Jewish studying. But, whereas these acts of confirmation used to be within an established and generally accepted "system" of Judaism, for example, the synagogue, today's Jewish identification often lacks the support of such a group system. However, similarities and parallels to past constellations may be found: The almost ritualized form of the Jewish funddrive gathering, in which the Jew publicly identifies with the Jewish group by announcing his contribution is a phenomenon worth sociological investigation.

In modern Jewries, identification is for all practical purposes a process of selection. The Jew acknowledges his Jewish identity by choosing from a number of possible ways of being Jewish. At the same time, at least in most countries, the Jew making his identification has to merge into his preference given circumstances which are beyond the control of the individual. Such given data are, for example, Israeli citizenship for the Jew in Israel or American citizenship for the American Jew. Most important, forming a Jewish identity is rarely done by picking one out from a stock of ready-made models. Jewish identification is a "creative" process.

In a way, every person identifying himself as a Jew creates his own manner and form of Jewishness. Many of the community norms that fused Jews in the past into a rather unified group have fallen by the wayside. The closed pre-modern system of Judaism has been replaced by various Jewish group ideologies. Thus, once again one is obligated to raise the question of normative authenticity. Are there elements basic and indispensable in the variety of Jewish attributes that form Jewishness today? Is there a normative minimum? Simon Herman reported that his studies of Israeli and American students had found "that neither group saw much similarity between Israeli and American Jews. . . . On the other hand, the feeling of interdependence has grown. . . . This feeling of interdependence represents the minimal basis of Jewish belongingness in our time." We might want to compare this with Peter Y. Medding's statement (quoting Charles Liebman) that, commonly, Jewish organizations in the United States are ethnic solely in membership, not in content, and compare it further with the conclusion by Glazer and Moynihan, that "the cultural content of each ethnic group in the United States seems to have become very similar to that of others, but the emotional significance of attachment to the ethnic group seems to persist." Clearly, interdependence as "minimal basis of Jewish belongingness" appears to emerge as a fragile thing.

All the more, the questions remain: Is there a normative minimum? Are there articulations of Jewishness which are unacceptable, and if so, to whom and by which sanction? As was demonstrated by the "Who is a Jew" controversy in Israel or the claims of the "Jews for Jesus" movement in America, these questions are of acute practical importance.

Problems such as those formulated above carry beyond the domain of social psychology. The study of identification presupposes a reciprocal dynamic of perception and reality, and while the perception does not offer principal difficulties for being recognized and described, the Jewish reality does. Contemporary Jewish groups represent sets of identification patterns which are common to the group members. But the fact is that the Jewishness of Jewish group identities is constantly measured and evaluated by competing groups and this fact has considerable impact on group formation and maintenance. To use a strong word, Jewish identification had become a competitive undertaking. Ideally, it should not be so. Judaism, according to the belief, the instinctive reaction or the subconscious feeling of many, should be one, governed by one value system and representing basically one way of life and thought. According to this belief, affiliation and identification should be both uniform and constant. This is, of course, far from the truth.

John Murray Cuddihy in his somewhat bizarre, though always fascinating book, *The Ordeal of Civility—Freud, Marx, Levi-Strauss and the Jewish Struggle with Modernity* (1974) cites a number of patterns of Jewish identification and Jewish witnesses who declare them unauthentic and unrealistic—including even Marshall Sklare who is quoted as finding "the new definition of Jewishness as a religious identity, the new post-war redefinition of the descendants of the Eastern Jewish group as religious denomination . . . a highly convenient fiction which it is wise to cultivate." Such critique presumes more than the socio-psychologic analysis can provide or demonstrate. Simon Herman stated the insufficiency of merely attitudinal classification. I am confident he will extend his censure also to analysis along solely functional lines. Yet, these approaches are not entirely insufficient so long as they point to any particular sense of Jewishness which can be connected to an internal Jewish value system.

In exploring the relationship between such a Jewish value system and the variety of Jewish identification—in our days unfortunately too often no more than a spiritless compartmentalization of Jewish organizational or party activities—it is no longer convincing to summon the unifying Jewish spirit, the all-pervading *ruach leumi, Juedischer Geist* or the *génie du Judaïsme.* In 1840 Leopold Zunz characterized Jews and Judaism as "a collective entity which is not motivated by accidental purposes, which is built on historical necessity and which exists because it has an inner life, a living spirit." We no longer share Zunz's ideology derived from universal history and morphological historiography, nor do we find it possible to formulate the "essence of Judaism" so that it may serve as a normative authenticator of claims to Jewishness.

Historical evidence is used as one of the main authenticators of Jewish identity. Linking the group to the march of Jewish history is one of the strongest and best articulated features in modern Jewish identification. Yet, reliance on history also introduces a relativism which then acts in contradiction to the normative elements in Jewish identity. Historical relativism has the potential to erode the norms in Jewish identity. In the processes of Jewish identification historical and normative elements are usually intermingled and the mingling is made more complex by emotional, political, philosophical, religious and other factors. One merely needs to consider the internal complexity of each of these factors in order to arrive at an understanding of the difficulties facing the scholar who sets out to analyze Jewish identity.

The more one pursues this trend of thought, the more evident the limits of a merely socio-psychological investigation become. The method is appropriate in studying the variant patterns of Jewish *identification*; it is insufficient in exploring the character of Jewish *identity*. Identification refers to the process by which an identity is acquired or achieved. And I maintain that the patterns of identification do not necessarily or ever fully correspond to the patterns of identity. I do not agree with Mordechai Bar-On who regards "identity" as "the objective description of a condition which is mainly spiritual, whereas identification is the subjective description of the *same* condition" [italics mine]. And I refer to Zvi Gitelman's paper which demonstrates that changes in the identification process are not automatically followed by corresponding changes in group identity. An investigation of the patterns of identity independent of the investigation of the patterns of identification is necessary. It should take the form of a study of the various identity *structures* showing the *interrelation of the parts as dominated by the general character of the whole*.

An investigation of this kind will be typological in nature, resulting in sets of "type constructs" which in their totality cover the full gamut of Jewish identities. Old labels, such as religious, Zionist, secular, socialist, cultural, political, etc., are too broad and vague. They do not work any more. They have become inadequate to describe the complicated interlacing in the modern structures of Jewish identity. We need new meaningful delineations—for our scholarly as well as our practical self-understanding.

III

The Centrality of Israel and
Interaction among World Jewish Communities

Center and Periphery in Jewish Historic Consciousness: Contemporary Implications

Ephraim E. Urbach

Interdependence between center and Diaspora has been a concern of modern Jewish historiography since its inception. The significance of this concept is obvious in considering the ideological and political status of the present or future Jewish People. Views of two contemporary Jewish historians on the nature of this relationship may be taken as a starting point.

In the introduction to *Israel in the Diaspora,* Ben Zion Dinur, after examining some approaches to this problem by Jost, Graetz, Geiger, Teubler and Dubnow, concludes thus:

> A number of questions in Jewish historiography remain to be satisfactorily explained. Further elucidation is required not only of the extent of the historical role of the Jews in the Diaspora, the nature and value of their reciprocal influence between the Jewish communities in the countries of their dispersion . . . even the nature of the unity that binds Diaspora Jewry into a national entity bearing the brunt of events has not yet been defined or explained properly. As for . . . the question of the Land of Israel and its place in the history of Diaspora Jewry, this in truth has hardly been investigated.[1]

Such a conclusion and in particular the final statement are most certainly exaggerated. It was written, however, in order to draw attention to a problem which, in Dinur's view, had not found a satisfactory answer and, in particular, to emphasize the overall importance in Jewish history of the Land of Israel and its Jewish settlement. This importance, according to Dinur, does not stem simply from a longing for redemption amid persecution and oppression in the Diaspora, but from the distinctive historical-territorial character associated with the Jewish community in Eretz Israel and the

---

1. *Yisrael ba-Golah*, 2nd ed., Jerusalem, 1958, vol. 1, p. 30.

specific image it presented (which, he felt, was the result of historical continuity, independent existence, and a fully developed Jewish
life-style).

It is difficult for the reader to find adequate evidence for what
Dinur calls these "three basic facts" and to refrain from testing their
validity. It seems to have escaped Dinur's notice that he thus, a priori, contradicts the justification for beginning his history of the Jews
in the Diaspora with the Arab conquest of Eretz Israel. He holds that
although the majority of the Jewish People were to be found outside
the borders of Eretz Israel even before the Arab conquest, the existence of a nation scattered in alien lands was not a phenomenon peculiar to the Jews. He does not take as his starting point the abolition
of Jewish hegemony in Eretz Israel, but the expropriation of lands
owned by Jews and the emergence of a new national majority there.
It is not necessary to enter into a lengthy examination of Dinur's
premises. The best testimony is his own candid acknowledgment, at
the conclusion of his introduction, that every historical judgment is
subjective and is dependent upon time and the vantage point from
which the historian sees the past, even when he does so by means of
Dinur's principle: "historiography through the sources."

Trust in National Redemption

Yehezkiel Kaufmann in his *Golah ve-Nekhar*, published two
years before the first volume of *Israel in the Diaspora* appeared, sets
out to explain the actual position of the Jewish people in the present
era, and to find a national solution to the question of exile through
clarification of sociohistorical processes.

Kaufmann undertakes a very acute and unbiased analysis of
all proposals put forward since the end of the eighteenth century for
a solution to the dangers of assimilation. He condemns these proposals as illusory, since he considers that, although alienation and exile
have existed in varying degrees at all times and in all parts of the
world, in Jewish history they have become crystallized and have received a unique form; this form, through its own momentum, has
produced unique consequences. The Jewish People had no nationally inherited territory. Here is a genuine social reality that has wide
implications; lack of territory is not just a fabrication by those hostile
to Jews or a notion that can be dismissed as an outmoded conception
of a national society. Feelings of alienation, deeply rooted in the

consciousness of the Jewish People, will not be eradicated by political or social revolutions, so long as the Jewish People continue to retain their distinctive character or remain in their ghetto state. Belief in redemption through political-national assimilation, in the rights of minorities, in redemption through social revolution—these presuppose the abolition of primary instincts which claim national rights over a particular piece of land, and a resulting feeling of alienation fostered by a state of exile. Any hope of extinguishing these instincts is utopian, since it would be based on the abolition of national distinctions and the elimination of religion throughout the world.

These beliefs, according to Kaufmann, are eschatological and cannot be regarded as a real solution to the problem of the Diaspora. The masses of the Jewish People are still bound wholeheartedly to their Jewishness, which in many countries continues to create a cultural barrier between them and their neighbors. They cannot be expected to endure the difficulties of daily life in the hope that these difficulties will be abolished at some future time; nor can they live on hope of nirvana in the form of a "new humanity." The Jewish People are looking anxiously for redemption, but not the redemption of extinction or of annihilation through assimilation in the self-immolation of nirvana. For the masses of the Jewish People there is no road to redemption other than national redemption. This objective need of the Jewish People for national redemption is the primary source of the national movement in its different forms.

Religious Inheritance

Kaufmann's approach rejects the concept of a Jewish spiritual center in its various manifestations. He is particularly critical of the concept of Zionism as envisaged by Aḥad Ha-Am. In Kaufmann's view this does not differ from the Diaspora nationalism of Dubnow, both being postulated on a belief in future centers in the Diaspora and on a misconception of the operation of the religious factor in Jewish history. According to Kaufmann, there is no historical basis for belief in a national secular culture which can flourish equally in Eretz Israel or anywhere else, thus influencing Diaspora Jews and uniting them in the future. He strongly criticizes the idea that it is the ethical basis of Judaism that draws Jews together and enables them to exist as an entity in exile and dispersion. Although a lofty ethical code was developed among the Jewish People, their fate will not be decided, as Aḥad Ha-Am supposed, by virtue of this moral system. The Jewish People have always regarded their religious existence as the primary reason for their fight for their unique identity. It was not the force of external factors or the biological urge for existence which established its special place among the nations, but the innate power of the religious culture of Israel.

Kaufmann writes:

> Evidence of this is the fact that any sector of the nation which renounced its religion, whether voluntarily or by force, has been absorbed into the other nations. In this respect, the Judeo-Christians of antiquity did not differ greatly from the forced converts of the Middle Ages, nor whole groups which renounced their faith from individuals who were converted and left Judaism.
>
> Religion has always been the dividing line separating the Jews from other peoples, and every Jew who has gone beyond this line has been absorbed into the other nations. Ethnic, psychological, class or biological factors have never been sufficient to bind together any sector of Jewry that left the religious community or to shut the door in the face of assimilation. This fact constitutes the decisive evidence that there is nothing beyond and that the religious factor was the sole element which united the Jews and distinguished them from the other peoples in the countries of their dispersion.[2]

Diaspora Jewry did not possess a national culture which could maintain itself by its own strength. When the authority of religion was undermined, assimilation became a vital objective. In his recognition of this fact, Kaufmann rejects the idea of a center for Diaspora Jewry by singling out a number of positive aspects in the arguments of Berdichevsky, Brenner and Klatzkin. In Kaufmann's opinion, the national movement, during the process of its development, compromised on the ideal of Jewish redemption from the Diaspora and came to terms with the necessity for the Diaspora. The utopian argument foundered on the rocks of political Zionism. Aḥad Ha-Am demonstrated, by use of a simple calculation, that "the ingathering of the exiles was something supra-natural."

Kaufmann, however, considers that all the various forms of belief in redemption put forward in recent times are more utopian than the idea of redemption through the ingathering of the exiles. He holds that the national movement ought to implant a new concept in

2. *Golah ve-Nekhar*, 3rd ed., Tel Aviv, 1942, vol. 1, p. 199.

the national consciousness, side by side with the traditional religious conception—redemption by pioneer settlement, which is the converse of ghetto settlement. The ugly taint attached to Jewish character by their enemies during centuries of ghetto life is regarded by Kaufmann as concealing a vital colonizing spirit. The new national ideology directed Jews toward Eretz Israel, the Land of their forefathers, for which there existed, apart from the religious bond, a feeling of proprietorship. As a result of this feeling Eretz Israel has the strongest claim upon the Jew, who has shown that he can create a new form of settlement there. Kaufmann, however, does not evade the issue as to whether settlement in Eretz Israel can solve the problem of the future of the Jewish People throughout the world. It is worthy of note that he wrote the following in 1929, the year of Arab massacres of the Jews in Eretz Israel. (Although Kaufmann's conclusions seem naive in the light of later events, his skeptical prognosis deserves to be recapitulated, and not only for its bearing on the present situation.)

> The Jewish People claim Eretz Israel as the sole national right of a poor and wretched people to a foothold in the land of their forefathers. The opponents of Zionism who contend that it is thus performing the function of British imperialism in Eretz Israel argue in this way either out of naiveté or out of a malicious intent to pervert its meaning. Apart from this plot of land the Jewish People have no national territory, and they are aliens everywhere. Here only have they a historic right, and this they cannot surrender. Can settlement in Eretz Israel solve the problem of the fate of the Jewish People in the world? . . . Even if we overlook the political and economic consequences, we still cannot ignore the difficult and critical problem of the Arabs. This issue, which is problematic enough in a small part of historic Eretz Israel, would be even more difficult to solve in a greater Eretz Israel which would expand into the neighboring countries.
>
> Eretz Israel, it seems to me, is the only land in the world where two peoples have a right of ownership. . . . The Jewish People cannot renounce their sole historic national right in Eretz Israel. But it would be dangerous to dismiss or underestimate the fact that Eretz Israel is part of the land of the Arab population, which is already beginning to feel the stirrings of a national movement. . . .
>
> An ethnically mixed and antagonistic population is extremely dangerous everywhere, and infinitely more so in such circumstances. The Jewish population finds itself surrounded by the Arab population on every side. The history of all peoples in all places at all times does not encourage belief that the Arab population will have a different attitude to the Jewish population in its midst. The ethnographical situation

in Eretz Israel and all its neighboring countries, therefore, imposes limits on the area for Jewish settlement. There is no ground for dreams that this settlement could solve even partially the problem of exile.[3]

How therefore can the problem of exile be solved?

The Jewish People need a country, a new country. *They will hold on to Eretz Israel as long as they can*, but they will have to seek the solution to the problem of exile in another country also—and perhaps even in other countries. . . .[4]

Is territorialism in any way a betrayal of Eretz Israel?

Eretz Israel will remain eternally engraved on the hearts of the Jewish People. The settlement which is being created there will certainly always be the heart of the Jewish nation in whatever place they may be living. The sacrifices which the people are making for it are not in vain. Nevertheless, the solution to the problem of exile will not be found here. . . . History has imposed this experiment on the Jewish People so that after centuries of wandering they should seek a new national land. No romance can transfer this destiny from them.[5]

Where is this Land?

Certainly the Jewish People will not find it by themselves. But there is hope that a country will be found when the problem of Jewish redemption again becomes an international issue. *For the problem of exile is indeed not an internal Jewish problem, but an international problem in the full sense, as Herzl understood it.* The problem of maintaining Judaism is an internal Jewish question only. But the problem of exile, the Jewish problem, is a general problem which also concerns the other nations. For two thousand years the Jews in the Diaspora have lived in special quarters alongside the Gentile peoples. Unending jealousy and rivalry, contempt and hatred, violence and murder have flourished in the wake of this ill-fated proximity, and like a terrifying and menacing specter the "wandering Jew" has wandered "eternally" among the Gentiles.[6]

3. *Ibid.*, vol. 2, pp. 467–470.

4. *Ibid.*, p. 471.

5. *Ibid.*, p. 475.

6. *Ibid.*, p. 473.

In the light of the events which we have since experienced—the Holocaust of European Jewry, the failure of all international conferences and plans of governments to find a new land to solve the Jewish problem, the establishment of the State of Israel and the wars in which it has been involved, the attainment of independence by the states of Africa and Asia and the course of their relations with Israel—it is difficult not to notice the obvious contradiction between Kaufmann's arguments when dealing with the proposals of others and the lack of these criteria when he states his own conclusions. Moreover, in the first part of the book, which deals with the period prior to emancipation, he enumerates many principles which have no basis except in the deductions of the author himself.

It seems that the opposing views of Dinur and Kaufmann, which are both widely distant in outlook as well as in the starting point of their investigations, overestimate their ability to find a solution to the complex web of history. There is a danger in drawing mechanical conclusions about the past based on events of the present and in paying insufficient attention to the role of the unexpected or accidental, which may reverse or disappoint expectations and contradict assumptions. This has been a pitfall not only for Dinur and Kaufmann but also for other scholars who have attempted to lay down principles and draw conclusions from the development of Jewish history, conclusions which generally contradict the attractive theories of historical cause and effect.

The Dispersion

There is no intention here to investigate the problem under consideration throughout the panorama of Jewish history; only evidence from the period of the Second Temple and the centuries following its destruction will be examined here. It is obvious that the relationship between the center and the Diaspora was dependent on the extent of the former's political, religious and institutional hegemony. The loss of those, or their restriction, deprived Eretz Israel of its character as a center, for in no way can yearnings for the past or obedience to its traditions or even sporadic return be regarded as evidence of the firm relationship between a national center and its Diaspora.

At the beginning of the Hasmonean period, a letter sent to the Jews of Alexandria and Egypt urged them to maintain the festival of

Hanukkah, although they had not experienced that miracle themselves (*II Maccabees*, ii:17–18). It reads: "May the Almighty who saved all His people and who gave His inheritance to all of us, and the kingdom and the priesthood and the Temple as He promised in the Torah, speedily have mercy upon us and gather us up from all the earth under the Heavens and from every place." Here "the kingdom, the priesthood and the Temple" are considered the center, which is the inheritance of the whole nation. At the same time the situation of Jews outside Eretz Israel is regarded as one which is transitory and must be stabilized.

In the book of Ben Sira the worshiper expresses the hopes and expectations bound up in redemption with these words: "Gather up all the tribes of Israel that may settle on the land as in former times." However, to the Jews in the Diaspora (originally called, in Greek, the "dispersion"), the existing situation did not appear as exile, that is, as the result of doom and punishment, but as the outcome of emigration and expansion.

Philo states that "one country cannot support all the Jews because they are many in number" (*Against Flaccus*, 25). He also emphasizes that cities inhabited by Jews for generations were regarded by them as their native towns, towns in which they had been born and grew up. Indeed, they had come to many as colonizers when they were founded initially (*ibid.*, 46). At the same time, Philo regarded Jerusalem as the central city not only of Judea but of numerous countries, and he saw the dispersal as a transitory and temporary phenomenon. The eschatological future was the day on which "the dispersed will arise in the countries of the Greeks and of the barbarians, in the islands and the continents, and will travel from every side to the place appointed for them . . . and when they come they will rebuild the cities that have been destroyed, the wilderness will flourish again. . . . The enemies who rejoiced in the times of their misfortunes, and who ridiculed them . . . will recognize that they have wronged not a wretched and downtrodden people but a noble nation whose honor shines forth again after it had been dimmed for a little time."

It may be assumed that with these words Philo expresses a feeling that was prevalent in broad sectors of Hellenic Jewry. To the eyes of the outsiders, the presence of Jews throughout the settled world (*oikoumene*) and their links with Jerusalem was a prominent feature. Mommsen depicts the situation in these words:

> In the course of establishing cities, which continued for generations to an extent that had never occurred previously or subsequently, the Jews were in the vanguard, so much so that it would not be unusual to find them aiding the Hellenization of the Orient. In particular this applied to Egypt. Alexandria, the most important of the cities founded by Alexander the Great, to which large numbers of Jews migrated after the conquest of Eretz Israel by the Ptolemies, was as much a Jewish city as a Greek one. The local Jewish community was at least equal to that of Jerusalem in size, in resources, in scholarship and in social organization. In the period of the early empire there were approximately eight million Egyptians and one million Jews, whose influences exceeded their numerical weight. A similar situation obtained in Antioch, the Seleucid capital. Constitutionally, the Jews formed a "state within a state," and they were not governed like the local inhabitants by the Hellenes.[7]

Strabo writes: "The Jews of Alexandria have a head of the nation (*ethnarch*) who governs the people, and adjudicates audits and supervises contracts and ordinances as though he were the head of an independent state." (Josephus, *Antiquities, xiv, 117*).

The religious influence, its penetration of the Gentile world, the reciprocal penetration of Greek elements into Judaism, proselytization, the Judaization of individuals and of the kingdom of Adiabene in the reign of Tiberius, all are evidence of the influence of Judaism. On the other hand, the predominance of the Greek language—the translation into Greek of the Scriptures and of the ethical work of Ben Sira by his grandson, the whole corpus of Hellenic literature and development of the allegorical method of biblical interpretation, all witness a concomitant phenomenon which was accompanied by an extreme trend toward assimilation.

Yet, in spite of this, the Jewish community remained united. Jerusalem was its symbol, the Temple was the temple of all Jewry, the half-shekel due was sent to Jerusalem, and every Jew endeavored to make a pilgrimage to the Temple Mount at least once in his lifetime. Jewish learning remained as much a joint possession of the scholars of Alexandria and Babylonia as of those of Babylonia and Jerusalem. Mommsen's comments on the subject merit our special

7. Th. Mommsen, *Römische Geschichte*, 2nd ed., 1885, vol. 5, p. 488.

attention: "The feeling of Jewish identity also existed among circles which had moved far away from the inner core of the religion."[8] "Neo-reform Judaism" (as Mommsen calls it) "did stray too far from its antecedents, like neo-paganism"; thus the Jews, living in the Greek milieu, and using the Greek language, adhered with particular tenacity to the forms of the Jewish religion if not to its substance. In all important matters and particularly in instances of external pressure and persecution, the differences in Judaism seemed to disappear, and while the Jewish state (Mommsen cals it Rabbinerstaat) had no formal importance, yet in certain conditions it could appear "a threatening power." The full accuracy of this last observation has been corroborated by the rich store of papyri discovered after these words were written. Their content and its importance for our subject will be discussed later.

A theory, differing in no small extent from the above view but helping to illuminate the subject, is that of the eminent savant Ernest Renan. Faithful to his maxim "the people as an eternal Referendum," he writes:

> The Jews in the period of the Second Temple at first displayed the same type of patriotism that was subsequently evinced by the Parsees, the Armenians, and to a certain extent by the modern Greeks. It is a patriotism of merchants scattered in every locality, each one acquainted with the other, a patriotism which does not found states, but autonomous communities in the midst of other states. The Jews of the Diaspora created independent churches with their own officers and councils in the cities where they resided. In some places they had an ethnarch or alabarch with almost royal privileges. They lived in their own districts separated from the general jurisdiction, in havens of peace and happiness, and regarded by the rest of the population with resentment and hostility. In general, poverty was more common than any wealth. The period of the large estate owners had not yet arrived. That began in Spain in the time of the Visigoths. The primacy of the Jews in the financial sphere was a result of the lack of aptitude of the barbarian races, of the scorn in which the church held financial knowledge and its primitive conception of lending and interest. If a Jew was not wealthy he was poor. He did not benefit from middle-class conveniences, he was able to bear poverty easily. What he was able to do even more was to combine his most lofty religious feelings with an outstanding business sense.[9]

8. *Ibid.*, pp. 496–497.

9. E. Renan, *The Apostles*, J. H. Allen, tr., Boston, 1898, pp. 242–243.

Even Renan adds a generalization to the effect that theological eccentricity does not inhibit activity in the practical sphere, and he cites numerous examples from England, America and Russia, mentioning the *Raskolniki* and the Latter Day Saints. He records:

> Jewish life, as it continued before the State of Israel, had a quality which engendered happiness and good will, and of fellow feeling for one another. Their hearts clung to the past, and this was the same past. Their lives were enveloped in a warm embrace by religious traditions. The Romans seldom penetrated their residential districts. The Jews aroused varying reactions in the surrounding world. A pamphlet like that of Apion achieved a wide circulation and many writers drew from it.
>
> On the other hand, many were attracted by the Jews and there were numerous converts to Judaism. To the Jews Roman civilization appeared the embodiment of oppression and ugly vice. In their own circle life was full of joy and interest, as we find among Jews today in the most wretched synagogues of Poland and Galicia.[10]

Renan's description, which may be termed a sociological-typological summary, is not quite so appropriate for the period of the Second Temple as it was for a later age. Nevertheless, it may be admitted that not only did he anticipate later scholars in a number of issues but his approach was also much more objective than that of some present-day sociologists. Sir Karl Popper, for instance, says merely that "their retention in ghetto-life in Eastern Europe up to 1914, and even subsequently of ossified forms of Jewish tradition is extremely interesting."[11] Pertinent to the subject under consideration is the fact that Renan makes no reference to the status of Eretz Israel and its central role. It would have been more correct if he had applied his remarks to the centuries following the destruction of the Temple, but for the preceding period, Mommsen gives a much truer picture.

Center and Diaspora

The Jews of Egypt exerted a certain influence on political factors affecting the destiny of the Jewish center. When Cleopatra

10. *Ibid.*, p. 248.

11. Karl R. Popper, *The Open Society and Its Enemies*, 5th ed., 1966, vol. 2, p. 301, n. 56.

wished to take over the kingdom of Alexander Yannai for Egypt, Hananiah, son of Onias, told her that such a heinous offense would turn all the Jews of Egypt into her enemies. There is also reliable evidence to support the statement of Josephus Flavius that the Jews of Egypt enabled the Roman armies to enter the country in the times of Gabinius (57 B.C.E.) and of Caesar (47 B.C.E.) because of the influence of Hyrcanus, who was undoubtedly also motivated by other political considerations.

On the other hand, the political character of the center made its mark on the political status of Diaspora Jews. The writ of Claudius granting rights to Alexandrian Jews was largely the work of Agrippa, though, at the same time, Claudius deemed it necessary to warn the Jews of Alexandria not to conspire against him or to admit Jews coming to the city from Syria or Egypt by sea. It may be assumed that by "Syria" he meant Eretz Israel, from which many Jews came to the aid of the Jews of Alexandria in their conflicts with other inhabitants. Similarly, there is evidence from this period that Jews from Tiberias hastened to help their brethren in clashes in Antioch. Philo describes with religious enthusiasm the procedure for levying the half-shekel Temple dues, the guarding of the money and its conveyance to Jerusalem. The dues from the half-shekel were not applied only to the needs of the Temple and its sacrifices; the dues were also used to strengthen the walls of Jerusalem and its bastions (as well as to repair the conduits) and to furnish all the needs of the city (*Shekalim 4:2*). When he arrived in Jerusalem Philo found a king and a high priest ruling the land, and judges and law officers and elders ruling the Sanhedrin. Agrippa I is described warmly as a righteous king.

Philo indubitably was aware of the way in which King Herod and his successors conducted the affairs of state, and he certainly had knowledge of high priests who were not always chosen for their lofty principles. The reality was not ideal, yet it filled the heart of Philo with pride and superseded all his philosophical allegorizing. In this respect Philo's attitude toward state institutions was no different from that of the sages of his day who were living in Eretz Israel. However, as citizens of the country, they often took up the cause for justice against the ruling Establishment. It is interesting that Philo makes no mention in his writings of the Temple of Onias in Leontopolis. However, the *Halakhah* (law) displays a tolerant attitude towards his temple, which had been built by Onias IV. It was actually the temple of a military colony owing its existence to personal ambitions which had suited the politics of Ptolemy Philopater when he was involved in a war with Syria. At any rate, the Mishnah (*Menahot* 13:10) states that (if a man) says of his sacrifices "I will sacrifice it in the temple of Onias" he should offer it in the Temple, but if it is offered in the temple of Onias he has fulfilled his obligations. This temple does not seem to have been regarded as a competitor of the Temple in Jerusalem. When Raban Gamaliel the Elder sent out his cyclical letters from Jerusalem he addressed them "to our brethren in Upper Galilee . . . and to our brethren in lower Galilee . . . to our brethren of the South . . . to our brethren the Exiles in Babylon . . . and to all the Exiles of Israel" (*Sanhedrin* 11b). In the neighborhood of the *Lishkat ha-Gazit* (Chamber of Hewn Stone) in the Temple there was a *Lishkat ha-Golah* (Chamber of the Diaspora) [*Middot* 5:4]; while in Jerusalem there could be found synagogues of the Alexandrians and of the people of Cyrene and Cilicia (*Tosefta Megilla* iii:6; cf. also Acts of the Apostles vi:9).

The destruction of the Temple and the abolition of independent Jewish hegemony in Eretz Israel terminated the relationship between Diaspora Jewry and the Jews of Eretz Israel, that is, of a people in dispersion toward its natural center. However, the struggle for the restoration of Jewish hegemony continued until the Revolt of Bar Kokhba and in the political sphere for a short time afterward. The war against Rome brought in its wake a chain of violent outbreaks between the Jewish communities and the Hellenic populations in all the countries of the dispersion. Even though the origin of the conflict was the struggle of the Jews for their legal rights, the war in Judea was not without influence. Josephus (*Wars* viii, 12) relates the activities of the survivors among the Zealots who managed to escape to Egypt. According to him they were unable to arouse the Jews to immediate revolt as they had succeeded in doing in Cyrenaica. Nevertheless, the spirit of the revolt was not forgotten and in the reign of Trajan the disturbances developed into a full-scale war, which continued from 115 through 117 C.E., affecting the Jews of Cyrenaica, Libya, Cyprus, and even as far as Mesopotamia. The disastrous consequences of this war are viewed in the Talmud and the Midrash with consternation: "At that time it was said the horn of Israel is cut off" (*Palestinian Talmud * Sukkah* v:1,55b).

*Hereafter, P.T.

The events in Eretz Israel in the period known as the "War of
Quitus" (Quietus) and the years which preceded the Bar Kokhba
Revolt, years of persecution that were thought to precede the Re-
demption, are among the most obscure and complicated chapters in
Jewish history. It is not possible to enter here into a detailed exami-
nation of those times. The point of interest for this inquiry is the Bar
Kokhba Revolt and its initial successes, which find expression in the
coins struck at the time and in Talmudic sources (*Tosefta Ma'aser
Sheni* i:6; *P.T. loc. cit.; Babylonian Talmud** Bava Kamma* 97b).
The revolt again roused the Jews of the Diaspora, and evidently a
number of them were among the combatants.

The failure of the Bar Kokhba rebellion and the demographic
changes which began to affect the position of the Jews in Eretz Israel,
in addition to the persecutions which followed, did not end the attempts to restore the center of leadership. However, these attempts
remained sporadic. Even the authority of the academies in Eretz Israel was circumscribed. They were wholly dependent, on the one side,
upon the personal qualities of their leaders, and, on the other, on the
willingness of Jewish centers outside the country (in particular, Babylonia) to accept a measure of subordination to their jurisdiction.
Even a patriarch such as R. Yehuda ha-Nassi, who, in his office, combined learning with aristocratic status and sagacity with personal
wealth, and who dressed in robes worn by royalty, regarded the Babylonian Exilarch as a rival (*P.T. Kilayim* ix:3). It was evidently at the
start of his period of office that Hananiah, nephew of R. Jehoshua,
attempted to transfer to Babylonia the right to intercalate the year.
The account of this incident, as reported in both the Palestinian
and Babylonian Talmuds (*P.T. Nedarim* vii:40a; *Sanhedrin* i:19a;
B.T. Berakhot 63b) already reflects the arguments that were later to
be voiced on this matter in discussions concerning the jurisdiction
of Eretz Israel vis-à-vis Babylonia. It is expressed in such inter-
changes as "I have not left behind scholars like me [i.e., of my cali-
ber] in Eretz Israel"; the dictum "For from Zion will go forth Torah
and the word of the Lord from Jerusalem" was even countered by
another: "From Babylonia will go forth Torah and the word of the
Lord from Nahar Pekod." The emissaries of R. Yehuda ha-Nassi succeeded in quashing this attempt, but during the patriarchates of his
grandsons and when the great yeshivot of Babylonia reached the

**Hereafter, B.T.

height of their achievements, the prerogatives of intercalation of the
year and of appointing (=*minui*) scholars (the term used in Eretz Israel for the Babylonian equivalent of *semikhah*), did not at all reflect
the relationship of a center to its diocese.

Primacy of the Center

Residence in Eretz Israel was without doubt considered a religious act. However, economic conditions and difficulties with secular powers, which had existed from the period of the Tannaim, led a
number of scholars to leave for Babylonia, either for short periods or
permanently. When R. Akiba went to Nehardea to intercalate the
year he found a scholar, Nehemiah of Beth Deli, who cited *Halakhah*
in the name of Rabban Gamaliel the Elder (*Yevamot* 16:7). R. Simeon
ben Yohai deprecated anyone who left Eretz Israel even during times
of scarcity and famine. His statement that "Elimelich was among the
great men and benefactors of his people but because he went to live
abroad he and his sons died, and the rest of Israel survived on their
Land" (*Tosefta Avodah Zarah* iv:4) in all probability referred to the
notables and philanthropists of his day. Not all scholars followed the
example of R. Eleazer ben Shammua and R. Johanan Ha-Sandlar who
"were going to Nisibis to study with R. Judah ben Bathyra; when
they reached Sidon, they recalled Eretz Israel, they raised their eyes,
and their tears flowed, they rent their garments, and they recited the
Scripture: 'And you will inherit it and you will live in it, and you
will perform all these laws and precepts'; and they said, 'the precept
of living in Eretz Israel is the equivalent to [fulfilling] all of the
precepts in the Torah.' They turned around and went back to Eretz
Israel."

There were scholars who shed tears and rent their garments,
and also read this scripture, yet did not return (*Sifre*, Deuteronomy,
par. 10, p. 146). Many pronouncements against the exile (*Galut*) are
to be found in Talmudic sources, for example: "The *Galut* is hard to
bear and it outweighs all the punishments in the Torah" (*Sifre, ibid.,*
par. 43, p. 100); R. Eliazar said, "Jews who live outside the country
are idol worshippers" (*Tos. Avodah Zarah, loc. cit.*). Nostalgia for
Eretz Israel could find satisfaction in fulfilling injunctions which applied to the Land of Israel, such as was described as "the act of Thad-
deus a resident of Rome" (*Pesaḥim* 53a). It is told that in one place
R. Joshua and R. Gamaliel came upon children who were playing

at setting aside the heave-offerings and the tithes and declaring, "Our brothers in the Land of Israel are performing likewise" (*P.T. Sanhedrin*, vii:3, 24d). The words of R. Johanan, "our rabbis in the *Golah* used to set aside heave-offerings and tithes until the *Rovin* came and abrogated them" (*P.T. Hallah*, iv:9, 60a) probably refer to Babylonia. There is an ironical twist to the Midrashic account: "You find that when the Jews were exiled they would observe the laws of the sabbatical year, and the gentiles would deride them saying 'in your own country you did not keep the sabbatical year'" (*Lamentations Rabbah*, 1:4). Throughout the period of the Amoraim until the Savoraim the scholars of Babylonia used to send *halakhic* inquiries to Eretz Israel and to accept the rulings of its scholars. Even in matters of civil law they did not hand down rulings on their own, but acted on the authority of the scholars in Eretz Israel. This continued even in the time of Abbaye and Rabbah when status of the academies of Eretz Israel was in decline (*Gittin* 88b; *Bava Kamma* 84d).

There were indeed individuals who rebelled against the primacy of Eretz Israel. R. Jehudah, a disciple of Mar Samuel, went so far as to expound this principle as follows: "Whoever emigrates from Babylonia to Eretz Israel transgresses a positive biblical precept" (*Ketubot* 110b). However, even though not a few scholars of Babylonia went to settle in Eretz Israel, the nature of the existing relationship could not restore Eretz Israel to its position as a center. Resh Lakish, who perceived the change that had taken place, explained the absence of the Holy Spirit (*Ruah ha-Kodesh*) during the Second Temple period as follows: The Jews of Babylonia had failed to respond to the call of Cyrus for the return of the exiles—"Whosoever there is among you of all His people—his God be with him—let him go up." The Almighty said, if all the Jews go up, the Divine Presence will rest there [on the Second Sanctuary] and if not they will be able to avail themselves only of a *Bat Kol* [Heavenly Voice] (*B.T. Yoma* 9b). In the generation after Resh Lakish the scholars of Eretz Israel applied the scripture: "If she be a wall" (*Canticles* viii:9) to mean "Had Israel returned [united in a body] like a wall from the Exile, the Temple would not have been destroyed a second time" (*Canticles Rabbah* viii:9). The reason for the destruction of the Second Temple is here attributed to a failure at the very beginning of the period. The explanations offered had a specific implication, since they were voiced by scholars of Eretz Israel who had little sympathy for their Babylonian colleagues (*Canticles R.*, loc. cit.; *B.T. Yoma* 9b). Perhaps even more expressive of absence of sympathy or even of direct hostility is the explanation given to the delay in the return of the exiles which began with the emigration of Ezra: "Ezra and his associates and his following did not go up [to Eretz Israel] at that time. Why did not Ezra go up at that time? Because he had to complete his studies with Baruch ben Neriah. But should not Baruch ben Neriah also have returned? It is recorded that Baruch ben Neriah was a heavy man and aged, and was unable to travel even in a litter" (*Canticles R.,* v:5). The sarcasm of this allusion is unconcealed, and there is also recognition that Eretz Israel was no longer the Jewish center.

Ascendancy of Babylonian Ritual

The numerous documents that have come to light in the Cairo *Geniza,* include evidence of cultural activity in various spheres in Eretz Israel, as well as information on its academies. The documents show that even after the termination of the patriarchate and during the savage persecutions which took place at the end of the Byzantine period following the Arab conquest of the country, the Jewish population in Eretz Israel continued to maintain itself there. In the Geonic period, however, the attitude of the scholars of Babylonia toward Eretz Israel underwent a radical reversal. Not only was no place allocated for teaching the *Palestinian Talmud* in the Babylonian academies, but the Geonim of Babylonia set out to impose the legal norms of Babylonia and ritual observances in Eretz Israel. They explained the difference in the ritual followed in Eretz Israel as the result of confusion following the persecutions and destructions there. Some zealous Geonim even tried to transpose the promises of the prophets and their mission and apply them to Babylonia.

Thus Ben Baboi, a second-generation member of the school of R. Yehudai Gaon, states: "Even in the era of Messiah, they do not see the messianic tribulations, as it is written, 'Ho, Zion, escape thou that dwelleth with the daughter of Babylon' (Zechariah ii:11)— escape from wicked Edom and from its Exile, for what is Zion but an academy distinguished (the word used—*metzuyanim*—is a play on the name Zion] for its teaching of Torah and piety, as it is thus written: 'Be in pain, and labour to bring forth oh daughter of Zion like a woman in travail,'" (Micah iv:10; see *Tarbiz* 2, bk. 4, p. 396; *Tanhuma,* Noah, par. 3).

The actual date of transfer of the academy of Eretz Israel from

Tiberias to Jerusalem and the designation of its head by the title
"Gaon" are not known, but in the eleventh century it regained status
similar to that of the Babylonian academies, due to the impact of two
outstanding personalities. The Geonim in Babylonia were generally
members of well-connected families, but they also included scholars
without such family connections, and the office of Gaon did not pass
by inheritance from father to son. However, in Eretz Israel, nearly all
the Geonim whose names are known came from three families, one
of which claimed to be of Davidic descent, while the other two were
of priestly lineage. The principal office-holders in the academy were
also sons of the Geonim. This situation certainly did not benefit the
institution. Of the two Geonim mentioned (who were also distinguished scholars), the first was R. Aaron ben Meir, a strong and severe personality, known principally because of his controversy with
Saadiah Gaon. The second, R. Solomon ben Judah, was noted for opposite qualities; he followed the tradition of Hillel. Open rivalry between the academies of Eretz Israel and Babylonia developed over
distribution of charitable funds and over support to communities
and individuals. The protagonists were of the stature of R. Sherira
and R. Hai Gaon. Nevertheless, the presence of outstanding scholars
who settled in Eretz Israel, such as Nahmanides, Samson of Sens and
Jehiel of Paris, did not turn it into a center of the Jewish world. The
sources which have been quoted show no definite awareness of the
existence of a center after the Patriarchate of R. Yehuda ha-Nassi. In
fact, efforts of both R. Yehuda and his grandfather Rabban Gamaliel
of Jabneh did not go beyond an attempt to restore the central authority of Eretz Israel. The awareness of exile and philosophy which
conceded the right of existence in dispersion lie outside the scope of
this paper. The dictum of R. Eleazar, "The Almighty only sent Israel
into exile among the nations so that proselytes might join them,"
was the legacy of the generations who took pride in the influence of
the religion of Israel even as they lived in a Gentile environment.

Others saw the extent of the dispersion as a factor preventing
extinction of the Jews in the world (Pesaḥim 87b). In contrast to this
view is the argument put into the mouth of Haman: When the king
contended that extermination of the Jews might cause a vacuum in
his realm, Haman pointed out that the Jewish people were dispersed
throughout his territory and therefore no void would be created (B.T.
Megillah 13b). The accepted view, however, is to be found in the

dictum that "The *Galut* is hard to bear, and it outweighs all the punishments in the Torah" (*Sifre*, Deuteronomy 10, 3). The Babylonian scholar, R. Samuel ben Isaac, who settled in Eretz Israel at the time of R. Johanan, formulated the significance of Eretz Israel as a center by his exposition of Jeremiah xiii:7—"My soul shall weep in secret for your pride"; "Because the pride of Israel was taken from them and given to the Gentile nations" (*Ḥagigah* 5b).

The removal of both Jewish sovereignty and independence in its own land was the reason for the termination of Eretz Israel as the Jewish center. Without this precondition, any attempt to prove its continuance as a Jewish center cannot succeed, and all the concepts of center and dispersion in Jewish history are merely reconstructions without basis in fact.

From *Altneuland* to *Altneuvolk:* Toward an Agenda for Interaction between Israel and American Jewry

Gerson D. Cohen

Our Current Situation

The Yom Kippur War changed nothing except to reveal that, with respect to the Jewish situation, nothing had really changed. What the war did achieve was to discharge a series of shock waves through the world Jewish community which bestirred at least a segment of Jewish leadership to confront the Jewish situation not in terms of ideology but in terms of reality. The Yom Kippur War was a heavy price to pay for unwillingness to confront important things as they are, but there is no point in bemoaning the past. Our task is to become wiser for the future. Unfortunately, we have not yet considered many fundamental implications of the realities of the Jewish situation.

This paper is predicated on the following assumptions:

1. The Yom Kippur War is not over. (For that matter, the Israeli War of Independence, begun officially in 1948, is still in progress; but that is a technicality which it will serve no useful purpose to dwell upon here. What concerns us at this juncture is that chapter in the war that jolted the Jews, the Arabs and the world at large into varying forms of "reassessment.") There is only a lull in hostilities, while both sides feverishly prepare for the next hot confrontation.

2. While the Israeli defense forces are alert to the possibility of another round, Jewish leadership seem to be doing very little, if anything, to prepare the Jewish People as a whole for *its* role in the next round or to reorient it in the light of *realistic* expectations. Part of that preparation ought to include cool but intense planning for internal and external orientation. The Yom Kippur War has revealed Jewish leadership to be woefully inadequate on that score, and, indeed, to be functioning on levels that are frequently enough so wide of the mark as to border on the phantasmagoric. To continue in ways

that are not apposite to our needs and to the realities of Jewish and world public opinion is to betray some of the moral fatigue that has overcome a considerable portion of the political leadership of the free world. For Jews to continue to talk to Jews as though we are all united in spirit and only need more money, *aliyah,* unity is to reflect a total insensitivity to reality: to the erosion of solidarity within the Jewish community in Israel as well as in the Diaspora on basic questions of Jewish policy, chief among these being Israel's political stance on indirect negotiations with the Arabs on the one hand, and to the Jewish identity crisis in Israel no less than in the Diaspora, on the other.

3. Israel's political crisis has revealed in full light of day that the dynamics of Jewish history—particularly with respect to Jewish physical security—are as operative with respect to the State of Israel as they have been with every Diaspora community. Jewish safety and security have always depended on a strong central authority that will clearly throw its weight in defense of Jewish clients. (That weight need not necessarily be through the contribution of military personnel, but may consist of materiel, money, or even threats; however, the posture of the guarantor must be clear and unequivocal.) From the point of view of physical security, the Jewish situation in Israel is today not very much different from that of the Jewish community of Elephantine in 411 B.C.E., of the Jews of Northern France and the Rhineland in 1096, of the Jews of Spain in 1391, or of the Jews of the Ukraine and Poland in 1648. This perception, alas, has become an unspeakable heresy with respect to the State of Israel, for it affirms that the physical-political position of Israeli Jewry is not *qualitatively* different from that of the Jews of the Diaspora during the last two thousand years and more. But that is exactly what I am saying, not out of a desire to shock, but out of a conviction forced upon me by my own reading of the totality of Jewish history.

The difference in potential Israel quantitative response to physical threat is, of course, so vast as to obscure the similarity with pre-State history. Israel clearly has capacities for maneuverability and of retaliation that are so great as to make its posture a significant factor even in the policy of the superpowers. But, in the final analysis, this means that Israel can elect not only to die in dignity, but to make the world pay for the consequences so heavily as to make the destruction of Israel too expensive an option *for the present.* However, such considerations are not *essentially* different from those which prevailed in the ancient or medieval world. Now, as then, it was often in the interest and capacity of the overlords of the Jews to protect their wards against total destruction; but now, as then, this interest is not a flat surety of the immutable allegiance of these protectors to Israel's safety. The *possibility* of the withdrawal of such loyalty and support on the part of the United States, for example, should by now be perfectly evident. It should be equally evident that the erosion in the traditional American posture toward Israel cuts across party lines and, however distasteful to admit, has even engulfed some American Jews in positions of political influence in the United States.

4. The virtual state of shock that has overcome many Jews now that American leadership is reassessing its policy reflects the chasm between Jewish assessments and what should long have been evident. Both the unbounded sense of confidence and the state of shock reflect a knowledge of Jewish history that spans the years from 1967 to 1973: the unshakable conviction that a superpower like America will inevitably perceive its interests today as it did a decade ago and that it will meet any challenge to this perception of its interests rationally and determinedly; in short, that a Jewish reading of American interests and responses is the only rational one.

On the other hand, even if we should grant that Israel's claims and posture are so cogent that they must convince anyone, we must recognize a counter-possibility. Anyone even faintly acquainted with Ibn Khaldun must consider the possibility of a great nation permitting itself—indeed, beckoning—to be overrun by barbarian hordes whose 'aṣabiyya is strong enough to overthrow mighty empires precisely because the barbarians themselves have no empire to lose.

However, the issue must be squarely faced. America is, today, an ailing nation. That it will ultimately overcome its malaise I, for one, have little doubt. But I also happen to be Jewish and, therefore, Jewish interests are primary with me. As a Jew, I cannot wait for America to be awakened to reality or to my perception of reality; for the alarm bell that will jolt America out of its present political-moral paralysis may well only be the kind of experience that finally awakened the West in 1939 and America in 1941. It will be of small comfort to us Jews to have served as a catalyst for the restoration of America to corporate sanity and to resolute and unequivocal behavior. Catalysts, alas, are often disposable chemicals. . . .

5. The danger the Jewish People faces gives promise of being one of long duration and, at the same time, is a clear and present one; it is a danger which requires proximate responses, not ideological or eschatological ones. Politics is the art of the possible, and we are now desperately in need of sound political thinking. To invoke an illustration of ideology guided by realism, I would suggest that the genius of the fathers of the State of Israel was not their achievement of the miraculous—that is, the impossible—but their perception of the limits of the possible and the probable. In times of crisis they also faced up willingly to action based on the absence of alternatives. In meeting today's crisis, we should consider all current options, not yesterday's hopes and dreams.

In the present situation it is pointless to fritter away our energies on a Zionist ideology of mass *aliyah,* or on a discussion of interaction between Israel and the Diaspora that makes of mass *aliyah* part of an unspoken agenda to which a successful colloquy will lead. That will not take place for the simple reason that most Jews of the world feel no personal need for it. (I say this even granting the absurd assumption that a vast concentration of Jews in Israel would provide a sufficient counterpoise to the superpowers in their formulation of policy. And, in the final analysis, it is not the Arabs but the superpowers that will determine whether there is to be a war or not, or what its outcome is to be. That is what happened in 1948, in 1956, in 1967 and in 1973.) We do ourselves a disservice if we ignore the fact that the major portion of Israel's Jewish population immigrated there only out of an absence of alternatives, that is, out of desperate physical need, not necessarily conviction. Need may have changed to conviction, but for the overwhelming number of Jews now living, this is not the case. The time, the money, the energy spent on patently unrealizable Zionist programs can be, must be used to meet the real internal danger—the erosion of Jewish solidarity and morale. We are in a state of danger that I presume to diagnose as a crisis, for our physical survival and corporate health are intertwined with our morale, that is, our willingness to die for a cause which we believe to be so worthwhile as to make of Jewish life a transcendent cause.

6. The crisis is not one of the State of Israel but of the *People* of Israel, that is, the whole Jewish People. A calamity for Israel would constitute a real—not merely a moral—calamity for world Jewry. Accordingly, an erosion of Jewish morale in the United States is a threat to all Israel. An erosion of the solidarity of Jews in the

State of Israel with the Jewish community of the world is a threat to
the State of Israel itself. Signs of this erosion are already a fact, not
merely a possibility. We can, alas, no longer afford to assume that a
mere threat to Israel will arouse and mobilize the whole of the Jewish People behind the State of Israel. The processes of assimilation,
secularization, and rebellion against institutional authority in Israel
as well as in the Diaspora have gone too far to be dismissed. Moreover, even within the ranks of the committed there is an increasingly
audible murmur of doubt about the soundness of Israel's policies in
the arena of international politics. I am not happy about these rum-
blings. Indeed, I confess that they alarm me, for they are now coming
from quarters on which we thought we could rely. But it is sheer folly to ignore them. Moreover, they will not be silenced by appeals
or leadership tours. The situation, I firmly believe, is reversible, but
it must first be acknowledged and confronted.

The Contemporary Jewish Situation

So far, my assumptions. From all this, I can proceed to a number of, what appear to me to be necessary, attitudes and proposals.
Since Jewish solidarity and unity of purpose will be key factors for
the survival and quality of Jewish life in the trying years ahead, I
propose that we make our prime concern the Jewish People and their
collective spirit. This paper will, accordingly, deliberately dismiss
issues such as "the centrality of the State of Israel" and concentrate
instead on concerns that are apposite, in my view, to *our present
Jewish situation.*

The last phrase betrays my point of departure, my underlying
assumption. All Jews now share a Jewish situation in common,
whether they live in Israel, the United States, or any other free country in the West.[1] To debate the place of Israel in the Jewish situation
is to concede the possibility that it may not be a central, that is, indispensable, unexpendable, *vital part* (in the physiological sense of
the term) of the Jewish People. I refuse to consider that possibility. In

1. Those who are not free and would like to be, have but one obvious concern. With
respect to them, those of us who are free also have but one apposite concern: to liberate them to make their own choice! Further, for those of us who are free, there are
many Jewish situations that are local in character and, accordingly, of little relevance
to this paper. I am concerned here only with those that engulf the whole free part of
the Jewish People irrespective of its place of domicile.

the formulation of collective Jewish policy and ideology, the disappearance or weakening of Israel as a vital organ of the Jewish People is beyond the realm of rational consideration. For better or worse, I am incapable of considering options for Jewish life without a State of Israel. Moreover, for better or worse, I am incapable of thinking about any policy or program for Jewish life anywhere in the world without taking into account, as an element of *crucial* importance, the effect or implications of that policy or program on and for the State of Israel. Israel is a vital part of my Jewish body and mentality.

On the other hand, I also find the alternative of exclusive or even predominant concern for any one of my vital parts an absurdity. I do not know which is more central to my body—my heart, my liver, my kidneys, or my nervous system. Exigencies may compel me *temporarily* to devote the major part of my attention and energies to the repair and strengthening of one vital part but not to the measuring of its relative importance or to the abdication of concern and responsibility for other parts. To insist on, or even to give lip service to, the centrality of the State of Israel in the life of the Jewish People is to me an absurd shibboleth in terms of the *practical implications of such a principle.* Does it mean that a healthy and creative Diaspora is less important than a healthy Israel? If so, I find the phrase repugnant and unspeakable. In this sense, it is a relic from the days when Zionism was fighting to gain recognition as a vital component of Jewish life and when Israel was struggling to gain recognition, even from Jews, of its indispensability to the Jewish body politic. That day is long gone. To insist on a point that is now axiomatic is to raise doubts about its certainty in the minds of the proponents of the statement.

Recent events have determined our agenda for us. Our task is to articulate afresh the meanings of Jewishness in the modern world and of the educational techniques for the inculcation of those meanings to Jews everywhere. Clearly, not all Jews will agree on the meaning of Jewishness and its implications, but there are enough to pool their energies to meet common Jewish problems or, to put it differently, to confront the common problems emerging from our Jewish situation in terms that are equally apposite to Israel and the Diaspora. A vital component in the explication of Jewishness will have to be an elucidation of the historic factors underlying the situation common to Jews everywhere in the world. Another essential element will be a reformulation or reaffirmation of the interrelated-

ness of Jews everywhere and of the implications of this interrelatedness. It will shift our central concern to the Jewish people and to the
elements that must be mobilized to activate as many as possible of
our people in pursuit of common goals—proximate as well as ultimate—in Israel as well as in the Diaspora. It is a task for a generation,
one that must undo or redirect programs and ideologies of almost
two centuries.

The State of Israel and Jewish History

The State of Israel and the vital components of its body and
character came into being for good and compelling reasons, reasons
that the founding fathers of the state or their precursors may have
had grounds to believe would convince the Jews and the world at
large. Some of these arguments have totally convinced some Jews,
and some have convinced many Jews in part; most Jews have responded affirmatively to Israel in one form or another, either for
Zionist reasons or from other motivations. However, the majority of
Jews have refused to commit themselves to classical Zionist formulations and their implications in terms of personal and existential decision: I mean such formulation as the negation of the *galut*, making
Israel a kinetic spiritual center of their lives, and relegation of the *galut* to an inferior status in the scale of Jewish values. That is the reality and it gives every likelihood of continuing to remain so for the
foreseeable future. Indeed, within the foreseeable future, the safety
of Israel and the well-being of the Jewish People as a whole depend
on the continuity of this pluralist Jewish response to the question of
Jewish identity in the modern world. Classical Zionists have become
a new orthodoxy in Jewish life, and their perceptions and form of
speech have assumed a fundamentalist coloration that is alien to the
thinking of most Jews in the free countries of the Diaspora as well as
of many Jews within the State of Israel itself.

In retrospect, the rejection of classical Zionist ideology by the
overwhelming number of Jews the world over should have been
clear from the very first days of the Zionist movement, for most Jews
regarded Zionism even as Pinsker and Herzl did, that is, as a measure of last resort that had been forced on the Jews. While many Jews
may have been sympathetic to the rebirth or renewed expression of
an age-old Jewish hope of a return to the historic homeland, most
sought quite different solutions to the sorry Jewish plight.

Some, and let it never be forgotten that they were not insignificant in number, felt that the solution to the so-called Jewish question lay in social revolution and in elimination of class warfare. Millions of Jews gave their assent to Communism and Bundism as their new form of Judaism. Indeed, even among the early Zionists there were some who shuddered at the thought of any kind of Jewish society other than a Socialist one in their ancient, new homeland. Historical events of one form or another have made a historic memory of that dream in all its variations. As a living doctrine for the orientation of Jewish society as a whole or even Jewish society in the Jewish State, it may yet be revived, but at present provides no rallying point either in Israel or in the free Diaspora. However, the collapse of the socialist dream did not appreciably swell the ranks of Zionist activists. Many former communists and Bundists now support the State of Israel, but only in the sense that most Jews of the Diaspora do, as a good and necessary solution for Jews other than themselves.

Most Jews have also rejected a second course that not long ago had the character of a mass movement of sorts—assimilation as a solution to Jewish *Angst*. This, of course, in no way implies that many Jews do not continue to be lost to the Jewish community through indifference or intermarriage; but few, if any, still deliberately choose this way, that is, with the *articulated* purpose of putting an end to their Jewish identity. Indeed, even cultured Gentiles no longer plead for the disappearance of the Jews through total and active assimilation. The acerbity of would-be humanist-universalists (read: Christian polemicists) such as Julian Benda against the Jews for continuing to insist on their discrete, corporate identity sounds far more remote than the mere five decades that separate those fulminations from our day. Here, too, a variety of circumstances have made this course of action as an expression of an *ideology* unfashionable, if not downright shameful. But, once again, bankruptcy of assimilationalism did not result in an appreciable turn to *aliyah*.

The overwhelming number of Jews who chose to respond to the intolerable conditions to which they had been subjected in the nation-states of central and eastern Europe chose a third course, namely, migration to the West, especially to the Western hemisphere. Here, too, the Jews chose a variety of Jewish courses of action—socialism, assimilationism, secular nationalism, religious affiliation and reform (with a small "r"—including Conservatism,

Reform, Reconstructionism, and American-style Orthodoxy). Religious affiliation provided the umbrella for an ethnic identity that was acceptable within the framework of the American melting and leveling pot. But whatever the style of Jewish identity and behavior they chose, westward migration and integration proved to be the course of action most appealing to and enduring for the greatest number of Jews of the free world.

In sum, any rational reading of Jewish history will reveal that for most Jews, Zionism in the real sense—that is, *aliyah* and settlement—was a last recourse for Jews who chose to continue to live as Jews in dignity and who wished simultaneously to achieve a dignified acceptance into the family of humanity.

This last element—acceptance into the family of humanity—had been the great proximate eschatological drive of Jewish intellectuals of all colorations, including Zionists, in the nineteenth and twentieth centuries. This was what Judah Loeb Gordon pined for when he urged Jews to be Jewish at home and human [*sic*] outside. By any assessment, the promise of rebirth on ancestral Jewish soil did not capture the hearts of most Jews—at least, if we judge Jews by their actions. The overwhelming number of Jews now living in Israel immigrated there for lack of alternative. Even thousands upon thousands of refugees from the Holocaust as well as citizens of Israel itself opted for migration to free countries of the West.

All this should be too well-known to require recapitulation here. But recapitulation is precisely what it does require, for many in the State of Israel as well as in the Diaspora have so muted the facts of Jewish history as to make the real appear a failure or even a betrayal of the *accepted* ideal. What has consequently happened is that even relatively sophisticated Jews in Israel and in the Diaspora have no basic understanding of the course of events that led to the emergence of the two great poles of contemporary Jewish life— Israel and North America. Worse still, the refusal or inability to confront the realities of contemporary Jewish history has left a goodly portion of world Jewry—in Israel as well as in the Diaspora—bereft of any real sense of Jewish peoplehood. This is particularly true for secularized Jews, who have no sense of kinship with Jews of the present or of the past, that is not rooted in their sense of rejection by the nations of the world. With them there is no positive drive for kinship or a sharing of destiny and goals. Hence, the problem of Jewish identity is not merely one of self-awareness with respect to Gentile society but of kinship between one Jewish community and another. The Jews are largely unequipped to recognize or accept the continuity of Jewish history and, consequently, of Jewish kinship and confraternity in contemporary secular society.

Zionist spokesmen have never been able to come to terms with the reality of modern Jewish history—that is, with the legitimacy of the free choice of the masses of Jews; and they have made their unwillingness to face reality the basis of the Jewish history and ideology that they have imparted to the Jewish youth of Israel. The consequence has been a growing spiritual chasm between secularists and many religiously oriented Jews of Israel on the one hand, and enlightened Jews of Israel and the Diaspora on the other. Only the memory of one Holocaust and the real threat of another holds most Jews together. This is a tenuous thread and one which, as I have already indicated, shows signs of fraying. The threat of another Holocaust may be temporarily effective—and I will be the last to deny its possibility—but it is not likely to make Israel an *enduring center* in the real life of Jews. It certainly does not appear likely to stimulate Jewishness, that is, real Jewish commitment.

Zionism, like many other modern Jewish ideologies, has often misread and frequently distorted Jewish history for the sake of an ideal to which I believe all Jews should not only subscribe, but in which I would like to find ways for them to participate. However, its misreadings and distortions have confused many Israelis and Diaspora Jews and left them totally at a loss on their common ties, common destiny with, and, accordingly, common duties to the Jewish People as a whole. To many Israelis Jewish identity appears to be as existentially problematic as it is to many an assimilated Jew of the Diaspora. This can be graphically experienced by looking at the secularist Israeli in the Diaspora, who is more often than not a Jew lost to the Jewish community. This, I submit, is a situation as harmful to Israel as it is to world Jewry. If Jewish identity is a primary concern of the State of Israel, the situation is an indictment of classical Zionism. It is also a product of the characteristic features of the cultural and spiritual life of Israel. The Yom Kippur War merely brought to the surface the tension, which had long been sensed and occasionally expressed, between Jewish and Israeli identity in the minds of many Israelis, and this has been communicated to many Jews in the Diaspora.

Furthermore, the Yom Kippur War uncovered the vacuum created in the minds of a whole generation by the cultivation of an illusion that the establishment of the State of Israel had fundamentally changed the dynamics of Jewish history. Many Jews seem to have simply forgotten that the Jewish State can only survive in a world that insures its survival, and that in a largely hostile world—as devoid as ever of any underlying commitments to principles of morality—only a strong guarantor with clout to back up Israel will insure its survival. Israel, after the Yom Kippur War, was jolted by the discovery that it was part and parcel of Jewish history, that some of the syndromes of *galut* survival were by no means at an end even in the State of Israel.

What is more, the Yom Kippur War made it evident that anti-Semitism is still very much alive and that, if the reports in the press are to be credited, an Egyptian ambassador knew what he was doing when he appealed to the people of Argentina to join in a movement to destroy the Jews. Curiously, the Jew of America is far better equipped to confront such an obscenity than the Jew of Israel, for the simple reason that Israel based its morale to a considerable degree on a chain of illusions that is fundamentally oblivious of, if not downright hostile to, the conditions actually attendant upon Jewish identity, survival and solidarity even today. Many Jews of the Diaspora are aware of this attitude on the part of Israelis and mutter in muted protest, because, they fear, now is not the time to fight this battle officially and publicly.

The significant point about these widely recognized characteristics of the mentality of many in the State of Israel is that they make it evident that the Jewish State has been in large measure shaped by yardsticks of modernity and humanism formulated by, and appropriated from, the Gentile cultural tastemakers of Europe of the eighteenth and nineteenth centuries. Israel, in consequence, in many ways conforms to the syndromes of African black nationalism so aptly portrayed by the Italian sociologist Vittorio Lanternari.[2] Not the least dangerous of these appropriated values is the condescension to, contempt for, and sustained (though unsuccessful) effort at the rejection of Jewish "landlessness" and of the Jewish characteristics supposedly associated with *galut* and *galutiyut*. These epithets often reflect Gentile notions that Jewish history in the Diaspora was a chimera—that only with the establishment of the State were Jews restored to an active role in world history as a corporate group. In other

---

2. Vittorio Lanternari, *The Religions of the Oppressed,* a study of modern messianic cults, trans. Lisa Sergio, New York, 1963, 1965.

words, Gentiles determined the yardsticks by which twenty centuries and more of Jewish history could be brushed aside as inconse-
quential, parasitical, pariahlike. (Bruno Bauer, von Treitschke and
Werner Sombart—the list could be extended endlessly—would,
doubtless, take great satisfaction in the successful influence that
their so-called objective analyses of Jewish history and character
have exercised over the Jews!) The need for a land, a language, an
army, a productive economy, a machinery of government came to
Jewish consciousness out of secular considerations and largely
thanks to the castigations of anti-Semites—often of the most liberal
and genteel kind, described so aptly by Professor Uriel Tal—who
simply would not accept Jews into their society as Jews. Alas, many
Jews have made their own those highly invidious appraisals of the
Jews along with the *healthy stimuli* these rejections generated in our
people. Yehezkiel Kaufmann's protests against the spiritual destruction that we inflict on ourselves by our assent to those Gentiles has
not yielded a sufficient reassessment of the roots and overtones of
Jewish collective responses to modernity. *Galut* is still a badge of
shame in the dictionary of many; solidarity with—and dependence
on—a people of *galut* a source of confusion.

What I have said—and perhaps a good deal more—is at least
equally true of the overwhelming proportion of Jewish life in the
Diaspora. In America, for example, religious affiliation for the majority of religiously affiliated Jews is a form of acculturation to the mod-
ish style of life in America. As assimilation progresses, Jews paradoxically often express their Americanization through synagogue
affiliation. Much of this, of course, is simplistic, but it is deliberately
put this way to point up the common paths chosen by Jews *in* Israel
and *out* of it in their drive to become part of the family of modernity.
It is also put this way to emphasize the tremendous hurdles that
must be overcome if we are to recapture a definition of Jewishness
that will transcend political and geographical limitations. In short,
Zionism is as much confronted by the problem of Jewish identity as
is the assimilated Jewish Diaspora.

All this has come to pass because Zionism, like the other Jewish patterns of behavior in modern times, represented an effort not
only to find a physical and spiritual haven for the Jewish People, but
a desperate effort *to put an end to classical Jewish history* in a way
that Jews perceived that history for two thousand years. Did Georges

Friedmann not reflect more than his own appraisal (or was it also a hope) when he saw in Israel the beginning of *The End of the Jewish People?* Hence a whole generation of Jews was reared in Israel not only to look down on Jewish history and the creativity of fifteen centuries but also to be ignorant of it!

A recently published Israeli high school textbook, entitled *The History of Israel in Contemporary Times* (note: not of the State of Israel, but of *Israel*) that begins its story with 1897 speaks worlds. With one stroke of the pen the name of Israel has been confined to the State of Israel, which, in the mind of the author and of his readers, is synonymous with *verus Israel*. All of contemporary Jewish history is now measured by its relationship to the Land of Israel. This may be legitimate ideology, but it is hardly history, and hardly the kind of historically grounded ideology that will provide the young Israeli with the spiritual armament with which to confront world Jewry and Jewish reality. The real and total people of Israel, the literature of Israel, the pride of Israel, the real history of Israel (in which "Israel" means the Jews)—the stage for which is and has been the globe!—are suddenly driven from—or at best into a corner of—Jewish consciousness. In consequence of this planned ignorance, American Jewish youth have a lot more in common with Israeli youth than is often recognized or acknowledged. The textbook mentioned is not an accident. It is a consequence of widespread modern Jewish assent to the glorification of the Bible and the biblical period—ending significantly in 73 C.E., and for the more sophisticated in 135—and the denigration of virtually all subsequent Jewish history and literature until Herzl. (For those who probe the significance of this attitude toward Jewish history, I would recommend a glance into Justin Martyr, Paulus Orosius, Emil Schuerer and Martin Noth.)

Moreover the textbook in question is not an isolated phenomenon. It actually represents a carefully organized and formidable armada of new rituals, new forms of leisure, new yardsticks of cultural taste, and highly sophisticated techniques of Jewish fundraising and budgeting. The same armada determines with a fair degree of effectiveness the parameters of Jewish pluralism and dissent. We are all the losers—and many of our children stand in danger of total spiritual bankruptcy—for having failed to see that neither the world at large nor the Jews can or will accept the directives of even the most charismatic secular Jewish leadership.

Toward a New Renewal

There are fortunately enough Jews of like mind, alert to the spiritual state of affairs, to give good reason for hope that our efforts at a spiritual renewal of the whole Jewish People are by no means devoid of legitimate hope. Israel was born in the face of far more disheartening circumstances. In Israel as well as in the Diaspora our people have a core of spiritual nobility among young and old who are eager to serve their people and shape Jewish destiny in keeping with transcendent commitments.

The following suggestions for sustained, meaningful and productive interaction between Israel and the Diaspora are predicated on the assumption of a common destiny even in the face of total absence of external pressures. In the first place, a sustained relationship must be predicated on a policy of mutual kinship and respect. An expectation of solidarity will require taking counsel before issuing directives. More important, confraternity must face up to the underlying problem of kinship of spirit. It must confront the question not of why *be* Jewish but of why *transmit* this Jewishness. Jewish education is indeed a priority task for Jewish leadership, but the only rationale for such education is that it is part of the mandate of Jewishness. I have no problem about why *I* am Jewish. I do have a problem about educating my children to be Jewish in certain ways in the hope that they, too, will do the same for their children. To ask them to be Jewish because Israel will need them might well be a self-serving betrayal of their conceivably alternative and better interests. To educate them to a notion that Israel is central to their lives simply because they are Jewish is, to say the least by any nonreligious yardstick, a *non sequitur*.

Israel can occupy an indispensable place in Jewish life only if it becomes and remains part of an inseverable dimension of greater centrality—*the centrality of the Jewish People*. To this, I hasten to add that even the Jewish People can only perpetuate its centrality if it, in turn, is a consequence of a higher mandate—and that is the destiny that made the Jews, sustained the Jews, motivated the Jews as Jews until very recent times—namely, the Torah. Only a religious, that is, transcendent, mandate can lead to a sense of consanguinity between my children and Jews of Moroccan origin living in Israel. Apart from that religious mandate, apart from the covenant that underlies such a mandate, no demand of loyalty on my part or anyone else's makes any sense.

For a while, to be sure, Nazism and the Holocaust made an aggressive affirmation of Jewishness, on any basis, even one devoid of a religious foundation, a necessity. Many Jews are aware of this and, accordingly, live on a holocaustology as a surrogate for theology. I find theologies predicated on the Holocaust an effrontery. The Holocaust should have generated a new anthropology, perhaps a mass contrition and religious return, but it is not for me a basis for life. Any articulation of Jewishness will have to include a response to holocausts, of the past and of possible future ones, but it will also have to take into account the possibility of peace and goodwill among all men in the face of which we must still be Jews.

For two hundred years the masses of Jews have resisted such a confrontation with their Jewishness, for they sincerely believed in the soteric power of other, secular eschatologies. Indeed, there is still no good reason for Jews to reject alternative eschatologies except this—that Jews stand under the command of a covenant with God that has made them members of a unique People. I do not contend that this is a pleasant answer, one that will satisfy emotionally. The renowned rabbinic homily, *kaffah aleihem har ke-gigith,* affirming that the Torah was imposed upon the Jews betrays not a little resentment on the part of some Jews of ancient times about their destiny. I contend that it is the only answer I know that gives cogency to the demand for acceptance of Jewishness and for some orientation to the identity we seek to preserve and cultivate.

As a consequence of my Jewishness I not only can, but do and must, feel a deep kinship with other Jews that transcends citizenship and time and place. As a Jew, I find the demands of secular nationalist totalism as a yardstick of legitimate loyalties an idolatry. I feel a special relationship with the Land of Israel, for my being a Jew makes it my Land. I feel a special sense of solidarity with the State of Israel, for it is the institutional embodiment of my people's relationship to its Land. But that Land derives its special place in my life from my religious heritage. But I am also a member of the American Jewish community. As a Jew, indeed, I am at home to varying degrees in any Jewish community. That means that my Jewishness not only gives me ties with Jews everywhere, but places special obligations on me to Jews everywhere. It further means that my Jewishness is to be expressed and experienced wherever I happen to be. It means that wherever I happen to live I must participate in the life of that Jewish community, for only through community can my Jewishness come to adequate expression.

Accordingly, my spiritual home is *Jewland*, and my life is forever being oriented—consciously and unconsciously—by my Jewish identity, by the covenant into which I was formally ushered shortly after my birth. The Jewish People is my family, for its God is my God, its Land is my Land, its Torah is mine, its destiny is mine. In short, I am obliged to be concerned for the quality, shape and content of Jewish life everywhere.

I firmly believe that as a Jew, I have duties to the Land of Israel and hence even to its State. But, by that same token, I believe that every Jew of Israel has a relationship and duties to Judaism, to the Jewish People and to the Jewish community everywhere. If we are one people, born and sustained by the identical covenant, sharers of one destiny and of common goals, we must be trained to identify with each other actively. The real center of our life must be our Jewishness. This Jewishness will generate multiple loyalties—to the Land of Israel, to the people of Israel (i.e., the Jews), to the Torah of Israel (i.e., Judaism). Such loyalties, I venture to suggest, will generate more *aliyah* than the present basis of appeal, for it will generate needs for Jewish ambience, Jewish idiom and Jewish kinship. In any event, it will certainly inhibit the almost automatic alienation from the Jewish community that is currently the case in the majority of those who leave the Land of Israel.

America as a Pivotal Element in Jewish Life

Now it happens that I am a native son of the largest Jewish community of one country in all of Jewish history. It is still a relatively young community, only now beginning to adjust in Jewish terms to the challenges and opportunities of an environment for which there is no model or precedent in all of Jewish history.

It is important to lay some stress on this last point, for it is only in the light of its unprecedented characteristics that one must, in large measure, understand the character, the shortcomings, and the achievements of this huge aggregate of Jews. From the perspective of what American Jews might have done as Jews, given the resources at their disposal, American Jewry may fairly be said to have achieved precious little. Given the level of sophistication and attainment of its members in many walks of life, its Jewish ignorance is abysmal. Few of its leading communal spokesmen have any real knowledge, let alone understanding, of Judaism, Jewish history,

Jewish literature. But one cannot in justice totally dismiss American Jewish cultural and spiritual accomplishment or confine it to its vast communal organization or philanthropic endeavors. American Jewry has many notable achievements to its credit. Among them are its vast networks and aggregates of institutions that perpetuate, cultivate and mediate the Jewish heritage, Jewish consanguinity and Jewish solidarity. These institutions are all the more notable for their voluntaristic and pluralistic character. They are the product of the determination and dedication of a minority of American Jews, but they set the pace and provide the yardstick for American Jewish identification. The professional class of American Jewry—scholars, rabbis, educators, social workers—are a lonely crowd, mirroring and disseminating to a relatively small audience the deep passion and commitment they bear for Jewish tradition. They have, thanks to the motivations of Jewish communal leadership, often had to bear in near silence the abuse not only of their ideological opponents but of those whose cause they have spearheaded.

It is an accepted truism that Jewish education in America has been an egregious failure. By statistical yardsticks, that assessment is unchallengeable. But there are some streaks of genuine light in that darkness, too. American Jewry is the only Diaspora community in the free world to have produced its own native scholarship and educational personnel. All branches of American Judaism and Jewry have been able to draw on their own constituencies to reproduce themselves—for the rabbinate, for Jewish scholarship, for Jewish education. Only American Jewry can boast that it has provided the overwhelming number of teachers of Judaica in the hundreds of American universities where Jewish subjects are part of the accepted academic agenda. This last point should also not be drowned in a subordinate clause. It was in America that the Jewish tradition first attained legitimacy as part of the university curriculum and consequently as part of the spiritual fabric of the society as a whole. American Jewry has been the seedbed for considerable Jewish theological expression, much of it in quest of an enlightened response to modernity in terms of Jewish faith and commitment. Moreover, and this is a matter of no small moment, American Jewry has contributed Jewish scholars even to the highest echelons of Jewish scholarship in the State of Israel itself.

It is a matter of record that Zionism and the State of Israel provided an indispensable measure of the vigor, pride and motivation that underlie even the limited achievements of American Jewry. Whatever knowledge of, and expression in, Hebrew exists in America must be credited to Zionism. I go further and assert what I cannot prove but know to be true: the Jewish pride in Jewishness that I have seen emerge and grow in America in the last thirty years is in large measure a direct consequence of Zionism and of its program and achievements.

The State of Israel—its prehistory as well as its history—must be acknowledged as one of the formative progenitors of a rapidly maturing American Jewry. But Israel must recognize that every being has a life and legitimate drives of its own. American Jewry could not possibly have fashioned its Jewish milieu by the yardsticks of European or Israeli Jewry. It must do so in terms apposite to American life and in terms that are apposite to its own aspirations and needs. Many of the drives and dreams of American Jewry have paralleled those of Israel's founding fathers. Many of these aspirations and ambitions represented a desire to break with the characteristic features of the Jewish past and to break with many of the basic values and forms of the Jewish past.

History, however, has had a cunning of its own by which it has shaped American Jewry. Paradoxically, America provided a stimulus that may or may not be a blessing but a fact with which we shall have to reckon. It not only tolerated Jews; in many ways it encouraged Jews to be Jewish. America has not done so unequivocally or without ambivalence, and the ambiguity of the American attitude is mirrored in the texture of Jewish life in America. But whatever the case, Jewishness in America has had to be articulated in terms of a positive rationale, not necessarily in terms of response to persecution or exclusion from the mainstream of society. In other words, America has compelled thinking and sensitive Jews to reaffirm and articulate a Jewish faith, and a Jewish *raison d'être*. Jewishness has had to be grounded both for Jews as well as Gentiles in an ideology that transcends the accident of birth as well as political loyalities and aspirations.

America, in short, has compelled Jews who would be Jews to confront the totality of their heritage and to take a stand with respect to their religious identity and covenant. Most American Jews, obviously, can and do avoid the confrontation. But a community is characterized by its greatest spokesmen, and the spititual spokesmen of American Jewry had to adopt a rhetoric that America would treat as acceptable and legitimate. That religious rhetoric then took on a momentum of its own. It compelled Jewish leaders to articulate new ideologies of Jewishness, new formulations of Jewish religion, new interpretations of Jewish peoplehood. That rhetoric—to the bafflement of many Israelis—enabled, nay stimulated, Jews to identify with Jewish nationalism and yet resist the call of the Yishuv to come and settle in the ancient homeland. American Jewry saw itself as part of a renewed people but refused to become part of a renewed Jewish political entity.

In the presence of those Jews who have elected to settle in Israel, and in the presence of those who by choice, accident of birth, or sheer lack of an alternative have joined in building this new Jewish society and culture, many American Jews stand in awe and not a little envy. On the other hand, most American Jews who share in this awe and envy also reflect an ability to identify with everything Jewish without undertaking *aliyah*. They share a constant concern for and involvement with Israel and its life. Nevertheless, they feel no compelling drive to uproot themselves. Clearly, they have found an alternative way of responding to the demands of their Jewishness. They also, I believe, pine for a new, common vocabulary. Can it be done, and if so, how?

To the first question, I can only reply that as a Jew I feel that it must be done, if only for the reason that Israel and the Diaspora need each other. For one of the two to assume that the other is more in need of its sibling than vice versa is a counterproductive, perhaps even a self-destructive, posture. But I believe a common renewal must be achieved for intrinsic reasons underlying our Jewishness. The world stands at the brink of moral collapse. We can survive as a people only if we have our own spiritual wellsprings and drive.

As for the second question, I am clearly pushing for a reorientation of Israeli education in favor of Jewishness in which the Diaspora is treated not only with respect but with pride of fraternity, common vision and common destiny. I believe that American Jewry must strive to Hebraize itself anew with far greator vigor than ever before. I do not put much stock in the sustaining power of a Jewish theology devoid of vocabulary and rituals that do not reflect contemporary Jewish rebirth. I certainly am not suggesting that Jewish orthodoxy is the path to take. Much of institutionally organized orthodoxy has, in my view, discredited itself in Israel and in the Diaspora religiously, morally and politically. In other words, not only do

I not regard modern institutionalized orthodoxy as the authentic Judaism, I regard it intellectually and religiously sterile. Its strength derives from its affirmation of what is authentic and indispensable: Judaism as a vocabulary of life that transcends in importance any human institution. Orthodox youth reflect a model dedication to Israel, for it is the land of promise and the Holy Land. The remainder of the Jewish People must find ways to appropriate these values and translate them in ways that do not make of Jewry an ecclesiastically ruled or oriented body politic. But from the Jewish experience as well as from the classics of Jewish tradition, we must learn that the terrain and obligations of Jewishness are confined not only to the State of Israel but to wherever Jews live.

The first step is to confront the high school text that I mentioned earlier and all that it bespeaks. Israel and America must get to know each other and understand each other with mutual respect and sense of kinship. An immediate and necessary consequence of such a posture will be a massive effort at the reorientation of Jewish rhetoric. Let us not make light of rhetoric. It is often a stumbling block between nations. It is often the source of blessing or catastrophe within families. The Jews of Israel will have to stop looking at the Diaspora in ways reminiscent of anti-Semitic theory and stop being defensive about everything Israeli. Israel has achieved such glory in many areas that it can afford to be an equal brother, not a spoiled child. All of this can be summarized in focusing on the implications of two words: Israel and *galut*. Israel must be understood as much greater in age and dimension than the State of Israel. The State is only one aspect of Jewish rebirth. But the State is not the sum and substance of either Jewish identity or of Jewish eschatology. And these two categories embrace the whole of the Jewish People not only of our day but of every age.

The *galut* is a theological-geographic category, not a moral or esthetic one. It generated not only the State of Israel but our perception of our Jewishness and a heritage of which we may be as proud, to use an understatement, as any people on the face of the earth. Accordingly, even as the age of Enlightenment and emancipation waged a massive attack against Jewishness, it will be our task to regenerate our perception of it in Israel and out of it.

Mutual respect and kinship also imply reciprocity. Even as the Diaspora must continue to send its youth—particularly, those training for communal leadership—to Israel for study, training and work, Israel will have to send some of its best youth to the Diaspora for the same purpose. Israel will profit by sending some of its more promising youth to America to study not only electronics and business management but also how to be Jews in the modern world. Above all, it will have to orient those of its sons and daughters who go to the Diaspora for study and/or work to identify with the Jewish People there. Jewish education, particularly the orientation to the Jewish past, will have to be revitalized, and purged of its Lanternari-syndromes. In this post-emancipatory era, the perceptions of neither Mendele nor Toynbee are valid for the *galut*. To maintain them betrays the kind of *galutiyut* mentality that Israelis claim to despise.

*Inter*action in respect, kinship and spiritual consanguinity between Israel and the Diaspora will necessitate frequent meetings and discussions between Jewish leaders on questions of Jewishness and Jewish interests and goals in different parts of the Jewish world. Above all, it requires that Jewish policy with respect to the Jewish People be formulated not with an eye on one center of the Jewish People but on all vital parts of the Jewish People.

The Interaction of Israel and American Jewry — After the Holocaust

Irving Greenberg

Analysis of the continuing interaction of Israel and American Jewry must take into account the fact that both communities operate in the shadow of the Holocaust. This event has affected Jewish fate and destiny as has no other in almost 2000 years. The Holocaust has also affected the impact of the other major Jewish event of the present millennium — the rebirth of the State of Israel. While the birth and life of Israel were bound to influence deeply Israel-Diaspora relations, the Holocaust has changed the terms of the interaction and its outcome.

In 1966 Leonard Fein predicted a strong and immediate tendency to estrangement between American Jews and Israelis. Stanley Lowell, then President of the American Jewish Congress, bluntly rejected *aliyah*, indicating that he would support America should there ever be a war between Israel and the United States.[1]

The history of the past ten years when the Six Day War and the Yom Kippur War intervened is part of these misjudgments. Much of the impact of the wars was felt because they powerfully evoked the memory and ongoing spiritual force of the Holocaust in Jewish life. Indeed, fear of another Holocaust was dominant in American Jewry in May, 1967.[2]

Failure to take the Holocaust into account has affected the debate over "the centrality of Israel"—a term frequently criticised

1. Leonard J. Fein, "Convergence and Divergence," *Congress BiWeekly*, vol. 34, no. 7, April 3, 1967, pp. 17–19; no. 8, April 17, 1967, pp. 20–22. Stanley H. Lowell declared that he put his American citizenship before his Jewishness, *New York Times*, June 15, 1962. (After visiting Israel in the summer of 1967, Lowell retracted the above.)

2. A. Gottschalk, "United States of America: Perspectives," *The Yom Kippur War—Israel and the Jewish People*, Moshe Davis, ed., New York, 1974, p. 39; Mordecai Waxman, "United States of America: Perspectives," *ibid.*, p. 66. Arthur Hertzberg, "Israel and American Jewry," *Commentary*, vol. 44, no. 2, August 1967, p. 72.

as being the ideological rationale for denying the legitimacy of the *galut* or for philanthropic neglect of the Diaspora's needs. Moderates on the Diaspora side have called for modifications of this image — the two-foci or ellipse theory.[3] Others in Israel and the Diaspora have argued for different metaphors; but the Holocaust has undoubtedly established Israel's centrality. Had Israel come into being without a Holocaust . . . , had the Allies and world Jewry acted effectively during the years 1942–1944 . . . , the Diaspora and its relationship to Israel might now be different. But since the Holocaust was not held in check, this argument is an exercise in futility.

Israel's Centrality: Demography and Culture

Since the Holocaust, Israel's centrality for the Jewish People has become a stark physical, biological fact.

In 1939, the population of the Yishuv in Palestine was approximately 400,000 out of 16,700,000 Jews throughout the world, or two and a half percent of the world Jewish population. Even that figure exaggerates Israel's portion, for over 200,000 were refugees brought to Palestine during the early phases of the Holocaust. Within two years of the founding of the State of Israel, the population numbered 1,115,000 out of almost 12,000,000 Jews — some nine percent of the world Jewish population. (Again most of the additional population consisted of Holocaust survivors who came to Israel because they had learned the lesson of the Holocaust.) Today the percentage has reached almost twenty-two percent.[4] American Jewry is greater in number — but it is declining demographically.

By destroying East European Jewry, the Nazis smashed Jewry's biological center—the only major center before World War II with a significant natural increase, except for North Africa from which Jews also came to Israel after 1947.

Both Dieter Wisliceny and Rudolf Hoess (the commandant at Auschwitz) report Eichmann's conviction that he had struck Jewry a

3. Simon Rawidowicz, *Bavel vi-Yerushalayim*, Waltham, 1957, vol. 2, pp. 646 ff., 680 ff., 879–909. Leo Baeck, "The Mission of Judaism," *World Union for Progressive Judaism Report*, Sixth International Conference, 1949. p. 80.

4. Leon Shapiro, "World Jewish Population," *American Jewish Year Book*, Morris Fine, ed., 1941, vol. 42, p. 592. In 1939 — 424,373 Jews in Palestine/15,757,000 Jews in world, *ibid.*; in July 1950 — 1,115,000 Jews in Israel/11,500,000 Jews in world, vol. 52, 1951, pp. 195 ff; in 1973 — 2,806,000 Jews in Israel/14,150,000 Jews in world, vol. 75, 1974–1975, pp. 561 ff.

blow from which it would not recover. He believed that Western Jewry was too assimilated and lacking in demographic vitality to compensate for these losses.[5] Had the State of Israel not come into being, Eichmann's boast would have been confirmed by now. No other Jewry has a natural increase; all are in various stages of population erosion due to declining fertility and rising assimilation.[6] Israel is the primary, perhaps the exclusive, hope of rebuilding the shattered body of the Jewish People.

Despite growing world overpopulation, the Jewish People has decreased to a dangerously low degree due in good measure to the Holocaust. As a result of the occupational, income and geographic distribution of the Jews, they are concentrated in the culturally open sectors of society. No group in an open society can avoid intermarriage in significant numbers. For many decades, Catholic intermarriage in America was at a considerably higher rate than the Jewish, but the Church kept growing because its high birthrate more than canceled out its losses through exogamous marriage.[7]

Sheer numbers also create an important *spiritual* force. A diminished population means less ability to sustain the cultural institutions and resources which nourish identity and creative spiritual existence. For example, in the contemporary culture Judaism has still not achieved a full synthesis and a renewed way of life. Cultural and religious renewal, therefore, is necessary over a broad range of areas—ethics, philosophy, liturgy, as well as in its institutions. Such renewal calls for great skill in combining dialectical and even conflicting phenomena—reconciling the universalist and particularist thrusts; attaining deep involvement in worldly matters without losing the sense of transcendence; creating high-level community relationships in a society which emphasizes individualism and self-fulfillment; encouraging prayer in a secular age. A very small part of the population is able to take the initiative in such endeavor; however, the new trends then spread to the population at large.

Renewal of the Catholic Church started with a range of orders,

5. Dieter Wisliceny, affidavit dated November 29, 1945, printed in *Nazi Conspiracy and Aggression*, Washington, 1946, vol. 8, p. 610; Rudolf Hoess, *Commandment of Auschwitz*, London, 1959, p. 215; Irving Greenberg, "Adventure in Freedom or Escape from Freedom? Jewish Identity in America," *American Jewish Historical Quarterly*, vol. 55, no. 1, September 1965, pp. 18–19.

6. U. O. Schmeltz, et al., ed., *Studies in Jewish Demography — Survey for 1969–1971*, Jerusalem and London, 1975, pp. 12–15.

7. Greenberg, *ibid.*

journals and schools which then explored the new themes. Less than one percent of its population was involved, but among the Catholics one percent represented 5,000,000 people: There was thus sufficient human power to create a variety of liturgical experiments, new schools of philosophy and seminaries, political revitalization movements and journals. In the case of the Jewish People, one percent represents 120,000 people scattered throughout the world; as a result, it is impossible to sustain the necessary institutions and settings. Since there is unlikely to be one master solution for the much needed spiritual renaissance, a wide variety of explorations, institutions and organs is essential. Considering the subdivisions of the Jewish community—religious, secular/kibbutz, city/Orthodox, Conservative, Reform—the problem of accumulating a critical mass for renewal becomes even more obvious and pressing. Thus, the quantity problem becomes a negative factor of the first magnitude in the quest for spiritual quality.

It has been estimated that thirty percent of the Jews alive in 1939 were killed in the Holocaust. It is estimated that over eighty percent of the Jewish scholars, rabbis, full-time Torah students alive in 1939 were dead by 1945. By wiping out the concentrations of Jews most sheltered from modernization and most resistant to assimilation, the Holocaust intensified the exposure of the remaining Jews to dissolution and assimilating factors. In the past, East European migrations renewed American Jewry when the initial wave of immigrants had become almost totally assimilated or had disappeared. A parallel, if less total, stabilizing phenomenon was also evident in Western Europe.[8]

Before World War II, there were two major Jewish communities where Jewish languages were native tongues and Jewish culture could be developed in a Jewish language — Eastern Europe and Israel. A vital culture must have its own language, a fact which is especially true in the Jewish situation. Even Aramaic Jewish culture flourished because mastery of its language maintained the connection with the classic sources and their language. The Nazi onslaught reduced Jewry to one major Jewish language center: Israel. The Yiddish-speaking communities of the United States and the Argentine are fast disintegrating under the impact of the general culture.

8. Charles Bezalel Sherman, *The Jew within American Society—A Study in Ethnic Individuality*, Detroit, 1961, pp. 157 ff.

American Jewry could create an important English language
Jewish culture if it made a persistent effort. But since this culture
would not have its basis in the classic sources, it would lack vitality
and continuity. This does not mean that the culture and religion developed in Israel are automatically well suited to the Diaspora—perhaps the opposite is true. But the potential vitality and centrality for
the future may be incomparably greater because of the linguistic-cul-
tural infrastructure found only in Israel today.

Jewish sovereignty and majority status lead to much broader
cultural resources too—including universal Jewish education. While
the Israeli population is still only twenty-two percent of the world
Jewish population, eighty percent of the children receiving Jewish
education in all day schools are studying in Israel.[9]

Israel is not free of assimilation. Through its media,
advertising, education and citizens' travel abroad, it is exposed to international culture and values. Should the Arab-Israel conflict be resolved, this could have serious consequences on marriage, identification, and so on. For the present, however, the majority status of
Jews reduces the salience and magnetism of Gentile culture and supports continuity of Jewish memory, history and institutions. Even
the alienated Israeli is in a setting which reduces considerably the
chance of intermarriage. Thus his children may be revitalized as
Jews—a much less likely occurrence in a similar Diaspora situation.

Without Israel the demographic future of the Jewish People
would become hopeless and the cultural situation more restrictive.
The bulk of committed Jews throughout the world, being survival-
ists, instinctively recognize that Israel is a matter of life and death for
them and give Israel a positive emotional and philanthropic centrality in Jewish life. Attempts to dismiss this centrality as the ideology
of an assimilating Diaspora leadership which prefers not to invest in
indigenous Jewish culture are trivializing abstractions,[10] and most
Jews grasp this obvious and crucial fact at once.

---

9. Moshe Davis, *Beit Yisrael be-Amerikah*, Jerusalem, 1970, pp. 406–412. Professor
Alexander Dushkin correctly defined the day schools as the standard of satisfaction of
Jewish education. The Talmud Torah/Sunday Schools are so marginal that there is a
general conviction among Jewish educators that they are of little value.

10. Hannah Koevary, "Giving to Israel—We Gain and We Lose," *Sh'ma* 4/62, November 30, 1973, pp. 14–15.

Israel's Centrality: Fate and Meaning

The Holocaust had an even more profound impact on the relationship between Israel and American Jewry in the realm of Jewish fate, meaning and self-understanding.

The Nazis attempted literally to put an end to Judaism. They succeeded only partially. The Holocaust did bring the end of *galut* Judaism: the Jewish way of life and meaning predicated on Jewish lack of power which accepted exile as normative even though it was not "at home" in it. For two millennia Jewish culture stressed social and communal cohesion and a sense of tradition which would enable the community to outlive this period of exile. Jews could have little or no effect on the overall framework of society. Instead, they sought a social definition which allowed Jewry to function according to its own values and rules within as wide a latitude as possible.

The community could only adjust to a given fate. It did try to soften and even anticipate blows by bribery, intercession, flight—or by rebuilding after a tragedy. This policy succeeded because Christian anti-Semitism was ambivalent and contained elements, positive and negative, which validated Jewish existence. As the Jewish chroniclers noted, the Lord was gracious to Israel and scattered her among the nations so that if one community was crushed, others thrived or came into being (*Pesaḥim* 87b).

Over the centuries these values became less provisional and more internalized as ultimate norms so that a "waiting-for-the-Messiah" ideology became more authoritative. Such passivity, however, should not be exaggerated. Would-be Messiahs received strong support — an indication of the presence of tinder ready to be set afire. Moreover, one may look upon the spread of Kabbalah as a way of "taking charge of one's fate." According to Lurianic Kabbalah particularly, Israel, by fulfilling its internal religious-spiritual service, could bring the world to perfection and lead it to the coming of the Messiah; that is, could change its fate. Even Hasidism, which sought to "domesticate" Messianism so as to avoid further untimely outbursts of Messianic movements, gave hope that the Jew could affect his destiny through spiritual activity.[11] Still, in the political arena,

11. Gershom Scholem, *Sabbatai Sevi — The Mystical Messiah 1626–1676*, Princeton, 1973, pp. 6–22, 44 ff. See also Scholem, "Toward an Understanding of the Messianic Idea in Judaism" and "The Messianic Idea in Kabbalism," *The Messianic Idea in Judaism*, New York, 1971; "The Neutralization of the Messianic Element in Early Hasidism," *ibid.*, pp. 176–202.

in its fundamental societal structures, in collective capacity for self-defense, *galut* Judaism assumed that Jewry was a satellite of God and History.

However, modernity struck deeply at *galut* Judaism. It undermined the sense of distinctiveness by accepting Jews and promising them full equality; it undercut continuity by substituting national languages and cultures. It weakened the Jewish sense of purpose and ultimate destiny. It tore at the idea of *galut* by making the existent reality for Jews so attractive that they no longer desired to be redeemed from it. "Berlin is our Jerusalem" — or as the first American Reform Congregation put it: "Charleston is our Jerusalem."[12]

The absolute realization of modernity should presumably have put an end to Diaspora Jewry and *galut* Judaism. Modern culture, which generated ideas of a national self-realization, stimulated a Jewish return to Zion, especially after hopes of integration into national cultures were dashed by cultural anti-Semitism and pogroms. At the same time, the powerful assimilationist forces of modernity led many Jews to identify completely with national or universal subcultures—revolutionary, humanist or intellectual. Modern culture was so magnetic, it seemed that only a small minority would choose Israel and rebuilding of the Jewish political reality. Far greater numbers—indeed the bulk of the Jewish People—would in all probability be swept into the universal relinquishment of Jewish existence. This perception brought on counter-reactions, including Jewish religious responses which insisted that *galut* Judaism could be saved by rejecting both modernity and Zionism. There were also various Diaspora nationalist responses which insisted that *galut* Judaism would be saved if it was based not on religious but on national, secular culture.[13] Except in Eastern Europe where modernity was slower in penetrating, groups subscribing to these ideas were doomed to minority status. By the 1930s most Jews were non-Zionist or even anti-Zionist: the active, committed Jewish community (except in Palestine) was clearly integrationist, almost assimilationist.

The Holocaust shattered this constellation, dramatizing the awesome fact that modern culture was more efficient and deadly in its

12. W. Gunther Plaut, *The Growth of Reform Judaism*, New York, 1965, pp. 8–9.

13. Simon Dubnow, *Nationalism and History, Essays on Old and New Judaism*, Koppel S. Pinson, ed., Philadelphia, 1958, Part 1, pp. 73–241; Joseph Wanefsky, *Rabbi Isaac Jacob Reines: His Life and Thought*, New York, 1970. pp. 5–36.

destruction than the Dark Ages. Due to a combination of modern technology, greater efficiency and bureaucratic norms, erosion of taboos and ability to create great concentrations of power, total annihilation of the Jews under Nazi power became possible. The norms which modern society flattered itself as having developed—liberalism and humanitarianism, universal rights, the rule of law—failed to protect the Jews. The Allies in their fight for democracy, the Church representing religion, or the world Jewish communities representing kinship ties, did no better. Universalist norms often served as a cover for lack of response. The death camps could not be bombed because general military objectives came first—this was a war to save mankind, not solely a Jewish war. These norms weakened the victims' perception of danger and undermined their resolve to resist.[14]

The Holocaust demonstrated clearly that only the power and ability to organize in defense of one's fate can create a potentially moral reality and protect future victims. This lesson was grasped not only by Jews but by many other national groups and minorities. The period after World War II has been marked by a proliferation of liberation movements; all have in common a strong sense of actual or potential victimization status. Not infrequently, partisans of such movements use Holocaust terminology to describe their situation and justify their movements.

Similarly, the Holocaust transformed an overwhelming number of Jews who wished to remain Jewish into Zionists, that is, supporters of the need for a Jewish State. American Reform Jewish leadership started to change in the 1930s during the early days of Hitler; not until the Six Day War drove home the full consciousness of the Holocaust as a recurring event did the majority of American Reform Jews give high priority to support of the Jewish State.[15]

For most Jews the Holocaust brought about the end of *galut* Judaism. In the light of the Holocaust, even Jews who choose Diaspora comfort realize the absolute necessity for Jewish sovereignty in

14. Greenberg, "Cloud of Smoke, Pillar of Fire: Religious and Ethical Implications of the Holocaust," *Auschwitz: Beginning of a New Era, Proceedings of a Conference*, Eva Fleischner, ed., New York, 1976, Sect. iic; Alexander Donat, *The Holocaust Kingdom: A Memoir*, New York, 1965, pp. 100, 103.

15. Leonard Fein, et al, "Attitudes towards Israel," *Reform Is a Verb*, New York, 1972, pp. 65–73. Cf. Marshall Sklare, *Jewish Identity on the Suburban Frontier*, New York, 1967 (especially pp. 214–249, 322–326), with T.I. Lenn and Associates, *Rabbi and Synagogue in Reform Judaism*, Hartford, 1972, pp. 234–252.

Israel, so that self-defense can be organized. Jews must be able to wield that power in their own interests, they must be able to call on the resources of force, available only to sovereign nations in the modern world.

Many observers have scorned the tendency of Diaspora Jews, especially after the Six Day War, to overidentify with the Israeli army and martial heroism. But this is the direct outcome of the realization that it is a moral necessity for Jews to be able to protect themselves. Hence, the dominant tendency of Diaspora Jews to align themselves with such a position, except for those influenced by counter forces, such as certain liberal or left movements.

The belief that the Jewish problem can no longer be dependent on other powers for its solutions operates in another way, often misunderstood by Israelis. American Jews are much more involved in national politics and universal issues (for example, the opposition in the United States to the Vietnam War). These tendencies are frequently dismissed by Israelis as escape into universalism, betrayal of Jewish concerns or naiveté. While these negative factors do operate, equally important is the perception that what happens in the general society now decisively influences Jewish existence. While other Jewries are more restrained, American Jews are increasingly activist, especially in the formation of national policy toward Israel. As Holocaust consciousness intensifies, and the existence of Israel hones awareness, Diaspora Jews have steadily become more willing to confront their national governments on policies affecting Israel. Compare the behavior of the American Jewish leadership in 1956 to their actions in 1967 and 1974.[16]

The fact that this same leadership defers to the Israel government's policies and priorities is often imputed to the non-representative character of Jewish Diaspora leaders and the lack of an electoral process to choose those leaders. However, it is equally based on the recognition that Israel has created Jewish power—reflected in its ability to set up a general staff, brain trusts and planning departments. Despite the serious danger to Israel's existence and its urgent need for the financial help and political defense the Diaspora gives, pride of place is given to Israel.

16. See Gary Schiff, "American Jews and Israel: Community Relations in the Yom Kippur War" (forthcoming article); Daniel J. Elazar, "Overview," *The Yom Kippur War—Israel and the Jewish People*, pp. 1–35.

Diaspora ideologists and people with religious reservations about Israel have made much of the paradox that Zionism, instead of providing a cure for the Jewish problem, has created a vulnerable state, the most likely contemporary scene of a potential second Holocaust.[17] Yet contrary to such expectations, this fact has not led Diaspora Jews to greater independence. Holocaust consciousness has turned this into more total involvement with Israel. Committed Jews throughout the world realize that in the cruel and relentless present reality, there are no guarantees against another Jewish Holocaust. But Israel provides the possibility of fighting a recurrence—an enormously significant advance in thirty years. Compare the unchecked daily mass murders of the Einsatzgruppen in 1941 with the immediate retaliation to terrorist incursions in Israel of recent years.[18] The fact even now, after thirty years, that the Jews are not absolutely protected from a recurrence is a devastating moral judgment on the world and our modern culture, but Jews are thankful indeed for small favors.

Since American Jews perceive that if Israel were to be destroyed, they themselves would become highly vulnerable, there is a much stronger tendency to see the fate of both communities as inseparable. The operational consequences are a much higher level of fund raising and greater willingness to risk Jewish standing in the Diaspora countries for the sake of Israel than was true in the 1940s. The Holocaust has operated powerfully within Israel, giving great determination and thrust to its military effort.[19]

Perhaps Diaspora response is somewhat too one-sided after the Holocaust; perhaps one should be one-sided in such matters. Since the concentration of force leads to abuse and corruption, the Holocaust should evoke sympathy and responsibility for others, especially in the breasts of those who felt the pain of abandonment, of

17. Harry Gersh, "As the Old Zionism Begins to Fade," *Sh'ma* 5/92, April 18, 1975, pp. 254–256; Henry Schwartzchild, "Racism, the Unavoidable National Sin," *ibid.*, 6/104, December 26, 1975, pp. 28–29.

18. Raul Hilberg, *Documents of Destruction—Germany and Jewry 1933–1945*, Chicago, 1971, pp. 50, 51; *New York Times*, May 15, 1974 and May 16, 1974; cf. Greenberg, *Confronting the Holocaust and Israel*, New York, 1975, pp. 3, 4.

19. See Ofer Feniger letter, *The Seventh Day: Israeli Soldier Conversations*, A. Shapiro, ed., New York, 1970, pp. 189–191; Harold Fisch, "Jerusalem, Jerusalem," *Judaism*, vol. 16, no. 3, Summer 1967, pp. 259–265.

silence and indifference to their suffering.[20] Former victims, who remember they were strangers in the land of Egypt, should be
extrasensitive to the danger that they may inflict suffering on those
under their control.[21] Thus far, the Israeli use of military power has
been marked by a high degree of self-control—perhaps the still fresh
memory of the Holocaust operates here too. The notion that Diaspora
Jews, more likely to be morally sensitive, should, therefore, uphold
the ideal in the overall economy of world Jewry is a mistaken one.

Neither Israelis nor Diaspora Jews should be romanticized —
both suffer from the usual human limitations. It may be that because
the Israelis feel secure in their actual power, they are, so far, more
conscious of its dangers and, therefore, more capable of criticizing
its application.[22] Since American Jewry with its Holocaust anxiety
perceives Israel as more vulnerable than do the Israelis themselves,
they are less critical of Israel's application of power. As the future
unfolds, it will not be a neat Israel/Diaspora category that distin-
guishes people on this issue, but the relative sensitivity of people to
the Holocaust and its lessons.

Need for a Haven and the Law of Return

The Holocaust dramatized the fact that a refuge for the Jews is
an absolute necessity. Had there been some place where Jewish refugees were received willingly, hundreds of thousands, perhaps even
millions of Jews could have been saved.[23] Determined that never

20. Greenberg, "Cloud of Smoke," Sect. VIIIA; Greenberg, "New Revelation and New
Patterns in the Relationship of Judaism and Christianity," paper read at the celebration of the Tenth Anniversary of the Declaration of the Relationship of the Church to
the Jewish People of the National Conference of Catholic Bishops, December 16, 1975,
Washington, 1976.

21. Cf. Exodus, 22:21; 23:9.

22.This is counter to the "Response" by Richard Rubenstein in *Homeland and Holocaust: Issues in the Jewish Religious Situation*, Donald Cutler, ed., Boston, 1968,
pp. 43 ff., p. 50.

23. See David Wyman, *Paper Walls: America and The Refugee Crisis 1938–1941*,
Amherst, Mass, 1968; Henry L. Feingold, *The Politics of Rescue—The Roosevelt
Administration and the Holocaust*, New Brunswick, N.J., 1970; Arthur Morse, *While
Six Million Died*, New York, 1968; A. J. Sherman, *Island Refuge—Britain and Refu-
gees from the Third Reich 1933–1939*, Berkeley, 1973; Alex Weisberg, *Advocate for
the Dead—The Story of Joel Brand*, London, 1958.

again would there be such a situation, the newly declared State of Israel passed the Law of Return, which guaranteed just such a haven for all Jews. In the fifties, implementation of this law led to years of austerity in the Israeli standard of living. The law is motivated by self-interest too. More Jews are needed in the upbuilding of Israel and improvement of its security situation. But the admixture of self-interest that is part of human reality in which ethical or religious imperatives are realized does not cancel out the ideal. Also there is an ongoing cost to the Law of Return—its implementation leads to constant criticism of the State and pressure by Orthodox Jewry. The law is used against Israel in racist slogans; in propaganda, especially of the Left; by those who say that only if Israel "de-Zionizes" and gives up this law will she have peace and be accepted by her Arab neighbors, and by non-Jews who spread the image of Israel as practicing religious discrimination.[24] Weakening of public support for Israel, especially in the United States, could be very costly and increases the possibility of renewed genocide. The reluctance to repeal or weaken it is sustained by the Holocaust memory—a bond which links the Jewish communities.

This law plays a powerful, often unstated, role in support for Israel among American Jews, who are aware that in the event of another Holocaust in the Diaspora, it is absolutely critical that such a haven be available. In countries where the situation is already explosive (in South Africa, for instance), Jews give generous support to Israel. Whatever disagreements arise between Israel and the Diaspora, the Law of Return is a powerful bond of mutual interest which maintains a high level of cohesion. Diaspora Jewry's self-interest is an important balance wheel to centripetal tendencies built into the difference in the condition of Israel and the world communities.

As Holocaust consciousness grows stronger, American Jewry is becoming less affected by domestic governmental pressure and shows a greater willingness to acknowledge the centrality of Israel and give it support in all ways, including political.

24. Consider, for example, the argument of the Kuwaiti representative at the U.N., Dr. Abdallah al-Sayegh, in favor of the resolution condemning Zionism as racism. "In a country in which there is a law called the Law of Return, permitting a Jew who has never been to Palestine to 'return' and a policy prohibiting a Palestinian from actually returning to his home, both on the basis that the first is a Jew and the second is a non-Jew, how can a country like that be described as a democracy, and how can the label of 'racism and racial discrimination' be questioned in application to that particular country?" (quoted in The New York Times, November 12, 1975, p. 16).

Whenever the threat of a Holocaust appears over Israel —as in the period prior to the Six Day War and during the Yom Kippur War—the moral-existential impossibility of sustaining the resultant loss rallies American Jewry even more fiercely and totally to Israel's side. The threat to other Jewries—Argentinian, Syrian, even Russian—has never evoked the same intensity of response, because the threat to Israel has been more directly military and total, and because the media convey Israel's position to Jews more forcefully than that of other Jewish communities. Russian Jewry comes closest to Israel in arousing intense feeling, but it is not perceived as facing genocide. American Jews feel that Israel's birth and its survival have been the main offset to the Holocaust and the foremost re-creation and legitimation of normal Jewish life after the destruction. A threat to its existence, therefore, is intolerable. Other Diaspora communities could be destroyed without confirming the final triumph of the Holocaust, but if Israel were to be annihilated the Holocaust would be complete.

When fears for Israel's existence were at their height after the Yom Kippur War, rabbis and others in America argued for a Yavneh alternative, insisting that American Jewry must affirm and ensure Jewish survival.[25] This view was overwhelmingly rejected by the masses of American Jewry. This is the clearest possible testimony of the centrality of Israel to Jewish existential meaningfulness—both secular and religious.

Israel as the Central Post-Holocaust Jewish Religious Phenomenon

Human values and redemption in actual history are so central to Judaism that any great historical tragedy challenges the meaningfulness of existence and the credibility of the Jewish religion. Great catastrophes have inevitably been followed by major reformulations of Judaism. The dimensions of the Holocaust were so great that the entire Jewish religious framework was put into question. The reestablishment of Israel so soon after the Holocaust was necessary for the survival of religious meaning. Chief Rabbi Herzog stated this

25. Rabbi Joseph R. Narot's letter to *The New York Times,* January 30, 1975; Arthur E. Green, "A Response to Richard Rubenstein," *Conservative Judaism,* vol. 128, no. 4, Summer 1974, pp. 26–32.

openly in 1949 when he defended his support for the creation of Israel, although the existing religious instrumentalities could not cope
with or contain the actual functioning of the State. This is suggested
in Rabbi Joseph B. Soloveichik's classic *Kol Dodi Dofek*.[26] Elsewhere, I have written:

> If the experience of Auschwitz means we are cut off from God and
> hope and the covenant may be destroyed, then the experience of
> Jerusalem means that God's promises are faithful and God's people
> live on. Burning children speak of the absence of all values, human
> and divine; the rehabilitation of one-half million Holocaust survivors
> in Israel speaks of the reclamation of tremendous human dignity and
> value. . . . Israel's faith in the God of History demands that an
> unprecedented event of destruction be matched by an unprecedented
> act of redemption and this has happened.[27]

In a generation when Job-like suffering all but obscured God's
presence, Israel is the sign out of the whirlwind of renewed dialogue
and divine Presence which provides Jews with strength to endure.
In a generation of destruction, re-creation of life is the central
religious statement. The reborn State of Israel is this fundamental
act of life and meaning of the Jewish People after Auschwitz.[28]
Whatever the criticism of its religious shortcomings, Israel's major
contribution makes the entire religious claim credible. This is so important that American Jews have steadily forced a more central role
for Israel in religious life despite the resistance of many of the religious institutions.

The most widely observed *mitzvah* in the Diaspora Jewish
community—reaching far beyond synagogues—is contributing to
the United Jewish Appeal and Israel Bonds. From year to year, celebration of *Yom Haatzmaut* (Israel Independence Day) has grown,
despite the many reservations expressed by institutional leaders. For
more and more Jews, the primary Jewish experience of celebration has
become the pilgrimage to Israel; others encourage Israeli art and its

26. Isaac Herzog, "Kovetz Zion," *Ha-Torah veha-Medinah*, vol. 7, pp. 9 ff., Joseph B.
Soloveichik, "Kol Dodi Dofek," *Ish HaEmunah*, Jerusalem, 1968, pp. 65-106; note
also pp. 77 ff., 80-82.

27. Irving Greenberg, "Judaism and Christianity after Auschwitz," *Journal of
Ecumenical Studies*, vol. xii, no. 4, Fall 1975, p. 538.

28. *Ibid.*, pp. 544-545.

music in the home. Even if these are not always on a high level, they bespeak powerful emotions.

In the 1950s with the great suburban migration of American Jews, the centrality of the synagogue was proclaimed, especially in Conservative and Reform circles. The religious force of Israel is so strong, however, that the synagogue in America has lost ground steadily. The Federations and United Jewish Appeal have increasingly become instruments in the search for Jewish education and religious experience. The synagogue leadership, especially rabbis, have resisted the trend in vain because it draws strength from the strong Israel orientation. Instead, the synagogues have been drawn into its orbit—through pointing up the presence of Israel in the synagogue liturgy; through becoming a service agency for support of Israel by means of rallies and fund raising in the Six Day and Yom Kippur Wars; through inclusion of a year's study in Israel for rabbinical students in the Conservative and Reform movements. In American Jewry, Reform still has the strongest spiritualizing tendencies which are in constant tension with the realities of a flesh and blood Israel. As a result, in the Reform Rabbinate one is likely to find spiritual views critical of Israel's limitations. However, the development among laymen of a more particularist religious consciousness, oriented toward Israel, has overwhelmed this tendency.

A similar phenomenon is taking place within Orthodoxy. Despite recurrent criticisms of Israel's non-religious character and violations of the *Halakhah,* Orthodox leadership has partially, though reluctantly, conceded Israel's religious normativeness. "Against their will, many of them now answer, Amen." The Chief Rabbinate of Israel hesitated to declare Israel Independence Day a religious holiday and prescribed Hallel (thanksgiving prayers) without a blessing. It was swept by the enthusiasm of the people into decreeing Jerusalem Day (the celebration of the unification of Jerusalem after the Six Day War victory) as a full holiday—no mourning although it occurs in the *Omer,* a mourning period, and Hallel with a *berakhah,* the full blessing. At the height of the S.S. *Shalom* controversy and the earlier "Who Is a Jew?" debate, Rabbi Joseph B. Soloveichik warned: "Do not force us (the Orthodox) to choose between the State of Israel and the Torah of Israel." The Lubavitcher Rebbe has been highly critical of Israel in the recent "Who Is a Jew" controversy; and leadership of the Yeshivah world, closely linked to fundamentalist

Orthodoxy, has been very reserved about Israel on many issues. Yet they have not been able to fulfill their threats of sanctions. Holocaust consciousness, especially in the war periods, has been so overwhelming that even their own following has given full support to the State of Israel.

In 1967, a bitter fight over autopsy policies was superseded by a call to all Yeshivah students to demonstrate for Israel. These circles increasingly participate in Israel Day parades, in rallies against the PLO and such events—despite the double-pronged opposition of the Gedolim (Sages) to Israel's secularity and to public demonstration. In the grim days of the Yom Kippur War, the Satmar hasidim—bitter opponents of the Zionist State—were finally silenced by the rest of Orthodoxy; even Satmar's own internal groupings brought forth a demand for full identification with Israel. Despite the swing to the right within Orthodoxy in the last decade, the religious leadership has had to accept greater centrality for Israel—or find its followers deserting on this issue.[29]

New Cycle in Jewish History

The overall pattern of Jewish history suggests that a new phase in Jewish history is beginning. The destruction of the Second Temple ushered in a major new cycle—one in which the galut became the central given of Jewish existence. The Holocaust and the rebirth of Israel ushered in a major cycle characterized by Jewish sovereignty and self-determination.

Attempts to throttle such a development have been unavailing: the Yom Kippur War struck more cruelly than the Six Day War at this development, but the physical force and the funds provided to protect this growth were again greater than ever. This is not to claim that there are single-track directions in Jewish history, since events and human decisions affect the outcome. For example, the destruction of the Temple did not end major Jewish settlement in

---

29. Cf. Soloveichik, ibid., p. 27, with Joel Teitelbaum, Al ha-Geulah v'al ha-Temurah, New York, 1967; Israel Rubin, Satmar—An Island in the City, Chicago, 1972, pp. 226–227.
After Yom Kippur 1973, a Satmar group which organized demonstrations against Israel evoked tremendous criticism. This group, excommunicated on the grounds that it had no permission from the Beis ha-Midrash of the Rebbe to do this, has set itself up as a community in Lakewood, N.J. (The above information was supplied by Rabbi F. Schoenfeld of Young Israel, Kew Garden Hills, N.Y.)

Israel, nor did it halt attempts to re-create Jewish sovereignty for centuries afterward. Even the cultural-religious reformulations (new institutions, values, observances) were multi-optional. Gradually, however, the meaning and values of life were adapted to existence in exile, and became more dominant. As Jews responded to a wide variety of cultures, events and challenges, Israel became fantasy, hope and dream, while the main Diaspora centers became the focus of Jewish survival and creativity.

A similar unfolding could be projected during the coming millennium. Much will depend on Jewish communities still in existence: the strength of enemies or undermining cultural forces; the nature of Jewish leadership which emerges in each settlement; and the ability of the community to cope with challenges to physical existence or transmission of the meaningfulness of Judaism. Many Jews do perceive this decisive turning point: the Jewish People as a collectivity has returned to the active center of history. Millennial dreams and ideals can be fulfilled if the community wills it. Fantasies about Messianic perfection, the creation of religious models and talk of Jewish uniqueness will now have to meet the test—or be abandoned. This is critical for the Diaspora as for Israel.

It would be foolhardy to be sanguine about a flowering of Jewish culture, religion and social ethics—or population. Yet the Jewish People has in its hands the vehicle and opportunity to realize itself in full view of the world and with less chance of self-deception or of denying the problems. Israel is so central to the Jewish world, that were she to fail, Diaspora Jewishness could hardly begin to retain its credibility.

Jewish tradition and memory could prove inadequate to cope with the situation. On the other hand, the entire range of the tradition and history—without *a priori* exclusions—is likely to be explored in the search for effectiveness and meaning. Thus, we face a religiously and culturally explosive period. The development is temporarily masked by preoccupation with the upbuilding of Israel and the struggle of existing institutions to maintain inertial movement.

Just as Diaspora Jewish leadership over two millennia gradually passed to rabbinic and communal personnel, it may be anticipated that there will be a change in cultural-religious patterns with leadership passing to the political leaders of Israel. Indeed, the decisions of the political elite have already set much of the priorities and concrete applications of Jewish values in life today.

Toward a Post-Modernist Jewish Culture

There is a striking contrast between Israel's centrality in Jewish demography and self-understanding and its considerably more limited role in the cultural life of Diaspora Jewry. Many valuable educational programs of interchange and education for Diaspora Jews have been organized in Israel—university and Yeshivah study, special institute courses for youth, community leaders and future teachers, as well as a great variety of informal educational experimental settings. In certain fields of Jewish studies, Israeli scholars and universities set the standard for Jewish scholarship throughout the world. Israel also sends personnel to the Dispersion as teachers, scholars and youth leaders; yet, the role of Israel and Israeli culture is marginal in Diaspora Jewish culture.

The negative interpretation—that Israel's centrality grows out of the weakness of Diaspora Jewish life—is a contributing factor to that poor quality and is cover for the perpetuation of a Diaspora Jewish leadership with low levels of Jewish commitment and identity.[30] This may be partially true. Yet the United Jewish Appeal leadership attracts more emotional, personally committed Jews who tend to support particularist Jewish activity and philanthropy. Those who believed in "America First," or Diaspora priority, tend to be more marginal Jews and prefer to help non-sectarian Jewish institutions —as, for instance, hospitals. In New York City, the United Jewish Appeal, the Israel-oriented organization, was separate from the America-centered Federation group until last year. Again, the Federation of Jewish Philanthropies had one of the lowest ratios of fund allocations for Jewish education.[31]

Technical factors also inhibit Israeli cultural influence. American Jewry carries on most of its Jewish life and culture in English, but processes of translation and dissemination are slow. The language gap thus limits Israel's contribution to Jewish education in the Diaspora. Israeli textbooks are less practical because the language level is too high for Diaspora elementary and high schools. Obviously, Israel differs from each of the Diaspora Jewries. The latter also differ from one another because they take on the coloration of their

30. Arnold J. Wolf, "Leadership: What We Say vs. What We Do," *Sh'ma*, 5/93, May 2, 1975, pp. 261–263.

31. S. P. Goldberg, "Jewish Communal Services, Program and Finances," *American Jewish Year Book 1972*, Philadelphia, 1972, vol. 73, pp. 236–287.

geographic, national cultures. There is, in addition, the problem of resistance due to Diaspora institutional interests.

Jewish minority status had a powerful effect on the development of Conservative and Reform Judaism and, to a lesser degree, modern Orthodoxy. Israel's Jewish majority and its rich Jewish environment have made possible a much more polarized religious secular dichotomy. The Gentile influence has obscured for Israel the valid insights of Conservatism and Reform, even as the obverse has made Israeli religious life and models far less exportable to the United States. Orthodoxy in Israel lags far behind that of the United States in developing a spiritual leadership and vehicles that have had to confront modern culture or acknowledge the pluralism of Jewish life.

Nevertheless, these factors can be overcome. The Institute of Contemporary Jewry at the Hebrew University is making a serious effort to enrich the development of parallel studies in the United States. More systematic use of Israeli academics and teachers in Diaspora educational institutions would help, but a shortage of personnel of the right caliber among those prepared to serve abroad is a restricting factor.

At present, much of Israel's culture and academic achievement is within the parameters of Jewish culture in modern civilization. Israel is a small outpost of Western civilization and what it can offer is available in Diaspora countries in more indigenous forms. Sometimes the sheer size and variety of the Diaspora world, especially in the United States, makes a qualitative difference and gives Israel minor status. Yet the Holocaust experience has created a desire for a post-modern Jewish consciousness and culture. Israel possesses unique advantages in unfolding such a development, but it lacks institutional resources and settings designed to carry out this task.

The Holocaust challenged the hegemony of fundamental assumptions of modernism within the Jewish world. For an ever-increasing minority, it set in motion a reconsideration of the policy of integration and assimilation and provided alternate norms for a more independent and critical attitude toward modern culture. Thus, it could be said that the Holocaust polarized existing tendencies—driving more Jews into highly assimilationist settings and others in more vital Jewish directions. It stimulated a new receptiveness to Jewish existence and life-style in people who were too deeply rooted in modernity simply to reject modern culture. The powerful

existential impact of the event opened up the situation; but there is
need for cultural, philosophical, and sociological validation of these
insights and the formulation of a new relationship between Jewishness and dominant cultural norms.[32]

The perception of freedom of identity and the weakening of
ascribed status is a pervasive value in contemporary culture. These
values have grown out of the quantum leap of human power and
control, through medicine and technology, backed by the development of democratic and universalist norms. The freedom to be protean is seen as the source of human dignity and liberation—even
from biological limits.[33] This weakens the sense of Chosenness and
the pull of Jewish existence. In an open majority Gentile culture,
most Jews, thus released, moved toward universal majority status.
The Holocaust has challenged this on two levels. It suggests that
"proteanism" is illusory—Jewishness is "given" and decisive to
one's fate. The sense of choice only creates illusions which weakens
the victims' perception that they are also part of the destruction to
come.[34] The Holocaust has also suggested that the breaking of organic relationship and deracination itself may be a major source of this
pathology which erupted at the very heart of modernity.[35] A post-
modernist articulation of this insight is crucial to a coherent, Jewish
sense of group existence. Most Jews will not retreat from modernity
with its broadening of human dignity and individual opportunity
offered to a premodern "Jewish soul." A dialectical incorporation of
these modern values is essential.

The same is true of the power of the universal pattern in modern culture. The extent to which universal visions are still unchal-
lenged despite the Holocaust is the extent to which Jews are still assimilating or becoming anti-Israel or anti-Semitic. Unreconstructed

32. Greenberg, "Values and Goals," *Yavneh Studies,* New York, 1962, vol. 1, no. 1,
pp. 47–49, "Toward Jewish Religious Unity: A Symposium," *Judaism,* vol. 15, no. 2,
Spring 1966, pp. 134, 137–139. See also Emil Fackenheim, Elie Wiesel et al., "Jewish
Values in the Post Holocaust Future: A Symposium," *ibid.,* vol. 16, no. 3, Summer
1967, pp. 269 ff; Emil Fackenheim, *God's Presence in History,* New York, 1970. ch. 3.

33. Robert Jay Lifton, "Protean Man," *History and Human Survival,* New York (n.d.),
pp. 315–331, reprinted from *Partisan Review,* Winter 1968, pp. 13–27.

34. A. Margaliot, *Hitpatchut ha-anti-Shemiut ha-Nazit m'Tchilatah v'ha-Teguvah ha-
Yehudit Ayle-ha,* Jerusalem, 1970; testimony of Abba Kovner, in personal conversation with the author, June 25, 1975.

35. "Cloud of Smoke," Sect. vii Bb.

socialist and liberation ideologies still furnish cover for attempted genocide on the isolation of Israel. The rough outlines of the critique are known: the abstraction of universalism and its inability to do justice to the unique; the need for plural sources of identity to prevent totalitarian control; the covert particularisms which frequently exclude Jewish validity within many universalist philosophies; and a challenge to the excessive claims of science and social science methodology and epistemology. Liberation from the tyranny of these categories would pave the way for positive Jewish confrontation with Jewish group existence. Even existence in the natural Jewish community of Israel does not guarantee that these questions will not become critical in the face of the enormous sacrifices demanded for continued Jewish existence.

Science, rationalism and the empirical tradition struck at many aspects of Revelation uniqueness and particularist Jewish values. The post-Holocaust situation has legitimated a new scholarship, more autonomous and critical of the assumptions which forced Judaism into unsuitable categories or reduced its credibility by covert manipulation of the terms of discourse.[36]

Modern biblical scholarship has shaken the traditional claims of authority. The original modernist formulations were a remarkable intellectual achievement but they did little justice to the meaningfulness of the biblical literature. A critique of this reduction in significance started within the scholarly tradition itself, some of the criticism coming from Jewish scholars who even speak of differences between Jewish and non-Jewish intellectuals in approach and conception.[37] The argument grew out of post-Holocaust Jewish assertiveness and greater awareness of the limits of the so-called universal scholarly standard. However, this is not a Jewish project. The work of the scholars of the *Heilsgeschichte* school at Göttingen, which gives a post-critical affirmation of God's acts in history, grows out of the post-Holocaust cultural disillusionment with the tyranny of modern categories. It rejects secular absolutism which cuts off

36. An example of such scholarly analysis is to be found in Emil Fackenheim, *Encounters between Judaism and Modern Philosophy: A Preface to Future Thought*, New York, 1973.

37. Nahum Sarna, "The Bible and Judaic Studies," *The Teaching of Judaica in American Universities*, Leon A. Jick, ed., New York, 1970, pp. 35–40; William Hallo, "Biblical Studies in Jewish Perspectives," *ibid.*, pp. 43–46.

God's presence in history—because the unquestioned hegemony of modernity was shattered in the Holocaust.

A major investment in developing new terms and a more sophisticated epistemology could recover the riches of the tradition. This would destroy both the procrustean bed of modernist assumptions and the fundamentalist literalism which loses the power of the *Sitz im Leben* of the tradition. Some scholars hesitate to develop these areas because of academic orthodoxy. A willingness to explore these areas—with great sophistication to avoid special pleading or teleological scholarship—is the cutting edge of a new autonomous Jewish culture. Only a fully participating, yet critical, culture can maintain itself in the emerging open society. Israelis should take the lead in this area. Living in a Jewish environment with heightened Holocaust consciousness, they could be more independent and more institutionally supported in such a thrust. However, this initiative presumes a psychological liberation from European and American university models—without retrogressing from methodological achievements.

Another area calls for extensive exploration of values and development. For certain reasons, including freedom of inquiry and methodological gains, the university has renounced this area. Since university norms became regnant and the university received the major investment of society's funds, the result was a shrinking in the cultural salience of values and of settings in which to pursue them. Value exploration today usually takes place in settings which restrict freedom of inquiry, and are built on unscholarly conceptions. Yeshivot and other religious education settings are an example of this. The Holocaust literature shows how value-free science and scholarship can be used to liquidate people; "Hitler's Professors" also dramatize the problematics of the separation of scholarship and character. Of the twenty four defendants at the *Einsatzgruppen* trial, nine were lawyers and eight were other professionals, ranging from professors to clergymen.[38]

New settings must be created—perhaps nourished and surrounded by the university—where serious study and the implications of scholarship can be explored without regressing to parochial

38. Max Weinreich, *Hitler's Professors—The Part of Scholarship in Germany's Crimes against the Jewish People*, New York, 1946; "Cloud of Smoke," Sect. IIb, especially n. 16; George Steiner, *Language and Silence*, New York, 1970, and Elie Wiesel, in "Jewish Values," *ibid.*, p. 282.

pleading. This new model should develop academic religious study of the past three decades and clearly must involve more articulation of values than even that discipline has achieved. Despite the difficulties involved, the ontological legitimacy of values and the need for Jewish coherence call for the creation of such centers, which, in serious interplay with the university, will explore growth of values and role models such as are required by the post-Holocaust moral situation and Jewish culture.

An associated issue is the question of the symbolic, mythic and liturgical representation of the Holocaust and the rebirth of the State. Professor Gershom Scholem has pointed out that these developments, more than scholarship, have determined the impact of great events on Jewish religion and culture.[39] Today, these processes cannot continue in ignorance or contradiction to scholarship—if they are to be credible. Again, a post-modernist position is needed. Israel is the natural setting for the creation of symbols which would lead toward her becoming a spiritual center and a major source for Diaspora religious and cultural development.

Israel can play the same role in religious development. The modern period has tended to favor prophetic values in religion, but prophetic stances are inadequate for real power situations. Prophets may rely on spiritual power and make absolute demands for righteousness. Governments have obligations to protect people. Calling on the *halakhic* resources of the tradition—or creating equivalents— to judge specific situations, to reconcile conflicting claims and changing facts, becomes crucial. It means linking ultimate ends and proximate means in a continuing process. That cannot be done without some involvement in guilt, partial failures and compromises. Still, the historical record shows that even limited participation in the realm of the possible often leads to a surrender to the status quo—unless judgment is continually refreshed through exposure to prophetic norms. The development of Israel is a test of Jewish dialectic capacity—to live a normal life with abnormal moral discipline and sensitivity. It tests the effectiveness of Jewish tradition and memory in inspiring Jewish people not to do unto others what was done to them when they were powerless. Ability to develop these

39. *Interpreting the Holocaust for Future Generations: Proceedings of a Symposium,* New York (n.d.). This symposium was conducted at a meeting of the Memorial Foundation in Geneva on July 9, 1974. Professor Scholem made his point in the discussion on the papers presented.

areas would give moral centrality to Israel. Indeed Israeli achievements are needed by American Jews seeking to apply Jewish norms
to the realities in which they function.

Finally, the problem of enjoying affluence and freedom of expression—without becoming selfish or forfeiting group dimensions
of existence—is a central problem of the emerging post-modern
world. Perhaps there must be a surfeit of affluence before a critical attitude to it can be developed. In that sense, America may be ahead of
Israel. Yet the strength of the *halutzic* traditions, the training for sacrifice demanded from a citizen army, and the still powerful pockets
of traditional values in Israel are potential sources for such models.
While interaction of the Diaspora and Israel is needed for this development, Israeli ability to realize a better society would give Israel
moral primacy—to match its primacy in Jewish fate and destiny. Ultimately, that will be an important factor affecting *aliyah*. Unless a
catastrophe occurs in the Diaspora, Jews who seek to give primacy to
their Jewish values and to realize them in society will be the main
settlers in Israel. It may be naive to overestimate the role of ideas as
against material considerations or the role of violence in history. But
the re-creation of Israel and the thrust of Diaspora Jewish life after
the Holocaust show that hope and dreams are at times more powerful than objective forces.

Joint commitment and cooperation in preventing a recurrence, and re-creating life, would appear to be the most promising
paths toward a post-modernist Jewish unity and presence in the
world.

A Reassessment of Israel's Role in the Contemporary Jewish Condition

Immanuel Jakobovits

My views on the current situation and its travails are based on my firm commitment to the authentic Jewish teaching that the tortuous course of the Jewish experience, especially as related to the Land of Israel, is determined primarily not by capricious or fortuitous forces beyond our control, but above all by the merit and spiritual fiber of our own people. Our prophets expressed the special relationship between Providence and our fortunes or misfortunes in covenantal terms; the doctrine of reward and punishment in the Bible is invariably applied to Jewish existence in the Holy Land. The leading contemporary Jewish historian Salo W. Baron, in the opening to his monumental *Social and Religious History of the Jews,* recognizes the same mystique of the Jewish experience in the constant manifestation of what he calls history vanquishing nature, that is, normal or natural processes being superseded by special laws governing all of Jewish history.

This mystique is the wider significance of the centrality of Israel, now increasingly evident not only in Jewish life but also in world affairs and indeed in the consummation of the human purpose. The mere fact that a tiny people, restored to a little land, with few natural resources, continues to be close to the very heart of the major political, economic and strategic upheavals besetting the entire world in a universal crisis of unprecedented proportions, affecting the fortunes of superpowers and small nations alike—this in itself is the surest indication that the timeless drama of God's special relationship with Israel is far from played out. A numerically insignificant people cannot fill the front pages of the world's newspapers for over quarter of a century without serving a special purpose in the evolution of man's history.

Morally and existentially, this centrality finds expression in

283

those very double standards that are applied to Jews and Israel by the world community. Instead of simply decrying this abnormal feature in the way we are treated, we should accept it in part as a tribute by the world to the superior moral standards expected from the Jewish People; it should also serve to remind us that we cannot escape our historic assignment as moral pioneers and pathfinders among the human family, wherein we are destined to play a unique role in order to vindicate our equally unique record of triumph over all odds as an eternal people.

The all but complete disregard of these considerations, at least as a major factor in appraising the extraordinary features of our contemporary condition, is as incomprehensible as it is depressing. Since the untimely passing of Yaacov Herzog,[1] I do not know of a single ranking personality, in or near the seats of power in Israel or outside the country, who views the convulsive events of our times through specifically Jewish eyes as he did, who interprets current happenings and trends in the light of the forces governing Jewish history and the dynamics of Jewish thought. This deficiency applies not only to secularist leaders who conduct Jewish affairs of state as would statesmen, politicians or diplomats of any people facing our dilemma. I look vainly even to our religious and rabbinical Establishments for an interpretation of our national fortunes and misfortunes, an interpretation which bears the unmistakable hallmark of distinctly Jewish perceptions. Men of piety and learning may have succeeded to the priestly functions of spiritual leadership in biblical times. But the Hebrew prophets are without heirs today; the whys and wherefores, the questions on how to put together the jigsaw pieces of our jumbled world intelligently—these remain unanswered. The perplexed are not guided, at least not by a corporate voice of the Jewish national conscience, and the imperatives of Israel's moral impact on human affairs are altogether ignored in an abrupt disengagement from the prophetic ideals of Judaism.

In the attempt to bring Jewish perspectives to bear on our tribulations, my comments may be critical and perhaps even harsh. Yet I claim a right to express them—a right, indeed a duty, shared by all Jews in the Diaspora who are committed to the cause of Zion.

---

1. See his volume published posthumously, *A People That Dwells Alone*, New York, 1975.

Diaspora Jewry's Reactions

I have, for a long time, been urging more regular (though in-formal) consultations between a wide representation of Jewish lead-ers in the Diaspora and Israeli policy makers. Such consultations should explore fundamental policies on matters of major common concern as, for instance, educational and political reforms, Israel-Diaspora relations, and even the current peace negotiations—for the following reasons:

1. To secure our aid for Israel's needs, her emissaries never fail to tell us that we are partners. But there can be no partner-ship without participation, any more than taxation without repre-sentation. In part, the now growing rift between Israel and the Dias-pora is caused or aggravated by the imbalance in relations between them—the feeling that Diaspora Jews are expected to sign blank checks to underwrite policies over which they have no control or influence. Obviously, it is neither our right nor in our interest to ask for a vote on decisions which are the prerogative of Israeli citizens, but we do stake a claim to be consulted, if our partnership is to be genuine.

2. These decisions often crucially affect Jewish interests everywhere. I am not only referring to issues like "Who is a Jew," or Soviet Jewry, or bi-national relations with countries harboring large Jewish communities. The very security of Jews in Britain, as else-where, is now largely determined by Israel's place and image among the nations. Moreover, the centrality of Israel in Jewish life is, or ought to be, such as to make the Jewish character of the State, or the status of Jerusalem, the direct concern of every Jew, wherever he happens to live. On the question of Jerusalem, I believe our claim would command far greater force and sympathy if it were advanced not merely by politicians on behalf of a government and its citizens, but as a religious title by World Jewry, just as Islam, at Lahore, asserted a Moslem, as distinct from Arab, claim to the Holy City. Israel, far from encouraging and enlisting the involvement of World Jewry at these levels, has tended to spurn it, thus weakening the very bonds she purports to cherish and to require.

3. Times as critical as the present demand contributions to Is-raeli thinking of the finest Jewish brains and talents, wherever they are to be found. Additionally, Diaspora Jews may well have the

advantage of relative distance and objectivity so essential in reaching vital decisions. The Talmudic rule that "a witness cannot be a
judge" is of more than legal significance. Just as the genius reflected
in a master painting cannot be appreciated if one stands too close to
the canvas, so events cannot be evaluated unless one stands at a certain distance from them. Confinement within embattled Israel since,
and even before, the State's foundation is bound to be conducive to a
siege mentality, circumscribing some wider visions and tending to
produce a myopic view of world currents and opinions. For example, as we now, in our international loneliness, denounce the hostility of nations and bend every effort to mobilize their support, there is
a rather hollow ring to the much hailed statement attributed to Ben-
Gurion: "What matters is what Jews do, not what non-Jews think." It
epitomizes a frame of mind which breeds a cynical indifference to
the wider world—an outlook as natural to Jews inside besieged Israel as it is often irritating to those outside. The latter are obviously
more exposed and sensitive to the reactions of their fellow citizens
and therefore better able to provide the proper corrective, were they
consulted. The statement clearly defies the whole concept of *kiddush
ha-Shem* (sanctification of the Divine name), whereby, in the
past, we were greatly concerned about the good name of Jews and
Judaism among non-Jews.

In two of the above examples—the status of Jerusalem and the
cultivation of international goodwill—the application of specifically
Jewish commitments might have made a difference in our present
plight. All three points also underscore the religious principle of *kol
Yisrael arevim zeh la-zeh,* that all Jews are corporately responsible
for each other, sharing a common liability, a common destiny, and—
now more than ever—a common fate. Not since the beginning of our
dispersion at the end of the first Jewish Commonwealth have all Jewish communities been so interdependent as they have now become
through the rise of Israel.[2]

---

2. Vital as the partnership is between Israel and the Diaspora in their interdependence
today, it is still subject to considerable resistance on both sides. The average Israeli
and his Government deem unwarranted the Diaspora Jew's claim to participation and
interference in matters affecting the way of life and security of Israel. Conversely, the
average Diaspora Jew prefers to remain aloof for fear of being charged with "dual loyalities." The result is mutually perilous. In the Diaspora this attitude attenuates
any meaningful identification with Israel. True, Israel calls for support, arouses
pride, anxiety and sympathy—but Jews do not look to the Land as theirs in any realistic sense, as is evidenced by the mistranslation in an American *Haggadah* published

The Agranat Commission, assisted by countless commenta-
tors, probed into the setbacks of the Yom Kippur War and their traumatic aftermath. But Jewish history does not operate simply in terms
of military logistics or political equations. If it did, we would have
disappeared long ago. Happily for us, the logistics were illogical,
and the equations did not balance. How lamentable, therefore, that
there has been no high-level inquiry into some of the more profound
factors responsible for our disastrous reverses, into miscalculations
and intelligence errors which transcend the incorrect deployment of
troops or electronic gear. What needs to be reexamined in the light of
present realities are the premises and visions, the very axioms of
faith, on which the Jewish State was built and developed.

These prologamena lead me to my main theme.

The Zionist Credo

The primary motivation of secular Zionism has always been
the belief that the restoration of Jewish sovereignty would "solve the
Jewish problem" by eliminating the abnormality of the Jewish condition. This belief inspired the early forerunners of political Zionism
as it stimulated the policies of their successors. Pinsker's *Auto-
Emancipation* was "rooted in the desire to engineer the acceptance
of the Jews as equals in the modern world" by removing them "from
the situation of abnormality surrounded by hatred to a territory of
their own where they would become a normal nation." Further,
Herzl in his *Judenstaat* argued that "the Jews could gain acceptance
in the world only if they ceased being a national anomaly" (see *Encyclopedia Judaica*, 16:1043–4). Though later influenced marginally
by Aḥad Ha-Am's "Cultural Zionism" and by Weizmann's "Synthet-
ic Zionism," essentially the Zionist credo has remained the same to
this day. National equality became the magic formula which would

---

by a Conservative rabbi, "and may He lead the *homeless of our people* in dignity to
our ancient homeland" (Prayer Book Press, 1959, p. 41) instead of "and may he lead
us . . ." In other words, Israel is not for us, but for the *homeless*. In Israel, again, the
refusal to take counsel with Diaspora Jewry breeds unconcern and nonidentification
with Jewish affairs outside. This lack of interest is similarly manifested by the thousands of Israeli students in our midst, and it deprives the leadership of Israel of the
perspectives indispensable in reaching some of the most fateful decisions ever made
in Jewish history—on which the future of all of us depends. As the Talmudic phrase
teaches, "a captive cannot release himself from prison," Israel cannot be delivered
from her siege without outside help and advice.

put a quick end to all the suffering and persecution caused by the anomaly of Jewish exilic existence.

Alas, the Yom Kippur War, if not its antecedents, finally shattered this illusion. Immeasurable as the State's achievements are for Jews inside and outside Israel—far outweighing the costs exacted—the one thing the State cannot achieve is to turn us into a nation like all other nations, losing our historic identity as a unique people.

The reverse has happened. Far from having "solved the Jewish problem," Israel has highlighted it. Jews are today as different, as "peculiar," and as lonely as they ever were. They are subjected by the international community to those very "double standards" which it was the dream of secular Zionists to eliminate in the process of making us "equals." Indeed, through Israel, the abnormalcy of the Jewish condition, with all its attendant perils, has now been extended from individual Jews and scattered Jewish communities to the Jewish People as a whole. The welfare of Jews everywhere depends on Israel's survival. Only the semantics have changed. Anti-Semitism has become anti-Zionism, and instead of sporadic pogroms we have periodic wars and the constant threat of terrorist outrages.

The price exacted because of this illusion exceeds the failure to "solve the Jewish problem." In pursuing the phantom of equality and the mirage of normalization, the whole ethos of our national existence has been deleteriously affected. Instead of exporting the values peculiar to the Jewish spirit—from humility, integrity, moral excellence and profound faith to the discipline of life acquired through the regimen of religious observances—we all too often imported from our exile the materialism, the social and moral depravities to which we had been exposed. In the end, the benefits of equality have eluded us. The nations still do not treat us as equals, while the liabilities of equality afflict us. Like other peoples, we now sadly also have rising rates of crime, drug addiction, divorce, corruption in high places and even murder—scourges which used to be unknown in Jewish society.

The drive toward normalization has perverted many of our national values and aspirations. We take greater pride in that which we have in common with others—army, parliament, universities —than in aspects which distinguish us particularly—the religious soldier, Jewish law, the great academies of Jewish learning.

Weakening Jewish Commitment and Security

Paradoxically, whereas the establishment of the Jewish State greatly intensified Jewish consciousness and identification in communities everywhere, it has also weakened the Jewish spiritual commitment. In the Diaspora many Jews have found vicarious expression for their Jewish identity in the existence and support of Israel. For them, living as Jews by proxy has conveniently replaced the personal discipline of Jewish living. In Israel, again, a large number of Jews have found in their national allegiance a substitute for traditional Jewish observance. For those Jews the Diaspora has become the vicarious haven of their residual Jewishness, as is poignantly attested by the many Israelis who, surprisingly enough, discover their Jewish feeling and identity only when they visit communities abroad and find communication with their faith and with fellow Jews in the synagogue. Thus, Jewish statehood helped to accelerate the secularization, or despiritualization, of Jewish life both at home and abroad, leading to an ever-widening gap between Jews and the Jewish tradition.

Another dimension of the loss incurred by the abandonment of Jewish traditional values directly affects the very security of the State, as for example, the problem of the Arab refugees. Even if we could do little or nothing to solve the problem, surely as Jews—faithful to our ethical heritage of marked sensitivity to the sufferings of the stranger and the homeless—we should not have left it to gangs of murderous terrorists to draw the world's attention to this stain on humanity. Had we cried out in protest against the intolerable degradation of hundreds of thousands of human beings inhumanly condemned to rot in wretched camps for a generation, had we aroused the world's conscience over a tragedy of such magnitude, we might have prevented the growth of a monster organization which has already destroyed so many innocent lives. Now, with the blessing of the world community, that problem threatens the very existence of Israel more acutely than the Arab armies ever did.

Again, had we not neglected the teachings of Jewish ethics on abortions (at the average rate of 40,000 annually since the foundation of the State) and birth control, making the birth rate among Arabs *inside* Israel more than twice as high as that among Jews, the Jewish population would now be over five million. This number

would include at least two million more Sabras, without incurring
the colossal financial outlay and the problems involved in the trans-
portation and absorption of immigrants who number but a fraction
of this estimate.

For those conditioned by decades of secular Zionist teaching
and propaganda (including the principal fund-raising campaigns) to
limit their vision of Israel's purpose to that of providing a haven of
Jewish security, the shock waves likely to be produced by the collapse of this ideology may be devastating. The first impact is already
felt in declining *aliyah* (immigration) and increasing *yeridah* (emigration) rates and the blighting disillusionment which has driven
some of our youth (long since alienated from our traditions) to ask,
"What are we fighting for?" Others have been impelled to challenge
the justice of Israel's cause and yet others to question even the purpose of Jewish survival.

Not surprisingly, only the religious element is now immune
to this erosion of faith, as it is to the inroads of assimilation on the
wider front in the grim battle for survival. Attracted to the Land of Israel by its holiness more than by the security it may offer and to the
Jewish People by intense love of Judaism rather than by accident of
birth, these skull-capped young men and modestly clad women now
constitute the bulk of western *aliyah.* (In fact, the religious segment,
amounting to no more than 10 to 20 percent of the community, com-
prises about 60 percent of the recent immigrants.) They are the last
to swell the emigration or social drop-out rates and the first to preserve the pristine idealism and pioneering spirit, in war as in peace,
which has sustained us through our martyred history and formerly
enthused the Zionist movement. Even among recent Soviet Jewish
immigrants a survey indicated that, while none of the "religiously
observant" and only 14 percent listed as "traditional" contemplated
leaving Israel, 21 percent of the "nonreligious" and 72 percent of the
"anti-religious" admitted that they did not wish to remain in Israel.[3]

3. *Extracts from the Proceedings of the International Leadership Seminar on Soviet
Jewry,* Jerusalem, March 1975, p. 20. Similar trends are to be found in a study on attitudes among 17-year-old high school pupils in the Tel Aviv area. When asked, "Are
you prepared to accept emigration from Israel by an Israeli who is unable to find work
in his chosen field?" 69 percent of the "religious," 59 percent of the "traditional" and
only 40 percent of the "nonreligious" pupils replied in the negative. See Chaya Zuck-
erman-Bareli, "The Religious Factor in Opinion Formation among Israeli Youth," *On
Ethnic and Religious Diversity in Israel,* Solomon Pell and Ernest Krausz, ed., Bar-Ilan
University, 1975, p. 66.

Moreover, the strictly observant are now the only segment of our people, inside and outside Israel, to be secure against the ravages of shrinking numbers. Enjoying an exceptionally high birth rate and a virtually nonexistent rate of defection by intermarriage and assimilation, they are dramatically increasing their proportionate strength compared with other groups. This increase is perhaps as much as four or five times that of the average Jewish growth rate which, for most Jews, in terms of identification, is often less than zero. Considering that these "intensive" Jews scarcely face the problems of dropouts or crime, one may well discern spiritual echoes of Darwin's "survival of the fittest."

The lesson seems obvious; yet those in need of that lesson refuse to acknowledge or learn it—at a cost which may soon become catastrophic, for the problem goes much deeper. The question "Why Jewish survival?" troubles not only spiritually impoverished Jews; it bedevils the world at large.

Why Survival?

History is, and always was, brutal. Nations, like individuals, come into being, then die. Greater and more powerful peoples than we have disappeared; no one mourns or misses them. Who would grieve if we vanished, especially when millions die in a world undersupplied with compassion? After 4000 years of existence, far beyond the life span of other nations, we may be thought to have had a fair run; and even without the Jewish People, science, the arts, industry and agriculture would still continue to develop.

Jews are today widely regarded as a troublesome nuisance, a principal factor in many of the world's gravest crises and perils: the Middle East powderkeg, the oil boycott, the energy crisis, the threat to détente and trade relations with Russia—not to mention the traditional scapegoat role of Jews in times of economic depression. In the public image, Jews create problems rather than solve them.

What is to justify, then, our claim to national survival and our demand for the world's support and sympathy, even at the risk of economic collapse and the possibility of nuclear confrontation, as happened in October 1973, and might well happen again? Surely the answer can only lie in our special role as "a light unto the nations," as an exceptional people, as a model society determined to enrich mankind with incomparable contributions, as has been the case in the past. Surely our stricken world needs the uplift and inspiration of our unique Jewish heritage no less today than in pagan antiquity when we blazed a lonely trail which was eventually to guide humanity to the uplands of civilization and moral progress.

If we were the one people on earth who, through idealism and ethical behavior, had discovered how to eradicate crime and licentiousness, social inequality and selfishness, how to practice self-discipline and serve others, how to preserve the marriage bond—in short, how to sanctify life and make righteousness a national goal— our image among Jews and non-Jews alike would be vastly different. We would not be traumatized by the problem of Jewish survival as the leading item on our national agenda for the first time in history. It is surely no accident that three entirely novel questions, never previously asked or debated in our long annals, have been raised simultaneously: "Who is a Jew?", "What is Jewish identity?", "How do we insure Jewish survival?" The moment we no longer agree on the essential qualities and definition of a Jew, Jewish survival becomes problematical.

Our fundamental objectives, then, call for revision if Jewish survival is not to be meaningless or even questionable. A secular Jewish State, itself a contradiction in terms, simply cannot be viable. Moreover, without reliance on our religious Covenant and Divine promise, we cannot assert either a legal or historical title to the Land for so long ruled and occupied by others. It is the future of Judaism, therefore, even more than of the Jewish People (who are but its instrument), which is at stake. Its preservation must become the ultimate goal in our present struggle. There cannot be Jews without Judaism any more than there can be Judaism without Jews.

The futility of wresting the Jewish experience from its spiritual moorings should have been apparent even from a cursory acquaintance with Jewish history, or indeed from any realistic appraisal of Israel's purpose. Surely our forebears did not endure such cruel martyrdom "for sanctification of the Divine Name," or offer thanks daily to the Almighty that "He has not made us like all the nations of the earth, nor like all their multitude," so that eventually we should glory in being a people like all others or that we should boast the finest army in the world. Is it reasonable to establish a Jewish State as a bulwark against individual assimilation only to find that it is turning into a vehicle of national assimilation?

Proposed Counteraction

Alarmed by such trends, which moreover accentuate the threat to the unity of our people at a time of extreme danger, I recently contacted a select group of about thirty leading intellectuals and opinion-makers. These people reside mainly in Israel; all are well-known in public life, though none hold political office. I argued that: 1) the association of religion with politics was divisive and counter-productive; 2) persuasion was more important than coercion in strengthening Israel's spiritual defences; and 3) above all, at the heart of Israel's demoralization and polarization lay the failure of its educational system, whereby two-thirds of our children were completely estranged from the faith and traditions which had preserved and united us in our past tribulations. I invited those intellectuals to support a proposal calling for a moratorium on all new religious legislation; then, safe from partisan arguments, the stage should be set for the introduction in all Israeli schools of a daily period of religious education, to be given by teachers deeply committed to a program which would be implemented by the Ministry of Education and administered by a special statutory authority of a nonpolitical character.

The responses were highly interesting, but disappointing. All those consulted were more or less agreed upon the need and its urgency, even to the extent of endorsing the plea for religious education in principle as an antidote to existing spiritual starvation. But no one was really prepared for the crunch—the leap of faith, as it were, over the gulf between recognizing the malaise and administering the cure. Several of those who responded feared that any inclusion of religious instruction in the regular day school syllabus would create resentment. (In Diaspora Jewish day schools the exclusion of religious instruction would be unthinkable.) A renowned scholar-general wrote: "If Orthodox teaching were introduced as the sole expression of Judaism, it would present no less a danger to Jewish unity than the politicization of religion. Should not the courses and prayers, therefore, be conducted by the various religious trends?" (This would imply that children in Israel should be entangled in the arguments and divisions from which their fellow Jews in the Diaspora are still happily protected. A professor of Hebrew Law doubted whether formal instruction in spiritual values would even appeal to Israeli youth and if there were enough teachers in whom religious commitment was combined with Zionist orientation. Perhaps we should send *shlichim* (emissaries) in reverse. While he largely agreed with my contention that the key lay in education rather than in legislation, he still regarded the legislative process as an essential tool with which to promote the religious character of Israel. He wanted rabbinic attitudes to become more flexible; yet he urged that school courses should apply Jewish law and ethics to modern conditions. (But the problem can hardly wait until the dynamic process in the evolution of Jewish law has run its course.)

To the plea for "a renaissance of the *Halakhah*" (Jewish Law), I could only reply: The development of the *Halakhah* as a response to the changing needs of the times is an organic process which cannot be hastened artificially. In this age of instant communication and pushbutton answers to complex problems, we tend to be impatient, forgetting that computers are useless in reacting to the promptings of the soul or in dealing with eternal values. Nearly 500 years elapsed between the Exodus from Egypt and the building of Solomon's Temple—the first consummation of our religious ideals—and it took another 800 years to compose the Talmud as our religious response to the encounter with the Greek and Roman civilizations, as well as to the experience of national homelessness. Nor would a Sanhedrin be the panacea that is claimed by its diverse advocates (many of whom would be the last to submit to its rulings). Apart from serving primarily to strengthen the observance of the Law, it requires for its reestablishment two indispensable conditions: its unquestioned recognition by the majority of our people and the gathering together of seventy universally acknowledged sages qualified and willing to serve on it. Today, neither of these conditions can be even remotely fulfilled. Without them, the premature convocation of a Sanhedrin would only mock a venerated institution through popular indifference; and it might well exacerbate the dissension within the world religious community.

Most poignant was the reply to my proposal from a university president. Asserting that "the cement of Jewish unity" consisted of people who were traditional and who, even if not observant, recognized "that the things they do not observe are the commandments of traditional Judaism," he grieved over the Orthodox tendency "to become defensive" and to "write us off." He suggested the formation of a movement "that can only be led by Orthodox Jews themselves," designed to promote ethical virtues by personal example. The defensive approach should be replaced by "an outgoing program to spread a knowledge of the Jewish tradition in terms of the continuity of experience of the Jewish people throughout history" in fellowship with all Jews. (Allowing for all the sympathy evoked by such a cry for hands to reach out to him, the solution—putting the onus on Orthodox Jews only—still seems too vague and unrealistic to meet the immediate challenge.)

I sought to transform this correspondence into a meeting in Jerusalem to plan a campaign of action based on a consensus between us, but we were unable to move further. Once again, the sacred cow of the status quo—worshipped in religion, politics and all other Israeli establishments—remained inviolate.

The same inertia prevailed over earlier moves (advanced through more official channels) to counteract the appalling ignorance and indifference of Israel youth vis-à-vis Jews in the Diaspora—a major cause for estrangement in Israel–Diaspora relations and sometimes even mutual resentment. I had suggested the inclusion of regular courses on the history, structure and life of Diaspora Jewry in the Israeli school curriculum and far greater coverage of Jewish activities throughout the world in the Israeli press. This would nurture the identification of Israelis with other Jews just as they expected Jews abroad to identify with Israeli affairs and problems. Likewise, I wanted all Israeli students planning studies abroad to be adequately prepared before their departure so that they would identify with their host communities and enhance the good name of Israel. Such an identification would be warmly reciprocated by Diaspora Jews. Instead, there is a damaging liability to both Israel and the communities within which those Israelis live by the thousands (up to 3,000 in Britain alone) in complete isolation and apathy. They represent, after all, the most vital and potentially constructive element of the estimated quarter of a million Israelis now studying and residing abroad.

Regeneration of the Jewish Spirit

I acknowledge that there is today much soul-searching and a widespread quest for spiritual values, though evidently there is more sober concern at the grassroots of popular impatience than at the storm-resistant treetops of national leadership. This search for fresh thinking may indeed be the most hopeful portent to emerge from the agony of the immediate past. But what most people are seeking simply does not exist: a Judaism without religion, a faith without belief, a *Torah* without *mitzvot*. They are chasing shadows rather than substance.

The mysteries of Providence and Jewish history are such that the accepted roles of the 1967 and the 1973 wars may yet be reversed in regard to their effect on the consummation of Jewish purpose. The Six Day War, with all its ecstasy, may have induced one of the most calamitous recessions of Jewish spirit in our annals. Political and military attitudes apart, that war bred a sense of overconfidence, an inflexibility, a feeling of complacency, a disdain for the outside world and an extravagant taste for high living which spilled over into a moral pollution of the national character once distinguished by faith, integrity, selflessness, idealism and frugality. The Yom Kippur War, on the other hand, its heartbreak notwithstanding, may yet release invaluable spiritual energies and in a mighty burst of power redirect our destiny to its historic orbit.

The departure from the millennial norms of Jewish history and purpose and the confusion of means with ends may be illustrated by a striking homily. During the British Mandate, when thousands of Jews were refused permission to enter the "national home," it was said that the only thing wrong with the Balfour Declaration was a misplaced full-stop. That part of the text which reads, "His Majesty's Government view with favour the establishment in Palestine of a national home for the Jewish people . . . , it being clearly understood that nothing shall be done which may prejudice the . . . rights of existing non-Jewish communities . . . ," was phrased: "His Majesty's government view with favour the establishment in Palestine of a national home for the Jewish people . . . , it being clearly understood that nothing shall be done." However, this misplacement of the full-stop is but the response to our putting the full-stop in the wrong place in our claim to the Land. To this day, the principal dynamic of Zionism is the cry, echoed from the genesis of our peoplehood, "Let My people go!" But this is a travesty of history. Moses pleaded nothing of the kind before Pharaoh. What he demanded time and again was: "Let My people go, so that they shall serve Me!" By misplacing the full-stop, we turn the means into the end, forgetting the whole object of our redemption from Egyptian enslavement. Similarly, when, following the 1881 pogroms, Russian Jews pioneered the return to Zion, they called the movement BILU by the Hebrew initials of the verse in Isaiah (2:5): "House of Jacob, come and let us go"—full stop—instead of concluding the verse with the culminating words "in the light of the Lord." Without the final words, these slogans are a betrayal of Jewish destiny, doomed ultimately to evoke the nations' response that "nothing shall be done" to secure Jewish survival. Jewish freedom and independence are only vindicated "so that they shall serve Me" and go "in the light of the Lord" as "a light unto the nations."

Alternative Futures for Soviet Jewry

Zev Katz

The only prediction that can safely be made about the future is that it is unpredictable. This, however, does not deny the need for rational, systematic thinking about alternative futures. Full equality is impossible, historical truth is not grasped, complete justice (or happiness) is unobtainable. Yet, we spend our lives pursuing these ends. Were we to train our thinking in terms of (sometimes unthinkable) future alternatives, we might obtain a wider perspective which would lead to an early recognition of an adjustment to hitherto unknown developments. Jacob Katz posed the question: Was the Holocaust predictable? If the possibility of a Holocaust could have been conceived, perhaps the fate of European Jewry would have been different.

Basic Factors for the Jewish Future

In line with methodologies developed by Kahn, Brzezinski and Bell, this paper treats alternative futures for Soviet Jewry with special relation to "the centrality of Israel." But the specific needs to be seen as part of the following basic factors:
1) Future of the Soviet system
2) Development of Soviet-American relations
3) Future of relations between the U.S.S.R. and Israel
4) Future image of Israel and the West
5) Alternative developments within Soviet Jewry.
These basic factors may be further subdivided:
1) Future of the Soviet system—developmental patterns
    a) Status quo
    b) Military-nationalist regime
    c) Technocratic evolution
    d) Liberalization
    e) Degeneration and disruption

2) Development of Soviet-American relations
   a) Status quo (Kissinger-style détente)
   b) "Tough-bargaining" détente
   c) Sliding back to Cold War
   d) Intensified conflict with local hot wars
3) Future of relations between Russia and Israel
   a) Status quo
   b) Intensification of enmity; foci of hot conflict
   c) Normalization of relations
   d) Good relations
4) Future image of Israel and the West
   a) Positive image (peace, prosperity, progress in quality of life and social justice)
   b) Negative image (constant wars, internal conflict, economic and spiritual degeneration)
   c) Successful absorption (including a helpful attitude by old-timers)
   d) Faulty absorption
5) Alternative developments within Soviet Jewry
   a) *Aliyah* (immigration) to Israel
   b) Immigration to the West
   c) Assimilation
   d) Free Jewish life within Russia

Obviously, since we have 21 variables in five sets, a great number of combinations are possible. Here, only some of the more optimal and more detrimental combinations can be mapped out.

These relate to a combination of 1d (liberalization) with 2b (a tough-bargaining détente); 3d (good relations with Israel) linked with 4ac (a good image of Israel and the West, and successful absorption). Under optimal conditions, one would expect a favorable development in all categories related to 5: *aliyah,* emigration to the West, assimilation, as well as (for the first time since the Bolshevik Revolution) *free* Jewish life *within* Russia (5d). And vice versa, transition to a racial, military-nationalist regime in Russia (1b), or a disruptive degeneration (1e) there may trigger off pogroms and an intensification of anti-Semitism as well as a major wave of *aliyah* and emigration to the West (5ab), without any possibility of assimilation and free Jewish life (5cd). On the other hand, a conservative non-racial military-nationalist regime may actually be pro-Jewish in the sense of promoting *aliyah,* showing understanding for Jewish national goals and allowing a modicum of Jewish life in Russia. A technocratic system may lead to similar results, except that it may be very sensitive to a technological braindrain through extensive Jewish emigration.

II

Liberalization and the Jews

It is worth considering what would happen in the U.S.S.R. should there be a trend toward democratization.

Our grievance with regard to the present regime is so great that we are inclined to view *any* change as a development for the better. This is especially so with regard to democratization. Theoretically, a situation can be envisaged in which—under a liberalized regime—Soviet Jewry would become more like the Western Jewish communities: a highly developed, prosperous, and secure group maintaining close legal ties with Israel and Western Jewry, and a constant, though limited, *aliyah* to Israel. At present, such a possibility seems remote, since it would require not only a democratic Soviet system favoring good relations with the West and Israel but also the elimination of popular nationalism and anti-Semitism in Russia. Thus, a wholly beneficent result of liberalization in Russia should by no means be taken for granted. Actually, under Soviet conditions, democratization may become a dangerous and painful process for Jews for the following reasons:

1) Nationalism

A democratic regime will not be able to suppress the nationalist movements. While some of these may even be sympathetic to Israel and to Jewish cultural demands, their actual impact may be objectively anti-Jewish. For example, the *samizdat,* "Manifesto of the Democratic Movement in the U.S.S.R.," issued by Russian, Ukrainian and Latvian democrats, includes a paragraph of crucial importance and of some foreboding. It says that in the interest of preserving the national character of each national area in the U.S.S.R., the local nationality will have the right to regulate the influx of members of other nationalities into its area.

The general thrust of such attitudes is well known. The nationalities are even today struggling in various ways to promote only their own members into higher education, government positions and so forth. As a result, settlement limitations would be introduced. Though directed against *all* other nationalities, it may in practice turn into a new form of Pale of Settlement limitation, aimed mainly against the Jews.

2) Anti-Semitism

Democratization in Russia is possible only as a result of an intensive struggle between liberal and reactionary forces, but the latter will not give way easily. In such an entanglement, Jews will naturally figure prominently on the side of democracy. And, with equal regularity, anti-democratic forces will use anti-Semitism in the struggle. Events in Poland and Czechoslovakia in 1968 are only mild examples of what can happen in Russia in similar circumstances.

3) Increase in competition

Democratization would relax some of the economic and social controls, thus opening wider fields for competition. In such competition, some Jews are usually highly successful, and display high drive, great ambition and even brusqueness. Thus, intensified competition for positions and economic benefits may recreate conditions which breed some traditional forms of anti-Semitism.

4) Relaxation of censorship

In the conditions of Russia, this will open possibilities for direct expressions of anti-Semitism. Some *samizdats* have already reprinted writings of tsarist times which include anti-Semitic material, and there are right-wing theories which see Russian Orthodoxy as the mainstay of the country. Though not anti-Semitic by themselves, these writings imply the exclusion of Jews from full and equal citizenship in Russia based on such an ideology. (See *samizdat* publications such as *Veche* or *Slovo natsii*.)

5) Popular anti-Semitism

A nonauthoritarian political system in Russia will not be able to prevent the eruption and spread of long-suppressed mass anti-Semitism. Should there be a major crisis in Russia (e.g., war with China, civil disturbances), the masses and sections of the elite may naturally turn on the Jews and treat them as scapegoats. A wave of pogroms and even of mass annihilation could not be excluded in such circumstances.

6) Jewish uniqueness

Liberalizaton will allow large-scale emigration and autonomous organizations of Soviet Jewry to maintain wide-ranging ties with Israel and world Jewry. This will place Soviet Jews in a unique light in the eyes of the non-Jews in Russia. Paradoxically, this may become a source of anti-Jewish attitudes.

Future liberalization in Russia could perhaps be best compared with Jewish emancipation in Europe. The latter released the Jews from previous oppression and opened up possibilities for modern Jewish culture and political organization; but it also brought with it one of the greatest catastrophes in Jewish history.

III

Self-Liquidation and Preservation—Two Basic Variants

In actual terms, the future of Soviet Jewry can be presented as a continuum between two extremes: mass exile and holocaust on the one hand, and free Jewish life under a more liberalized regime on the other.

In the Addendum some simple calculations about the future of Soviet Jewry, based on two possibilities, are presented. Projection One assumes a process of speedy self-liquidation of Soviet Jewry. The total of Jews in 1970 is set at 2.5 million. This figure includes those with one Jewish parent and non-Jewish spouses, who could be candidates for emigration as "members of Jewish families." The *average* emigration ratio is fixed at 30,000 per year, and the *average* population change at 5 percent net decrease per decade, actually the case in the period between the Soviet census of 1959 and the year 1970. Obviously, an *average* emigration to Israel and the West of 30,000 a year may include years in which *actual* emigration could even reach 100,000, while in other years it might amount only to several thousand (e.g., as in 1970 when there were only 1,000 emigrants). As can be seen from this calculation, an *average* of 30,000 is an especially high estimate for the later period when the available number of potential emigrants is very small, since the total Jewish population after the year 2020 will amount only to several hundred thousand (see Projection One).

The projection of an *average* net decrease of 5 percent may also include fluctuations, including decades of an actual increase of several percent (as a result of natural increase and return to Jewishness), and decades of a much larger decrease of 10 to 15 percent (produced by total assimilation and negative natural increase).

Projection Two is based on assumptions favoring the nearly optimal preservation of Soviet Jewry: an estimate of 3 million Jews in 1970, an *average* emigration ratio of 20,000 a year, and a zero change in population which result from a balance between natural increase and decrease and between assimilation and return to Jewishness.

The calculations in the two projections are intentionally very simple so that they can be understood by anyone without special preparation in statistical methods. Further, their assumptions are rather schematic. Obviously, the purpose is not so much to obtain precise figures as to obtain a general idea of the possible direction of the process.

Results of Calculations

Even under the extreme assumption of a process of self-liquidation, Russian Jewry will still count 1.4 million in the year 2000 and 700,000 in 2020, almost fifty years from now (see Projection One). Under the preservation assumptions, there will be 2.4 million Jews in Russia in the year 2000, 2 million in 2020, and in 2070, almost one hundred years from now, there will still be 1 million (see Projection Two). Thus the end of Soviet Jewry is projected for the fifth decade of the twenty-first century under assumptions of self-liquidation and the third decade of the twenty-second century under assumptions of preservation.

With regard to the projections, several considerations which stem from historical experience should be taken into account. The logic of statistical projections does not necessarily reflect the logic of real-life developments. There are limitations to any phenomenon; after a period of a certain tendency, a counter-tendency usually sets in. Thus, after the first relatively large wave of emigration from Russia, certain limitations in the absorption of Russian *olim* (immigrants) and emigration possibilities from Russia may be seen more clearly. Although 250,000 Jews from Rumania went to Israel there exists even now the problem of Rumanian Jewry—still numbering some 80,000. The "problem of Jewry *X*" is not necessarily related to its numbers. We have a "problem of Syrian Jewry," though they number only several thousands. Polish Jewry remained a major problem for Poland and World Jewry even when it was diminished from a community of 3 million before World War II to several hundred thousand (1945–1956) and, later, to several thousand (1957–1969). Hungarian Jewry still exists, even though it is a small group (about 80,000), and is highly assimilated and isolated from world Jewish life.

Thus, it is clear that whatever the future degree of diminution of Soviet Jewry may actually be, there will be a Jewish community in Russia during any foreseeable future. "The problem of Jews in Russia" may also become much more acute than at present, no matter what their number in the future. Furthermore, should there be a prolonged cessation of Jewish emigration from Russia, or should the rate of emigration become considerably lower and the rate of assimilation and natural decrease less than projected, a sizable Jewish community will exist in Russia "forever."

IV

The Centrality of Israel for Soviet Jewry

In terms of the above discussion, how can Israel and world Jewry measure up to the challenge of the projected problems of Soviet Jewry? How can the concept of "centrality of Israel" be applied to the projected future of Jews in Russia?

The concept of Israel's centrality has been interpreted as one of building Jewish life around Israel in the following ways:

a) *Aliyah*
b) Political work for Israel

c) Financial support
d) Cultural interaction
e) Personal contact with Israel

In present conditions, the centrality of Israel with regard to Soviet Jewry turns around *aliyah* and the spiritual emanation from Israel. The latter relates to a multiplicity of Israeli contacts with Soviet Jewry, either directly (e.g., through Israel radio) or indirectly (e.g., by Israeli messages reaching Jews in Russia through Western Jewish visitors).

With regard to relations of Soviet Jewry with Israel and World Jewry, even the limited Jewish emigration allowed presently by the Soviets creates an entirely new situation. The 100,000 Russian *olim* in Israel and the 20,000 emigrants from the U.S.S.R. in the main centers of the West have already laid a foundation for a new infrastructure relationship.

As a result there is no single person (or family) in Soviet Jewry, who does not have a relative, friend, neighbor, or "fellow-workers" in Israel or in the West. Already, close contacts are maintained by letter, telephone, parcels, money transfers, and messages through Western visitors to Russia. Recent emigrants will at some time in the future be able to revisit their previous homes in Russia and meet with at least a few of their relatives and friends. Until the recent Jewish exodus, many Soviet Jews had relatives and friends abroad, but these connections which were very old had been discontinued for many years. Now, fresh, close connections are being established, as a result of which Soviet Jews are distinguished by new and unique characteristics. Alone among all Soviet ethnic groups, they acquired

a) an implied right to emigrate to Israel and—indirectly—to the West;
b) a network of close relatives and friends in Israel and the West.

Paradoxically, this unique situation of Jews in the U.S.S.R. is becoming a force for Jewish existence in Russia. The possibility of emigration is turning into a factor which may work in some ways for Jewish preservation. On the one hand, emigration means denuding Soviet Jewry of the most conscious, creative and active vanguard of Jewish life in Russia. Even if some possibilities open up for Jewish culture in the future, will there be someone to utilize them?

On the other hand, the Jewish renaissance in Russia, oriented toward *aliyah* and Israel, has become a powerful generator of new Jewish creative thought and of an informal embryonic infrastructure of Jewish organization and self-education in the U.S.S.R. By creating the category of "refuseniks," the Soviet regime itself has established the necessary conditions for this development. The beginnings of such possibilities are already seen in the embryonic Jewish movement for *aliyah*, in Jewish *samizdat*, in seminars on Jewish thought, and *ulpanim* for Hebrew and Jewish studies in Russia.

Thus, certain conclusions may be drawn from the foregoing: 1) it is neither possible nor desirable to evacuate Russian Jewry in a speedy way; a substantial number of Jews will remain in Russia for any foreseeable future; 2) under any of the alternative futures, there are slim chances for a free Jewish life and for a creative Jewish culture to develop in Russia; 3) under some of the alternative futures, Jews in Russia may actually face the danger of mass pogroms and annihilation. Israel and World Jewry must, therefore, do everything possible to use the new Russian-Jewish infrastructure in Israel and in the West as a resource for encouraging *aliyah* and emigration, and for spiritual emanation and contact with Jews in Russia for their continuous self-preservation. The centrality of Israel for Soviet Jewry will be enhanced if Israel becomes a center in which the foremost Russian-Jewish thinkers continue their creative search for self-understanding. Perhaps a major specialized center (institute) should be established in which Russian-Jewish *olim*—with the help of Israeli and Western-Jewish thinkers—will work on a series of studies and projects, the results of which will serve as material for a powerful spiritual emanation from Israel to Russian Jewry.

All other available instruments for such emanation will have to be prepared and utilized to the full: radio, worldwide television programs, publications, and participation in international conferences, exhibitions, competitions. (With regard to such emanation, the impact of normalization of relations with the U.S.S.R. needs to be investigated.)

The above discussion points unmistakably to the enormous challenges posed by the future alternatives for Soviet Jewry. Israel and world Jewry will have to live with this challenge for any foreseeable future.

Israel was the necessary condition for the Jewish renaissance in Russia. The centrality of Israel and the present infrastructure of newly settled Russian-Jewish communities in the West consisting of recent emigrants must now become the instrument for emanation to Jews inside Russia—both for the sake of further emigration and for their preservation as Jews as long as they remain there.

ADDENDUM

Projections About the Future of Soviet Jewry

Projection One: Self-liquidation through emigration and attrition

1. *Assumptions*
   a) The number of Soviet Jews in 1970 was approximately 2.5 million.
   b) An *average* emigration to Israel and the West of 30,000 Jews per year. Obviously, this means that in some years the actual number may reach 60,000 or 70,000, while in other years, it may be less than 10,000.
   c) An *average* attrition ratio of about 5 percent per decade, that is, between one census and another. Again, the actual ratio may fluctuate, reaching 10 to 15 percent in one decade, while in another decade, showing a *positive* net result: a natural increase may occur rather than a decrease, and a return to Jewishness rather than assimilation.

2. *Calculation*
   Decade of 1970–1979
   Actual emigration (to Israel and the West) 1970–1975 (rounded figures):

1970	1,000
1971	13,000
1972	32,000
1973	34,000
1974	20,000
1975	10,000

   Total for 1970–1975 110,000

Number of Jews in 1970	2,500,000
Actual emigration, 1970–1975	110,000
Estimated emigration for 1976–1979	
(4 × 30,000)	120,000
Total emigration, 1970–1979	230,000
Jewish total population in 1980	2,270,000
Attrition ratio of 5 percent	113,000
Jews in January 1980	2,157,000

Decade of 1980 through 1989

Estimated emigration	300,000
	1,857,000
Attrition ratio of 5 percent	92,850
Soviet Jews in January 1990	1,764,150

Decade of 1990 through 1999

Estimated emigration	300,000
	1,464, 150
Attrition ratio of 5 percent	73,200
Soviet Jews in 2000	1,390,950

Decade of 2000 through 2009

Estimated emigration	300,000
	1,090,950
Attrition ratio of 5 percent	54,550
Soviet Jews in 2010	1,036,400

Decade of 2010 through 2019

Estimated emigration	300,000
	736,400
Attrition ratio of 5 percent	36,820
Soviet Jews in 2020	700,000

Decade of 2020 through 2029

Estimated emigration	300,000
	400,000
Attrition ratio of 5 percent	20,000
Soviet Jews in 2030	380,000

Decade of 2030 through 2039

Estimated emigration	300,000
	80,000
Attrition ratio of 5 percent	15,000
Soviet Jews in 2040	65,000

End of the Jewish community in Russia by the year 2043.

Summary
1) Under these conditions, which assume a tendency toward self-liquidation of Russian Jewry, there would still be about 1.4 million Jews in the year 2000 and 700,000 in 2020.
2) Jews in Russia disappear totally sometime in the 2040s, mainly because a high *average* of 30,000 emigrants per year is assumed even for a population which has diminished to several hundred thousand.
3) Out of a total of 2.5 million, some 2.1 million will emigrate during a period of 73 years, and about 400,000 will be lost through assimilation and natural decrease.

Projection Two: Optimal conditions for the preservation of Soviet Jewry

1) *Assumptions*
   a) In January 1970 the actual number of Jews in the U.S.S.R. (including those assimilated and members of mixed marriages who are potential candidates for emigration) was 3 million.
   b) An *average* rate of yearly emigration to Israel and to the West of 20,000.
   c) Loss through assimilation balanced by natural increase, that is, zero change as a result of these factors.

2) *Calculation*

Jews in January 1970	3,000,000
Actual emigration, 1970–1975	110,000
Projected emigration, 1975–1979	80,000
Total emigration, 1970–1979	190,000
Jews in January 1980	2,810,000
Emigration in 1980–1989	200,000
Jews in 1990	2,600,000
Emigration in 1990–1999	200,000
Jews in 2000	2,400,000
Emigration in 2000–2009	200,000
Jews in 2010	2,200,000
Emigration in 2010–2019	200,000
Jews in 2020	2,000,000
Jews in 2030	1,800,000
2040	1,600,000
2050	1,400,000
2060	1,200,000
2070	1,000,000
2080	800,000
2090	600,000
2100	400,000
2110	200,000
2120	0

Summary

1) Under assumptions of optimal preservation, Russian Jewry will be counted as 2.4 million in the year 2000; 2 million in 2020, and in 2075 (i.e., one hundred years from now) about 1 million.
2) The disappearance of Jews in Russia is projected for the year 2120.

Diaspora Influence on Israeli Policy*

Charles S. Liebman

Influence may be defined as the exercise of power through direct or indirect threats of sanctions or promises of rewards by one party over another party, causing the second party to respond in a manner in which it would not otherwise have responded.

Diaspora Jewry exercises very little influence over Israeli public policy, but it is untrue to suggest that it exercises no influence. In religious policy, foreign policy, policy toward the World Zionist Organization (WZO), even economic policy, there are examples of Diaspora influence. Yet, it is fair to say that in adding up the factors that comprise the total of Israeli policies, Diaspora influence is slight.

On the surface, this is a surprising conclusion because the potential political resources which the Diaspora can bring to bear upon Israel are enormous. It is true that there is no individual political community which can be called the Diaspora, nor do Diaspora Jews perceive a distinctive Diaspora interest. It is also true that not all such communities, whether they are considered national communities or subcommunities (organizations or sets of organizations) within the national community, have enormous political resources. But there are at least a few communities which do possess these resources: their sheer size, financial contributions to Israel, and the relative influence which they exercise within their own countries (the latter being the most important factor)[1] provide them with enormous potential influence. First and foremost in this respect is the Jewish community in the United States.

Explanations for the absence of Diaspora influence can be summarized under three major headings.

*A revised version of this paper will appear as a chapter in a forthcoming book by the author: *Pressure Without Sanctions: The Influence of World Jewry in Shaping Israel's Policy,* to be published in 1977.
1. Interview with Binyamin Eliav, October 1970.

1. Limited Efforts at Influence

Israel is not viewed as a suitable object of influence by Diaspora Jews. As far as most of them are concerned, Israel represents Judaism. Since support for Israel is an affirmation of their Judaism, Israel has become extremely important to Diaspora Jews. However, their image of Israel and their relationship to Israel are devoid of political implications. Absent, for the most part, from the Diaspora's image of Israel is the vision of a different Israel (Orthodox Jewry does have such an image, which is one reason it has been the least reticent in pressing for changes). To most of Diaspora Jewry, Israel is functional as it exists today. American Jews, for example, give little or no thought to an alternative social or political system because it is not the particular system which is important to them. If the social system were grossly inequitable, if there were wide-scale discrimination or exploitation or abridgment of freedom, if Israeli foreign policy were suddenly to become anti-American, it would create acute embarrassment to American Jews, who are concerned, within the United States itself, with issues of social equality, minority rights and support of their country in foreign affairs. But short of such radical departures from the status quo, Diaspora Jewry is relatively unconcerned with Israeli policy.

The early Zionists had diverse visions of the state they sought to create. For some, it was to be built upon traditional Jewish law; for others, it was to be a spiritual center of Jewish culture and civilization; for the rest, it was to serve as an example to the world of how a modern state could function in accordance with principles of social justice, equality and liberty. To almost all, the vision included a universal dimension—Israel, by exemplifying a particularist vision, would also become "a light unto the nations."

The creation of the State of Israel and the exigencies of its fight for survival have dimmed the vision Jews once had of Israel. Yet, this dimming has been caused by other factors as well. The truth is that whereas Diaspora Jews now share the classic Zionist dream of a Jewish homeland, they have no Zionist vision. Israel, perhaps, has a particularist Jewish meaning for Diaspora Jewry: it is important to the Diaspora for *its* Jewish survival. But Israel has no universalist meaning for most Diaspora Jews. It is not integrally related to the variety of visions Diaspora Jews may have of a different kind of world, a different kind of society, a different kind of social order. Hence, the

Diaspora is not driven to press Israel into doing anything different from that which it is doing today.

Related to this is a second factor. Diaspora Jewry has very few special interests in Israeli policy formation. The interest investment and the stakes which Diaspora Jews have in Israel are not related to specific policies which Israel pursues. Whenever the stakes have been high enough, Diaspora communities did seek to influence Israeli policy makers. Take, for instance, South African Jewry in the case of Israel's attitude to South Africa; or the Orthodox groups in regard to religious policy; or the American Jewish Committee in regard to Israel's relationship with the World Zionist Organization.

Third, commitments and loyalties of Diaspora Jews to their own countries of residence raise the issue of legitimacy in any intervention in the internal affairs of another country.

Finally, enormous sympathy for Israel among Diaspora Jews makes them reluctant to exercise the sanctions within their power. This is indeed a partial explanation for Reform Jewry's reticence in pressing harder to secure equal rights in Israel. It even serves to explain the behavior of the most outspoken Diaspora leader, a man who, at one time, was the preeminent political leader of Diaspora Jewry—Nahum Goldmann. Goldmann became increasingly critical of Israel in the late 1950s, and, though he had powerful friends among American Jews, he never sought to utilize his position to pressure Israel. In his own words, "I just made speeches."[2] Goldmann believes that even if he had invoked other pressures, he would have failed. But the fact is that he was too deeply committed to Israel to experiment with sanctions.

2. Israel Unwilling to Legitimate Diaspora Influence

Diaspora influence has no legitimacy in the Israeli political mentality. Though this is less true today than it was in the past, the absence of legitimacy was more important in the past when Diaspora pressures were stronger and Israel was weaker and more susceptible to them. The initial premise is also less true of some segments within the Israeli political structure than of others, but, as a general rule, the Israeli self-image and its juxtaposition with that of the Diaspora Jew

2. Interview with Nahum Goldmann, October 1970.

deny a legitimacy to Diaspora influence which even foreign governments possess. Although this alone is not sufficient to explain the lack of Diaspora influence, it does help to explain the fierce resistance to Diaspora pressure that exists on issues where one might have assumed a far greater sensitivity to the expression of Diaspora values.

3. Lack of Political Means to Channel Diaspora Influence

Diaspora Jewry is not organized for the expression of its political interests within Israel. Only one organization reflecting Diaspora interests—the World Zionist Organization– Jewish Agency—is incorporated, however tenuously, into the Israeli political structure, but even this body is dominated by Israelis. Furthermore, organization of the WZO along political, rather than national, lines introduces cleavages within that organization and prevents the formation of Diaspora rather than Israeli interests. Nevertheless, one does occasionally find an expression of Diaspora interests—for example, the debate between Americans and Israelis about the obligation of Zionists to immigrate to Israel or the debate over selective immigration of North Africans in the 1950s.

The reorganization of the WZO along territorial (Zionist Federation) rather than party lines has increased the potential for the expression of particular Diaspora interests. However, reconstitution of the Jewish Agency and its separation from the WZO have also reduced the latter's area of authority within the Israeli political structure, although both groups are still potential sources for channeling Diaspora interests into the Israeli political system. Neither, however, is an intricate part of that system: they operate outside it rather than within. Both confront the Israeli Government *qua* government rather than as participants in the political policy-making process. An exception to this is the standing Committees of the Jewish Agency, which, however, have functioned until now at the level of technical rather than political policy formation.

Other organizations at the international and national level— the World Jewish Congress (WJC), B'nai B'rith, the Conference of Presidents of Major American Jewish Organizations, or the American Jewish Committee—have even less direct access to the Israeli political system.

Nevertheless, one cannot disregard the fact that there are differences of sensitivity to the Diaspora from different parts of the system. Within the government, the Foreign Ministry has regular channels for conveying information concerning the Diaspora. Indeed, one function of Israel's foreign representatives is to represent Israel to local Jewry and to convey information back to Israel concerning developments within the Diaspora. In addition, there is an advisor to the Foreign Minister for Diaspora affairs. The Foreign Minister, in turn, reports to the Prime Minister and to the Government on Diaspora Jewry. In the case of the United States, however, all Prime Ministers, particularly the last two, have their own ties; and while they may ask the opinion of Israel's representative in Washington, they are likely to arrive at conclusions based on independent sources of information.[3] Both the Foreign Office and the Prime Minister's office are sensitive to the Diaspora but the Ministry of Defense tends to see the relationship with Jewry as less central to Israeli affairs.

Among political parties, religious parties are the only ones that actively encourage the intervention of Diaspora Jewry. Consequently, they are also more sensitive to Diaspora demands, although the National Religious Party has rarely found this to be much of a limitation. The Independent Liberals are sensitive to the demands of Conservative and Reform Jewry; in fact their leader, Moshe Kol, initiated a meeting with Reform Jewish leaders. The Liberal Party, formerly the General Zionists, was at one time very closely associated with the Zionist Organization of America (ZOA), although the latter tended to reflect the policies of the former rather than vice versa. In general, opposition parties have often charged the Government with insensitivity to the Diaspora. But one suspects this is convenient political rhetoric rather than the reflection of a basic ideological position. Even Moshe Dayan, when he led the opposition party, Rafi, charged that the Government was not sufficiently open to Diaspora criticism. (Left-wing Mapam could be found, on occasion, defending American General Zionists against Ben-Gurion as in the 1950s.)

Having noted all this, we return to our basic point that with the exception of American Orthodox bodies, Diaspora Jews have no regular channel within the mainstream of the Israeli political system for conveying their interests and demands.

3. Interview with Yoam Biran, Office of the Foreign Minister's Advisor for Diaspora Affairs.

Israel-Diaspora Relations

Within the context of widespread and enthusiastic support for Israel, voices expressing dissatisfaction with Israel-Diaspora relations have increased in number and tone in the last few years. We do not refer to the voices of the New Left—the Jewish antagonists of Israel. They are simply unhappy with Israel and with Jewish support for Israel and are not the voices of rank and file Diaspora Jews. We do refer to certain Diaspora leaders, who, for a variety of reasons (to which we shall return), have expressed their dissatisfaction with the nature of Israel-Diaspora relations.

Their criticism takes several forms, which, I would argue, are related. Some complain that the Diaspora is overcommitted to Israel: it gives too much money to Israel at the expense of its own welfare and educational needs. For example, Guy de Rothschild, President of the *French Fond, Social Juif Unifie*, charged that French Jewry gave too much money to Israel, reducing the local community to a "distress budget."[4] He insisted on, and obtained, a redistribution of income from the United Jewish Appeal campaign in France.[5]

Then it is said that Israel is too prone to interfere in Diaspora affairs, as is voiced, for instance, in the statement that "many American Jews, who opposed the war [in Vietnam and] objected to Israel promoting the view that an American retreat from Vietnam would imply a renunciation by the U.S.A. of the use of power on behalf of a distant ally and might, in turn, lead to an abandonment of Israel."[6]

Further, it is suggested that Diaspora concern for Israel and the centrality of Israel in Diaspora affairs may come at the price of a weakened Diaspora. Dr. Gerson Cohen, present leader of the Jewish Theological Seminary, has stressed the need for an "autonomous and self-sustaining Diaspora tradition on American soil." According to American Jewish Congress president, Rabbi Arthur Hertzberg, himself a member of the Jewish Agency executive, it was unfortunate that fund raising for Israel had come to dominate the activities of the Jewish community to the neglect of Judaism which assures continuation of Jewish life.[7]

---

4. Interview with Jacob Tsur, former Foreign Affairs official and Ambassador.
5. *Jewish Chronicle*, December 15, 1972, p. 4.
6. *Ibid.*, February 3, 1973, p. 4.
7. World Jewish Congress, *Press Survey*, no. 3392, March 23, 1972. Rabbi Judah Nadich, president of the Conservative Rabbinical Assembly of America, expressed

A second set of complaints is concerned with the absence of Diaspora influence in Israel. In late 1972, the Conference of Presidents of Major American Jewish Organizations met in Israel. According to the press, those present said that "they wanted to play a more active role in criticizing defects in Israeli society, but implied that Israeli leaders were not willing to listen to criticism."[8] In an address before the annual meeting of the American Jewish Committee in May 1971, William Frankel, editor of the *Jewish Chronicle*, also stressed the necessity for a forum of Diaspora Jews which would advise Israeli leaders on Israeli policy directly affecting Diaspora Jewry. This opinion was echoed in a paper by the American Jewish leader Philip Klutznick, who suggested that consultations between Diaspora leaders and Israel are essential since "decisions made by the State of Israel affect the condition of all world Jewry."[9] Indeed, he raised the possibility of disagreement within world Jewry.

One might argue that the two sets of criticisms are mutually exclusive—one group demanding greater autonomy for the Diaspora and another insisting on the creation of a forum which, if anything, would increase Israel-Diaspora interdependence. Yet both reflect a dissatisfaction with the present balance of power between Israel and the Diaspora. In fact, Israeli recognition of, and respect for, Diaspora autonomy is more likely to be a by-product of closer ties than simply a result of a unilateral decision by Israel to be less involved in the Diaspora. The latter condition is likely to arise only if each side is completely disinterested in the affairs of the other—a condition which the critics themselves probably agree would be disastrous for world Jewry. They really want what Jacob Neusner has termed "a mature relationship,"[10] a relationship which would possibly emerge from a structure of interdependence different from that presently

concern that the immigration of young American Jews to Israel would remove an important element from the American scene and would endanger the future of Jewish leadership. He said that the time had come to devote more efforts to strengthening American Jewry, *The Jerusalem Post*, November 24, 1972, p. 3.

8. *The Jerusalem Post*, November 24, 1972, p. 3. Among those cited were Rabbi David Polish, president of the Association of American Reform Rabbis, who said that American Jews were concerned about the problems of morality in Israeli society and wanted to express criticism of Israeli internal affairs. Rabbi Louis Bernstein, President of the Association of Orthodox Rabbis in the United States, said that if American Jews are to identify completely with Israel, there must be mutual criticism.

9. Philip Klutznick, "Beyn Yisrael la-Tfuzot," *Gesher*, 18, December 1972, p. 22.

10. Jacob Neusner, "American Jewry and the State of Israel: Toward a Mature Relationship," *Jewish Advocate*, March 23, 1972.

prevailing; it would probably not result from a greater sense of autonomy and independence.

Obstacles to Proposed Solutions

The Diaspora cannot force Israel to a greater sensitivity nor, judging by all that has been indicated here, can it even "pressure" Israel to undertake basic changes against her will. What can and what should Israel do?

She can choose to ignore the problem—perhaps by confining herself to a rebuttal of charges made by her critics. Indeed, the late Louis Pincus spent considerable energy in the months before he died answering critics.[11] Instead of summarizing his major points, I have incorporated them into a rebuttal, sharper than any Israeli has yet offered. Perhaps this will be unjustly harsh and only exacerbate tensions, but I permit myself such a formulation because my sympathy is with the critics' sense of unease rather than with the self-satisfaction that is characteristic of Israelis. Israel's reply to the criticism of some Diaspora leaders could be stated as follows:

1. The sources of criticism may well be considered first. Critics certainly do not reflect the mass of Jewish public opinion in the Diaspora—not even the opinion of Jewry in affluent countries. Much of the criticism comes from rabbis and institutional or organizational leaders whose position of importance in the Diaspora, especially in the American Jewish community, has been displaced by the centrality which Israel has assumed in the eyes of most Jews. Some critics are people who are on the fringes of power and prestige and may be frustrated by new developments in Jewish life which have denied them greater power and prestige—who, to borrow a sociological term, are "downwardly mobile" in terms of prestige.

2. Israel has assumed an important role in Diaspora decision making, partly because Diaspora leadership is itself so second-rate. One need not be inordinately sensitive to heroic qualities to realize and appreciate that, for the most part, Israeli spokesmen in major Western countries are individuals of greater knowledge, understanding,

11. The clearest presentation of his views was his reply to Joachim Prinz at the WJC executive meetings in July 1973. I am grateful to Dr. Nathan Lerner for providing me with both the transcript of his statement and a corrected copy of that speech, which could not have been approved by Pincus more than a week or two before he died.

wisdom, articulation and sensitivity than are most Diaspora
leaders themselves. It is no wonder, then, that so many Diaspora
Jews are prepared to take cues from them rather than from indigenous leadership.

3. Assuming that Israel did agree to consult regularly with a forum
of Diaspora leaders, who would be represented in this forum? The
leaders of Jewish organizations? No one would seriously argue that
such individuals could represent the wishes or needs of Diaspora
Jewries. There are no representative leaders of the Diaspora. If Jews
could vote for their leaders, is there any question that Yitzhak Rabin,
Shimon Peres, Moshe Dayan or Abba Eban would get more votes
than the paper leadership of Diaspora Jewry?

   In addition to the question of representation, there are structural problems, one of which concerns the scope and nature of the
forum's authority. Should these Diaspora leaders deal with all of Israeli policy—for example, tax laws, foreign policy? How are areas of
authority to be delimited? Clearly, some matters ought to be left entirely to Israelis. But how does one determine the scope of the forum's authority and responsibility when it is so easy to demonstrate
that decisions in one policy area affect others? However impossible
it is to resolve the problem of "scope" in a theoretical sense, it may
be possible to do so pragmatically.

   A more serious question relates to the "nature" of the forum's
authority. Is the forum to be a purely consultative and advisory
body, or is it to be a decision-making body? If only consultative—
then Israel does not need it. She continually consults with Diaspora
leaders, and there are a number of forums (the reconstituted Jewish
Agency, the World Jewish Congress, the World Conference of Jewish
Organizations, or the World Zionist Organization) where Diaspora
and Israeli leaders meet and exchange opinions. But if the forum's
decisions are to be binding upon Israeli leaders, then one may well
question the propriety of nonresidents having such power in the decisions of a foreign country. More realistically, would Diaspora leaders want such authority, or, given the law of their own countries,
could they even legally exercise such authority?

   Finally, there is no one Diaspora interest. Any forum of Diaspora leaders is far more likely to pit one Diaspora interest against
another.

4. It is not necessarily true that Diaspora leaders are more aware of,

or sympathetic to, Diaspora Jewry's needs than are Israeli leaders themselves. No Jew is a greater "lover of the Jewish people" because he chooses to remain in the Diaspora. Despite all the criticism one may justly invoke against Israelis for placing their Israeli identity ahead of their Jewish identity, no one familiar with Israelis and American and Western European Jews could seriously argue that the American and European Jews are more concerned with the Jewish People than are the Israelis. This is true of rank and file Jews as well as of their leaders. A significant proportion of Diaspora Jewry would nôt be represented in such a forum—for example, the Jews of the Soviet Union—whereas other groups, such as the wealthy and the intellectuals, would in all probability be overrepresented (the former because they are the "joiners," the latter because of the deference of Diaspora Jewry to intellectuals). It is questionable, therefore, if any forum of Diaspora leaders can be trusted to represent the mass of unrepresented Jews more effectively than Israeli leaders.

5. The flow of money to Israel "at the expense of Diaspora institutions" reflects the wishes of the contributors themselves. In fact, the relative distribution of funds between Israel and the Diaspora is undoubtedly an autonomous Diaspora decision. The greatest reservation of the fund raisers represented in the reconstituted Jewish Agency concerns the share of their money which goes to the World Zionist Organization for expenditure in the Diaspora: that money is spent on education and cultural programs about which some of the critics express concern.

6. Israel and support for Israel are central expressions of Jewish identity today. Israel is the center of Jewish life because Diaspora Jews find no other form of expression which is quite so meaningful to them. It is a mistake to assume that if Diaspora Jews worked less or were less interested in Israel, they would work harder for, or be more concerned with, another Jewish institution or project.

7. A real crisis of survival is confronting Diaspora Jewry in the West, but voices from within the Jewish Establishment rather than from Israel confer a legitimacy on life patterns inimical to survival. It is not Israeli leaders who tell Diaspora Jewry that attending synagogue services or maintaining the ritual tradition is no more important than philanthropy—this was stated by an American communal and fund-raising leader in 1965 in speaking of the necessity to contribute

to local Jewish hospitals as well as to Israel. The statement was reported in the Anglo-Jewish press, but no outraged voices were raised from the Jewish Establishment against this distortion of Jewish values. It is not the Israeli establishment which condones intermarriage or argues that Judaism must accommodate itself to young couples who insist on intermarrying (this is said by a portion of the American Reform rabbinate). Israelis do not argue that day school education is undemocratic, or that it is wrong to seek government support for Jewish schools since that would violate principles of church-state separation, issues which apparently are more important than insuring adequate Jewish education to those who want it. It was mainly the American Jewish Establishment which raised these arguments, at least, until quite recently.

Israeli representatives abroad are urged to attend synagogue services, to send their children to Jewish day schools (they even get a special allowance for this purpose) and to respect Jewish tradition. It may be argued that not every Israeli representative complies with these suggestions. There are, perhaps, "ugly Israelis." (Thus, in one instance, an Israeli consul sent his children to a private Protestant school in a city which has a Jewish day school.) However, the Foreign Ministry relies on Israeli representatives abroad to observe the basic amenities of Jewish tradition. It was the Israeli Prime Minister who argued in 1970 that a particular law had to be amended (in the "Who is a Jew?" controversy), because it might otherwise encourage intermarriage in the Diaspora. Israeli leaders, highly sensitive to the dangers of assimilation, have devoted major efforts in recent years to the support of Jewish education in the Diaspora.

Thus, on the one hand, the American Jewish Establishment includes elements whose activity encourages assimilation, while Israel, on the other hand, is sensitive to, and anxious about, Diaspora survival. Quite apart from the fact, therefore, that activity on behalf of Israel is in itself a barrier against assimilation, the Jewish Establishment in the United States, for example, is no more concerned about (or is a better representative of) survivalist forces in Jewish life than is Israel.

8. Israeli representatives, one must admit, may not always adopt the proper tone in speaking to the Diaspora; they may sometimes appear abrasive and inconsiderate. Faced with enormous threats, its leaders cannot afford to be sanguine about its present military superiority. If

Israelis, therefore, sometimes put parochial above universal interests, if they tended to favor one political leader over another, or to
worry about the consequences of American Jewish positions of one
cast or another, they are hardly to be blamed. Why should Israelis refrain from pointing out their self-interests to Diaspora Jewry any
more than Diaspora Jewry should refrain from pointing out its self-
interests to Israel? In the last analysis, even Israel's harshest critics
do not suggest that Israeli representatives have done more than advise American Jewry—and in a severely restrained manner at that—
on various internal matters. (One suspects that what really disturbed
the critics was not that Israel tried to pressure American Jewry—
indeed, it did not do so—but that Israel did not share the peculiar
politically liberal proclivities of the majority of the American Jewish
Establishment.)

A Personal Conclusion

The problem of Israel-Diaspora relations today must be recognized for what it is—the problem of a very small percentage of Jews,
some living in Israel, others in the Diaspora, but all, for various reasons, unhappy with the present state of Israel-Diaspora relations.

I happen to be a part of that small group, but this must not
blind me to the unrepresentative character of my sentiments. I could
argue persuasively that the present state of Israel-Diaspora relations
is in the nature of a temporary "honeymoon" and that unless certain
actions are taken, relations in the long run will lead to serious estrangement. I am less concerned, however, about the future prospects of Israel-Diaspora relations than I am about the current state of
these relations. It is the latter concern which leads me to suggest a
new pattern of Diaspora involvement in Israel.

The problem of Israel-Diaspora relations is not one of political
representation. It is, rather, the far more difficult problem of political
values and political responsibility. Israel can afford to ignore its
Diaspora critics as unrepresentative, their criticism as unfounded
and their proposals as inept and impractical. But it cannot afford to
ignore the problematic aspects of Israel-Diaspora relations if it is to
remain true to the political values upon which the State was established. The problem, as I see it, is that Israel is becoming untrue to
itself. Diaspora Jewry has a corrective role to play, as, I believe, some
Diaspora Jews have sensed.

The founders of Israel never viewed the State as an end in itself. It was to be an instrument, primarily, for "ingathering the exiles"; in other words, it was to be an instrument to serve the Jewish People.[12] Ben-Gurion cotinually stressed a second function of Israel—to be a "light unto the nations." Whether the fulfillment of this universalist mission is or is not also the realization of a particularly Jewish value is relatively unimportant (although my own inclination is to believe, as did Ben-Gurion, that it is). The value, after all, is biblical.

These, then, are the core values and criteria by which Israeli policy ought to be guided and judged, though, obviously, they are not sufficient as policy guidelines. First, situations may arise where the application of one value must come at the expense of the other. (Theoretically, the decision on whether or not to challenge South Africa for its *apartheid* policy could have been such an example. In reality, it was not the principles of service to Jews versus ethical conduct which led to indecision but rather service to Jews versus Israel's self-interest.) Second, these values cannot by themselves necessarily guide the policy makers toward the decisions to reach in every given situation; they are not specific enough. Reasonable men will argue that the acceptance of German reparations was or was not a service to the Jewish People. Finally, other values, even if they are of secondary importance, must also be considered. Economic prosperity is an independent value which may be less important than serving the Jewish People or behaving in a moral way, but it is still a legitimate value. Yet what should one do when just a little self-interest, just a little violation in the spirit of a trade agreement, might bring a great deal of economic prosperity? Is Israel obligated to make economic sacrifices for the sake of marginal benefits that may accrue to Diaspora Jews? Was Israel, for example, obligated to build its ships in French shipyards because French Jewry asked it to do so, if it could build ships elsewhere more economically?

Israel's core political values, however inadequate for deciding

12. In leaping from Ben-Gurion's stress on "ingathering the exiles" to "serving the Jewish People," there is at least a superficial distortion of Ben-Gurion's views, though not, I believe, a basic untruth. Ben-Gurion and his associates, who stressed the value of "ingathering the exiles," were also defining "service to the Jewish People." In view of their own conception of Zionism and Galut, there was simply no other possibility for real service.

what precisely must be done, do provide a criteria for judging, in a very general way, the legitimacy of what was done. The judgmental role is not one which the Diaspora alone may exercise. Indeed, Israelis have a greater right to this role because it is they who bear the burden of fulfilling basic values. But it is also a role which they are less equipped to fulfill precisely because the burden is upon them. It is only natural that two processes should take place among Israelis. First, confronted with their immediate needs for survival plus myriad other values (for example, personal welfare, economic prosperity), Israelis are likely to forget the higher values to which their State is ostensibly dedicated. Second, they are likely to turn the State into an end in itself—to sanctify, as it were, the means. Americans, including American Jews, express a loyalty and love for their country, not because of America's mission or function, but because it is their country. Frenchmen, Englishmen and Russians do the same. Why should Israelis be different? One expects that Israelis, Arabs as well as Jews, will love their country not because it is a Jewish State, not because it is a noble State, but because it is their State. One expects Israeli national feeling to be no different in essence from American, British, French or Russian national feeling. One may consider this more or less unfortunate, depending upon one's universalistic cosmopolitan propensities, but it would be unrealistic not to expect it.

It is, therefore, important for the Diaspora to exercise a judgmental task, however restrained and circumspect. This is a necessary corrective to natural tendencies inherent in Israel to ignore, pay only lip service to, or rationalize away the basic values upon which the State of Israel was established.

A judgmental or critical role is the most appropriate political role for Diaspora Jewry, which cannot hope to become involved in the decision-making process. Decisions must be made by those who can be held responsible to a free electorate. Decisions must be made only by those who can assume the consequences for these decisions. There is no reason why Israel should not consult this or that Diaspora community, this or that individual, these or those leadership groups, and indeed it does so even now; but the decisions must be made by Israelis within the Israeli political system. Diaspora Jewry is not an integral part of that system; it cannot expect to be part of that system, nor should it be. But Diaspora Jewry's wishes must be part of the decision-making premises upon which the policy makers arrive at their options.

To some extent, this is already true, since Israel does take account of the impact of its decisions upon the Diaspora. However, the Diaspora could surely play a more active role. Israelis ought to assume that they must be answerable to Diaspora Jewry in a far more critical sense than is true today. Israel must sense that Diaspora Jewry is primarily concerned that Israeli policies be in accord with the two major values upon which the State was created and which serve as the basis for Diaspora Jewry's attachment to it. Diaspora Jewry has a right to insist that its involvement in Israeli life (which Israel itself has invited) should focus upon the expression of these two primary values. For example, Diaspora Jewry contributes funds to higher education in Israel. It should, therefore, have a right to ask how that higher education teaches values of service to the Jewish People or teaches the development of an ethically exemplary state. This very insistence on accountability to the Diaspora for fulfillment of these political values would serve to reinforce them in the Israeli consciousness. But there is also no reason why Diaspora organizations should not initiate activities within Israel that reflect their own concern with Judaism, Jews, and the ethical imperatives in, for example, Jewish-Arab relations.

The problem, of course, is that not only has Israel become less faithful to the basic political values upon which it was founded, but the Diaspora does not stress these values in its image of Israel. Israel has become functional for Jewish survival in purely symbolic terms. Consequently, there is a tendency to reify the symbols and forget the functional intention of Israel's establishment. Furthermore, through its reward system, Israel, consciously or unconsciously, promotes a leadership group which tends to accept Israel as it is rather than Israel as it should be. An article in the Israeli daily *Haaretz* made this point in the sharpest of terms:

> For Israel, interested primarily in mobilizing contributions and political pressure, it is more comfortable to make arrangements with the Montors, Schwartzes and Friedmans (past professional leaders of the campaigns to mobilize funds for Israel in the United States) than with the Silvers, Klutznicks or Soloveitchiks (American Jewish leaders with significant constituencies, who have been critical of Israel despite their basic sympathy towards the State). For twenty years, the

blessings of Ben-Gurion, Eshkol or Sapir became the certificate of legitimacy to community leadership.[13]

One hopes that this may change. A new foundation for Israel-Diaspora relations based upon criticism and self-criticism in the context of the mutually accepted values of Israeli society may cause greater discomfort, but in the last analysis will provide greater prospects for a long-term relationship. Not only will this help maintain Israel's Jewish identity, but it should also bring the more sensitive spirits in Diaspora Jewry to Israel to help insure that the State will continue to express those values to which they are committed and to participate in the process of their expression. Finally, it will eliminate the dangerous dichotomy of universalism-particularism which, we have suggested, is destructive of Jewish identity. The Diaspora Jew's responsibility to Israel would now, in fact, also become his responsibility to insure that Israel acts as a "light unto the nations." The Diaspora Jew would no longer have to balance his particularist Jewish obligations to Israel with the universalist-ethical obligations to which he is also committed.

Even though most Jews in the Diaspora and in Israel do not feel this way about Israel or about Israel-Diaspora relations, it does not mean that those who share a different perspective and vision, in both Israel and the Diaspora, should not act.

13. *Haaretz*, January 18, 1973, p. 12.

The Present-Day Relationship of State and Diaspora

Nathan Rotenstreich

In considering present relations between the State of Israel and the Diaspora, I am concerned mainly with the western Diaspora, more specifically the United States, both because my contacts with the latter have been more frequent and because of the obvious increase in importance of that segment of Diaspora Jewry.

We are still in the dark—and it is not for me to offer an opinion—about a new phenomenon: the importance which Russian Jewry attaches to the State, the existence of which has become a factor in their revival. This is no doubt a new aspect which is not without its impact on relations between the State and the Diaspora. Those of us who started out from the classic Zionist doctrine presumed, indeed believed, that any relationship between the Diaspora and the Land of Israel would first and foremost be one of succession; that is, the latter would supersede the former. In other words, the building up of the Land and its social and political consolidation would take the place of the Diaspora. Those theories were never properly formulated—nor could they be formulated. For what is meant by "succession"—is it a total succession or not? The historical process itself, the time of transition from the Diaspora to the Land, was regarded as a process of reassessment, of new values replacing old ones.

The decisive element, when considering the facts, and hence the problems connected with those facts, is that in reality one thing does not take the place of the other; there is coexistence between the western Diaspora and the State. That is the decisive reality of our generation. We must, therefore, take a fresh look at the facts from this aspect and see our doctrine through the prism of the completely new reality.

Emancipation and Autoemancipation

Classic Zionist doctrine assumed Jewish autoemancipation would take the place of the reality of Jewish existence in the European Diaspora. The many-faceted composition of that existence was based upon area of residence, mass persecution, individual persecution, persecution by various governmental authorities and the first signs of emancipation. Jewish autoemancipation was to be a new factor in the existence of the Jews which would replace that mixture.

In this respect it may be said, with regard to the western Diaspora, and above all to the American Diaspora, that there is coexistence between emancipated and autoemancipated Jewry. This is a new situation. It is a configuration which the classic conception of Zionism had not foreseen and for which it was not prepared.

Both autoemancipation and emancipation have gone through several crises. I do not deem it necessary to examine in detail the crisis which we ourselves are experiencing, the crisis of autoemancipation, for precisely during these times more than in any previous period has it become clear to us how high is the price we have to pay for the reentry of the Jews into world history. We have learned that the position of Jews who are playing a role in world history is neither idyllic nor ideal. They are participating in a process which entails all kinds of tensions, including a build-up of the tensions of international relations; and this history of which we are a part is characterized by international tensions which implicate us too. Further, our participation in world history has yet another aspect in that Zionism and its achievements serve, in a sense, as models for Arab nationalism. One of the great ironies of this historical involvement is the way in which the Arabs imitate Zionism in both its motivations and even its visible symbols.

Such is the price of participation in terms of world history. In a paradoxical, ironic sense we also have an influence upon the world around us. It can, therefore, be said that the crisis which we are experiencing is due to the fact that Zionism, which was born when there was some expectation of liberal world relations, now finds itself, at the time of its realization, in an entirely different world—a world based upon competition, tensions, a motley of nationalisms competing with each other, as well as a certain restructuring of the great powers.

Emancipation and the Messianic Ideal

Yet there is also a crisis in emancipated Jewry, especially American Jewry. This crisis is a consequence of the contradiction, whether open or veiled, between the objective progress achieved by that Jewry, enjoying the rights and opportunities bestowed on it by an unusual combination of liberal, democratic governments with rising economic power and influence and the dynamism of a technological society which is constantly being passed on to the people. Emancipated Jewry is becoming aware of the achievements of its emancipation at the same time that it is becoming awakened to the conviction that it is living in a messianic society in which a vision of justice, peace and interhuman relations and all that is part of the human ideal is formulated but not realized. On the contrary, by reasons of its sensitivity and its role in the academic community, American Jewry, even more than other elements of the population, is conscious of the fact that there is not necessarily any essential connection between the achievement of emancipation and messianism. History is hard and it presses even harder. The United States Government made mistakes in the Vietnam War; it is confused by the phenomena accompanying that war; it has made mistakes in its internal affairs. All this does not affect the achievements of emancipation, but it completely removes the halo from its position, the halo of a quite new historic era.

Awareness of Exile

It seems to me that we have passed beyond the "thirties," when American Jewry was engaged in a dispute within itself and with the classic Zionist doctrine as to its Diaspora condition; we still remember the attempts, which today are termed semantic, at differentiating between "exile" and "dispersion."

It may be said that, in recent years, American Jewry's awareness of the fact that it is living in exile has grown. There is a connection with the problem of ethnic minorities or rather with the ascendancy of ethnic minorities, which paradoxically enough has become more pronounced, especially in recent years. Jews who, because of the color of their skin and their social achievements, are counted with the majority have become more sharply aware of their exile. This realization is evidence of a new phenomenon in our time, the rising of a distinction between emancipation and awareness of exile. Awareness of living in exile is not necessarily connected, as was usually the case in the world of East European Jewry, with persecution and with residential or professional restrictions in certain areas.

Yet, in spite of this, or perhaps because of this, the wheel has not turned to a new quality of relations between western Jewry and the State of Israel or to the Zionist significance of the State. In other words, we are coexisting despite an ascendancy in the consciousness of exile and despite the fact that the reality of emancipation has lost its messianic meaning. This coexistence connects with several factors which I shall discuss in detail later.

Relationship Between Israel and the Diaspora

For the first time it has become clear that coexistence between the State of Israel as the fulfillment of Zionism and emancipated Jewry in exile does not mean simply that the one has not replaced the other. It also means that the extent of the State of Israel's dependence upon Diaspora Jewry has been increasing in recent years far beyond the dependence which existed when the State was created and far beyond the influence which western Jewry had on the establishment of the State.

The State of Israel has become dependent upon Diaspora Jewry for its daily physical, economic and political existence. The present troubled times have allowed for no essential clarification. The State has not clearly grasped its constant, it may even be said elementary, need of Diaspora Jewry; it may, however, have deepened its awareness of the existence of Diaspora Jewry and a conviction that without it the State of Israel cannot exist. We now encounter in literature, certainly in conversations, and even more so in deeds, a new argument justifying the Diaspora. This argument is not based upon the place of the Diaspora itself, its position, its power, its achievements, the opportunities it affords, the symbiosis between Jews and non-Jews and all that it implies, but is based on an assertion that the existence of the Diaspora is necessary for Israel, that it is needed as a support for Israel.

There is a second side to the argument: Israel needs the Diaspora because a strong Jewish Diaspora community is good for Israel —not as a Jewish reality, not as a source of Jewish creativity, but as a support. This means that we have reached a point where on both sides the need for support has become a more important basis for the relationship between Israel and the Diaspora than any other consideration put forward to clarify the relationship. Thus, it seems to me, we find ourselves in a situation where the coexistence of Israel and the Diaspora is based first and foremost on support.

This state of affairs is sometimes expressed in oversimplified terms. For instance, it is argued that the State of Israel takes so much from the financial resources of countries of the Diaspora that virtually no funds are left for the Diaspora's own needs. I am of the opinion that, but for the State of Israel, Diaspora Jewry would hardly have even those funds now left at its disposal. The Diaspora's powers of self-persuasion, for instance, with regard to an education system of its own, are rather limited. A serious system of Jewish education would require that everyone be personally involved, that everyone would wish to build a way of life, thus implying a new interaction between the Jewish community and the individual Jew—something that Diaspora Jewry did not achieve. Here, too, the situation has changed. The classic doctrine of Jewish Enlightenment used to counsel us: Be a Jew in your home and a human being outside it. Today, this has been reversed: Be a Jew in the outside world and a human being at home. A "Jew in the outside world" means a type for which the non-Jewish world makes allowances as a particular variant of Western culture or as a variant of Judeo-Christian civilization. This position suits the Jews very well. What little they can do is done not by virtue of their own initiative, but by virtue of their being dependent on the State of Israel. If they wished to invest the power they have in the organizational, cultural and economic fields, they would without doubt find opportunities to do so without conflicts of interest. Hence, something has happened to the quality of the relationship. The more the State of Israel becomes an object of support, the more it serves as an excuse for the Diaspora's failure to understand and support itself. I would even formulate it as their own lack of autoemancipation.

The basic approach has been altered. The Yom Kippur War enabled western Jews to regain their spiritual balance to a certain extent. They found two legitimate possibilities—would that they had made greater use of them! They could now differentiate between the State of Israel and its institutions, even between the Israel Defence Forces and the State. That is, they were given an opportunity to see the State of Israel as no longer monolithic, and they did not have to

accept all the obligations imposed on them, whether justly or unjustly, by virtue of their positive attitude to the State and its status. Indeed, they were given a legitimate chance to criticize. They were
also given an opportunity to regain a certain sense of proportion regarding the image of the Israeli "superman" who could work mira-
cles and who, in a moment, could find his orientation in the real
world. At the first seminar on "World Jewry and the State of Israel:
The Yom Kippur War," which was held in Jerusalem, December
1973, under the auspices of the President of Israel, those elements
were discernible. Those ideas have been given expression more in
discussion than in print, apparently because there is a certain fear of
the written word. Such a possibility I put forward as symptomatic of
the complexity of our present situation.

A New Interpretation of Centrality

The meaning of centrality has undergone a metamorphosis. In
a symposium published in *Judaism* on the American Jew and his image of himself, we found a new interpretation of centrality which the
majority of the participants shared or admitted. According to that
interpretation the future of Jewish life in America is closely linked to
the "plight of the State of Israel"—notice, not with the State of Israel,
but with its plight. In this I found confirmation of something I had
heard a few years earlier in the United States, when the expression
"Galutization of the State of Israel" was used. This meant that we in
Israel are close to the Jews of the United States because we are close
to an experience with which they are familiar—the experience of
predicaments and difficulties. Perhaps it was an emotional reaction to
the problem of the moment, but it may be that this was an interpretation arrived at through insight and through the impression created by
our problematic situation.

It is understandable that people want or are able to grasp an
idea only by translating it into a context with which they are already
familiar—and, unfortunately, the context they know is the archetype
of the Jew in distress; or it may be that the context they understand is
the problematics of the hour. It seems to me, therefore, that if we
wish to put matters into their proper perspective, we must turn from
the urgent problems of the present to the far larger coordinates of
history or ideology.

Primacy of Israel

I begin with a thought about a term which has gained curren-
cy among us and has even received official sanction: the centrality of
Israel. I may be susceptible to the influence of metaphors; at the same
time, I am convinced that this particular metaphor has become trite.
The metaphor of the center and its circumference has a linear dimension. It originated, as far as is known, from Ahad Ha-Am's conception, and on this point Professor Ephraim Urbach has said something
trenchant: The place of the State of Israel does not depend on the
quality of its creation but on its status. The concept of center and circumference, with all the meanings it has acquired, was connected
with the quality of the creation rather than the status of Israel. We are
fully aware that the creation, the quality of that creation, and the
problematics of Jewish creation in our generation are extremely
complicated. At any rate, the creation of the State of Israel does not
and cannot correspond to the idyllic model envisaged by Ahad Ha-
Am, that the center to be established in Israel would be a continuation of the literary creativity previously centered in Odessa and Warsaw. This is not possible. Things do not develop in that fashion—
they are accompanied by catastrophes, difficulties and stresses, by
demographic and international problems; the ideal Jew does not
emerge; no ideal type materializes. We must, therefore, see matters
in a completely different light.

I suggest that the concept of Israel's centrality in relation to
the Diaspora be replaced by Israel's preferential status, its *primacy*,
over the Diaspora. The idea of primacy seems preferable to that of
centrality; the former metaphor indicates that if there are conflicts
of interest between the Diaspora and the State of Israel, the interests
of the State would be preferred. However, I do not wish to deal
specifically with conflict situations, even though we have to take
them into consideration as possibilities of historical processes. I
would rather consider the primacy of the State of Israel from the
viewpoint of its status.

The State of Israel, as such, is, first of all, the culmination of
purposeful efforts by Jews; therein lies its basic difference from Jewish existence in the Diaspora. It is the outcome of conscious decisions taken by Jews. It is not a reality created by force of circumstances, but a reality which we wanted to create and establish from
the outset. Someone skeptically disposed toward the State of Israel

phrased it thus: "It was literally built into existence." I assert: Therein lies its *greatness*. The asserted element of artificial construction
should, I suggest, be seen as the essential element. Essential is surely
the opposite of artificial.

Jewish Historic Collectivity

A second point—closely linked to the first—is that the State of
Israel is the realization of the collective existence *ab initio* of the
Jewish People. It was originally established in order that the Jewish
People should have a defined and cohesive collective existence: not
a *post factum* collective existence in which Jews come together as
individuals, and the enlightened world allows them to form social
units and organizations which the world finds congenial, but a concentrated Jewish world which is defined by its collective character.
Thus, between the collective which is established from the outset
and the collective planned *post factum*, significance is derived from
the national idea, in accordance with the rhythm of Jewish history. A
collective, established as such from the very beginning, stands on a
higher level than collectives which come into being incidentally.

Many of the difficulties that we encounter are essentially
caused by the fact that the world has accepted the reality of Jews establishing collectives *post factum,* but it has not yet accepted the position that the Jews existed as a collective from the very beginning.
That Arabs are the medium of this opposition to planned collective
existence of the Jews is an accident of history.

We can convey this to the Diaspora without any embel-
lishment. Reverting to the matter of support which I have dealt with
earlier, we may say that there is a difference between helping brothers in distress and obeying the commandment to redeem captives,
and supporting the effort for the historical collective home of the
Jewish People. The second alternative possibly calls for a longer and
more sustained effort, but we know that some aspirations which appear to be long-range are actually short-range. That is the second
point in this concept of the primacy of the State of Israel.

The third aspect of preferential status is, without doubt, problematic, as indeed were the others, but this one is decidedly so. The
problem arises from the fact that according to the logic of the State
of Israel there is no structural difference between Jewish experience

and general human experience. The two must be complementary; they should find their total fulfillment synthetically, eclectically or coexistentially, but all in terms of a single existence. There is no way of separating what is human from what is Jewish or of excluding the human element from Judaism. There are indeed Jews who did not want and still do not want it to be so, and in that lies the root of their antagonism to the State of Israel. If, however, we start from the premise of the planned collective existence of the Jews and the place of such a collective within world history, we cannot escape from the human element in Judaism. The majority of the Jewish People in the countries of the West desire, at least symbolically, a Jewish existence—and a human existence. The State of Israel constitutes an attempt to escape from symbolism to reality, with all the problems that entails, even if it results in profanation in the transition from symbolic to real.

These three aspects are, in my understanding, fundamentally decisive even in the present circumstances. They do not militate against the coexistence of emancipation and autoemancipation. We are brought here to a new principle which contains old elements; that is, it contains a basis of the special quality of autoemancipation, but it also contains something new in that it emphasizes the image of Judaism and the image of the Jewish People as they are now. Thus, the metaphor of primacy or priority and preferability points rather more in the direction of dynamism than the metaphor of centrality, though it possibly brings into prominence complicated problems, indeed the real problems we face in this context.

If we want to interpret the situation in which we find ourselves here and now, we must consider both the changes which have taken place in that situation and the attempt to reinterpret Zionist ideology in terms of the new reality—a rethinking which may be of significance for the State of Israel as well as for Diaspora Jewry. It is imperative to do so in both directions, although there should be separate formulations—separate, not different—in each case, so that the stress is placed where the realities of the day demand it.

Toward an Israel-Diaspora Policy

by Eli Ginzberg

No approach to the theme "Israel and the Diaspora" can be severed from ideological and political considerations. Although a presumption of objective analysis is naive, there are better and worse ways of probing these complex issues. The naive individual, unable to draw upon the history and experience of a people who have lived with this tension for over 2000 years, is as limited as the Talmud student whose world is bounded by his parental home and the *yeshivah* where he spends most of his waking hours.

Changing Parameters

To set Israeli-Diaspora relations in perspective, it is necessary to consider the erosion of any assumptions of the immediate post-Balfour era. The rebuilding of the Homeland failed to elicit the whole-hearted support of any Jewry—East European, West European or American. Only the leaders of the Yishuv, and not all of them, saw much prospect of a true Homeland, much less a state, in their lifetime. One of the leading ideologists of the early post-World War I era was A. D. Gordon whose vision was limited to a Palestine dotted by a smaller or larger number of agricultural cooperatives. This was a vision of a Palestine that at best could absorb a few hundred thousand additional Jews.

At the end of World War II the equation had been radically altered. Most of Eastern European Jewry had been exterminated. They would never have a second chance to emigrate. But American Jewry, now highly prosperous and more self-assured, was no longer merely a bystander. Its dollars, if not its youth, would be available to help transform the Palestine community into a secure and viable state. By the early 1950s two of the preconditions were being realized—sovereignty and rapid growth of population. Security and economic development were still problematic. By the time the State of Israel had celebrated its twenty-fifth anniversary, in 1973, there was increasing ground for optimism that these two remaining conditions could be achieved, if not immediately, then in the forseeable future. Jerusalem was well on the way to reestablishing itself as the center of world Jewry for the first time since the Pharisaic era.

For the sake of didactic clarification, it may be useful to set out the parallel transformations that occurred during the same time-frame in the largest center of Diaspora Jewry in history, the United States. It was not until 1929 that the dominant leaders of American Jews (Louis Marshall and Felix Warburg) first succeeded in narrowing the gap between Zionists and non-Zionists. They provided the framework for the later, much broadened base of support. However, at the outset of World War II there was only a small cadre of politically active Zionists and a larger body of sympathizers. The involvement of American Jews with the settlement of Palestine in terms of money, not to stress manpower, was quite modest.

The refugee problem, the creation of the State of Israel, the new affluence of American Jews, and the repeated threats to Israel's survival laid the basis for much broadened and deepened support for Israel in the post-World War II era.

The ways in which American Jews relate to Israel reflect in the first instance how they relate to their Jewish identity. An analytic framework to probe these relations must allow for the entire gamut of possible responses among American Jews, from the ultra-orthodox who oppose the existence of the State on religious grounds to those who are in the process of disassociating themselves from their Jewish heritage and therefore ignore Israel.

An Analytic Framework

In order to capture the multiplicity of responses of American Jews to Israel it may be helpful to establish the following typology of Jewish identification:

a) The *deeply committed*, especially the observant;

b) The *strongly identified*, whose orientation is firmly rooted in background and personal values;

c) The *aligned*, who, through active membership in the synagogue and/or any other Jewish organizations, contribute actively to the maintenance of the Jewish community;

d) The *sentimental,* who respond to appeals for assistance but take little or no initiative in promoting communal activities;

e) The *indifferent,* passive Jews who take no positive steps to strengthen their identification, or that of their children, with Judaism;

f) The *rejecters,* who pursue a policy of disassociation with the aim of eventually severing their links with their Jewish origins.

In the case of the deeply committed, the strongly identified and the aligned, one can postulate the following in regard to Jewish content:

a) Among those who are deeply committed, the Jewish component in their lives takes precedence over all other values. Accordingly, they are deeply and continuously concerned about the well-being of Israel. Much the same is true for the strongly identified, many of whom find their identification essentially linked with all developments in Israel.

b) The aligned, by virtue of their organizational affiliations, are under continued pressure to respond to the problems of Israel, as well as to seek gratification from the State's progress.

c) The greatest variability exists among the sentimental, in whose case sentimentality may be translated into positive activity by the force of external events. However, their Jewish identity, if unactivated, erodes from lack of cultivation. The miracle of Israel has helped to strengthen their varied sentimental ties.

d) To the unconcerned and the rejecters, the future of the Jews and welfare of the State of Israel is largely a matter of indifference.

The Influence of Identity

Implicit in the foregoing analytic framework is the assumption that the manner in which Jews in the Diaspora relate to Israel depends in the first instance on how they view—and act on—their Jewish identity. This, naturally, does not preclude an important role for Israel in determining the nature of Jewish identity. In a world characterized by the growth of secularism, it does not strain the argument to emphasize that the trials and victories of the struggling State of Israel have provided substitute content for the majority of American Jews in whose own lives tradition and ceremonies play a diminishing role.

The deeply committed (except for ultra-orthodox anti-Statists) will be inclined to look to Eretz Israel for leadership in all matters Jewish, except for those areas where they have a specific interest in influencing the course of developments—as, for instance, Jewish law, Jewish scholarship and Jewish education. They will consider it incumbent upon themselves to contemplate *aliyah* and to make substantial personal sacrifices on behalf of Israel.

The strongly identified are likely to be more uncritical in their approach to Israel, especially if the source of their identification is primarily nationalistic. They will look to Israel to assume leadership in matters affecting Jews everywhere, with the possible exception of the United States. Many know too little about Jewish history, tradition and culture to develop strong independent positions. However, their continuing and determined support for Israel in financial and other spheres can be depended upon for the near and intermediate term. Even if this is not the appropriate place for extended inquiry, the question should be raised as to how long a significant number of American Jews will be able to sustain a policy of strong identification with Israel unless they live a life with Jewish content that is rooted in more than a renascent nationalism.

The place of Israel in the value structure of the aligned varies from those whose center of identification is specifically predicated on Israel to the considerable numbers of synagogue members who have never been exposed to a strong Zionist orientation. The continuing support of Israel by the aligned may be anticipated for the near term but is more problematic as the time horizon lengthens.

Only a major personal or community crisis is likely to elicit from the indifferent or the rejecters active support for any Jewish cause, including Israel. It is worth noting in this regard the marked change in the consequences of intermarriage today as compared to earlier generations. The figures affirm that more and more young American Jews are marrying non-Jews, only a minority of whom undergo formal conversion. On the other hand, it appears that many Jews with non-Jewish spouses remain identified with the Jewish community and that their children consider themselves Jews. In a world in which religious belief and practice no longer play a significant role among those who unequivocally consider themselves Jews, the significance of intermarriage in connection with identity must be reaffirmed.

The behavioral correlates of the diverse types of identification characteristic of American Jews with respect to Israel can be summarized as follows. The dominant pattern has been the long-time and continuing high level of philanthropic support. It is true that a high proportion of the total funds raised depends on the largesse of a relatively small number of large benefactors. On the other hand, it is also true that hundreds of thousands of Jews are approached and who respond, not once but repeatedly.

There is, however, no parallel commitment among American Jews when the support involves *aliyah.* Only small numbers even consider the idea seriously; smaller numbers emigrate; and still smaller numbers remain permanently in Israel. Although permanent emigration is a rarity, one must quickly note that ever larger numbers of American Jews do visit Israel for shorter or longer periods of time. The largest subgroup is represented by the perennial visitors; considerable numbers, in the tens of thousands, go every year or every other year. Smaller groups consist of the semi- and permanently retired, many of whom live part-year or full-year in Israel. Finally, an important and growing contingent is made up of younger and older students who spend summers, an academic year or even longer terms in Israel.

The one additional effort that American Jews make on behalf of Israel is to educate, inform and persuade leaders of opinion, particularly those who hold elective office, to adopt a positive stance toward the State of Israel. Convinced as they are that there exists a broad identity of interests between the United States and Israel in favor of maintaining peace and accelerating development in the Middle East, American Jewish leaders are not inhibited in their efforts to elicit the support of statesmen and politicians.

Patterns of Relationships

If one shifts perspective and asks what the dominant relationships between Israel and the United States have been, the following patterns can be identified. First, fund-raising activities: there has been a large-scale and continuing involvement of Israeli officials and leaders in the United States, both those serving abroad and others who are visiting emissaries. The representatives of the State of Israel range from Prime Ministers to young professors who have yet to make their mark. Since the primary purpose of the interaction between Israeli representatives and American Jews is to increase the enthusiasm and commitment of the latter, there is a selective process that guides the allocation of Israeli speakers—the most prestigious are reserved for the most affluent audiences.

While issues of security, immigration and absorption head the fund-raising agenda, year after year, the fact remains that a not inconsiderable part of the organized efforts of American Jews is in behalf of specific Israeli institutions or programs as the Weizmann Institute, the beautification of Jerusalem, the Hebrew University or the Hadassah Medical Center. Those who become actively engaged in such specific fund-raising activities usually acquire a deeper understanding of the directions which the people and institutions of the young State have set for themselves and of the problems that they have encountered and surmounted along the way. This degree of involvement often adds a significant Jewish content to the activity of those American Jews who become engaged in particular undertakings as distinct from the much larger number who are UJA contributors.

A still deeper level of relationship between the two Jewries takes place when Israel provides literary, educational and cultural values for American Jews, sometimes for the larger public as well, as in the case of Buber and Agnon. These range from the development of curriculum materials for day schools, afternoon schools and Sunday schools to tours of the Diaspora by the Israel Philharmonic, theatrical and dance troupes and other performing artists, and museum exhibits of archeological and creative interest.

Note should also be taken of the ever larger number of Israeli students, a high proportion of them Sabras, who through shorter or longer sojourns in the United States often come into close contact with American Jews. In the process they are able to communicate directly, often with deep feeling, the aspirations and ambitions that inform the actions of the young State, thereby providing their counterparts with a much better understanding of what the rebirth of Zion connotes.

Israel-Diaspora Relations—A Trial Balance

The foregoing summary of important characteristics of Israel-Diaspora relations (the Diaspora here being restricted to the United States) provides a background for assessment and policy directions. If the test of Diaspora involvement in Israel is to be *aliyah*, there is ground for serious concern. The number of American Jews willing to cross the divide and make a permanent commitment to Israel has never exceeded a few thousand per year, a figure which must be reduced by the not inconsiderable proportion who eventually return. However, if the test is less extreme and consists of involvement, reflected in continuing financial contributions and other forms of support, the ties must be adjudged to be strong.

What is less clear is the future trend in the relationship which will undoubtedly be affected by the changing fortunes both of the State of Israel and American Jews. If the siege in which Israel has lived her entire existence were miraculously lifted, there would be some basis for anticipating a diminution in the involvement and support of American Jewry: so much of their enthusiasm and support derives from an admixture of humanitarianism and an admiration for their out-numbered co-religionists, who are determined to fight for their lives in the midst of a hostile Arab world. But if the immigrant flow were to be vastly reduced and the external dangers moderated, the principal bases for support would be eroded. It might well be that new bases for continuing involvement could slowly be developed, but a largely secular American Jewry, knowing little and frequently caring less about the historical roots of Jewish experience, might lose interest.

There is little or no danger that such an eventuality would affect the deeply committed. The continued involvement with Israel is assured by the preeminence of Jewish values in their lives. But this formulation raises two related issues: How many deeply committed Jews are there likely to be in successive generations in the American environment? And what can be expected of the much larger numbers who today fall into the strongly identified and aligned categories?

Again, can one discern any significant contributions by Israel to the life of the Diaspora other than the overwhelming reality of its existence, problems and promise? The survival and strengthening of

the State of Israel may provide a sufficient fulcrum for a continuing
relationship, especially if crisis and quasi-crisis conditions continue
to dominate. But what if normalization or some approach to normalization were to set in? Would the existence of the State provide a firm
basis for continuing close relationships?

Some Policy Recommendations

This essay began with the stipulation that every discussion of
Israel-Diaspora relations was value-laden. There was no possibility
of any participant remaining unengaged, merely an objective observ-
er of the changing scene. Accordingly, I will not hesitate to confront
the implications of this stance by setting forth my recommendations
as to the policy and programmatic suggestions that the Israeli leadership should consider with the aim of strengthening their country's
relations to the Diaspora. In brief context they should aim to:

> provide as many points of linkage as possible in order that the
> greatest number of American Jews can find a formal basis for
> establishing and deepening their interest and support;

> avoid, as far as possible, policies and actions that will antago-
> nize the deeply committed, such as the Conservative rabbinate;
> reassess whether the considerable resources expended on stim-
> ulating *aliyah* might not be better directed to a less heroic ob-
> jective such as encouraging a larger number of young people to
> spend some period of time in Israel (a small number of whom
> would most probably decide to settle there);

> explore how the critically important fund-raising activities in
> the United States might be redesigned so that they could serve
> as a vehicle for giving American Jews more knowledge, insight
> and understanding of the values and goals implicit in their
> peoplehood;

> design, together with American Jewish leaders, intermediate-
> and long-range educational and cultural activities that would
> enable Israel to make a more effective contribution to the deep-
> ening of Jewish values in the United States;

> determine the range of Israel's assets which can be "packaged"
> to attract both small and large groups of American Jews to take

a more active role in the building of the State–from participating in archeological digs to entering into long-term development plans with an industrialized kibbutz desiring to expand its exports.

Concluding Observations

It is expected that Jews, especially Jewish intellectuals, will view any and every aspect of Jewish life with alarm. And the deeper their Jewish roots and commitments, the more likely that this will be so. What other lesson can be extracted from the recurring experience of a people who throughout history has been used as the scapegoat for the frustrations inherent in human existence?

Several years ago the late President Shazar was very critical of my failure to assume that the security of American Jews would ineluctably be undermined, sooner or later, by the hostility of the dominant majority. I did not preclude such a possibility but neither was I willing to predicate policy recommendations with such an eventuality in mind.

The implicit thrust of the present analysis is that the more immediate threat to the continued vitality of American Jewish life is to be found in the erosion of its Jewish base. While primary responsibility for reversing this erosion, or at least slowing it down, rests with the leaders of the American Jewish community, Israel can make a major contribution toward assuring that clear and present dangers are surmounted. It is up to Israel to see the situation as it is—not as she would like it to be—and to respond accordingly. Just as the Diaspora has little if any meaning without Israel, so too the survival and prosperity of Israel become much more problematic without a strong Diaspora.

Discussion

AVRAHAM HARMAN

When I read the word "post-Zionist" in Jerusalem I cannot refrain from shuddering, because for the last 40 years (going back to the 1935 debate on the Legislative Assembly under the Mandate), the core of the struggle is that we here refuse to give up our Zionism, and that we are conducting a struggle not for ourselves but for the whole of the Jewish People. Arafat says that there would be sweetness and light if we could give up our Zionism and forget the Jews of the Soviet Union, Latin America and the United States. We say "No," because it is our view that the Jewish People, which created the revived Jewish State, needs that State.

Jews survived hundreds of years in the *galut* for two reasons: first, they lived as extraterritorial, autonomous societies on the territory of the Torah; second, their relations with the societies with which they lived were foreign relations and not domestic relations. When the extraterritorial foundation of Jewish life in the Diaspora was eroded and broken up, the people decided that we needed a territorial basis for the continuity of a creative Jewish civilization. And we still face the question of how the Jewish People perpetuates itself in conditions of open, free societies, if they remain open and free.

The validity of the Zionist movement does not depend on whether there is mass *aliyah* or not. This is the only country in the world that has had an immigration during total war. Immigrants arrived in this country the day after Yom Kippur 1973. None of them was compelled to come—theirs was a Zionist *aliyah* in every sense of the word.

The Zionist (not post-Zionist) agenda today is more and more of the same, that is, more money, mobilization of political and public relations, influence, and *aliyah* for those who want to come. Israel is the central front in the Jewish struggle for existence. Moreover, the Zionist agenda includes the strengthening of Jewish life wherever it is and establishing priorities, foremost among them education in Jewish communities throughout the world.

One factor that can nurture Jewish resistance today is the

consciousness that our goals are identical with those that are needed to preserve the world. This is where the particularistic aim of the Jewish People coincides with universalistic requirements; if there is no room in this world for our polity, then there is no room for anything except chaos and brute force.

CHAIM PERELMAN

What do we mean when we speak of the State of Israel, of the Third Commonwealth? During long centuries we have spoken of *ahavat Zion* (love of Zion) as a characteristic of Jewish life, but this was only an ideal concept. One could read into it all kinds of values, aspirations and ideals. But once the State of Israel was realized, the situation changed—just like with a child. You may dream of a child with certain qualities, but once you have a child, you have to accept it as it is.

"Who is a Jew?" is a familiar problem, but in relationship to Israel there is another problem: Who is a member of the Jewish People, of the Jewish community? Does not the creation of the State of Israel necessitate new criteria? Is it enough today to be the People of the Book?

This is not only theory. In Belgium, for example, after the Yom Kippur War we organized the community, accepting only organizations which identified with the State of Israel. We recognize that Israel is the State of the Jewish People.

Today Jews throughout the world feel the impact of the State. They are the ambassadors of Israel abroad, but they may also be prisoners for the State, as are the Syrian Jews. The existence of the State may lead Jews back to the idea that they are a different people, as happened with the Russian Jews. That is not a religious problem—it is a problem of belonging.

Then there are practical consequences. The image of the State is vital for Jews everywhere, because it also determines the attitude of the non-Jewish population toward them. Jews throughout the world must present a positive image of Israel. But they cannot succeed unless the State of Israel, its government and population, help them to present such an image. It is important for our survival that our non-Jewish friends in Belgium, France and Germany have the best possible opinion of Israel. We are responsible for Israel as we are for the members of our family. But the government of Israel must know that Israel is the State of the Jewish People.

In Belgium, one percent of the community are organized Zionists. Zionists are just as borderline a phenomenon today as Jews who do not want to be committed to Israel. Hence to consider that the dialogue between the State of Israel and the Jewish People must be effected by Zionist organizations is some kind of fiction. The Jewish community must be organized and be the spokesman for Israel and for the Jewish faith throughout the world.

MOSHE RIVLIN

The reciprocal attachment between the Jewish People and the State of Israel must be based on four points: the historical tie, with all its spiritual implications; Israel's answer to the supreme tragedy of the Holocaust; Israel's ability to meet the actual problems of Judaism; the form of society which we are building in Israel and its potentiality as a magnetic force for the Jewish People.

Unfortunately, we are living at a time when the Holocaust experience is becoming increasingly meaningful; there is today much more knowledge—and much more apprehension—concerning the Holocaust. We cannot point to increased meaningfulness in the case of the other factors mentioned above.

When the State was founded, the answers were clear. It was obvious that the State of Israel was an immediate answer to the Holocaust—not only in the historical sense but as a practical answer to the problems of the Jewish refugee. It was clear there had to be a place in the world where the Jew can be master of his fate and where the Jew knows that he can find a haven.

When the State was founded and Israel saw the ingathering of exiles and the acceptance of refugees as her primary purpose, the vision and the reality became identical. It was only natural that the State of Israel, which had arisen out of blood and fire, should accept a thousand refugees a day without asking how they would be absorbed. Having accepted the refugees who came after the traumatic experience of the Holocaust—and together with them masses of Jews we saved from Iraq, Egypt and Yemen—we were determined to build something uniquely Jewish. This was clear to any Jew steeped in Judaism and Jewish values, as well as to the young Jew who had had no Jewish education but who appreciated what was being done.

Today we must ask ourselves whether we are providing an answer to the Jewish question. Recently there have been two worrisome developments—a sharp decline in the number of immigrants to Israel, and an increase in the number of "drop-outs," that is, those who leave the U.S.S.R. but do not come to Israel. We must look at these developments in perspective. For us, one of the signs of the centrality of Israel must be that it attracts immigration. Does it act as a focal point to Jews who see their future in this land; does it attract young people who see a challenge in joining us in the upbuilding of the State?

One thing which must come out of this discussion is a communication of the spirit. We must find a way to construct a framework wherein Jews from the Diaspora and Jews from Israel will see as their main function the elevation of the spiritual life of the nation and the building of a model society in Israel.

EZRA SPICEHANDLER

In the context of our discussion the term "Israel" itself really signifies at least three different concepts: *The State of Israel* as a political institution, *the People of Israel,* and *the Land of Israel.* Although all three concepts are interrelated and interdependent; they are by no means identical.

Obviously the *State of Israel* cannot command the political loyalties of Diaspora Jews who feel themselves to be loyal citizens of the countries in which they live. In the case of those Jews whose loyalty to the state in which they dwell has been impaired because they are denied equal rights under its laws and customs, the State of Israel may play a political role which it does not or will not play in countries of the free world. But the State of Israel can justly claim a primary role even in the free countries, within the broad area of inter-Jewish relationships, on the following grounds:

1) The Jewish policy of the State of Israel is ultimately determined by the Israeli electorate. The Israeli government is reponsible to the Knesset, which is elected through the democratic process. The Jewish community of Israel is the only large Jewish community which under law holds elections at regular intervals. This is a sad fact of Jewish life. Ideally, the Zionist Congress was to have been a democratically elected body. Unfortunately, often for reasons beyond the control of the Zionist movement, only one such election has been held since the outbreak of the Second World War. Consequently, decisions on Jewish policy made by Israel's political leadership have greater authority than those made by Jewish leadership in the Diaspora, which is by and large self-appointed.

2) The State of Israel, by reasons of its sovereignty and the administrative resources at its disposal, possesses instrumentalities of policy which enable it to collect data concerning world Jewry and to influence the Jewish policy of sovereign states through cultural, diplomatic, economic and other means.

3) The fiscal resources of the State of Israel—whether derived from taxation, intergovernmental grants and loans, or from contributions of world Jewry—are greater than those under the organized control of the Jewish communities of the Diaspora. The State of Israel is therefore better able than any voluntary organization to plan policies and execute projects beneficial to world Jewry—be they economic, migratory, cultural, or religious.

The People of Israel form the only Jewish community which enjoys the status of an ethnic majority, with all the cultural implications which such a status implies. Israel is the only country in which the Jewish religion has a privileged status and the entire fabric of Israeli society is permeated by Jewish cultural values and institutions.

In the area of Jewish studies Jerusalem has prevailed over Babylon. This is said with high regard for the achievements of Diaspora scholars and the great Diaspora institutions for higher learning. However, in terms of specializations, research budgets, scholarly publications and sheer numbers of students, the center of Jewish studies has long ago shifted to Israel.

The Land of Israel and the return of the People to the Land are concepts which have not yet been fully articulated. There are first of all the religious aspects today shared in different degree by the various religious groups within Judaism. Orthodox Judaism's stance is clear (although Neturei Karta are also Orthodox). However, on the other side of the spectrum, Reform Judaism has now joined the World Zionist Organization.

On the secular side, Ahad Ha-Am's assertion that the very effort to create the Yishuv will unite and revivify world Jewry has long ago been proved. The love of the Land and the People of Israel have been the most unifying force in contemporary Jewish life.

Arguments that the drain of funds to Israel has resulted in "starving" essential projects and programs in the Diaspora are easily dismissed by the statistics of Jewish fund raising. The UJA has set new standards for Jewish fund raising and pro-Israel activity has revived Jewish interest in Jewish cultural and religious life. Prior to the great campaigns, Jewish philanthropy resulted in relatively insignificant funds which were usually spent in the area of Jewish welfare with a general disregard of Jewish cultural and spiritual needs.

The primacy of Israel is, therefore, a fact of modern Jewish life. But the time has come to remove this subject from our Jewish agenda. Discussion in this area has been fruitful and stimulating but sometimes degenerates into arid theoretical quibbling. Jewish history will resolve the issue for all of us.

SIMON GREENBERG

Discussions on the relationship between the State of Israel and the Diaspora are not taking place in a vacuum, but in the light of the pressing immediate need that the State of Israel, for a variety of good reasons, has for a continuing and dramatic increase in its population.

The misunderstandings and acrimony that often characterize these discussions are due to the assumption that a positive attitude toward Jewish life in the Diaspora necessarily implies or encourages a denigration of the primacy of Israel and the urgency of Israel's need for *aliyah*, and that stressing the need for *aliyah* necessarily implies the expectation or even the hope that the Diaspora will disappear.

But the status of Jews and Judaism in the world depends upon both a vigorous State of Israel and a vibrant Jewish Diaspora. In the foreseeable future neither is, nor can be, self-sufficient. Israel is a geographically small state. If it should ever hold all or an overwhelming majority of the Jewish People it will indicate a serious diminution of the world's Jewish population. Israel needs the moral, political and economic support of a large, loyal Diaspora. The Diaspora to be Jewishly vibrant and loyal will need the constant religious and cultural replenishment that can come primarily if not exclusively from the developments that take place in Israel, for it is only the State of Israel that can offer to the Jewish religio-cultural heritage the basic conditions that will make possible the fullest realization of its potentialities.

Yet, Judaism without a Diaspora will be seriously impoverished. It will be in danger of becoming a geographically and ethnically limited religion, rather than the universally valid philosophy of life that it is today and has ever striven to be.

In Israel Judaism and the Jewish People face the challenge that inheres in the exercise of power. In the Diaspora they face the challenge that inheres in the environment's hostility or enticements. They have stood the test of hostility so triumphantly that many have concluded that they can do so only in a hostile environment. The honor of both requires that Diaspora Jews living in free democratic societies prove that it was not anti-Semitism but Judaism that kept the Jewish People alive.

This approach reflects the inextricable intertwining of the universal and the particular, of the religious and the cultural which characterizes the Jewish heritage.

It would contribute to the renascence and the clarification of Zionist thought if the aims of Zionism would be formulated so that without downgrading the primacy of Eretz Yisrael and the urgency of *aliyah*, this two-fold nature of the Jewish heritage would be clearly indicated. I suggest the following formulation which may serve as a preamble to a detailed program of Zionist activity.

"Zionism *aims* to make the religio-cultural heritage of the Jewish people an increasingly vital factor in molding the character of the individual Jew, and the Jewish People everywhere and of mankind. It *maintains* that the existence of a sovereign, politically democratic, physically secure, economically viable and spiritually sensitive State of Israel is indispensable to the achievement of that aim."

JONATHAN FRANKEL

The Zionist founding fathers—Pinsker, Lilienblum, Herzl, Nordau—set out to solve the "Jewish problem" by providing a homeland for those Jews who were driven by need or violence to leave their countries of birth. Already in the late nineteenth century it was apparent to acute observers that rabid anti-Semitism was on the rise in Europe and that quite soon England, the United States and other traditional lands of refuge would close their gates against further mass Jewish migration. So desperate was the situation in the eyes of these four leaders that they were ready to consider an alternative territory, should the entry to Palestine remain restricted. What was at issue here was an attempt to solve not the problem of "Judaism" but the problem of the Jews as human beings, threatened with physical destruction.

Classical Zionism, as represented by these leaders, set itself a strictly limited goal, which has been achieved since 1948. Close to two million Jews, who would in most cases have had nowhere to go, came to Israel. Those Jews who live amid crisis—in various South American countries, for instance—can hold their heads erect knowing that if anti-Semitism grows they have an alternative country which not only will accept them, but will also welcome them. The struggle on behalf of Soviet Jewry would hardly be conceivable if there were no homeland waiting for them.

This fact cannot give the Zionist any cause for self-satisfaction. The State of Israel was founded too late to save the bulk of European Jewry. Again, the Yishuv was only saved from total destruction in 1942–43 by the desperate victories at El Alamein and Stalingrad. And, today the future of this State with its three million Jewish inhabitants remains in doubt. Success in the past was only partial and does not of itself provide security in the future.

Nevertheless, this does not mean that the determination of such men as Lilienblum, Pinsker and Herzl to concentrate on the relatively narrow goal of solving the Jewish Question by establishing a Jewish State was erroneous. On the contrary, it revealed a strong grasp of the basic realities of Jewish life in the post-Emancipation era. Divided sharply in their fundamental beliefs and allegiances, the Zionists could not for a moment act effectively to solve the problems of Judaism as an ideology and a way of life. Only by opting for a clear-cut and limited political goal could the Zionist movement hope to unite behind it a large portion of the Jewish People. And only by opting for a genuine pluralism could it hope to hold together such diverse elements in one democratic framework.

The State of Israel is, and has to be, a direct heir to the Zionist movement and the Yishuv. It can only be as strong as its individual and competing constituent elements. If there is a spiritual vacuum in this country today, then the onus for filling it lies first and foremost on the voluntary and particularist movements (which are free, of course, to seek state aid for their projects and undertakings).

It was the goal of Zionism to permit the Jews to live a free life in their own country. Can Judaism really be so exhausted that it cannot hold its own in the ideological free-for-all of such a state?

ABRAHAM S. HALKIN

The problem of Israel and the Diaspora as a Zionist sees it ought to be: What can be done to revive among the Jews of the world a sufficiently strong desire to regard the implementation of the Zionist program as a worthy aim and objective?

I am not at this point talking of *aliyah*, desideratum though it is. I am deeply in sympathy with the desirability of creating an ethically and culturally superior state, although I do not think this goal is fundamental to the Zionist program.

I am sure that the State of Israel today has little with which to draw settlers from lands of comfort and opportunity. Although it is vitally important that changes be wrought in the life and culture of this country, the change which will make immigration more likely and make Zionist goals more relevant must take place in the Diaspora. What is needed is a reorientation by the Jews of America and elsewhere; a return to the earlier Jewish attitude to Eretz Yisrael; and restoration of the consciousness of *galut*, with all its implications.

I know that such a program will not win the support of those who do not accept the Zionist position, or of those whose faith in the realizable potentialities of the Jewish community of America is unshaken. I doubt that the program can affect the mature and the aging.

But those who consider themselves Zionists should be reminded of the Zionist decision in the past to dominate the education of the young in their cities. It should become clear to the educators and the administrators of Jewish schools that the child must learn that he is living in the *galut* and the *galut* is not home, while the historic Jewish aspiration is to return home. Although the educational approach may not increase *aliyah,* surprisingly, it will create a deeper consciousness of the duty of *aliyah* and of its likelihood.

DAVID LAZAR

Eretz Israel has remained "the Center" for Jews thanks to the permanent transmission of traditions, sentiments and customs in which religious practices have played a major role. Nostalgia for the "messianic return" was maintained by the vision of an idyllic pre-destruction Golden Age. However, in order to become a militant national movement a huge thrust was needed which could only be brought about by the breakdown of dreams of total emancipation in the West (epitomized by the Dreyfus affair), combined with the creative despair engendered by pogroms and anti-Semitism in Eastern Europe. Zionism blended the belief in the possibility of success of the collective Jewish enterprise and a socialist dream of redemption. It thus started what was to become the Yishuv and later the State of Israel.

Zionism and Israel have been manned by, and have catered to, many so-called secular Jews. Too much differentiation is made between practicing and non-practicing Jews. The role of the latter in Israel, both historically and existentially, has been basic. To begin with, in spite of being "secular Jews," they, mainly, created the "Center" and came to live in it. Then, because they inhabit the "Center," they are unlikely, even though secular, to be absorbed into the other nations.

It is in a way unfair to try and determine definitive aspects of Center and Periphery as we prepare for the third decade. Israel is only at the beginning of the road, not a final product. Centrality is properly defined because it makes allowances for an ongoing and expanding process. The greatness resulting from the materialization of the conscious will has rubbed off on an ever-increasing number of Jews who feel they are a part of this continuing creative movement, where Jews strive toward a Jewish solution to the Jewish problem. In this respect, the fact that Israel still struggles for physical survival and consequently has not yet found all the answers to the cultural, ethical and religious challenges of Jewish identity within a modern Jewish State does not minimize its centrality. Israel is after all the only *Jewish* State in the world. Jews are acutely aware of this and oscillate, as it were, between pride in a strong Israel and anxiety, reflecting the reawakening of the "minority reflex" in the face of physical danger. Both in 1967 (before the war) and in 1973 (during the war), a very large number of Diaspora Jews (including a sizable group of people who had never believed themselves capable of this kind of emotional reaction), felt very intensely that life would be intolerable if anything happened to Israel.

ZVI YARON

I would like to concentrate on the concept of normalization. It is superficial to be simply for or against normalization, particularly from a religious point of view. After all, the concept of the abnormality of the *galut* is not a recent idea. The idea of *galut* as an abnormal situation runs from the Maharal of Prague onward through religious writing, right up to Rabbi Kook and others. This means that a certain situation, regardless of physical, political, economic and social conditions, is a curse. I use this word although it may hurt all of us. The concept of *shekhinah be-galuta* means that the *galut*, in the sense of Jewishness and religious and cultural life, is not only wrong but evil. The question of Zionism, therefore, is not merely whether we can save Jews from distress, but how one understands the *galut* situation.

Israel can normalize religion. Israel may be more or less religious than other countries, but it is important that we create here a normal Jewishness, a normal religiosity, grappling with a situation where we have to be religious and Jewish in every respect.

In Israel there should be a widening of the scope of religious life. I am not referring to the important question of Reform and changes in the *Halakhah*, which can be developed anywhere—Cincinnati, London, or Paris. Only in Israel can there be a widening of the scope of religious life. Here we can apply, for instance, the concept of *tohar ha-neshek* (purity of arms), a matter of morality from the religious point of view in army life. There are in Israel new possibilities to mold religious patterns of living. But I do not think that religious Jews are sufficiently aware of these possibilities.

MARVIN FOX

I am troubled by the statements that have been repeatedly made to the effect that, "The Jews of the Diaspora are agreed that. . . ," or "The Jews of the Diaspora have rejected the notion that. . . ." The danger of projecting our own special attitudes and reactions on to the bulk of world Jewry is one that we must resist. I agree that the Holocaust and the establishment of the State of Israel are events which should have transformed the lives and the thinking of Jews everywhere, but I see little evidence, despite what we have been told, that this is in fact the case. So far as my experience goes, I would be forced to the conclusion that while a certain amount of lip service is paid by American Jews to the critical importance of these two events, they have not affected the life of American Jewry in ways that even approach transformation. Except for limited numbers, American Jews tend to live their lives as if little had happened, as if the cataclysmic and salvific moments of recent Jewish history had never occurred.

A second point should be noted. In the course of these discussions, it has been said by various speakers that Jewish identity must, in some way, be religious. They have stated repeatedly that a life which has Jewish substance requires a religious foundation. I share this conviction and am delighted to hear it expressed by those who are not the usual "official" proponents of such a view. At the same time, I cannot help but wonder whether we are all using the term "religious" in its normal meaning. Jewish identity which has a religious dimension rests on an affirmation of the reality of the transcendent, on the faith that God is ultimate reality and that we stand under His judgment. It is important to know whether those who speak of religion in these discussions share that view. It is equally important to know whether they believe that in this secularized age an appeal for such religious Jewish identity has any hope of truly succeeding in Israel and in the Diaspora.

Finally, since there were strong statements to the effect that *Halakhah* is essential for the building of contemporary Jewish life, but that such *Halakhah* must be made into a living force that can shape contemporary reality, we must recognize that this too depends on a faith commitment. Throughout the generations great *halakhists* were able to make the law into a sensitive and responsive Jewish social force. They succeeded not only by virtue of their learning and the strength of their leadership, but because they also saw themselves as working under a divine mandate and carrying out the supreme responsibility of teaching God's Torah to their own generation. Without this faith and the sense of responsibility which it presupposes, we cannot have an ongoing *halakhic* process. Without this faith religious norms become mere folkways.

ABRAHAM AVI-HAI

New-found statehood has dazzled Israelis and non-Israelis into believing that Israel is omnipotent, and the weakness of the Diaspora leadership, the lack of leadership of its spiritual heads and the spiritual poverty of its fund-raising leaders have led to reliance on Israel to do what they are unable to effect.

Just as the Diaspora once worked to create pioneering *haluziyyut* and helped to build the State-in-the-making through its Diaspora-based organizations, so now the Diaspora must create its instruments for the challenges of today.

If Israel has political or financial demands to make on the Diaspora, Israel's representatives speak and the Diaspora acts. Its manifold organizational structures raise the billions of dollars that create the demonstrations and the political pressures. These activities may be generated by Israelis but they are too important to be left in Israel's hands. So too, the Israel-centered mass movement of students, tourists, adult education programs, investors, and so on, must be built up in the Diaspora, for the Diaspora, by Diaspora groups and eventually for Israel's good.

The old modes, the Zionist party stranglehold on youth and education, as well as the general organizational inertia in the Diaspora, have stood in the way, while the State bureaucracy and ineptness must take blame for the failure to transfer personal investment and knowhow.

Post-1973 Israel should be able to admit its limitations. Our interdependence should create the new instruments appropriate to the Diaspora that has now come of age and which, with Israel and in Israel, will effectuate the programs required.

EPHRAIM BROIDO

It is very possible that while we go on debating our old-new issues at seminars, symposia and congresses, the game is already lost. It may well be that by the slow-travelling light of stars which went out long ago we see certain ideas and facts of the past as if they were still here. And yet what remains of the vital energies of post-Emancipation Jewry is being marginally employed in rebutting anti-Semitic accusations or pressuring the American administration about Israel, whenever the occasion demands, while fatally ignoring the crucial need for creating conditions for national and cultural regeneration.

If, for example, all that Jewish survival in America can aspire to is the maintenance of a component within American society, somewhat parallel to, say, the American Presbyterian Church, then Judaism in the United States may, at best, linger on for a short while, historically, before final disintegration sets in. But if this process is not too far gone, and if in various segments of American Jewry there is still the glimmering of the will to continue in the full sense, then we should get down to real work. If we are thinking of Jewish survival not just in terms of endurance with vague spiritual identities, but if, whatever our present tactics or past ideological usages, we feel that ultimately the only hope and meaning—and indeed justification—of our effort for survival is commensurate with our will and success in re-creating, in the union of territory, language and nation, the basis for a full-blooded Jewish civilization in the widest sense, there is no need to worry about the "centrality" of Israel. It is built into the Jewish psyche. There is need to worry about the center itself, about its strengthening beyond all possible threat. This can only be achieved by shifting—physically, numerically, intellectually, technologically—the center of gravity of Jewish life in the world, within one generation. There is no need to worry about the depletion of the Diaspora and the diversion of energies from it towards the State. Paradoxically, I believe that Jewish life in the Diaspora will become richer, not poorer. The more it is being depleted in a conscious collective effort, the more seriously it is involved in the actuality of a Jewish revival, by moving from the stage of sympathy and fund raising to active personal participation in building the State. Planned large-scale migration and settlement should go hand in hand with ensuring the Jewish re-education of Jewish youth in the Diaspora.

We have little time left politically and we have little margin culturally after the Nazi destruction of one-third of our people, which was the main base of the Jewish State in the biological and spiritual sense. We must not lull ourselves by formulas like "centrality," or the most dangerous of all tranquilizers, the old one of *Nezah Yisrael,* in the sense of "the eternity of Israel." We must face the realities of our history, of ever-dwindling remnants. We must make the *center,* not "centrality," secure, before forces of cultural and ethnic disintegration have done their work.

BENJAMIN AKZIN

The question to be discussed is not the place of Israel vis-à-vis the Diaspora, but the position of Israel vis-à-vis various aspects, temporal and eternal, of the Jewish People. There are two dangers when we talk about centrality. One is that of overconfidence, of assuming too easily that Israel holds, and will continue to hold, a central position. The other danger is that this position may be reduced in the future.

The meaning of Israel differs among various groups in the Diaspora. It does not mean the same for the Jewish community in the United States today, as for the community, or part of it, in the Soviet Union. It does not mean the same thing for the Jews in Sweden as it does for the Jews in Syria. Moreover, within each community there are also differences. There are those who regard Israel as essential to Jewish survival; others may regard it merely as important or desirable. It would be wrong to try to generalize and find a common denominator for all these attitudes.

The centrality of Israel is very much in danger because of the attitudes in Israel itself. In a way, these attitudes in Israel are more self-serving than the attitudes in the Diaspora. The attempt to assimilate is an old phenomenon in the Diaspora, but we now see tendencies toward estrangement or assimilation in Israel itself, whether on the part of the "Canaanites" or of those who like to call themselves Israelis and prefer not to remember or remind themselves that they are Jews. These tendencies contribute more than anything to cutting the link, whether it is a central and essential link or a secondary one, between us and the rest of the Jewish People.

How are we to define the nature of the link and the extent of the responsibility and participation of the Diaspora in Israeli affairs, and vice versa? Should this be regulated by feeling rather than by formulation and by what the British call, in their political history, conventions rather than statutes?

Today when we talk of Israel, we mean the State. That does not mean state fetishism, because obviously the State is only an instrument, which in Zionist thought is essential for a dignified survival of the Jewish People. We must not permit an erosion of this raison d'être of the State. Just as it may not be eroded by cutting down the Law of Return, so it may not be eroded by allowing further alienation between us and the Jews outside of Israel.

ARYE LEON DULZIN: Summary Comment

In discussions of the *centrality* of Israel it is quite irrelevant to reargue Zionist theory and to rehash the old debates about the negation of the *galut*. The decisive factor today is Israel's existential role in the life of the Jewish People—its *Sitz im Leben*. After the Yom Kippur War it is wholly pointless to discuss the problem of the *centrality* of Israel from the point of view of a so-called "pure" theory of

Zionism. The question today is whether, and to what extent, this centrality is a living reality. A further question should be whether there are weaknesses in the way the concept of centrality actually works. And finally, is it possible—on the basis of the present condition of the centrality of Israel—to make a meaningful prognosis of future developments in the relationship between Israel and Diaspora communities?

In considering the problem of centrality, even opponents of Zionism cannot evade the fact that the existence of Israel has radically transformed the self-awareness of Jews, regardless of their religious and social-political affiliations. There are, unfortunately, many Jews who are intent upon obliterating every vestige of their Jewishness; but the majority of Jews who uphold their Jewishness comprehend Jewish existence in terms of a Jewish State in Eretz Yisrael. This is true even of Jews who cherish the concept of equal status for the Diaspora, analogous to that of the ancient Jewish creative community in Babylon after the destruction of the Second Temple.

We may unquestionably assume that the State of Israel has basically changed the self-awareness of most Jews. Two questions remain: the precise meaning of this change in self-perception; and the ideological demands of Zionism and their consequences.

Regarding the change in self-perception, it is true that Israel has not yet achieved Ahad Ha-Am's vision of it as a cultural center of the Jewish People. But it is equally true—and on this point Ahad Ha-Am erred—that a cultural center can develop only out of a solid physical framework. Without the State of Israel, Ahad Ha-Am's center would be no more than a fascinating but hopelessly utopian idea. Now that we have our independent Jewish State, we have the means to fashion a society that will be suffused with Jewish creativity. So far, Israel's achievement lies in the fundamental changes it has brought about in Jewish life, both through its very existence and in the self-understanding of Jews. There are a number of other great Jewish communities: North America, for example, has twice the number of Jews that live in Israel. The fact remains, however, that there is only one Jewish community in the world which Jews everywhere hold in the center of their concern and aspirations.

Zionists are certainly not satisfied with this factual centrality. The challenge for Zionists is to give quality to the centrality of Israel, to make the Jewish State the cultural and spiritual center of Jewish values. For the essential meaning of Zionism is not only the continuity of Jewishness but the renaissance of Jewish life. The existence of the Jewish State is therefore to be considered the beginning of the redemptive process which will liberate the Jewish People from its bondage to other peoples and its subservience to other cultures.

As for the ideological demands of Zionism, it is fair to state that while the majority of Jews continue to reside in the dispersion, the State of Israel has already revolutionized the existence and the thinking of Jews. Although continuing to live as individual Jews in *galut*, the Jewish nation *as nation* is no longer in a state of exile. For *galut* is not only a matter of geography, it is also a question of psychology. Israel has done away with Jewish homelessness and it has thus achieved a significant measure of national liberation. But complete liberation and independence will be accomplished only with the ingathering of most Jews in Israel. Zionism has to be viewed as a process in the life and the history of the Jewish nation, beginning with the return to Zion and the renaissance of Jewish life in Eretz Yisrael, and continuing with the establishment of the State of Israel. But the final and complete achievement is still a long way off.

It is this incompleteness which characterizes, from the Zionist point of view, the weakness of the idea of centrality. For centrality implies that Jewish existence outside Israel is important in sheer weight of numbers, that most of the nation is still in the Diaspora living as a minority among other peoples. In many western countries the "minority" condition is undoubtedly characterized by freedom and affluence, while the group continues to be part of a much larger non-Jewish society.

On the other hand, although Israel continues to be dependent on other nations (and how many nations nowadays are entirely independent politically and militarily?), it has abolished the *sense of dependency*. Even when Israel is in dire danger, it does not merely try to survive, it pursues the struggle as an independent nation. Israel's problem is that it lacks the strength that derives from numbers. The total of three million is still very far short of Zionism's goal. To be sure, even while small in numbers, Israel has succeeded in transforming the nature of the Jewish confrontation with its enemies. But we shall have to cope with hostility so long as we have only three million Jews in Israel.

Anti-Semitism has always been one of the constants in Jewish life. Its expressions have changed, but it has not ceased to shadow —and endanger—Jewish existence. In recent years the old hatred has assumed a new name: it is now called "anti-Zionism." But it is still plain, unalloyed hatred of Jews. And this ingrained, traditional hatred cannot be overcome with a wave of some wand. It is the thesis of Zionism that anti-Semitism is a Gentile aberration that must be fought until it is entirely eradicated, and that this struggle must be waged from a position of strength—by the State of Israel populated by many more millions of Jews.

If anyone entertained hopes that anti-Semitism would fade away simply because Gentiles would be ashamed by the memory of the Holocaust, experience has brought bitter disappointment. Over-enthusiastic Zionists who felt sure that hatred of Jews would simply vanish in the face of the existence of a Jewish State have learned over the years to expect hatred to continue unabated and simply to reshuffle its arguments.

And so we return to the issue of the incompleteness of the Zionist achievement. By no stretch of the imagination can a state which contains less than 20 percent of the Jewish People be described as the ultimate achievement of Zionism.

The issue of *aliyah* is frequently presented as a need of Israel. But to present the case for *aliyah* in this manner is to diminish the Zionist idea. *Aliyah* is not only a need of Israel but of the Jewish People. It is altogether erroneous to speak of Israel and the Jewish People as separate units. *Aliyah* is part and parcel of Zionism. The Zionist view of *aliyah* implies a personal challenge to the individual Jew to take an active part in the fulfillment of Zionism, not to remain outside and consider from an objective distance both the merits and difficulties of settling in Israel.

Without *aliyah* the Zionist idea would have been doomed to oblivion. Zionism has been successful in achieving so much of its vision only because Jews actually returned to Zion. It is on this basis that Zionism stands and creates.

Interscript

Moshe Davis

This book begins and ends—in the middle.

It was so intended.

The first Seminar on Israel and the Jewish People met in the wake of the Yom Kippur War. As President Katzir states in his Foreword, the very same sorrow and questioning troubled spirits both in Israel and in the Diaspora. What emerged from the many reports and discussions at that meeting was not a coherent response to the questions, but a fusion of Jewish feeling: Israel—the State and People as one—had been attacked.

While comfort derived from the experience of coming together, the questioning persisted, and could not be denied. Moreover, all the participants felt—and expressed—that sober evaluation and reorientation to the global Jewish condition are a prerequisite to consistent world Jewish interaction. The Jewish People is at an historic turning point. As in past eras, *clarification of primary principles* in the contemporary idiom is imperative for creative Jewish survival. Hence the decision to establish a *Continuing Seminar* in which fertile minds of divergent viewpoints from a variety of Jewish societies would join in thought and program. Such confrontation should help focus the broadest possible range of knowledge and experience on the central issues facing the Jewish People in different parts of the world. In this new age of growing Jewish unity around the sovereign State of Israel, it is not inconceivable that a community of thought may develop ground concepts for an interdependent Jewish People, foundations which no single Jewish community can possibly expect to establish alone.

To will is not yet to achieve. Only after years of sustained effort may an international entity, formed out of disparate cultures and conditions, find it possible to evolve a contemporary formulation of Jewish history, experience and destiny. The present volume, which follows the one based on the Yom Kippur War deliberations, is the second effort in that direction. It seems to me that the book presents a mosaic of erudition and insight on the selected subjects it contains. But we are still very far from synthesis. That this should necessarily be so in the present state of Jewish existence is amply demonstrated by the varying positions and contradictions among the participants, particularly in the third section, which deals with the centrality of Israel and interaction among world Jewish communities.

Primarily the contributors to this book are not separated by deep ideological gulfs; nor do they differ significantly in their interpretations of the past. What does separate—and frequently divide— many of them is the way they apply the lessons from the past to the contemporary era. The difficulty is compounded by the different readings of the *present* condition of the Jewish People, readings which derive essentially from the different contexts of each diaspora situation. These variant readings which come to the fore in the total openness of the discussion, quite naturally reflect subjective evaluations of the world Jewish future. Thus, when most of the participants refer to the *Diaspora,* each tends to speak of his own diaspora. In fact, there are several diasporas even within the respective communities; indeed, the very term "Diaspora" requires careful reconsideration.

Significantly, the community of scholars and public figures assembled at the Seminar can be described as representing an "ingathering of cultures." Yet their respective contributions demonstrate how virtually every one of them falls back upon his particular cultural background and the particular problems of his Jewish environment. Take the European scene, where three or four million Jews in post-Holocaust countries are struggling to find some conceptual basis for their Jewish existence and identity. For Albert Memmi the accent is on the renewed surge of Marxism in Western Europe, while for Mikhail Agursky it is on Soviet dissidence; for the students of Latin America, North America, the Commonwealth countries, not to speak of Israel, markedly different problems come to the fore. In some instances basic issues were viewed in comparative context. But scholarly compartmentalization and contextual differences continue to prevail. Future seminars should make it their objective to develop a comprehensive approach to the evolving patterns of the physical, cultural and spiritual relatedness of the Jewish People.

Consider three central issues confronting the Jewish People today—anti-Jewishness, Identity, and the Eretz Yisrael-Diaspora nexus—examined in our volume. While it is conceivable in the present stage of Jewish knowledge to essay descriptive analyses of these issues in the *history* of Jewish society and ideas, I am bold to state that I am unaware of a single serious scholar who would undertake an authoritative analysis of contemporary world Jewish society in its totality. In other words, what we have learned since the beginning of the school of *Jüdische Wissenschaft* about the Jewish People across Time, we do not know about the Jews in our own times. At best, our vision is partial. What we need is a unifying vision.

For example, the use of the term "anti-Jewishness," introduced by Shlomo Avineri, is more exact than anti-Semitism in describing the new ugly syncretism of Moslem-Christian Jew-hatred, now a world-wide phenomenon. How European religious anti-Judaism and "scientific" anti-Semitism blend into this syncretic mold has been discussed extensively by Elie Kedourie in *The Chatham House Version*. It is widely known that on the American scene a drive is in progress towards the utilization of academic settings to buttress Arab economics and propaganda. This new academic presence will surely not confine itself to the realm of theology-history. While Avineri's thesis is fully supported by Moshe Ma'oz in his description of anti-Jewishness in Arab literature and media, Haim Avni and Mikhail Agursky emphasize other constructs in Latin America and Soviet Russia. The former stresses the trend towards meshing anti-Semitism with political governmental imperatives, and the latter discusses the enforcement of anti-Semitic acts as a pragmatic means of organizing Russian nationalism.

The entire discussion, while decidedly adding new information and interpretation, still leaves us with major open questions: Is there a particular Israeli perception and interpretation of anti-Semitism, as the late Maurice Freedman suggested? Does contemporary anti-Jewishness exhibit a genuinely novel force, as in the case of "anti-Zionism/anti-Jewishness" (cf. Emil Fackenheim); or is it only a matter of variations, that is, rationalization of well-known standard themes? Is it possible to deal radically with anti-Jewishness in all its deep-rooted manifestations?

The urgency to discover a unifying theory of Jewish identity is equally manifest. To believe in the existence of a monolithic Jewish community, whether in a particular country or on a world-wide basis, is to rely on myth. No single manifestation of Judaism can answer the needs of the different elements of world Jewry. Henceforth diversity, not uniformity, will have to be part of a comprehensive concept of Jewish identity. All the papers in this section—whatever the premises on which they are based—have this common denominator, namely, the assumption that the meaning of Jewish belonging has undergone a mutation. Further agreement exists that the essential causes of Jewish group attrition are internal; and that the sheer biological survival of the Jewish People is at stake because of such assimilatory factors as out-marriage and low birth rate—decisions influenced by the outer society, though not determined by it. In a word, the issue is the Jewish will to group survival.

What does *not* emerge from the papers and the discussion is agreement on the *directing idea* which delineates what it means to be a Jew, not only in the historical idiom, but also in a manner whereby the apathetic and non-identified but-not-yet-severed members of the Jewish People can discover their own desired place. Here I would particularly stress that in the search for this *directing idea* discussion can no longer be based exclusively on the experience and thought patterns of western Jewish communities in the past few centuries, but also on the re-emerging culture of the Asian-African Jews in Israel. In addition, the trials and experiences of Soviet Jewry inside and outside Russia will inevitably introduce new definitions of Jewish belongingness.

Unresolved questions remain: What are the expressions of Jewish identity peculiar to the Jewish communities in their respective countries? What are the prospects for the durability of a secular Jewish identity? If the problem in some societies is not primarily one of identification but of giving distinctiveness to a Jewish identity, what form can this distinctiveness take? What is the role of Jewish education in developing such distinctiveness? And ultimately: How can we weave the variety of Jewish identities into a texture of world Jewish unity?

Finally, we come to the framework—and perhaps in time, definition—of the Diaspora-State of Israel interconnection. We cannot blind ourselves to the obvious: the establishment of the State of Israel was an event in Jewish history so sudden and so overwhelming that, despite the hope of centuries, we are, as the Psalmist said about an earlier Return, "like unto them that dream."

What has transpired in our generation is yet to be comprehended. The Jewish People is at the very beginning of a national transformation. Because of the urgency of the hour, the impossible is attempted, namely, to define the nature of the convulsive force even as we are being forged anew by its impact. This explains, in the greatest measure, the differences and dissonances among the writers of the papers in the "centrality" section of this book and even *within* the respective papers.

Can the confusions and the contradictions about definitions and relationships be overcome? Perhaps, but only if we transcend the human and cultural lag and take present history, so to speak, by the forelock. That is to say, we need to contend profoundly with the meaning of *this* generation's history, fully reckoning with the physical and spiritual condition of the Jews throughout the world after the Holocaust. The "survivors" in Eastern Europe are severed from the body and the spirit of Judaism; and in Western Jewry, more than half, despite their material strength, are withdrawing from Jewish group identity. Above all, any formulation must take into account the motivating role of the State of Israel, its infusion of a will to live into the psyche of individual Jews and its progressively developing influence on Jewish collectivities in the various diasporas.

The State of Israel is not an end in itself, but a means towards the all-embracing objective of the vitalization of the Jewish People. Summarizing a longtime Zionist position, Gershom Scholem writes in his new volume *On Jews and Judaism in Crisis,* "I am convinced that the existence of Israel no less than that of the Diaspora depends on our placing the primacy of our connection with the Jewish people—its historic and present state—at the center of our decisions . . . we are first and foremost Jews, and we are Israelis as a manifestation of our Judaism. The State of Israel and its construction is an enterprise meant to serve the Jewish people, and if one deprives it of this goal, it loses its meaning and will not prevail long in the stormy course of these times."

My personal commitment to this proposition does not delude me into believing that it is broadly accepted either in Israel or in the Diaspora. The fact is, however, that basic questions of relationship are still being asked, and as long as they are unresolved, they must be dealt with soberly. What indeed is the optimum Israel-Diaspora relationship: dependence? interaction? solidarity? responsibility? And how can the reality of a sovereign Jewish State contribute to the self-definition of the Jewish People at a time when the majority of Jews remain in the Diaspora?

Specific questions in all three areas of this volume's discussions have been deliberately set down. They indicate the direction in which the Continuing Seminar is proceeding. Feeling is reinforced by clarification, and both await the hammering out of definitions not only of the selected themes of this volume but of such other basic issues as the meaning of Zionism today and the Judaic essence of Israeli society.

Mindful of the counsel of the ancient rabbis that one's home should be a *Beit Va'ad la-Hachamin*, not necessarily an assembly for decision-making but a "meeting-place for sages," President Katzir aspires to develop an international collegium for creative thought concerned with contemporary Jewish life. A refreshing mood pervaded the past seminars. Critical evaluation and response once again emphasized the truth that, in the realm of permanent interrelationship of Israel and world Jewry, we can most successfully rely on the authority of knowledge, intelligence and persuasion.